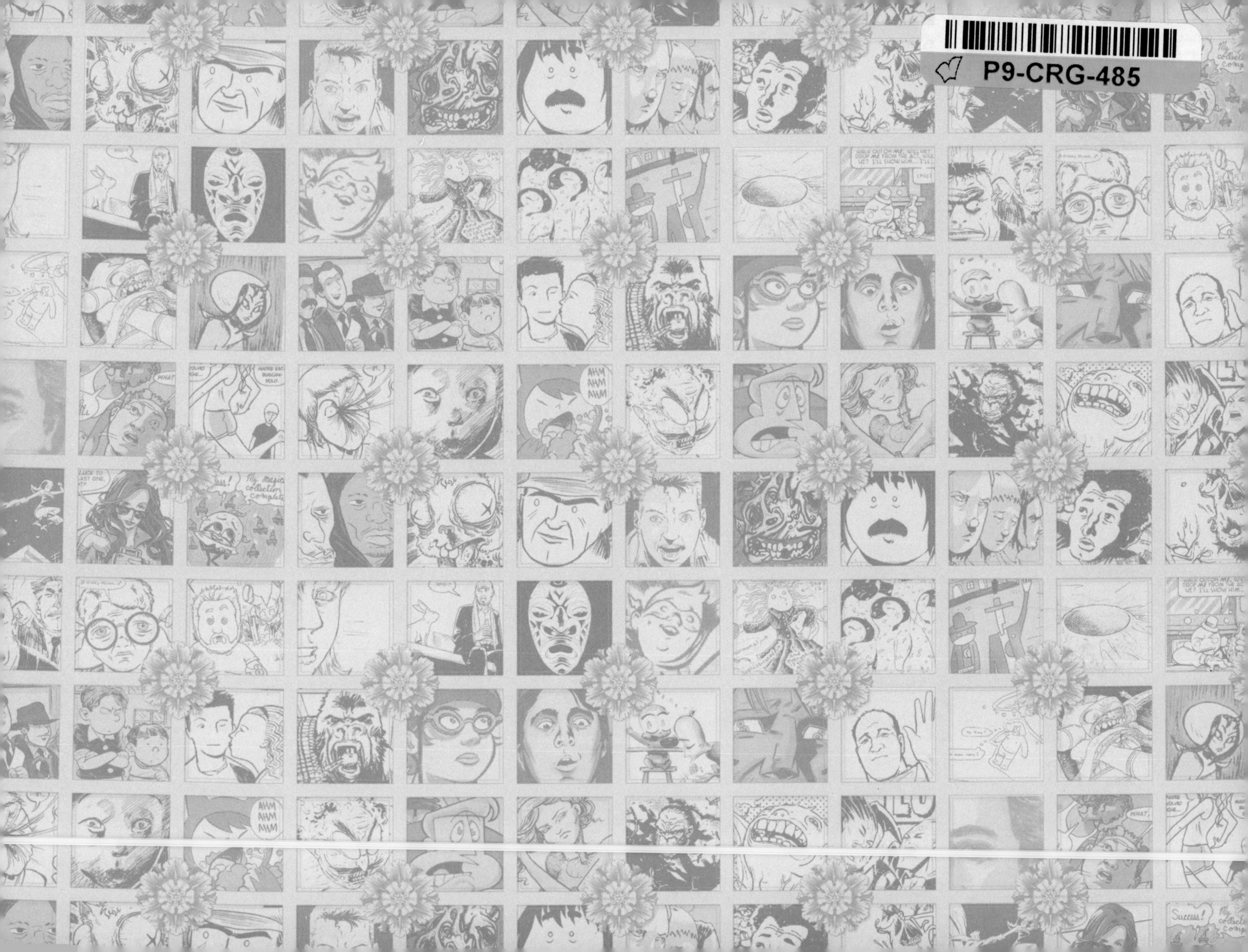
AHM
AHM
AHM
My magic collection complete
LUCK TO LAST ONE.
WHAT!

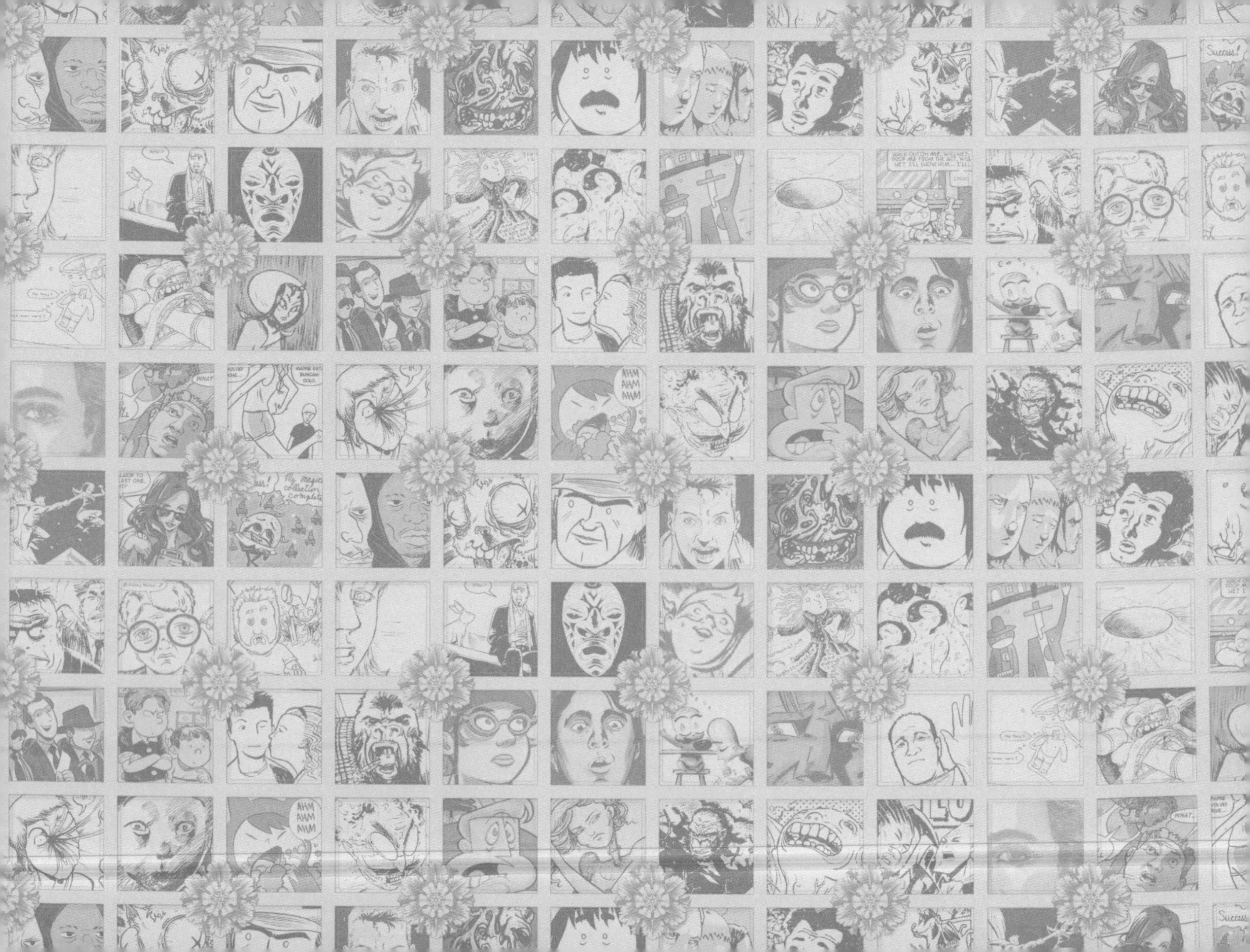

Success!
AHM
AHM
AHM
My magic collection complete

THE ACT·I·VATE PRIMER

IDW
PUBLISHING
San Diego, CA

Conceived by Dean Haspiel
Edited by Scott Dunbier and Dean Haspiel
Cover Art by Nick Bertozzi
Book Design by Joe Infurnari

THANKS: Jeff Newelt, Warren Ellis, XOXOs and DEEP6 Studios, and all the ACT-I-VATE fans.

ISBN: 978-1-60010-528-9

12 11 10 09   01 02 03 04

www.IDWPUBLISHING.com

THE ACT·I·VATE PRIMER

TABLE OF CONTENTS

❧ FOREWORD BY WARREN ELLIS ❧

❧ CREATOR BIOS ❧

FOREWORD

I think I've been asked to write the introduction to this book because I was the first person outside the group to do what you've just done: pay money to read their comics. ACT-I-VATE started out as a group project on the LiveJournal internet blogging service, run as a "basic account." LJ basic accounts are kind of crippled and not conducive to building an audience. Any idiot could see right from the start that ACT-I-VATE was a big thing, that would develop a big audience. So I sold some of my daughter's little friends into white slavery and used the money to buy them an upgraded account that gave them the space to do the thing with fewer constraints.

Which is much what you're doing right now. Buying this book allows the group to move into the future without having to worry about such things as Not Being Able To Eat, Ending Up Selling Their Skinny Bodies On The Streets, Donating Important Organs To Medical Firms While Still Alive And Actually Needing Them Quite A Lot, and so forth.

Some of you are opening this book having read the work of the collective online. Possibly you started at the beginning, as I did, and heard the rolling thunder of these remarkable talents letting rip right from the horizon. The sheer revelation of Michel Fiffe, Dean Haspiel becoming giant-sized and tearing off guitar riffs from five miles up, the media shock of zeitgeist'd Dan Goldman, the almost Beckett-like exactitude and funny wonder of Leland Purvis, and the louche Beardsleyesque comics-vaudeville of Molly Crabapple...just to pick a few off the top of my head. If you were there at the start, you know what I'm talking about and that's why you're here. For you and for me, ACT-I-VATE quickly became the best place for comics on the Web.

Some of you are opening this book having never read the work of the collective before, because it looks good or because it's been recommended to you. You're in on the ground floor, too, because none of us have yet experienced this as a print work. In fact, you're getting it better, because you don't have to cope with load times and LiveJournal being a clunky piece of shit. The weirdness of the net/print dichotomy that somehow still pertains even in 2009 means that an entire new audience will discover ACT-I-VATE right here. These are still New Comics. You're here just in time.

And if you're flicking through this and still deciding? Trust me. They were worth my money. They're worth yours. And what you're buying is a whole new view of comics.

That's why I think I was asked to be here. The reason I decided to be here is quite simply this: to thank them for doing it. ACT-I-VATE makes comics better.

-- WARREN ELLIS
BOILING ENGLAND
JULY 2009

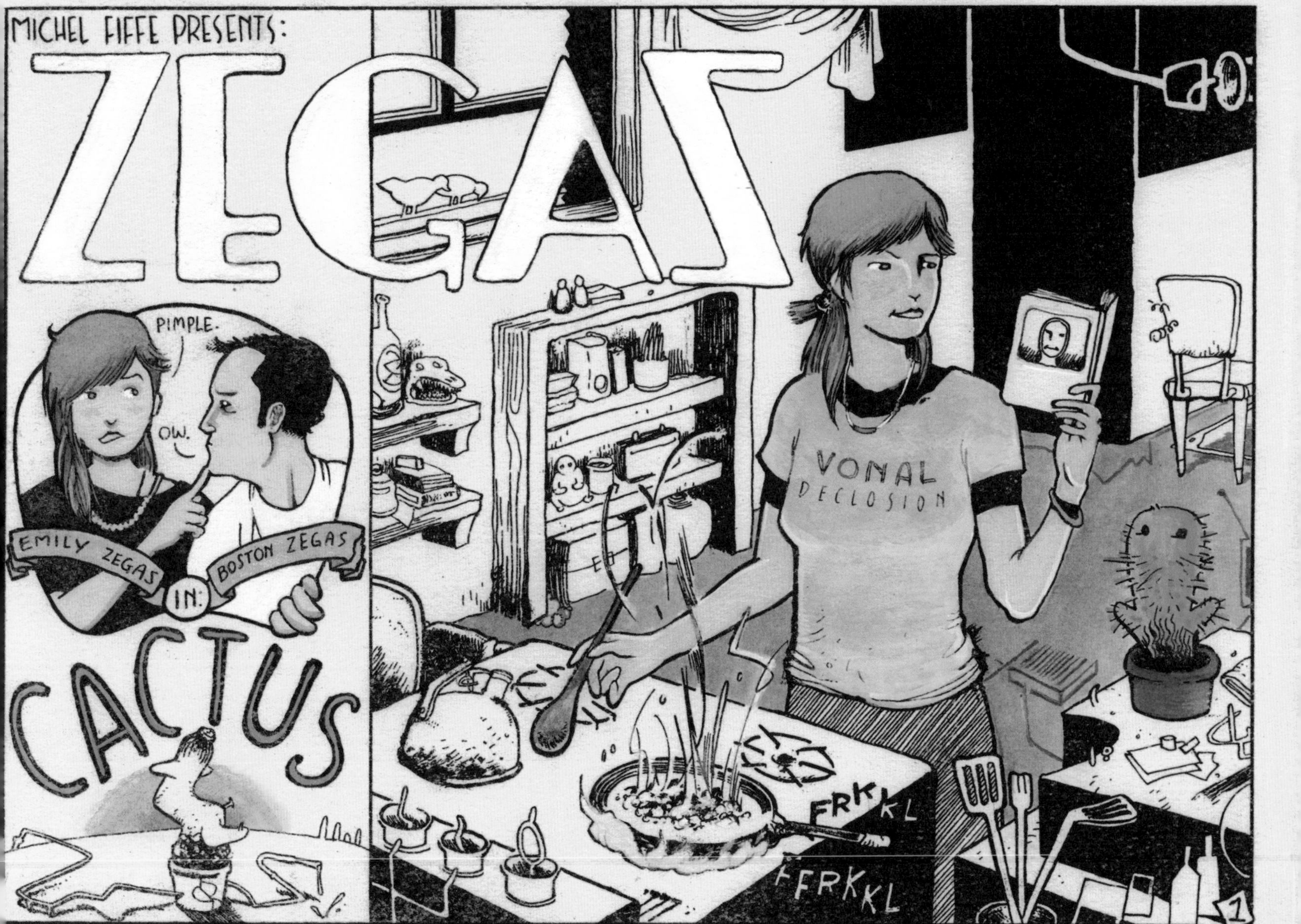
MICHEL FIFFE PRESENTS:
ZEGAS
PIMPLE.
OW.
EMILY ZEGAS
BOSTON ZEGAS
IN:
CACTUS
VONAL DECLOSION
FRKKL
FFRKKL
1

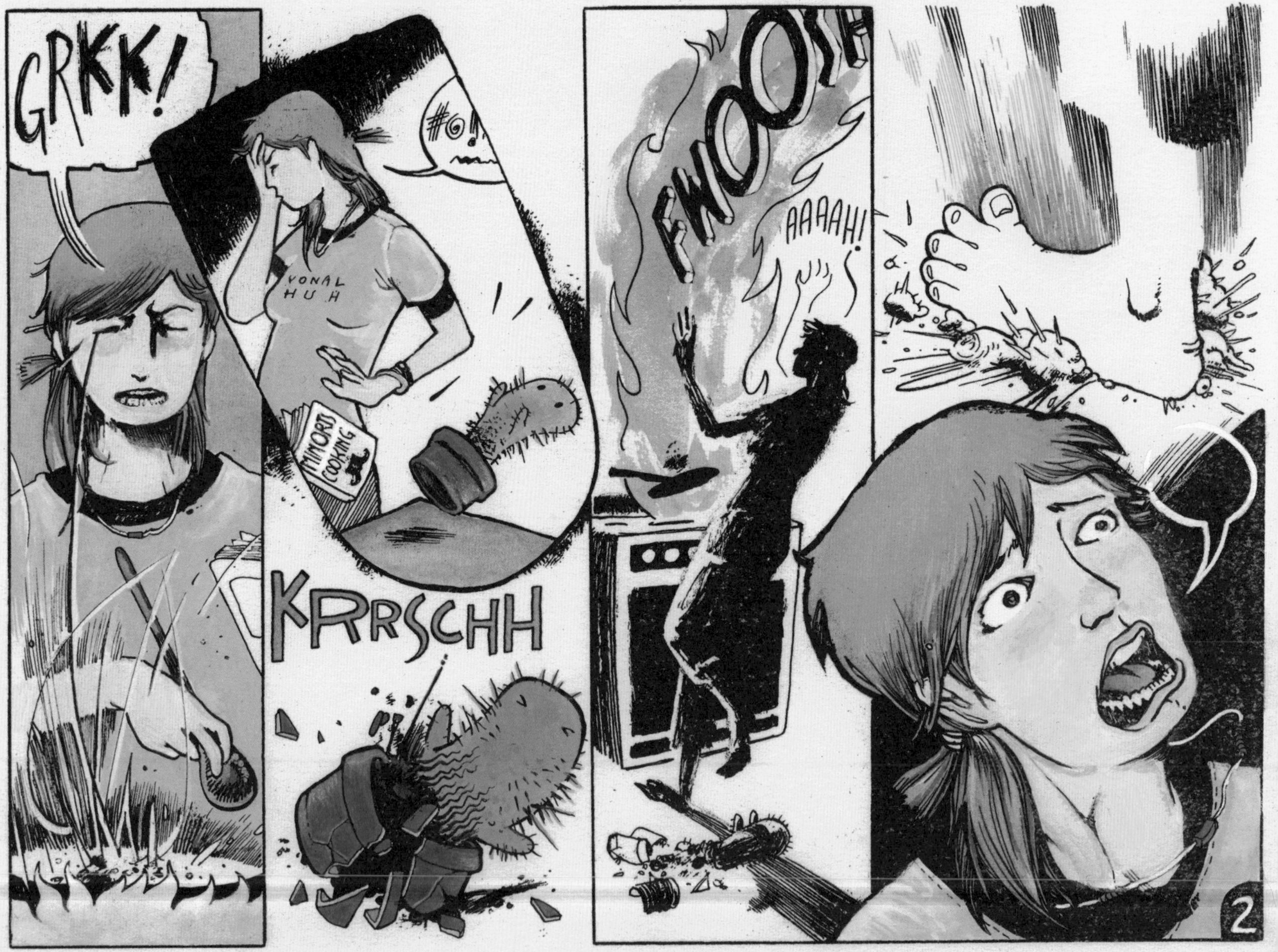
GRKK!
MIMORI'S COOKING
KRRSCHH
FWOOSH
AAAAH!
2

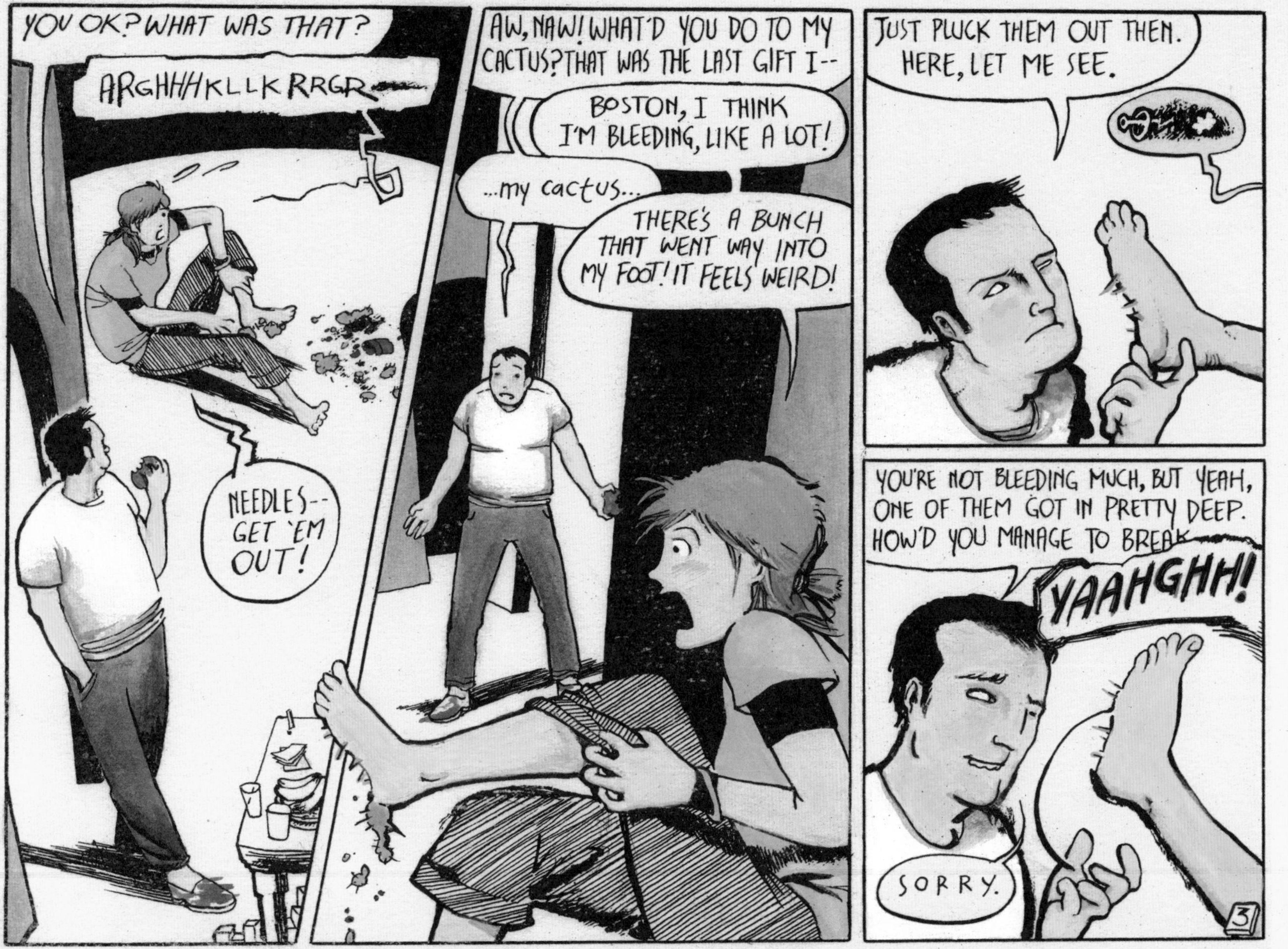
YOU OK? WHAT WAS THAT?
ARGHHHKLLKRRGR
NEEDLES-- GET 'EM OUT!
AW, NAW! WHAT'D YOU DO TO MY CACTUS? THAT WAS THE LAST GIFT I--
BOSTON, I THINK I'M BLEEDING, LIKE A LOT!
...my cactus...
THERE'S A BUNCH THAT WENT WAY INTO MY FOOT! IT FEELS WEIRD!
JUST PLUCK THEM OUT THEN. HERE, LET ME SEE.
YOU'RE NOT BLEEDING MUCH, BUT YEAH, ONE OF THEM GOT IN PRETTY DEEP. HOW'D YOU MANAGE TO BREAK
YAAHGHH!
SORRY.
3

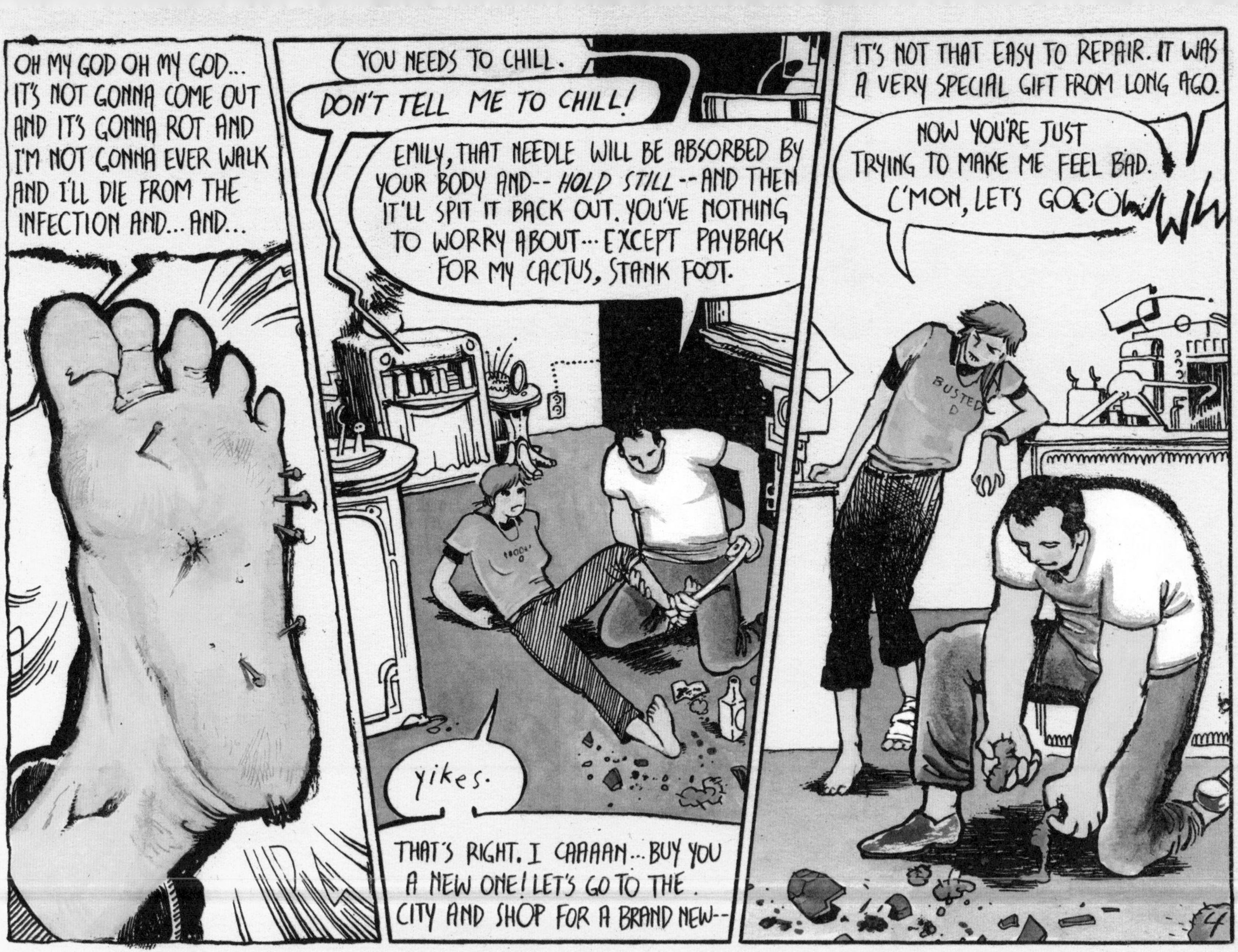
OH MY GOD OH MY GOD... IT'S NOT GONNA COME OUT AND IT'S GONNA ROT AND I'M NOT GONNA EVER WALK AND I'LL DIE FROM THE INFECTION AND... AND...
YOU NEEDS TO CHILL.
DON'T TELL ME TO CHILL!
EMILY, THAT NEEDLE WILL BE ABSORBED BY YOUR BODY AND-- HOLD STILL --AND THEN IT'LL SPIT IT BACK OUT. YOU'VE NOTHING TO WORRY ABOUT... EXCEPT PAYBACK FOR MY CACTUS, STANK FOOT.
yikes.
THAT'S RIGHT. I CAAAAN... BUY YOU A NEW ONE! LET'S GO TO THE CITY AND SHOP FOR A BRAND NEW--
BUSTED D
IT'S NOT THAT EASY TO REPAIR. IT WAS A VERY SPECIAL GIFT FROM LONG AGO.
NOW YOU'RE JUST TRYING TO MAKE ME FEEL BAD. C'MON, LET'S GOOOWWW
4

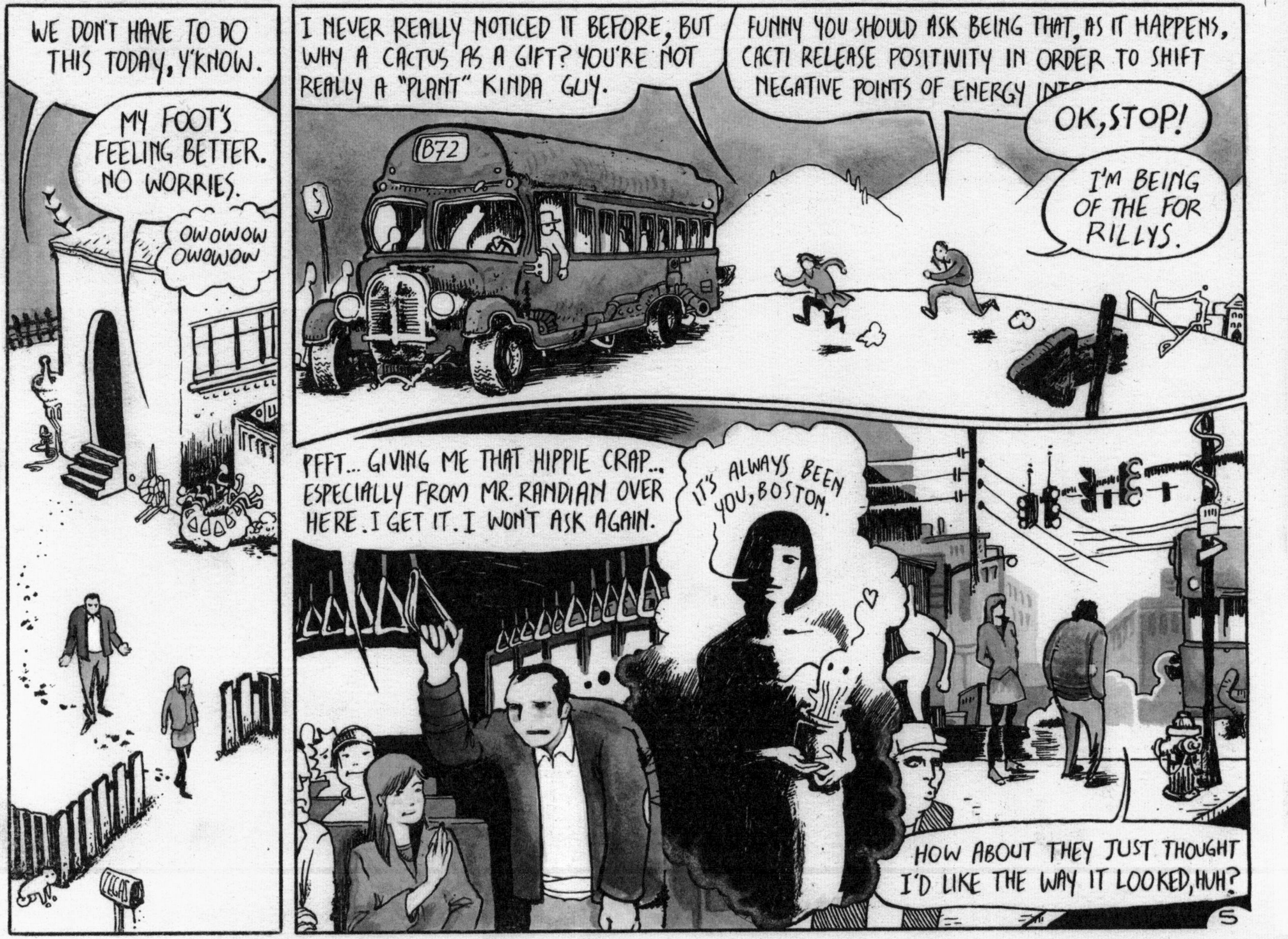

WE DON'T HAVE TO DO THIS TODAY, Y'KNOW.
MY FOOT'S FEELING BETTER. NO WORRIES.
OWOWOW OWOWOW
I NEVER REALLY NOTICED IT BEFORE, BUT WHY A CACTUS AS A GIFT? YOU'RE NOT REALLY A "PLANT" KINDA GUY.
B72
FUNNY YOU SHOULD ASK BEING THAT, AS IT HAPPENS, CACTI RELEASE POSITIVITY IN ORDER TO SHIFT NEGATIVE POINTS OF ENERGY INT
OK, STOP!
I'M BEING OF THE FOR RILLYS.
PFFT... GIVING ME THAT HIPPIE CRAP... ESPECIALLY FROM MR. RANDIAN OVER HERE. I GET IT. I WON'T ASK AGAIN.
IT'S ALWAYS BEEN YOU, BOSTON.
HOW ABOUT THEY JUST THOUGHT I'D LIKE THE WAY IT LOOKED, HUH?

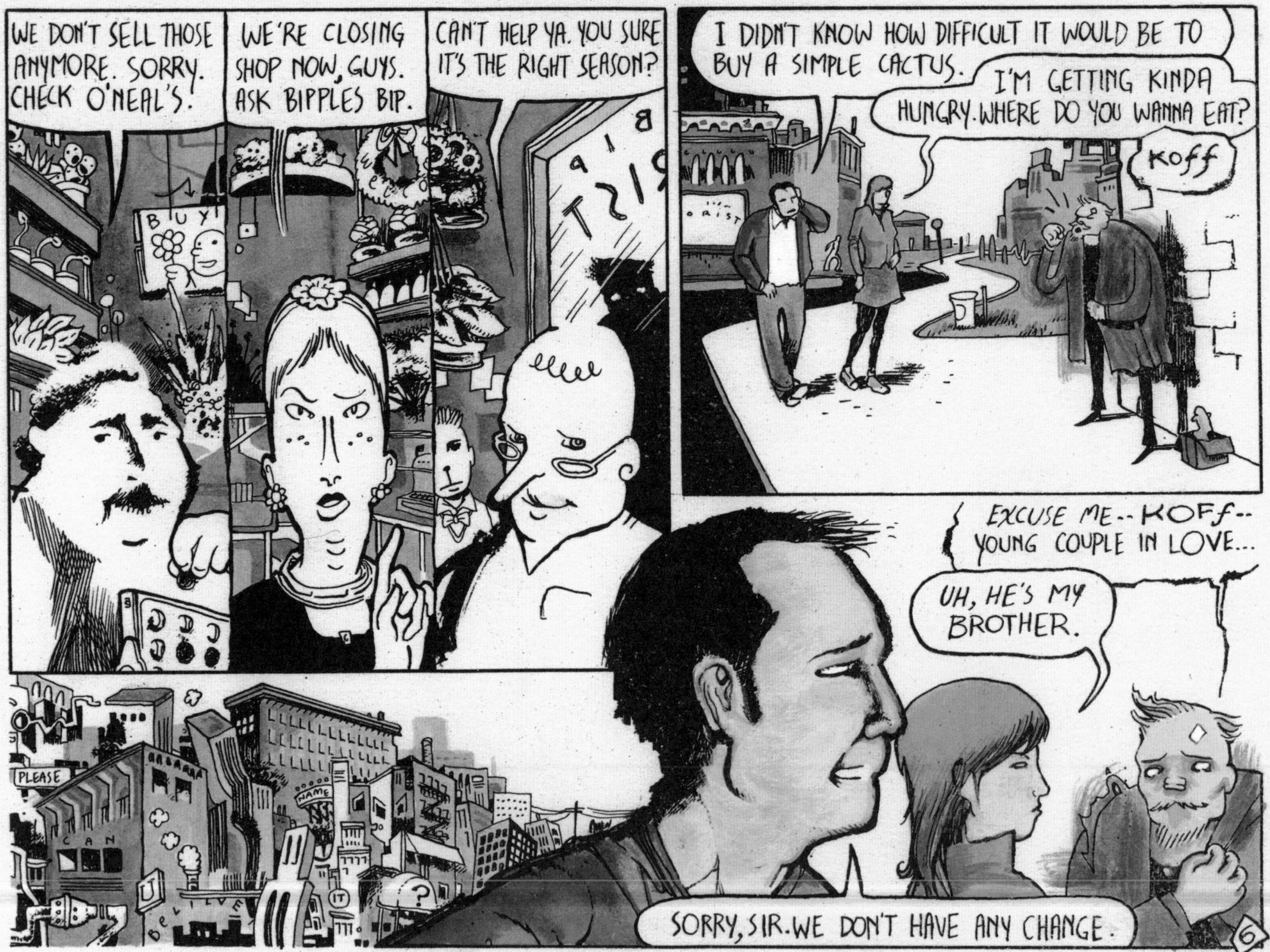
WE DON'T SELL THOSE ANYMORE. SORRY. CHECK O'NEAL'S.
WE'RE CLOSING SHOP NOW, GUYS. ASK BIPPLES BIP.
CAN'T HELP YA. YOU SURE IT'S THE RIGHT SEASON?
I DIDN'T KNOW HOW DIFFICULT IT WOULD BE TO BUY A SIMPLE CACTUS.
I'M GETTING KINDA HUNGRY. WHERE DO YOU WANNA EAT?
KOFF
EXCUSE ME.. KOFF.. YOUNG COUPLE IN LOVE...
UH, HE'S MY BROTHER.
SORRY, SIR. WE DON'T HAVE ANY CHANGE.
PLEASE
CAN
NAME
6

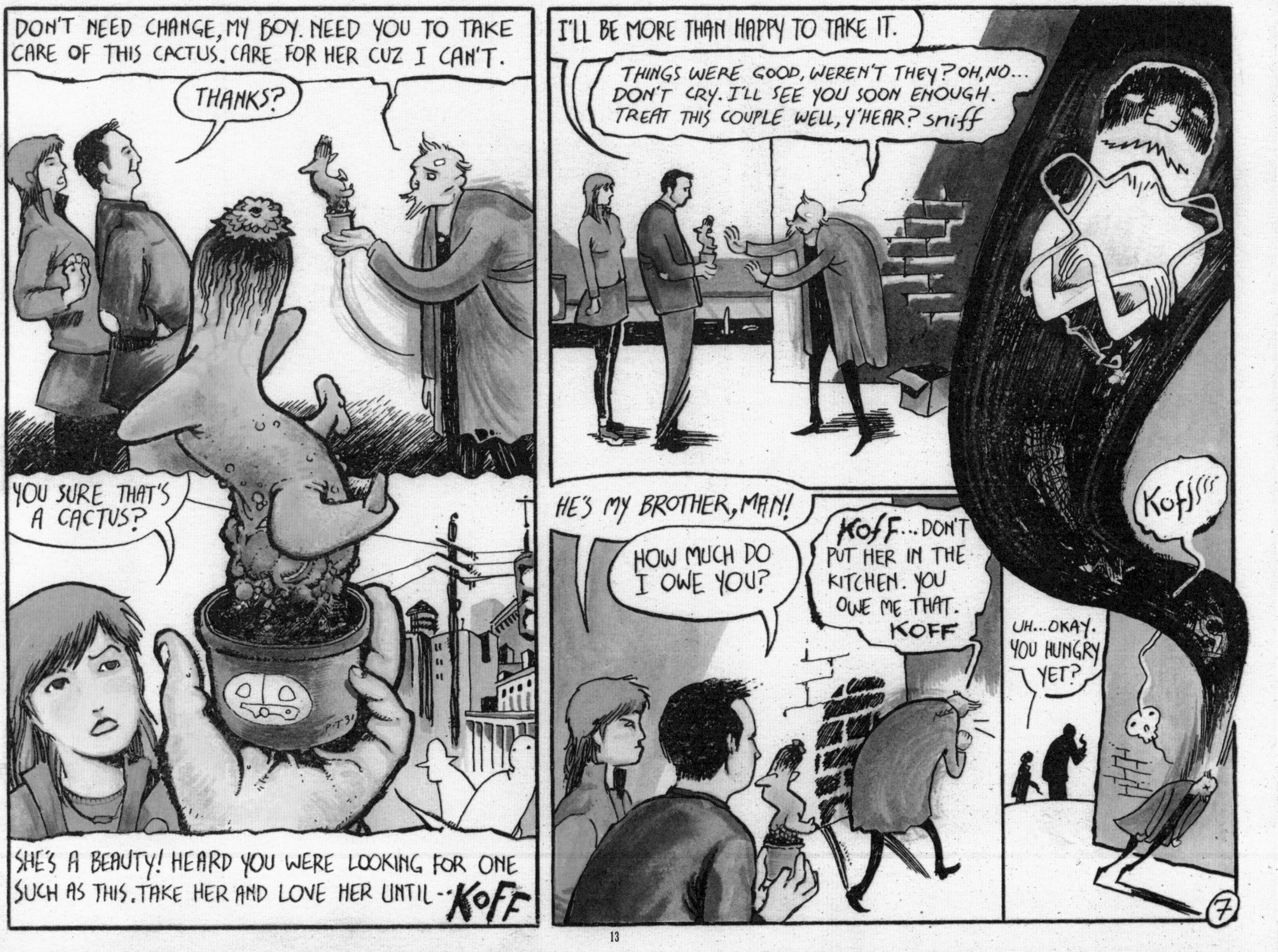
DON'T NEED CHANGE, MY BOY. NEED YOU TO TAKE CARE OF THIS CACTUS. CARE FOR HER CUZ I CAN'T.
THANKS?
YOU SURE THAT'S A CACTUS?
SHE'S A BEAUTY! HEARD YOU WERE LOOKING FOR ONE SUCH AS THIS. TAKE HER AND LOVE HER UNTIL--KOFF
I'LL BE MORE THAN HAPPY TO TAKE IT.
THINGS WERE GOOD, WEREN'T THEY? OH, NO... DON'T CRY. I'LL SEE YOU SOON ENOUGH. TREAT THIS COUPLE WELL, Y'HEAR? sniff
HE'S MY BROTHER, MAN!
HOW MUCH DO I OWE YOU?
KOFF... DON'T PUT HER IN THE KITCHEN. YOU OWE ME THAT. KOFF
KOFFSSS
UH...OKAY. YOU HUNGRY YET?
7

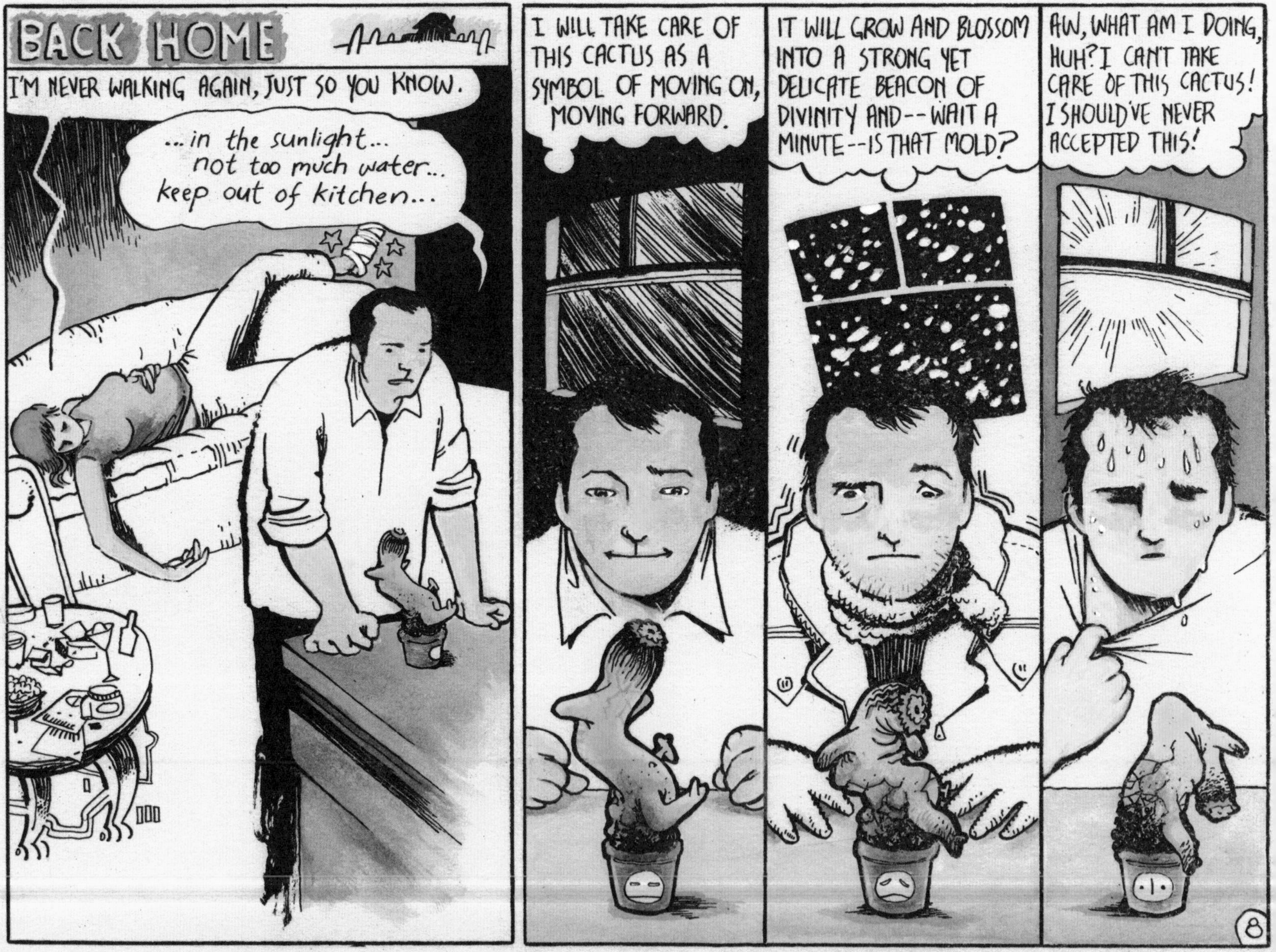
BACK HOME
I'M NEVER WALKING AGAIN, JUST SO YOU KNOW.
...in the sunlight... not too much water... keep out of kitchen...
I WILL TAKE CARE OF THIS CACTUS AS A SYMBOL OF MOVING ON, MOVING FORWARD.
IT WILL GROW AND BLOSSOM INTO A STRONG YET DELICATE BEACON OF DIVINITY AND--WAIT A MINUTE--IS THAT MOLD?
AW, WHAT AM I DOING, HUH? I CAN'T TAKE CARE OF THIS CACTUS! I SHOULD'VE NEVER ACCEPTED THIS!
8

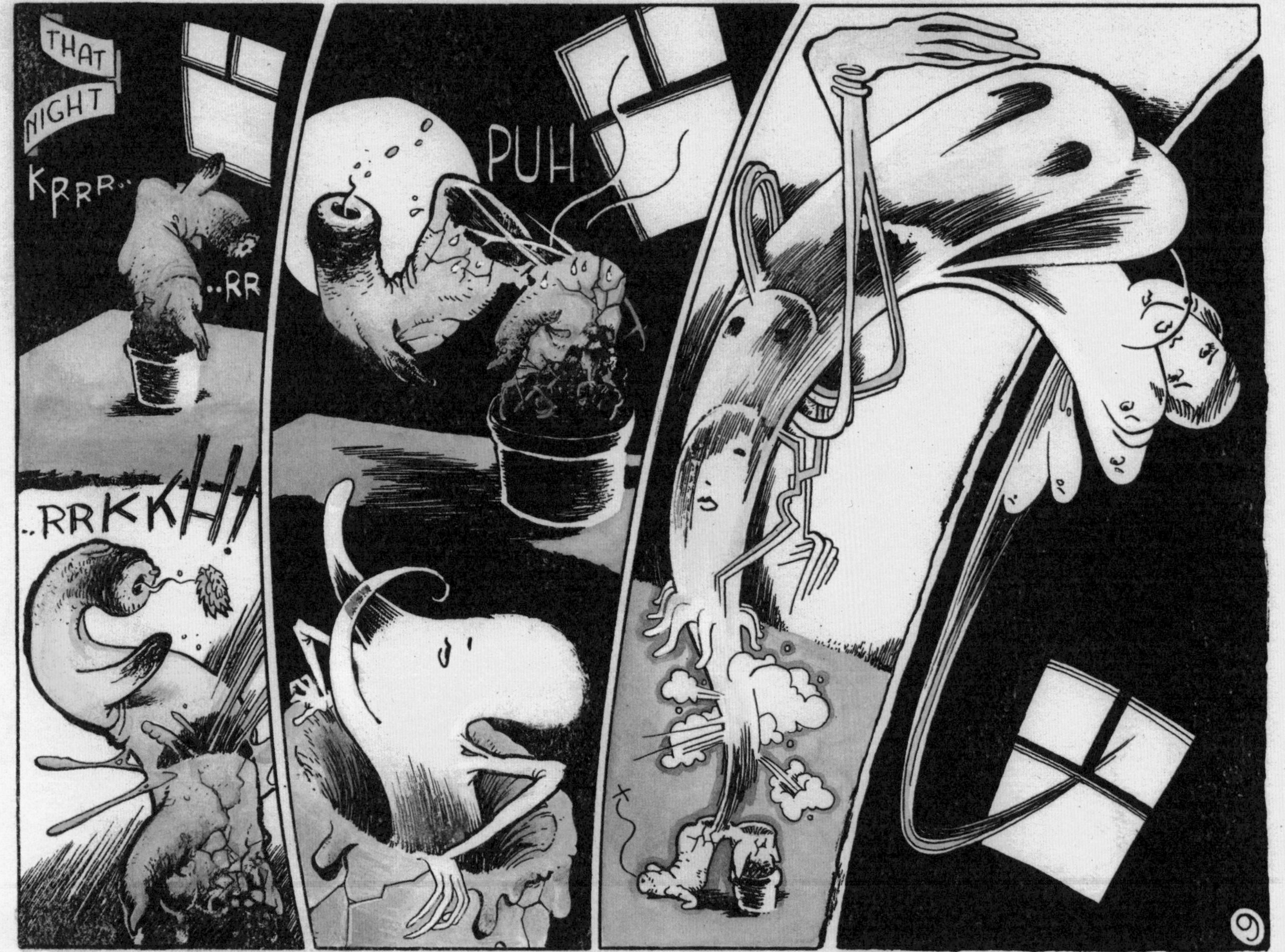
THAT NIGHT
KRRR..
..RR
..RRKKHH!
PUH
9

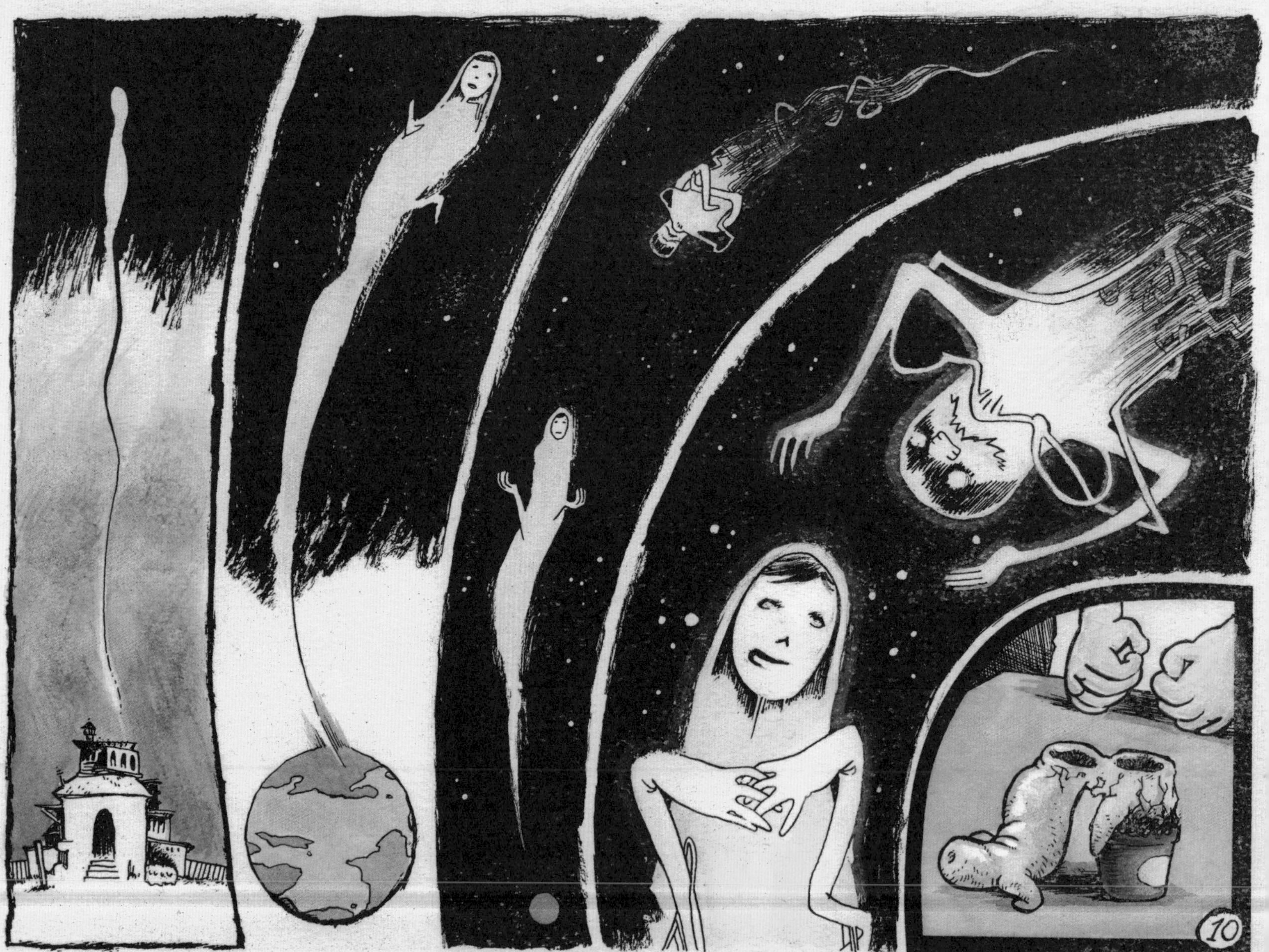
10

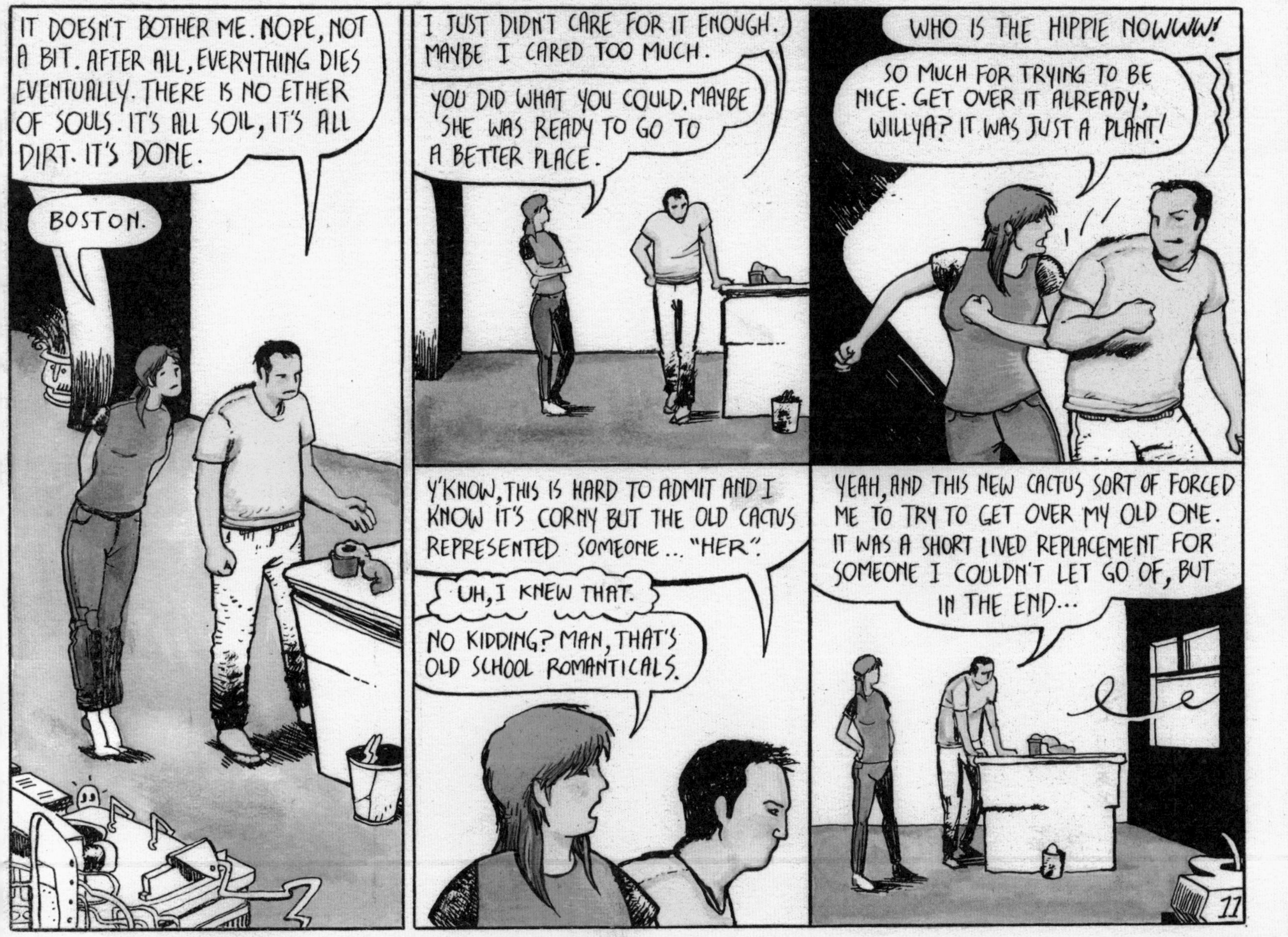
IT DOESN'T BOTHER ME. NOPE, NOT A BIT. AFTER ALL, EVERYTHING DIES EVENTUALLY. THERE IS NO ETHER OF SOULS. IT'S ALL SOIL, IT'S ALL DIRT. IT'S DONE.
BOSTON.
I JUST DIDN'T CARE FOR IT ENOUGH. MAYBE I CARED TOO MUCH.
YOU DID WHAT YOU COULD. MAYBE SHE WAS READY TO GO TO A BETTER PLACE.
WHO IS THE HIPPIE NOWWW!
SO MUCH FOR TRYING TO BE NICE. GET OVER IT ALREADY, WILLYA? IT WAS JUST A PLANT!
Y'KNOW, THIS IS HARD TO ADMIT AND I KNOW IT'S CORNY BUT THE OLD CACTUS REPRESENTED SOMEONE... "HER".
UH, I KNEW THAT.
NO KIDDING? MAN, THAT'S OLD SCHOOL ROMANTICALS.
YEAH, AND THIS NEW CACTUS SORT OF FORCED ME TO TRY TO GET OVER MY OLD ONE. IT WAS A SHORT LIVED REPLACEMENT FOR SOMEONE I COULDN'T LET GO OF, BUT IN THE END...
11

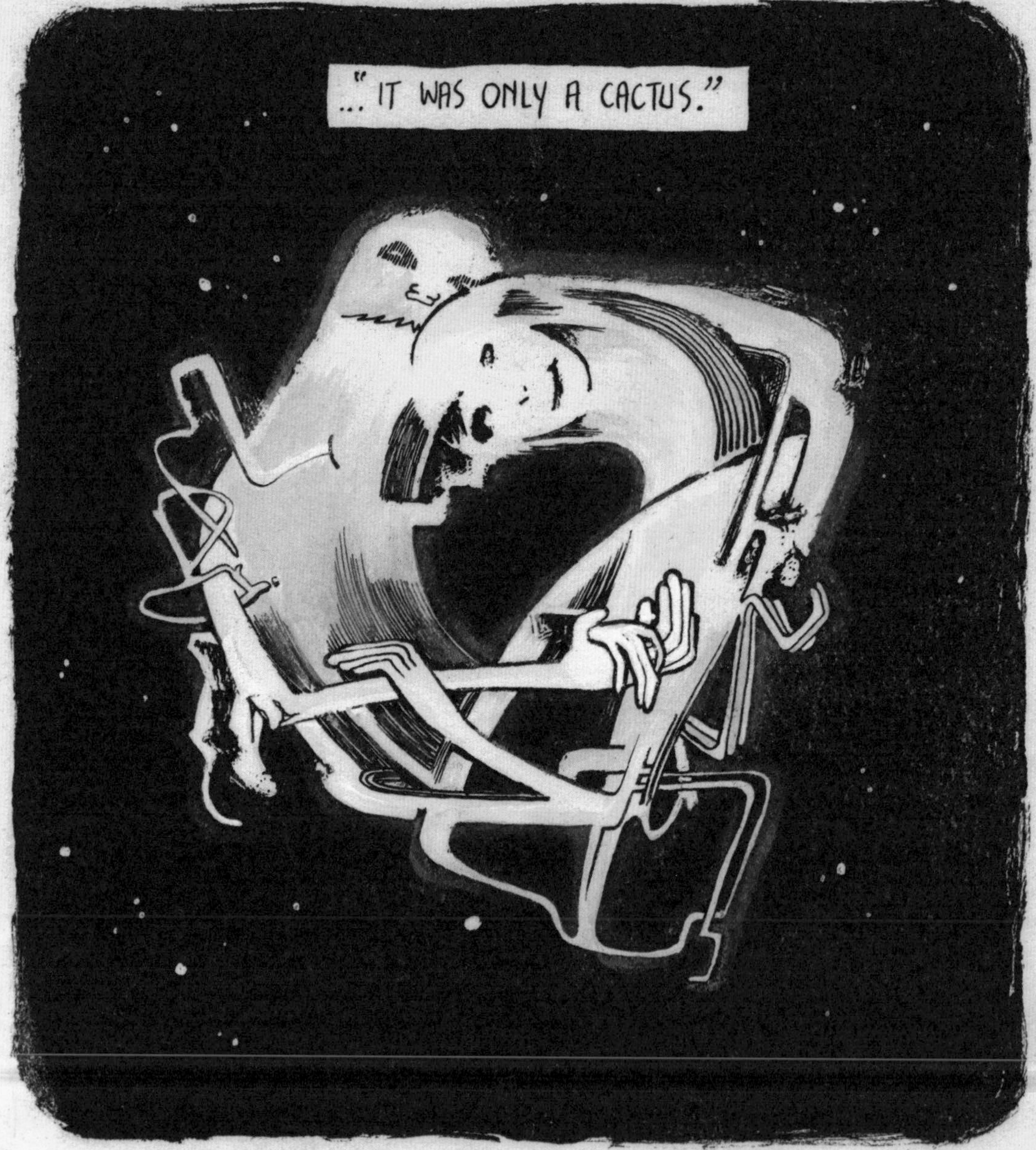
..."IT WAS ONLY A CACTUS."

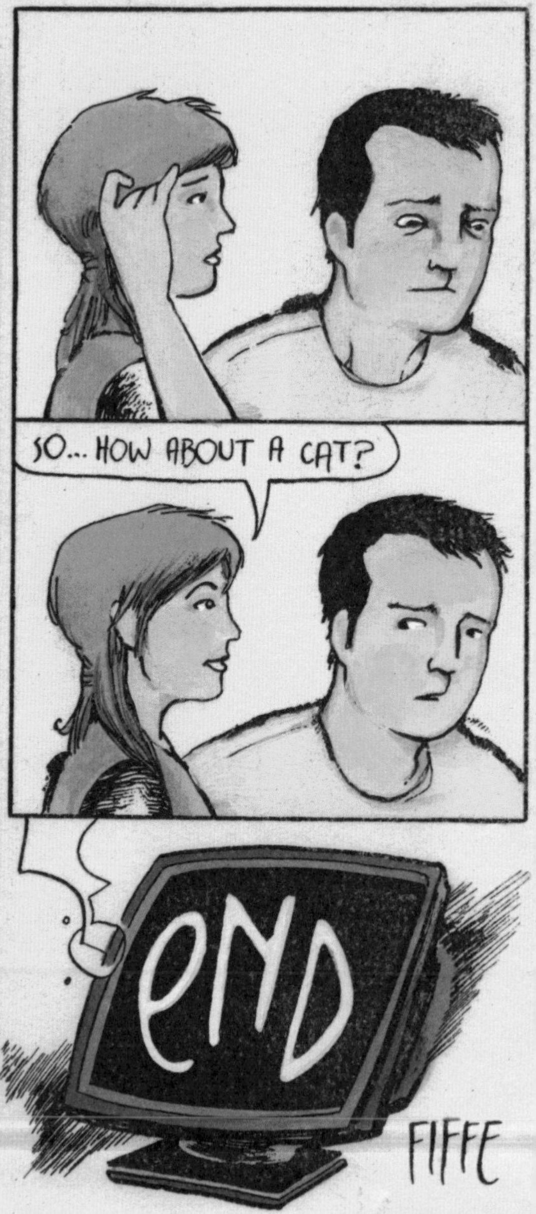
SO... HOW ABOUT A CAT?
END
FIFFE

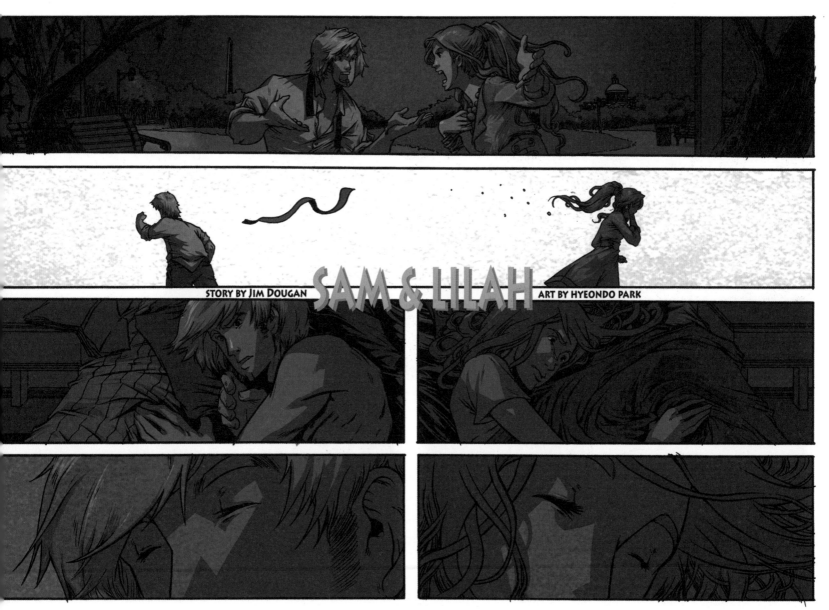

SAM & LILAH

STORY BY JIM DOUGAN   ART BY HYEONDO PARK

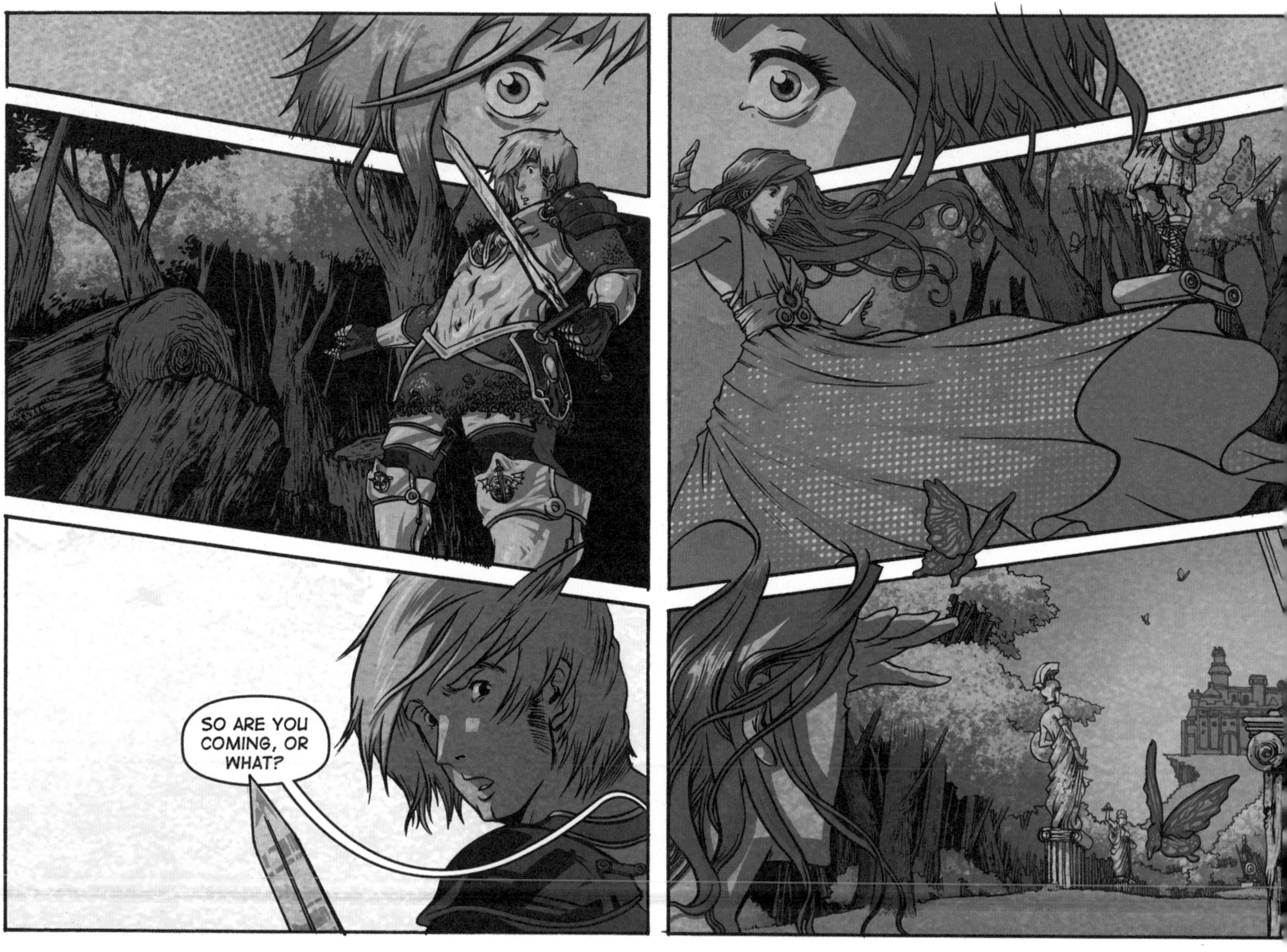
SO ARE YOU COMING, OR WHAT?

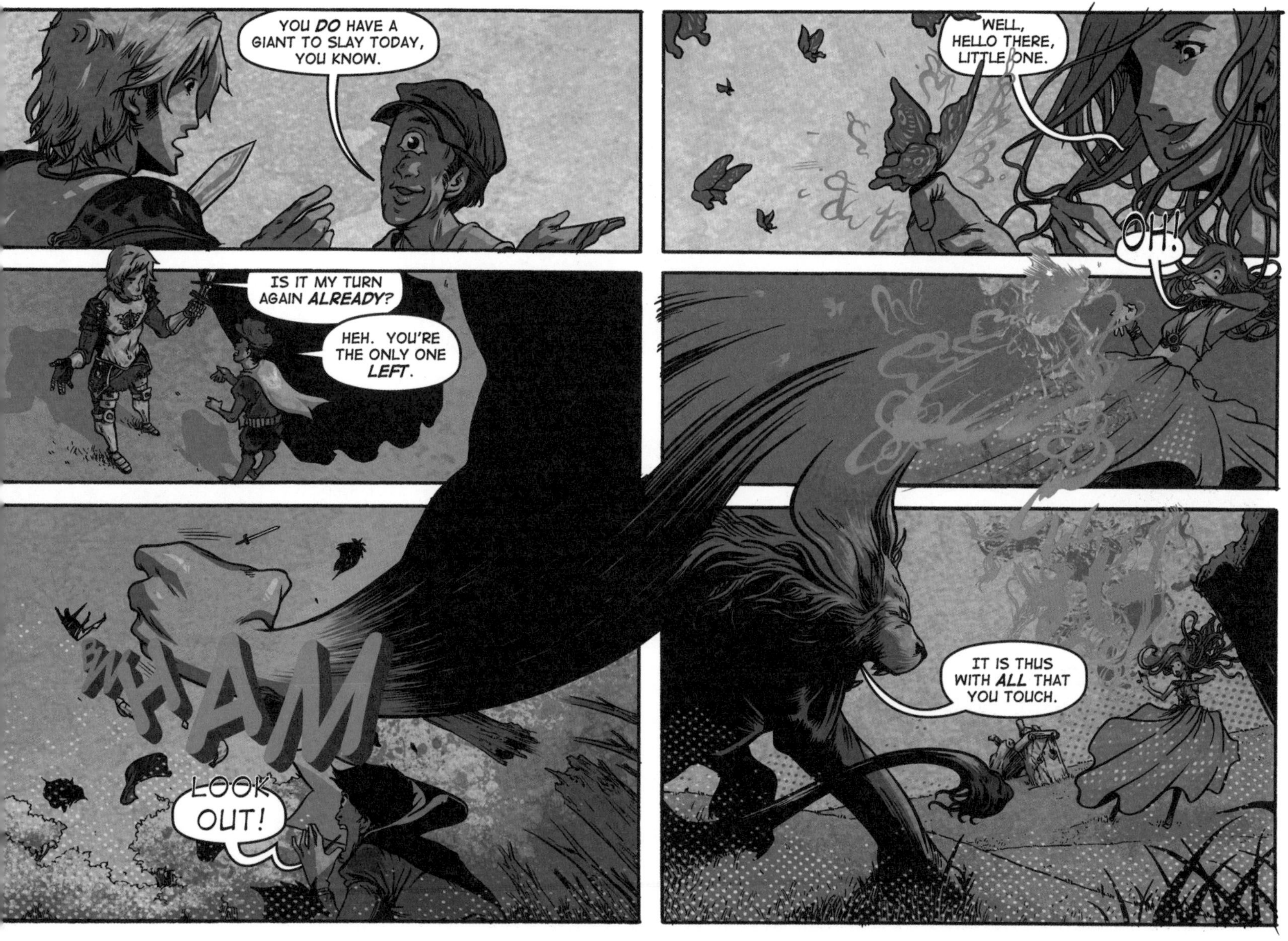

YOU DO HAVE A GIANT TO SLAY TODAY, YOU KNOW.
IS IT MY TURN AGAIN ALREADY?
HEH. YOU'RE THE ONLY ONE LEFT.
WHAM
LOOK OUT!
WELL, HELLO THERE, LITTLE ONE.
OH!
IT IS THUS WITH ALL THAT YOU TOUCH.

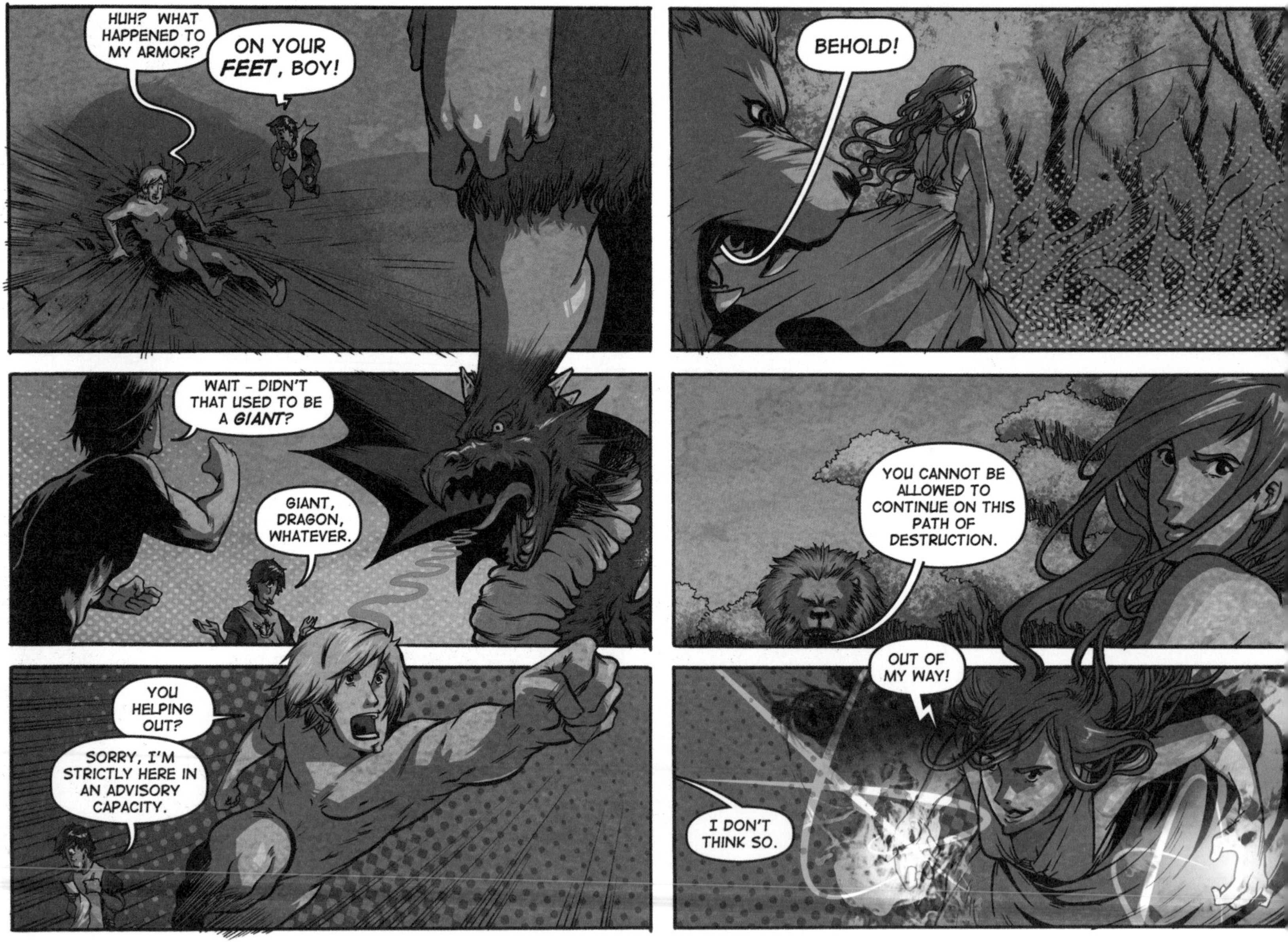
HUH? WHAT HAPPENED TO MY ARMOR?
ON YOUR FEET, BOY!
WAIT - DIDN'T THAT USED TO BE A GIANT?
GIANT, DRAGON, WHATEVER.
YOU HELPING OUT?
SORRY, I'M STRICTLY HERE IN AN ADVISORY CAPACITY.
BEHOLD!
YOU CANNOT BE ALLOWED TO CONTINUE ON THIS PATH OF DESTRUCTION.
OUT OF MY WAY!
I DON'T THINK SO.

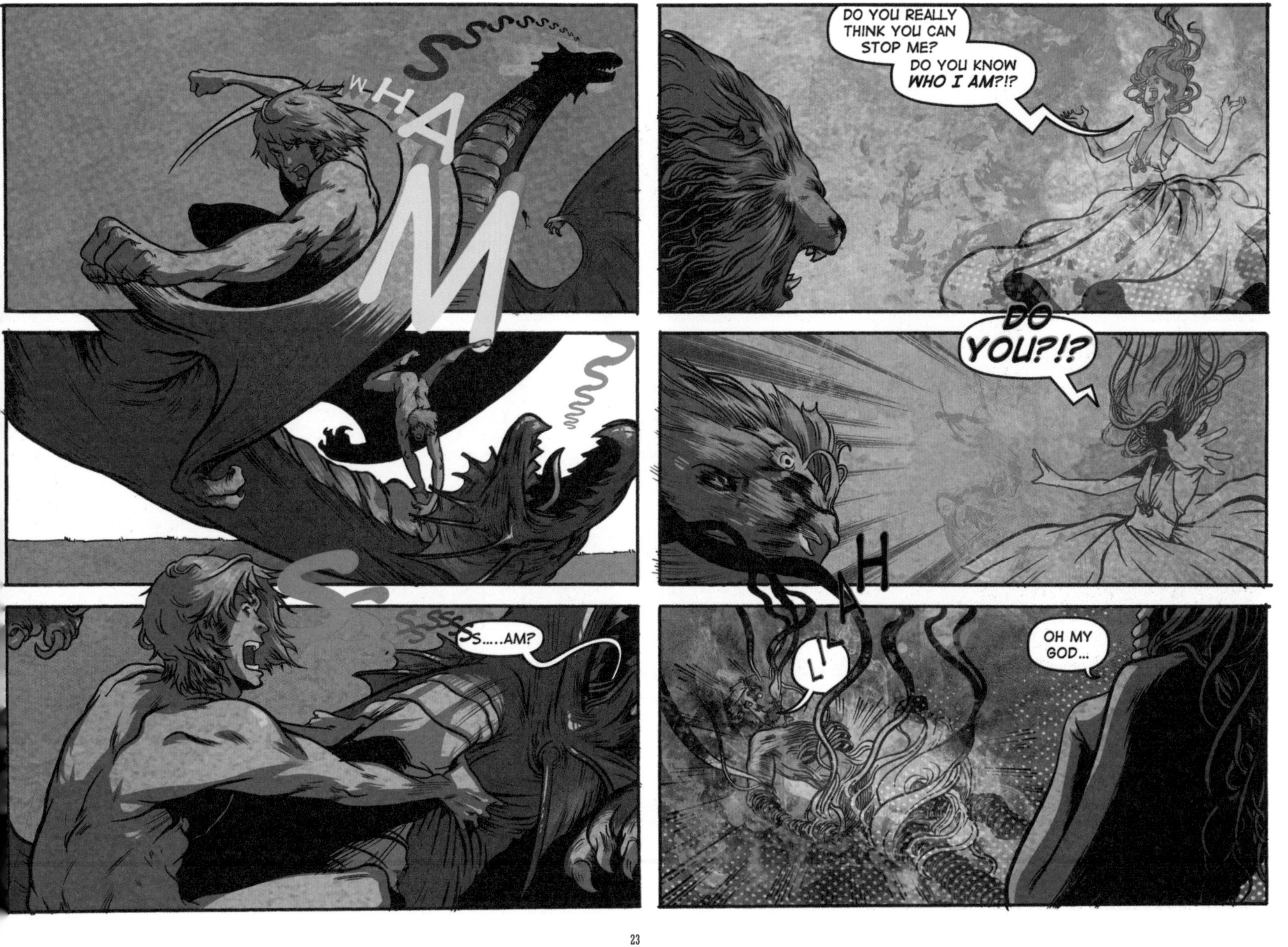
SSSSSSS
WHAM
DO YOU REALLY THINK YOU CAN STOP ME?
DO YOU KNOW WHO I AM?!?
SSSSSS.....AM?
DO YOU?!?
LILAH
OH MY GOD...

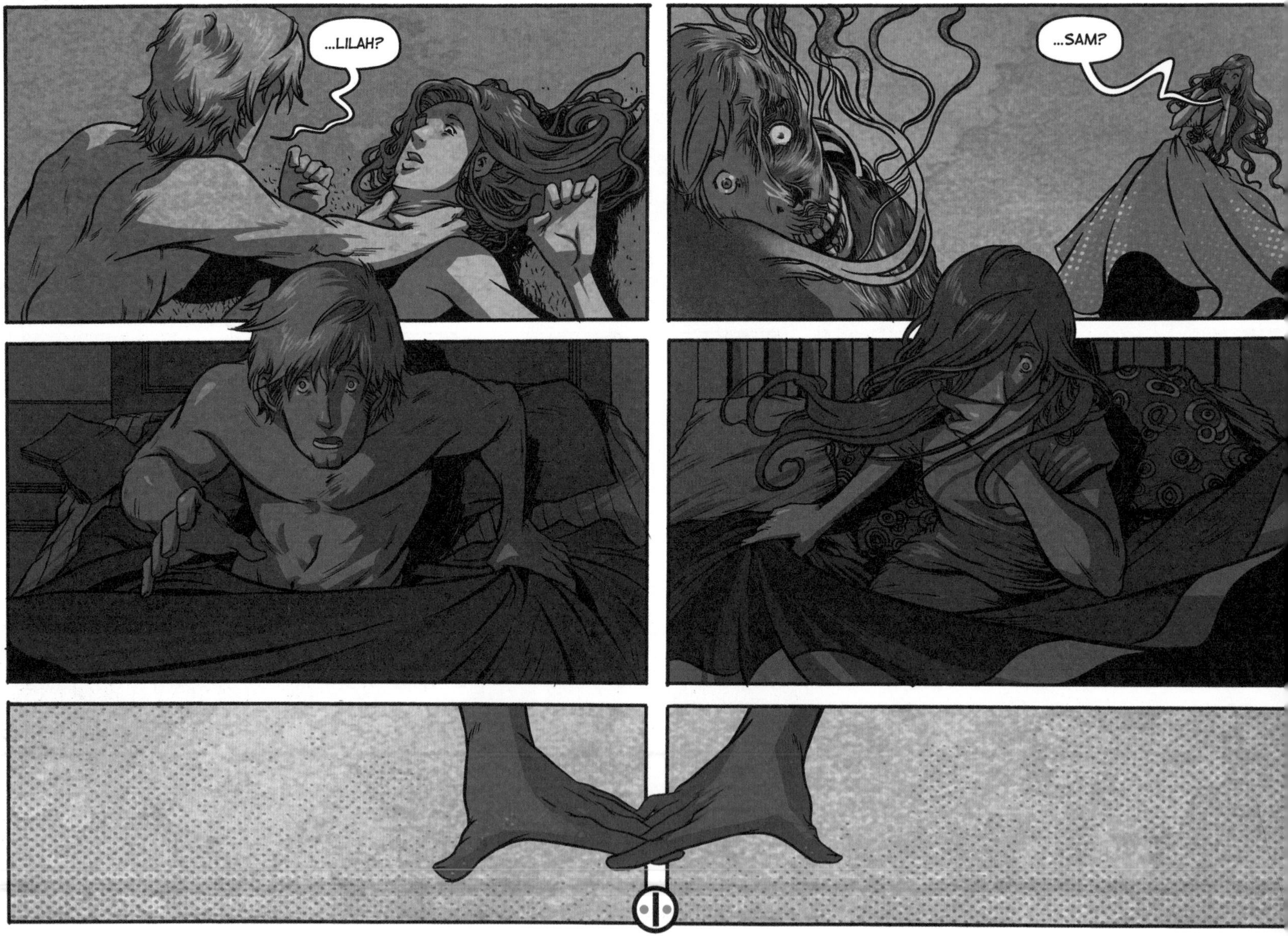
...LILAH?
...SAM?

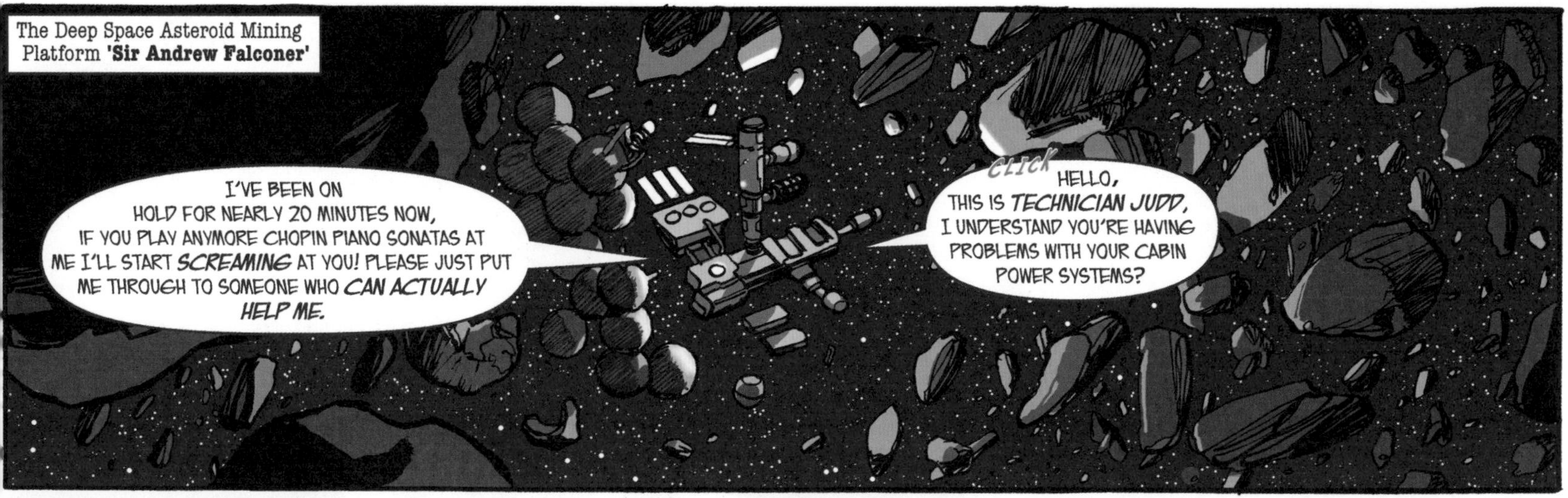
The Deep Space Asteroid Mining Platform 'Sir Andrew Falconer'
I'VE BEEN ON HOLD FOR NEARLY 20 MINUTES NOW, IF YOU PLAY ANYMORE CHOPIN PIANO SONATAS AT ME I'LL START SCREAMING AT YOU! PLEASE JUST PUT ME THROUGH TO SOMEONE WHO CAN ACTUALLY HELP ME.
CLICK
HELLO, THIS IS TECHNICIAN JUDD, I UNDERSTAND YOU'RE HAVING PROBLEMS WITH YOUR CABIN POWER SYSTEMS?

WHEN LILLY MET COSMO...

a prequel written & drawn by Simon Fraser

with colours by Gary Caldwell

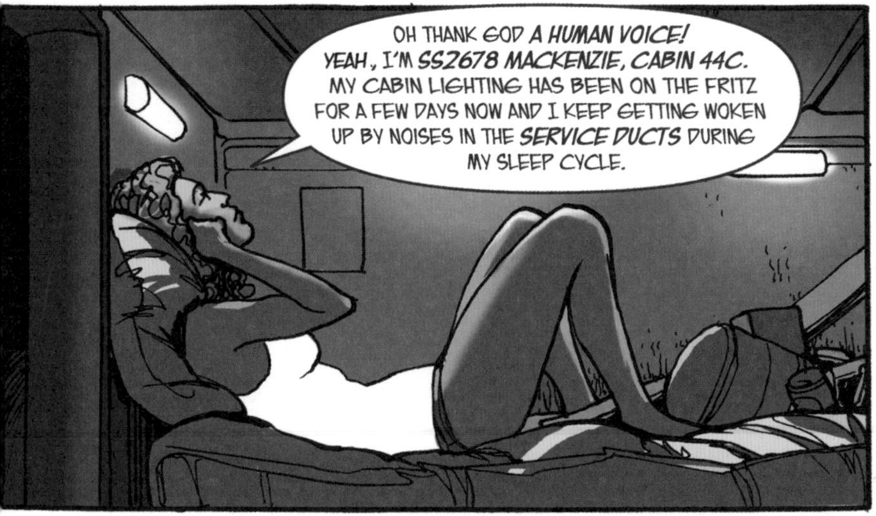
OH THANK GOD A HUMAN VOICE! YEAH., I'M SS2678 MACKENZIE, CABIN 44C. MY CABIN LIGHTING HAS BEEN ON THE FRITZ FOR A FEW DAYS NOW AND I KEEP GETTING WOKEN UP BY NOISES IN THE SERVICE DUCTS DURING MY SLEEP CYCLE.

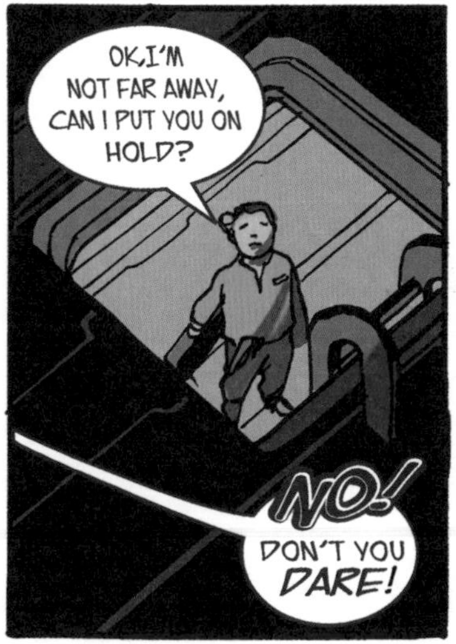
OK,I'M NOT FAR AWAY, CAN I PUT YOU ON HOLD?
NO! DON'T YOU DARE!

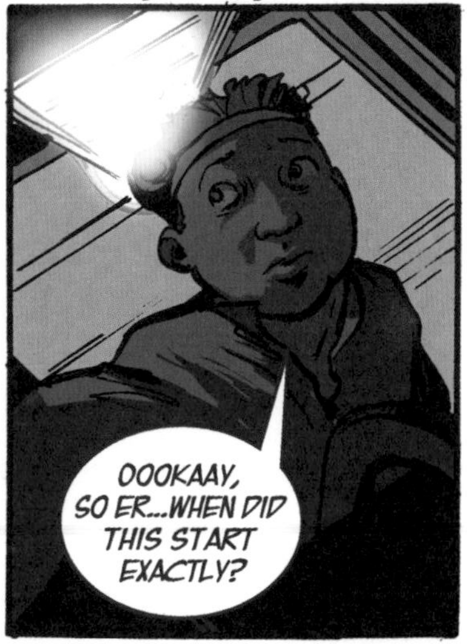
OOOKAAY, SO ER...WHEN DID THIS START EXACTLY?

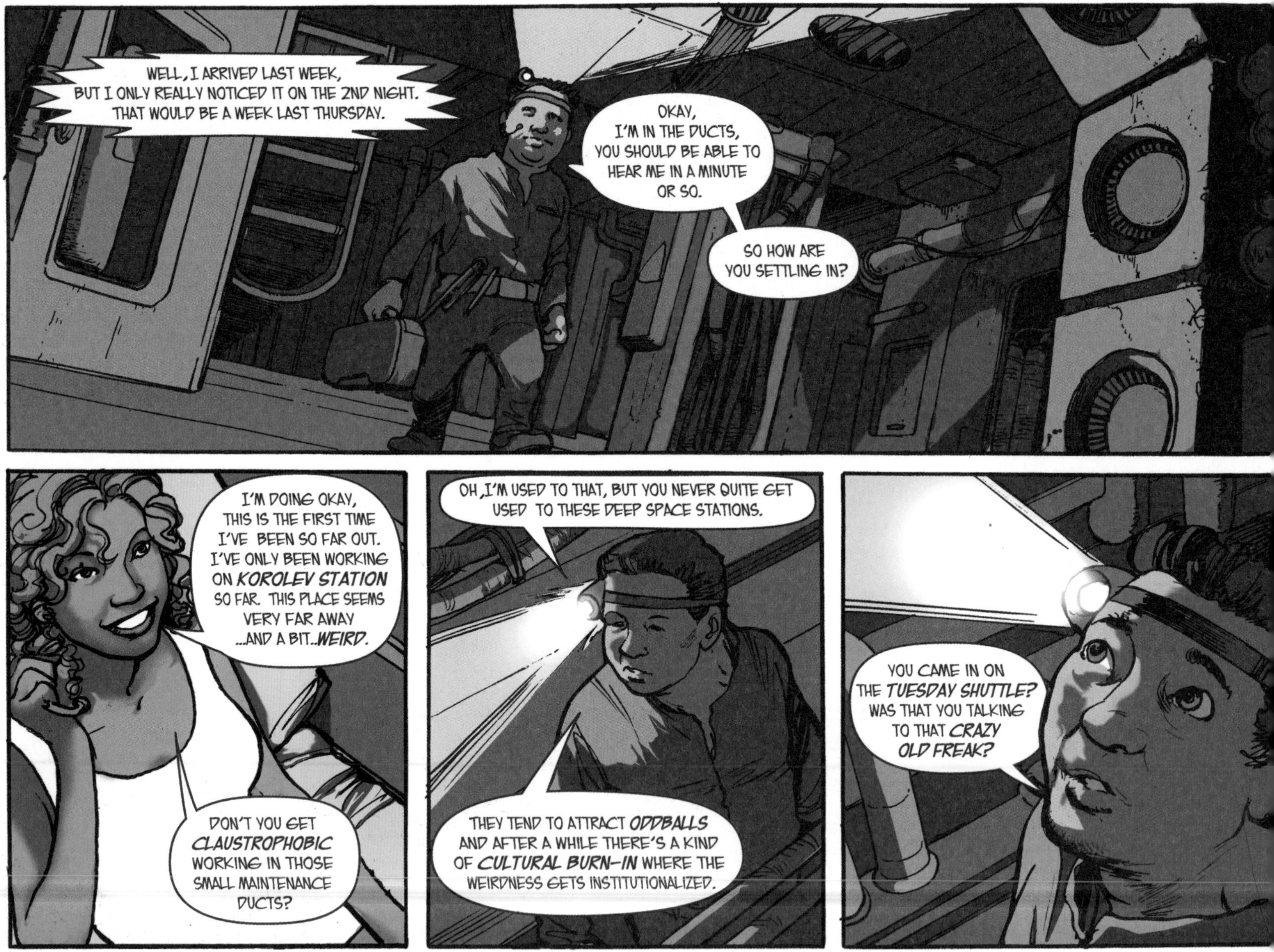
WELL, I ARRIVED LAST WEEK, BUT I ONLY REALLY NOTICED IT ON THE 2ND NIGHT. THAT WOULD BE A WEEK LAST THURSDAY.
OKAY, I'M IN THE DUCTS, YOU SHOULD BE ABLE TO HEAR ME IN A MINUTE OR SO.
SO HOW ARE YOU SETTLING IN?
I'M DOING OKAY, THIS IS THE FIRST TIME I'VE BEEN SO FAR OUT. I'VE ONLY BEEN WORKING ON KOROLEV STATION SO FAR. THIS PLACE SEEMS VERY FAR AWAY ...AND A BIT...WEIRD.
DON'T YOU GET CLAUSTROPHOBIC WORKING IN THOSE SMALL MAINTENANCE DUCTS?
OH, I'M USED TO THAT, BUT YOU NEVER QUITE GET USED TO THESE DEEP SPACE STATIONS.
THEY TEND TO ATTRACT ODDBALLS AND AFTER A WHILE THERE'S A KIND OF CULTURAL BURN-IN WHERE THE WEIRDNESS GETS INSTITUTIONALIZED.
YOU CAME IN ON THE TUESDAY SHUTTLE? WAS THAT YOU TALKING TO THAT CRAZY OLD FREAK?

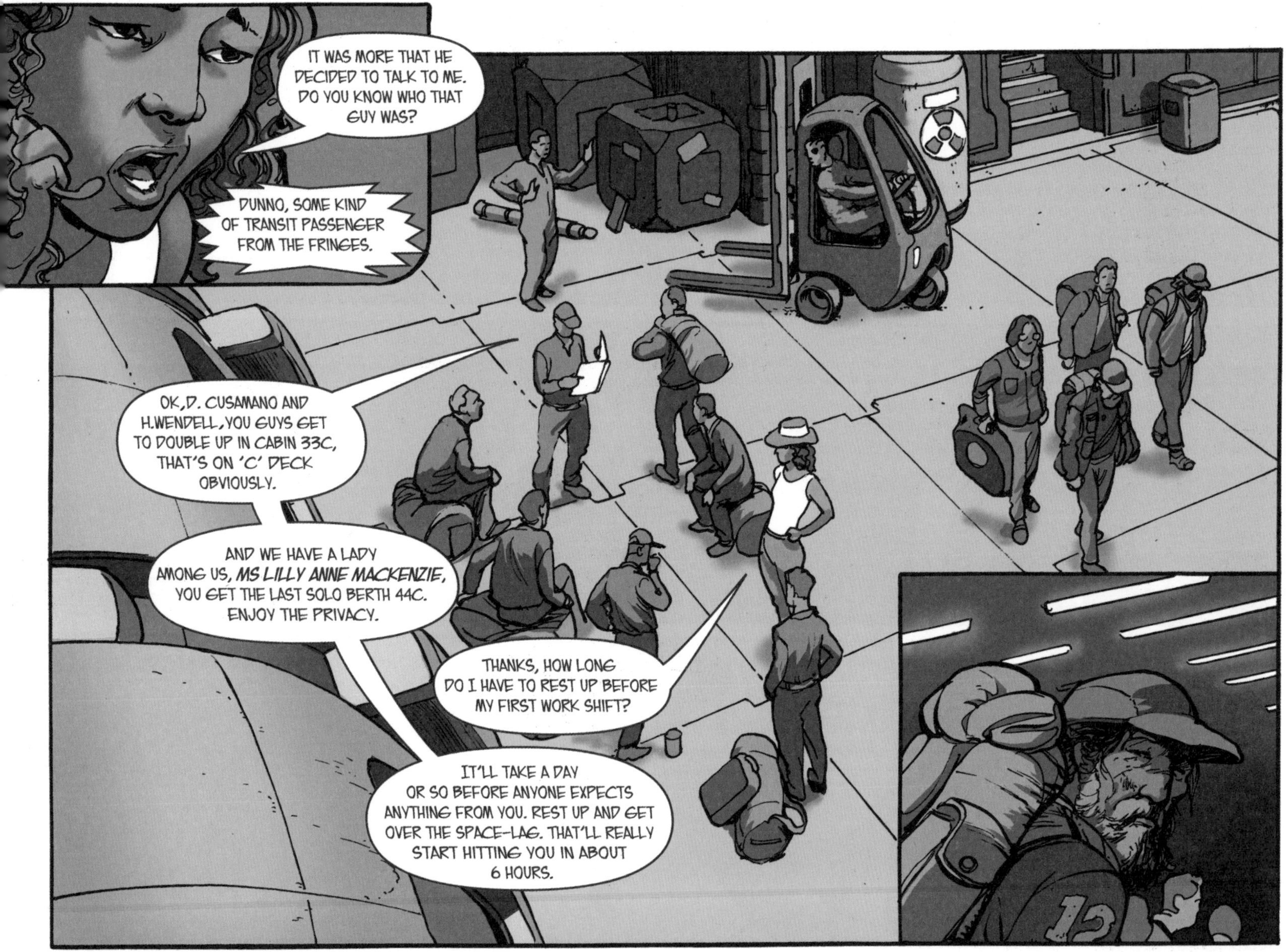
IT WAS MORE THAT HE DECIDED TO TALK TO ME. DO YOU KNOW WHO THAT GUY WAS?
DUNNO, SOME KIND OF TRANSIT PASSENGER FROM THE FRINGES.
OK, D. CUSAMANO AND H. WENDELL, YOU GUYS GET TO DOUBLE UP IN CABIN 33C, THAT'S ON 'C' DECK OBVIOUSLY.
AND WE HAVE A LADY AMONG US, *MS LILLY ANNE MACKENZIE*, YOU GET THE LAST SOLO BERTH 44C. ENJOY THE PRIVACY.
THANKS, HOW LONG DO I HAVE TO REST UP BEFORE MY FIRST WORK SHIFT?
IT'LL TAKE A DAY OR SO BEFORE ANYONE EXPECTS ANYTHING FROM YOU. REST UP AND GET OVER THE SPACE-LAG. THAT'LL REALLY START HITTING YOU IN ABOUT 6 HOURS.
12

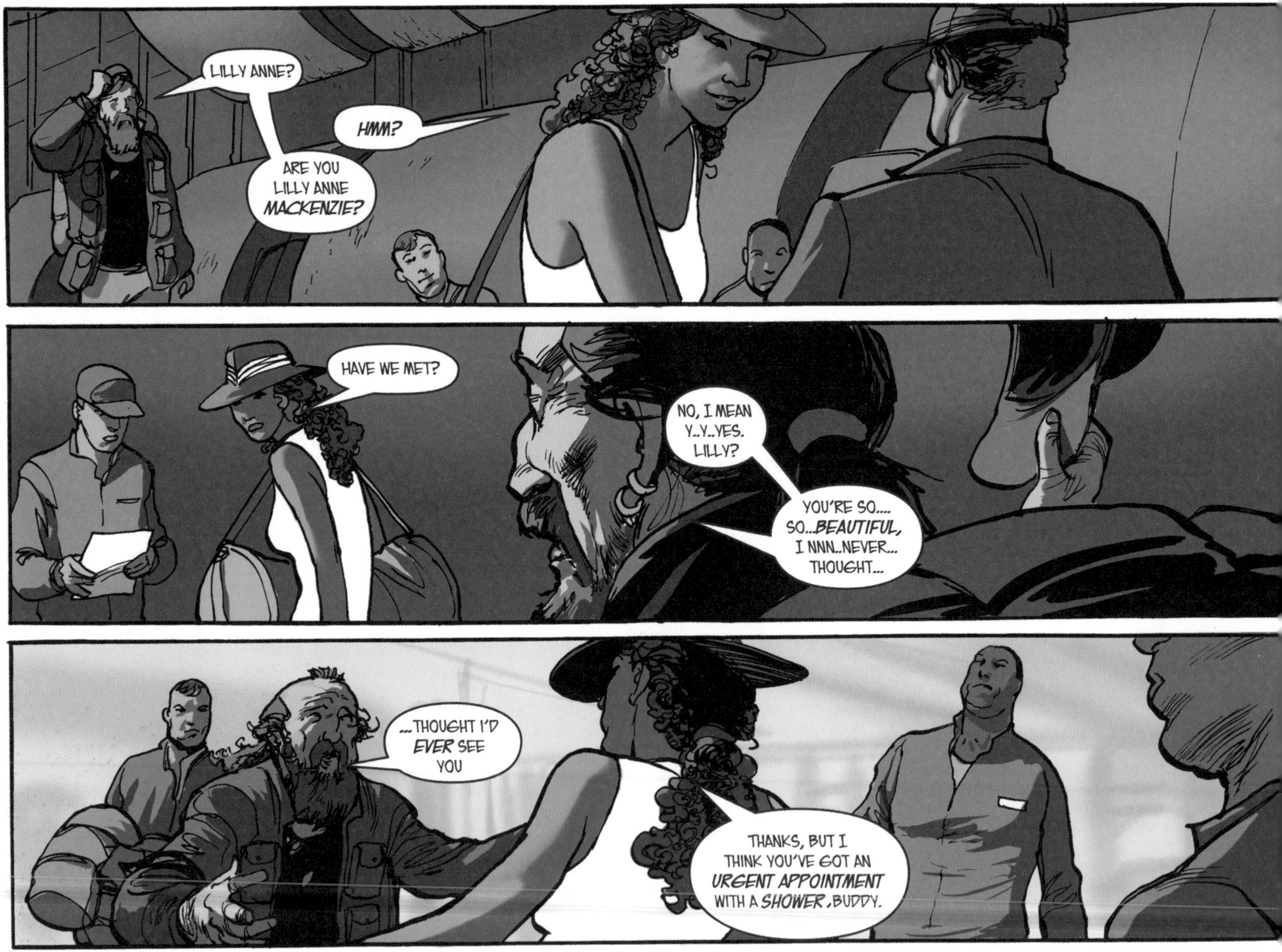
LILLY ANNE?
HMM?
ARE YOU LILLY ANNE MACKENZIE?
HAVE WE MET?
NO, I MEAN Y..Y..YES. LILLY?
YOU'RE SO.... SO...BEAUTIFUL, I NNN..NEVER... THOUGHT...
...THOUGHT I'D EVER SEE YOU
THANKS, BUT I THINK YOU'VE GOT AN URGENT APPOINTMENT WITH A SHOWER, BUDDY.

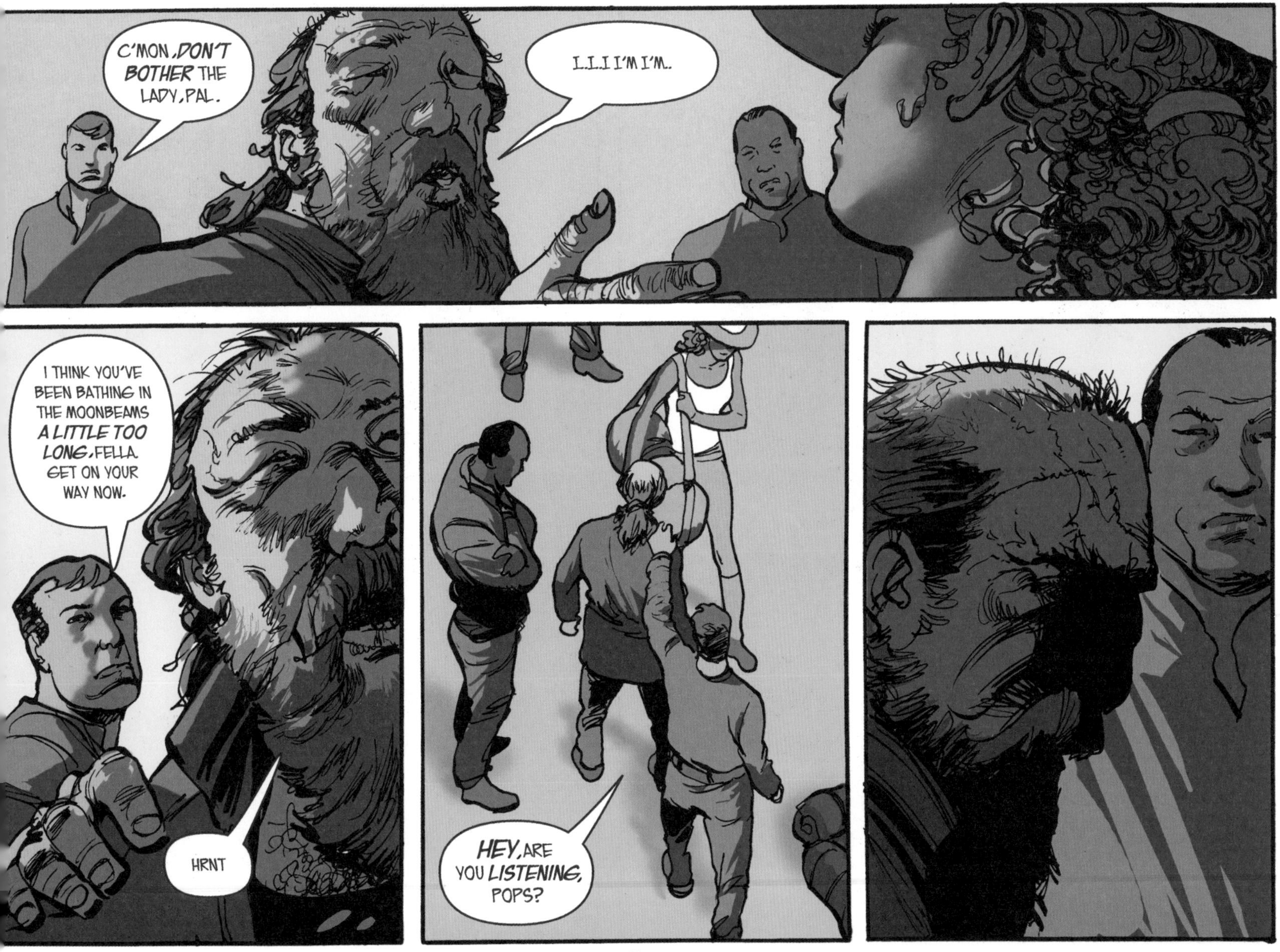
C'MON, DON'T BOTHER THE LADY, PAL.
I..I..I I'M I'M.
I THINK YOU'VE BEEN BATHING IN THE MOONBEAMS A LITTLE TOO LONG, FELLA. GET ON YOUR WAY NOW.
HRNT
HEY, ARE YOU LISTENING, POPS?

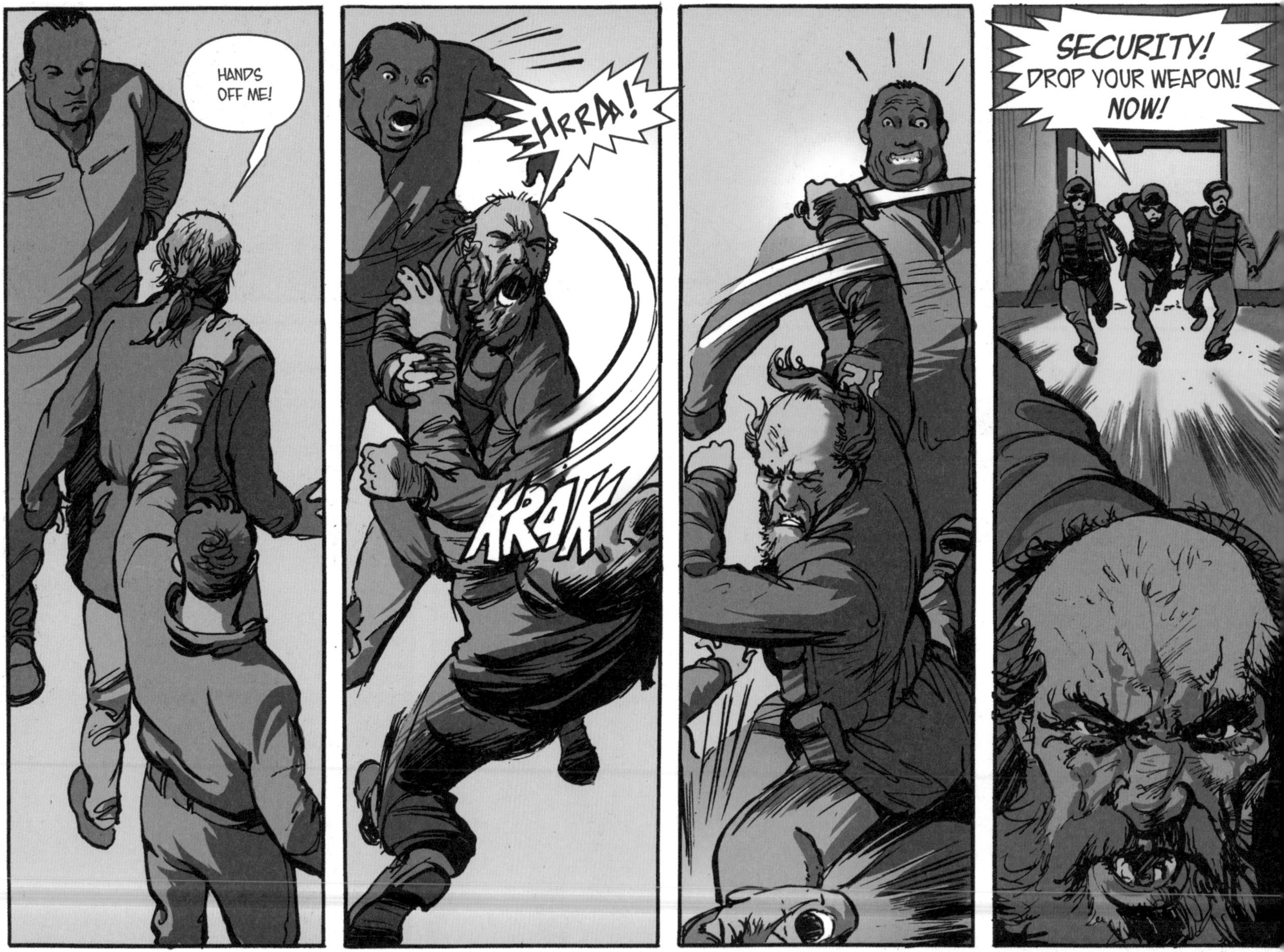
HANDS OFF ME!
HRRAA!
KRAK
SECURITY! DROP YOUR WEAPON! NOW!

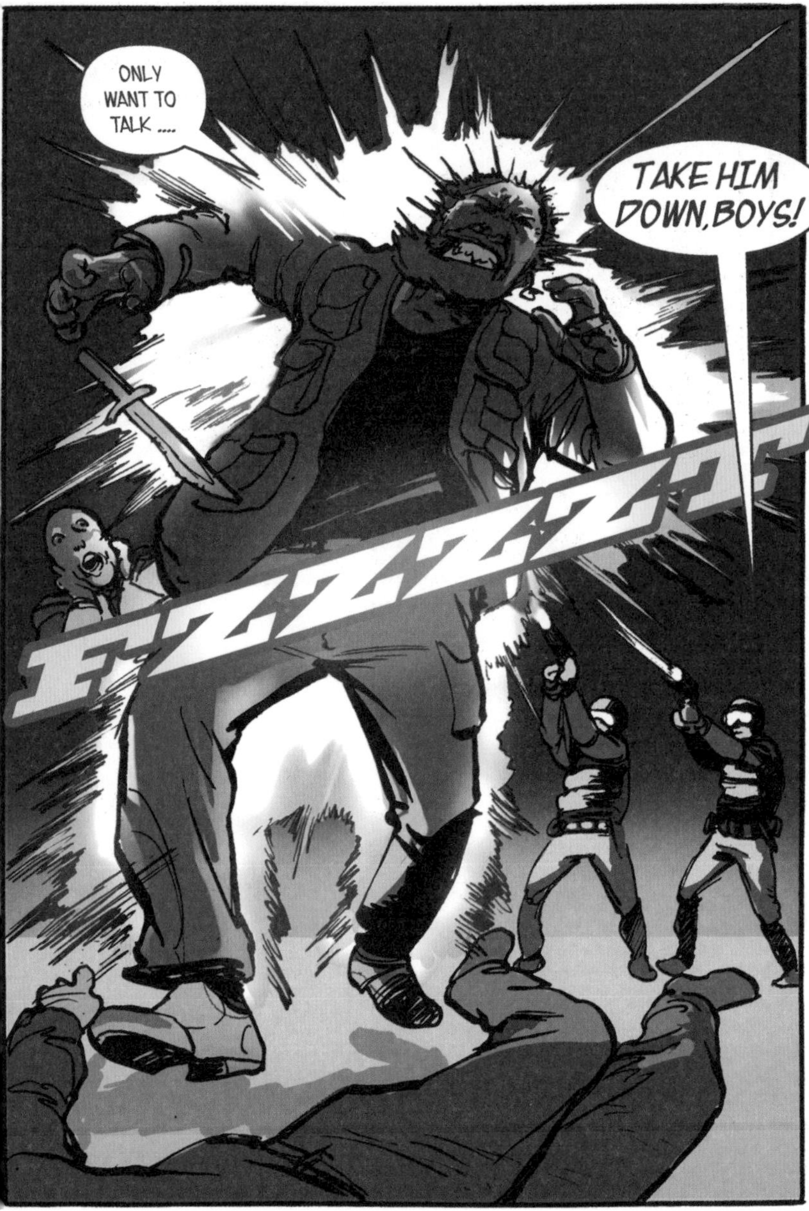
ONLY WANT TO TALK ....
TAKE HIM DOWN, BOYS!
FZZZZZT

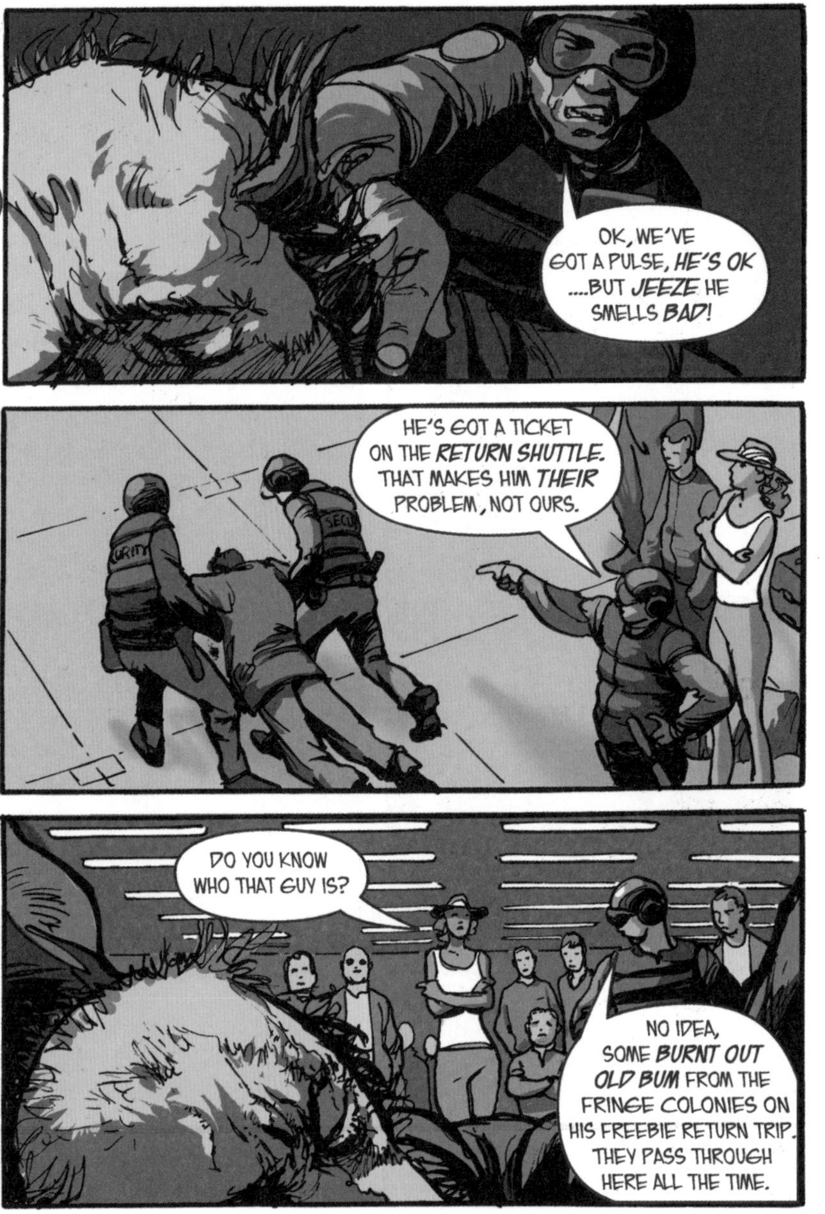
OK, WE'VE GOT A PULSE, HE'S OK ....BUT JEEZE HE SMELLS BAD!
HE'S GOT A TICKET ON THE RETURN SHUTTLE. THAT MAKES HIM THEIR PROBLEM, NOT OURS.
DO YOU KNOW WHO THAT GUY IS?
NO IDEA, SOME BURNT OUT OLD BUM FROM THE FRINGE COLONIES ON HIS FREEBIE RETURN TRIP. THEY PASS THROUGH HERE ALL THE TIME.

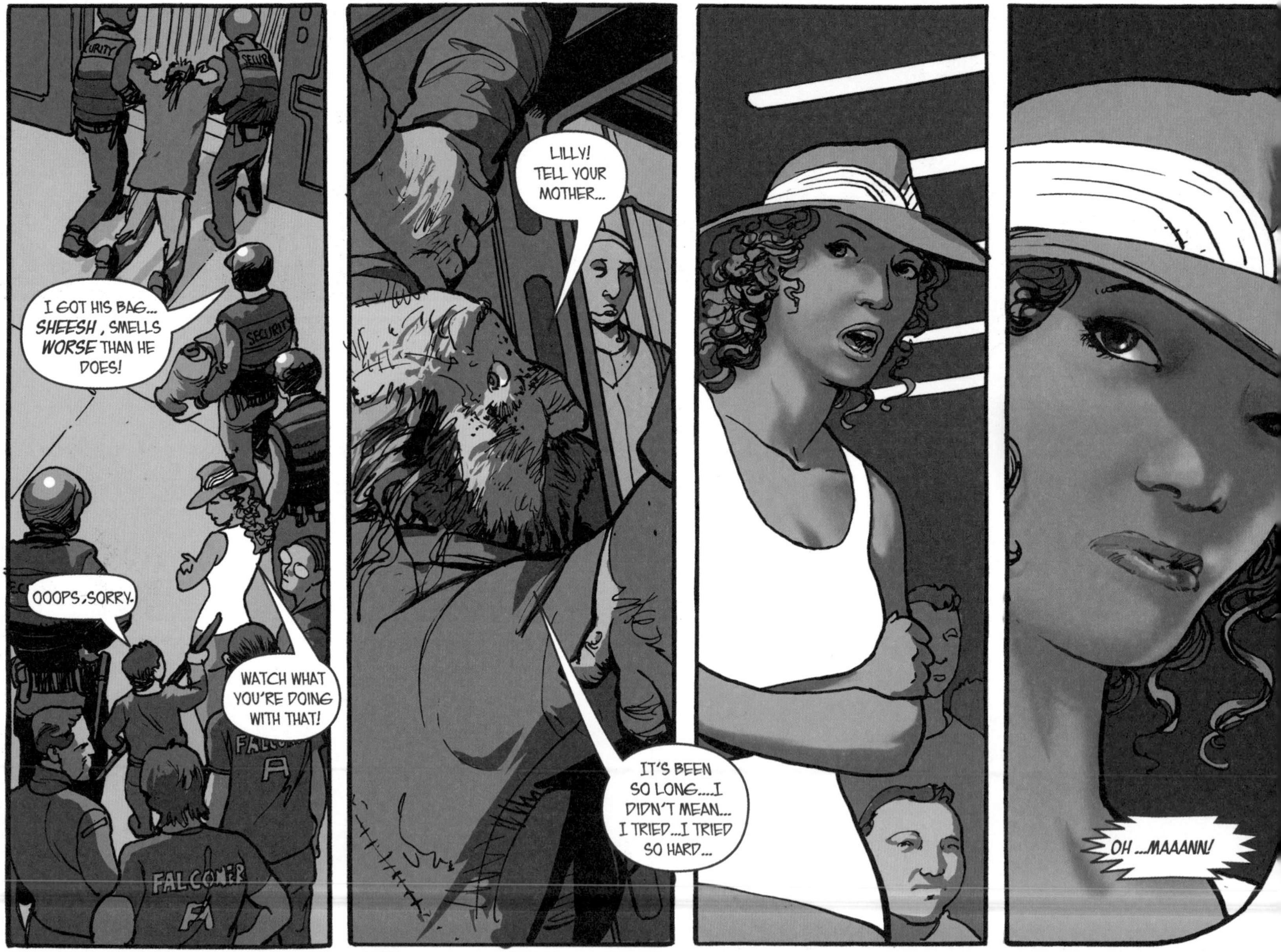
I GOT HIS BAG... SHEESH, SMELLS WORSE THAN HE DOES!
OOOPS, SORRY.
WATCH WHAT YOU'RE DOING WITH THAT!
LILLY! TELL YOUR MOTHER...
IT'S BEEN SO LONG....I DIDN'T MEAN... I TRIED...I TRIED SO HARD...
OH ...MAAANN!

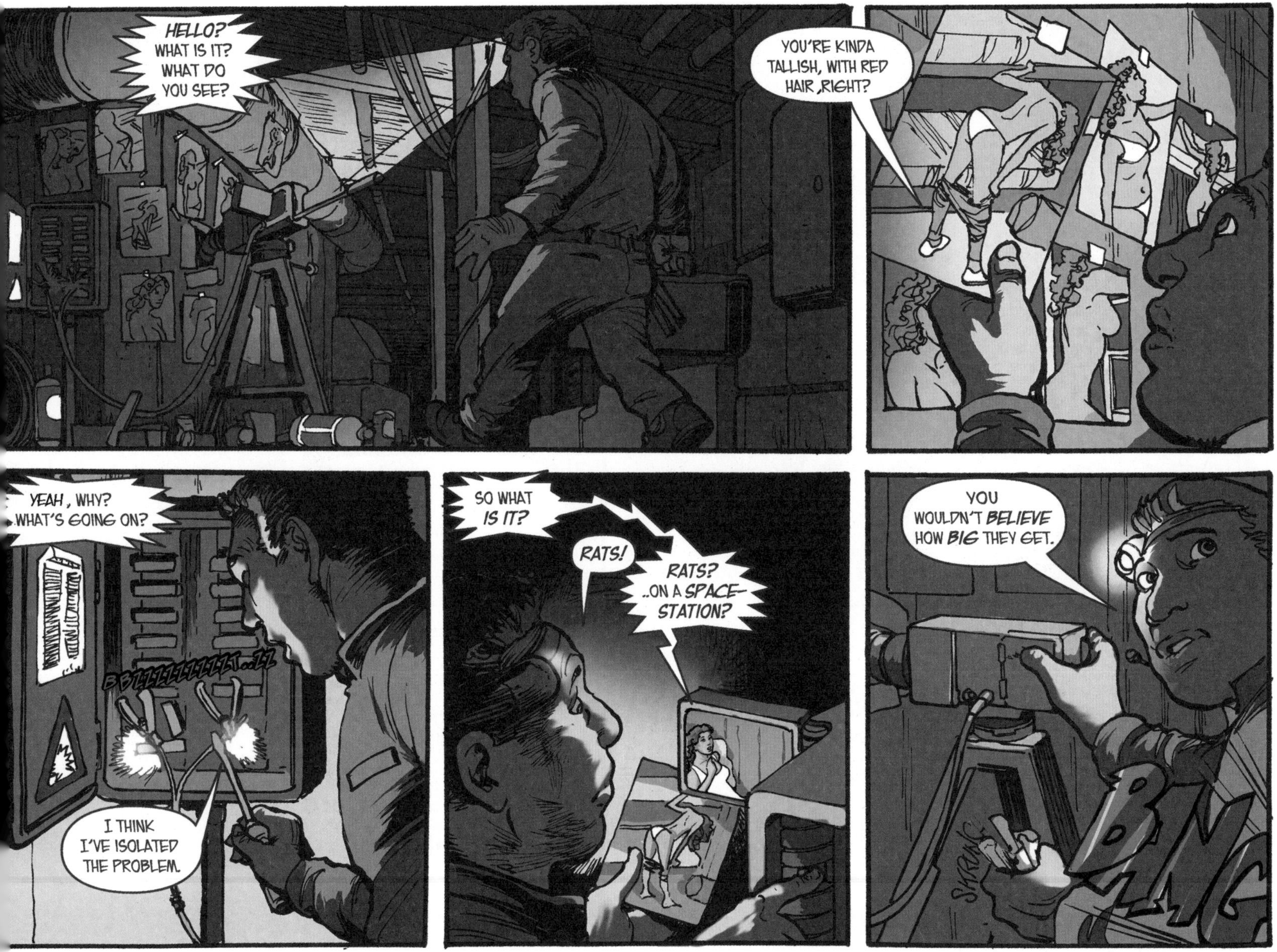
HELLO? WHAT IS IT? WHAT DO YOU SEE?
YOU'RE KINDA TALLISH, WITH RED HAIR ,RIGHT?
YEAH , WHY? ..WHAT'S GOING ON?
I THINK I'VE ISOLATED THE PROBLEM.
SO WHAT IS IT?
RATS!
RATS? ..ON A SPACE-STATION?
YOU WOULDN'T BELIEVE HOW BIG THEY GET.

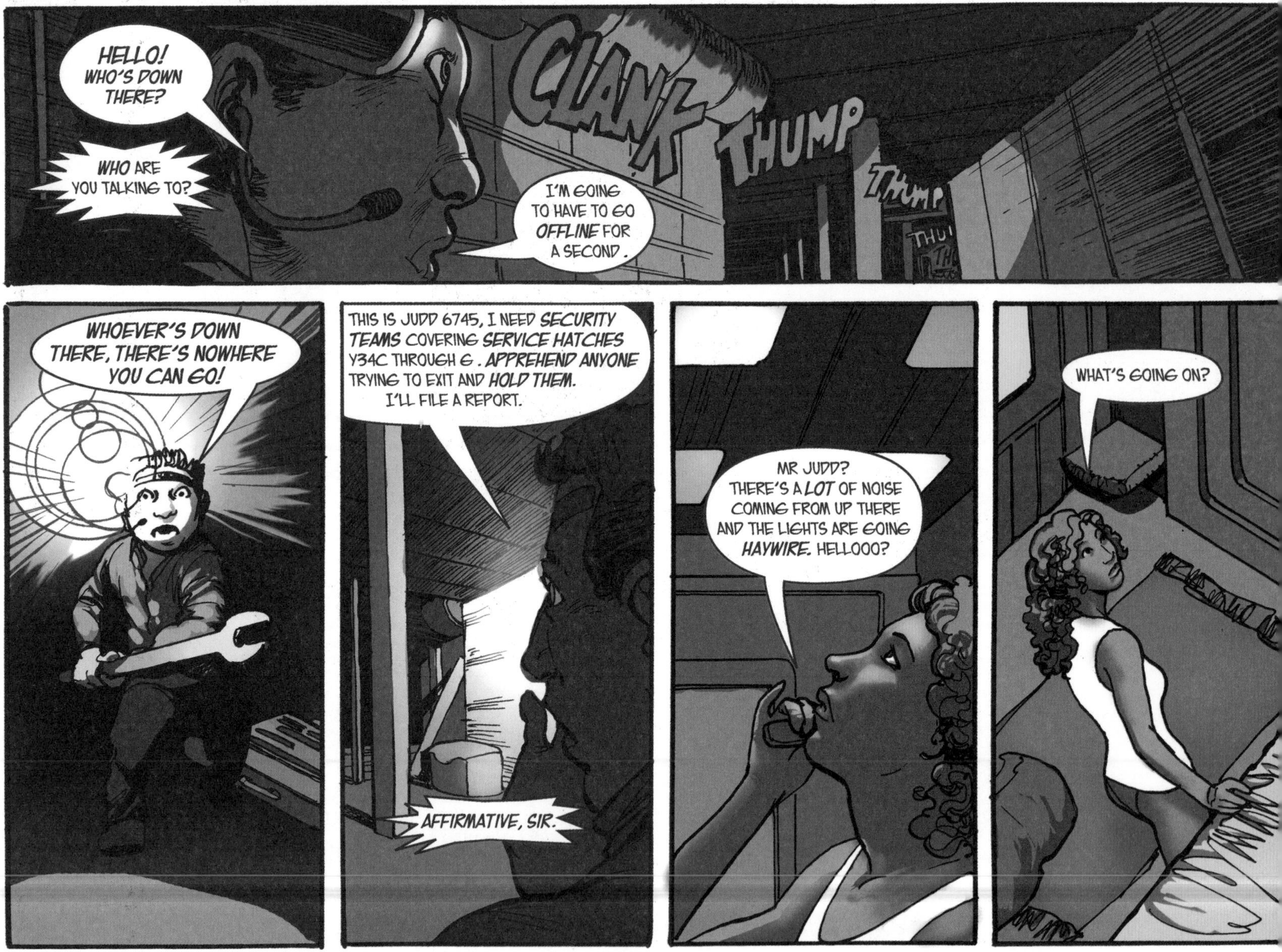
HELLO! WHO'S DOWN THERE?
WHO ARE YOU TALKING TO?
CLANK
THUMP
THUMP
I'M GOING TO HAVE TO GO OFFLINE FOR A SECOND.
WHOEVER'S DOWN THERE, THERE'S NOWHERE YOU CAN GO!
THIS IS JUDD 6745, I NEED SECURITY TEAMS COVERING SERVICE HATCHES Y34C THROUGH G. APPREHEND ANYONE TRYING TO EXIT AND HOLD THEM. I'LL FILE A REPORT.
AFFIRMATIVE, SIR.
MR JUDD? THERE'S A LOT OF NOISE COMING FROM UP THERE AND THE LIGHTS ARE GOING HAYWIRE. HELLOOO?
WHAT'S GOING ON?

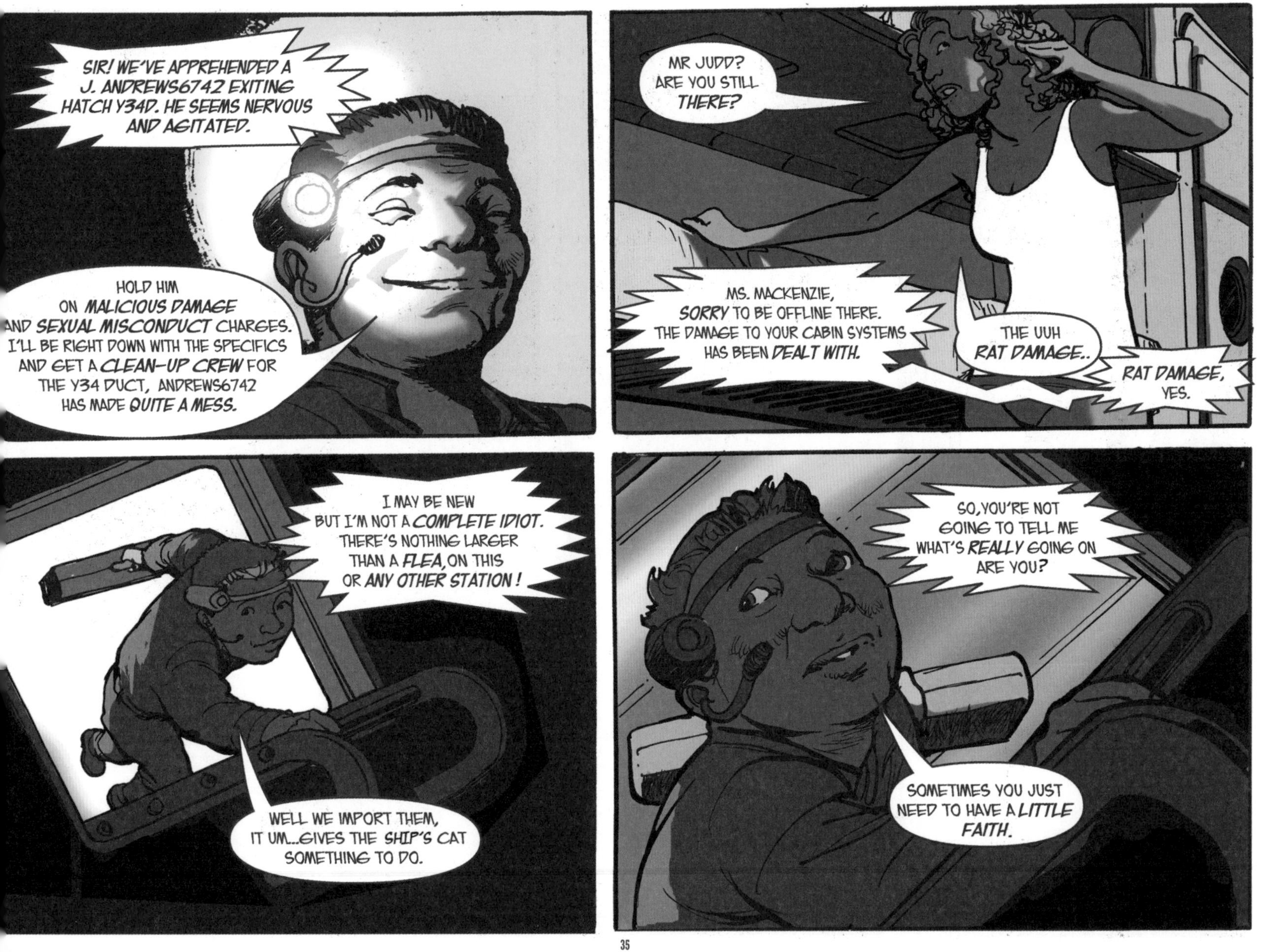
SIR! WE'VE APPREHENDED A J. ANDREWS6742 EXITING HATCH Y34D. HE SEEMS NERVOUS AND AGITATED.
HOLD HIM ON MALICIOUS DAMAGE AND SEXUAL MISCONDUCT CHARGES. I'LL BE RIGHT DOWN WITH THE SPECIFICS AND GET A CLEAN-UP CREW FOR THE Y34 DUCT, ANDREWS6742 HAS MADE QUITE A MESS.
MR JUDD? ARE YOU STILL THERE?
MS. MACKENZIE, SORRY TO BE OFFLINE THERE. THE DAMAGE TO YOUR CABIN SYSTEMS HAS BEEN DEALT WITH.
THE UUH RAT DAMAGE..
RAT DAMAGE, YES.
I MAY BE NEW BUT I'M NOT A COMPLETE IDIOT. THERE'S NOTHING LARGER THAN A FLEA, ON THIS OR ANY OTHER STATION!
WELL WE IMPORT THEM, IT UM...GIVES THE SHIP'S CAT SOMETHING TO DO.
SO, YOU'RE NOT GOING TO TELL ME WHAT'S REALLY GOING ON ARE YOU?
SOMETIMES YOU JUST NEED TO HAVE A LITTLE FAITH.

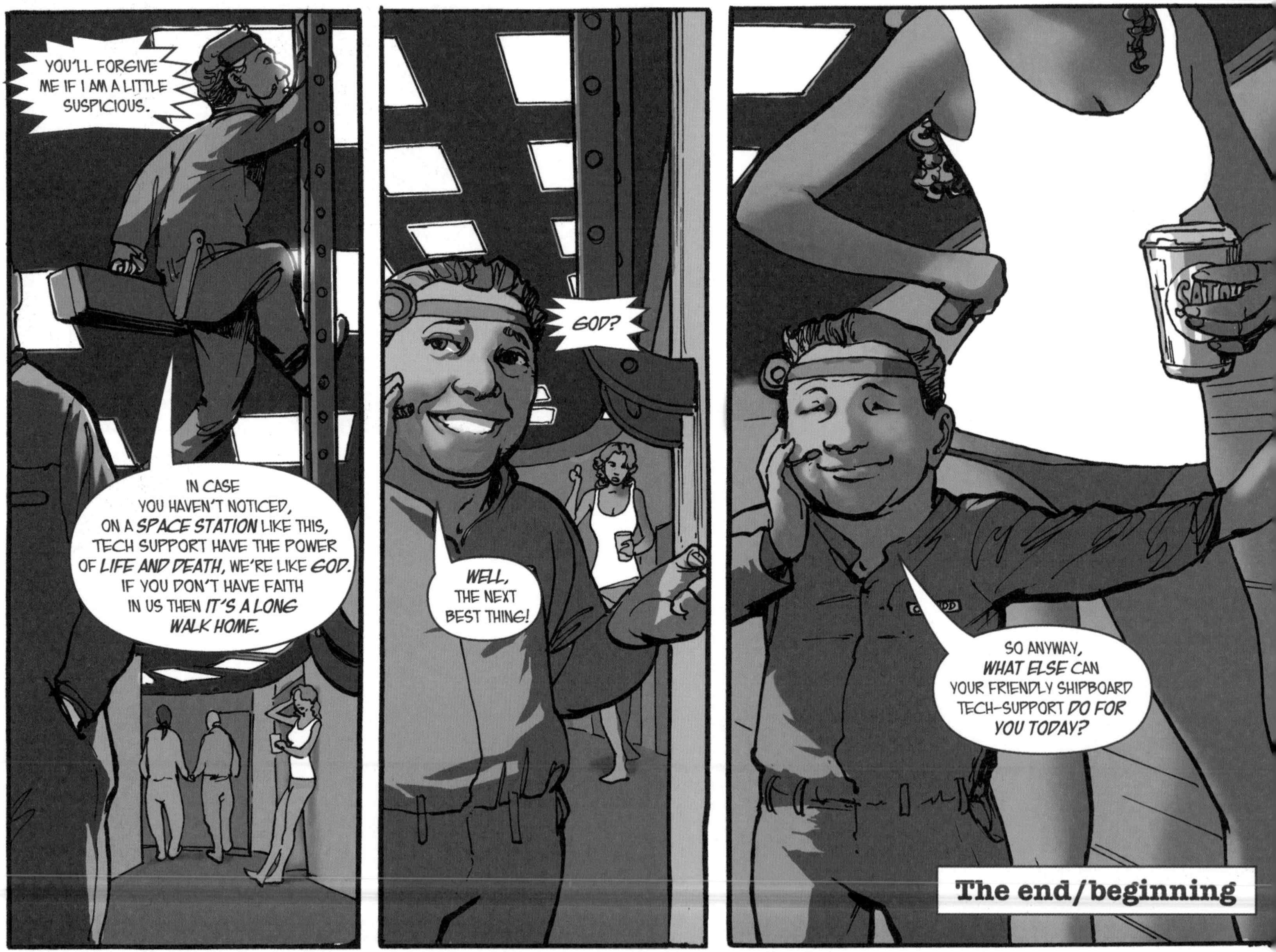
YOU'LL FORGIVE ME IF I AM A LITTLE SUSPICIOUS.
IN CASE YOU HAVEN'T NOTICED, ON A SPACE STATION LIKE THIS, TECH SUPPORT HAVE THE POWER OF LIFE AND DEATH, WE'RE LIKE GOD. IF YOU DON'T HAVE FAITH IN US THEN IT'S A LONG WALK HOME.
GOD?
WELL, THE NEXT BEST THING!
SO ANYWAY, WHAT ELSE CAN YOUR FRIENDLY SHIPBOARD TECH-SUPPORT DO FOR YOU TODAY?
The end/beginning

PRESENTING

FOR YOUR EDIFICATION *and considerable* ENLIGHTENMENT

A MUGWHUMP the GREAT ·cartoon·

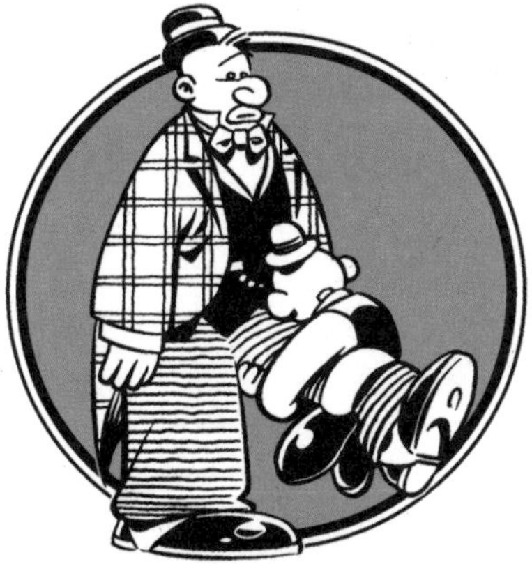

THE BOY WHO CAME TO STAY

AS PERFORMED BY MR. ROGER LANGRIDGE, ESQ.

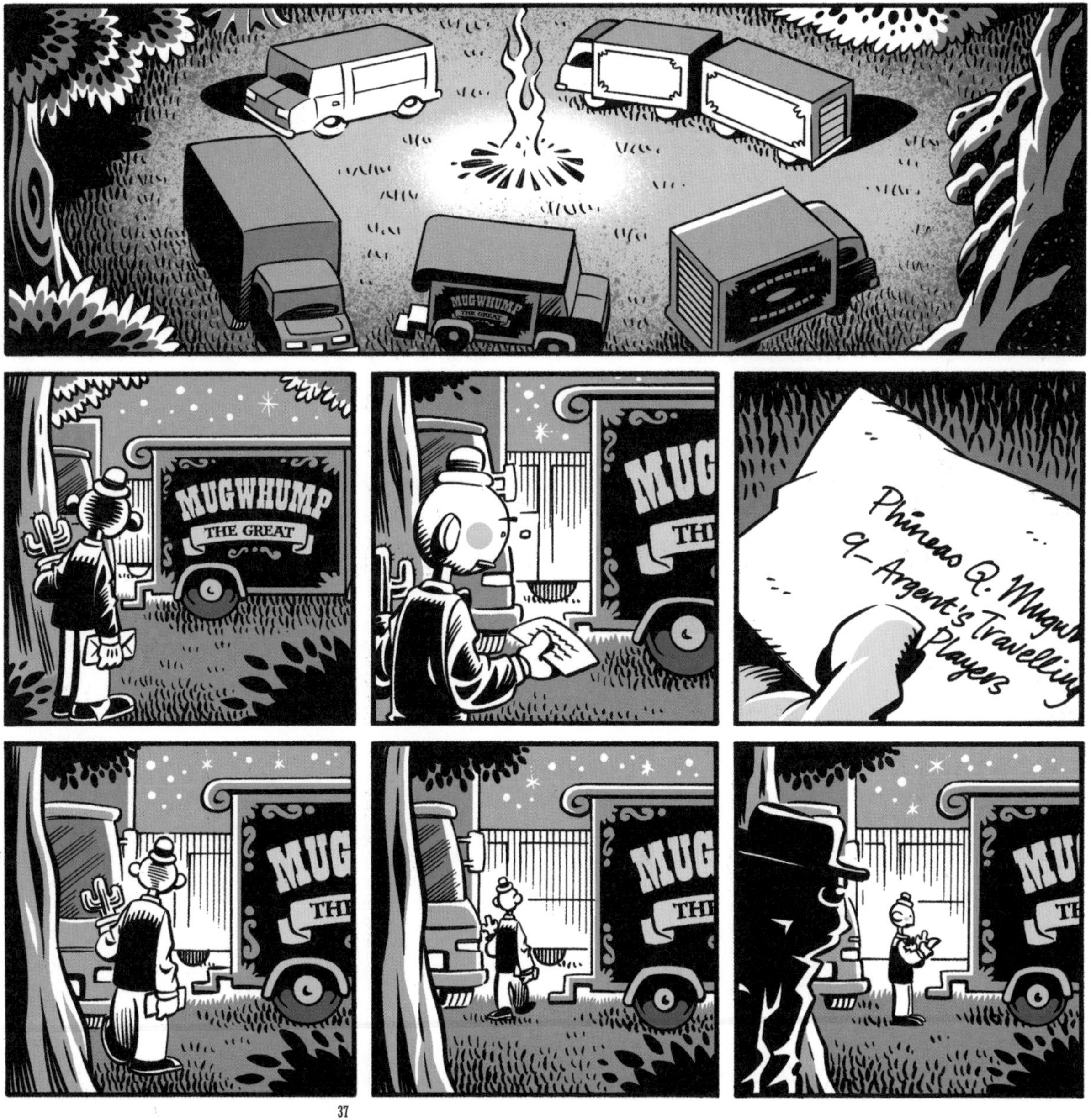
MUGWHUMP THE GREAT
MUGWHUMP
THE GREAT
Phineas Q. Mugw
9- Argent's Travellin
Players

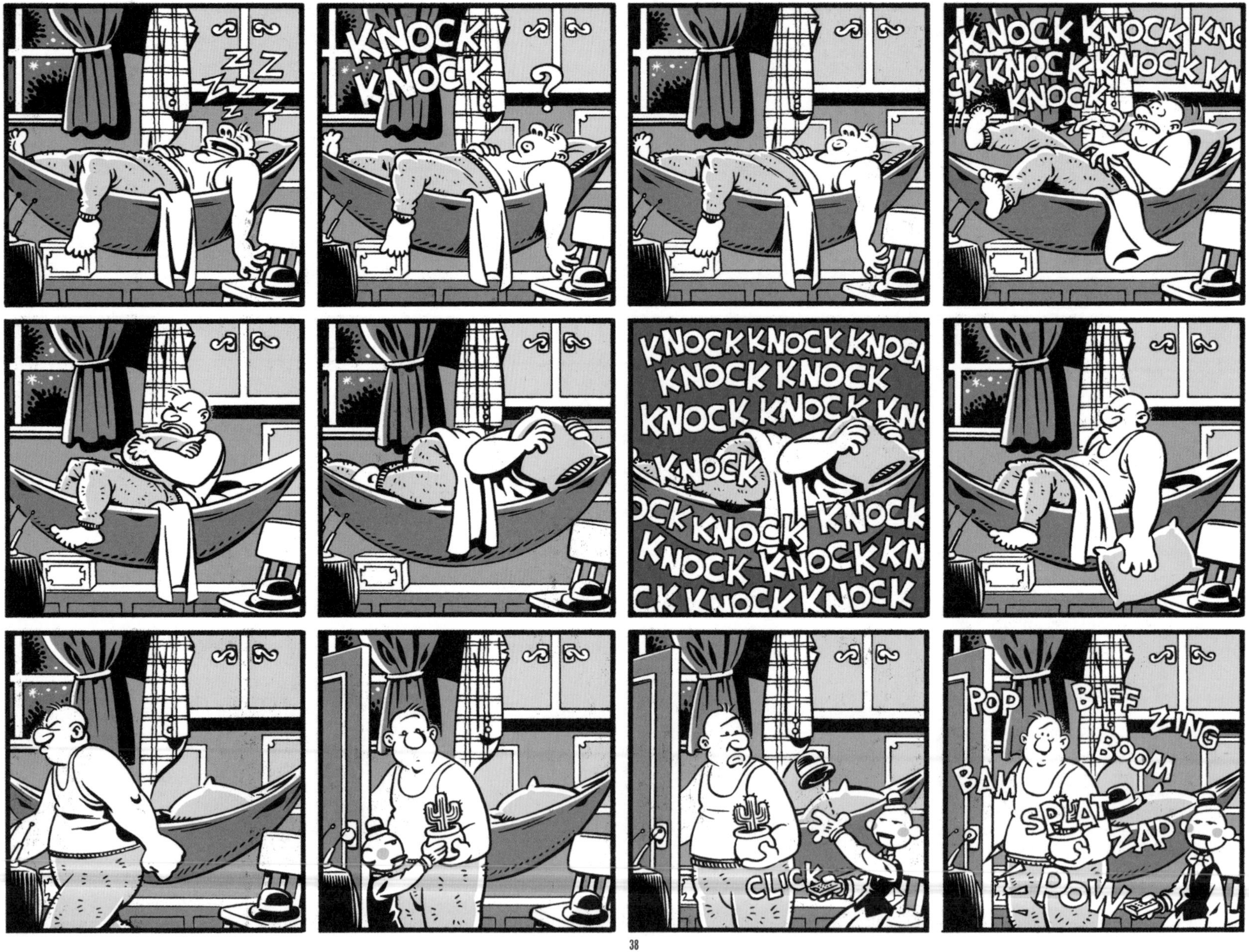
Z Z Z Z Z Z Z
KNOCK KNOCK
?
KNOCK KNOCK KNO
CK KNOCK KNOCK KN
KNOCK
KNOCK KNOCK KNOCK
KNOCK KNOCK
KNOCK KNOCK KN
KNOCK
CK KNOCK KNOCK
KNOCK KNOCK KN
CK KNOCK KNOCK
CLICK
POP
BIFF
ZING
BOOM
BAM
SPLAT
ZAP
POW

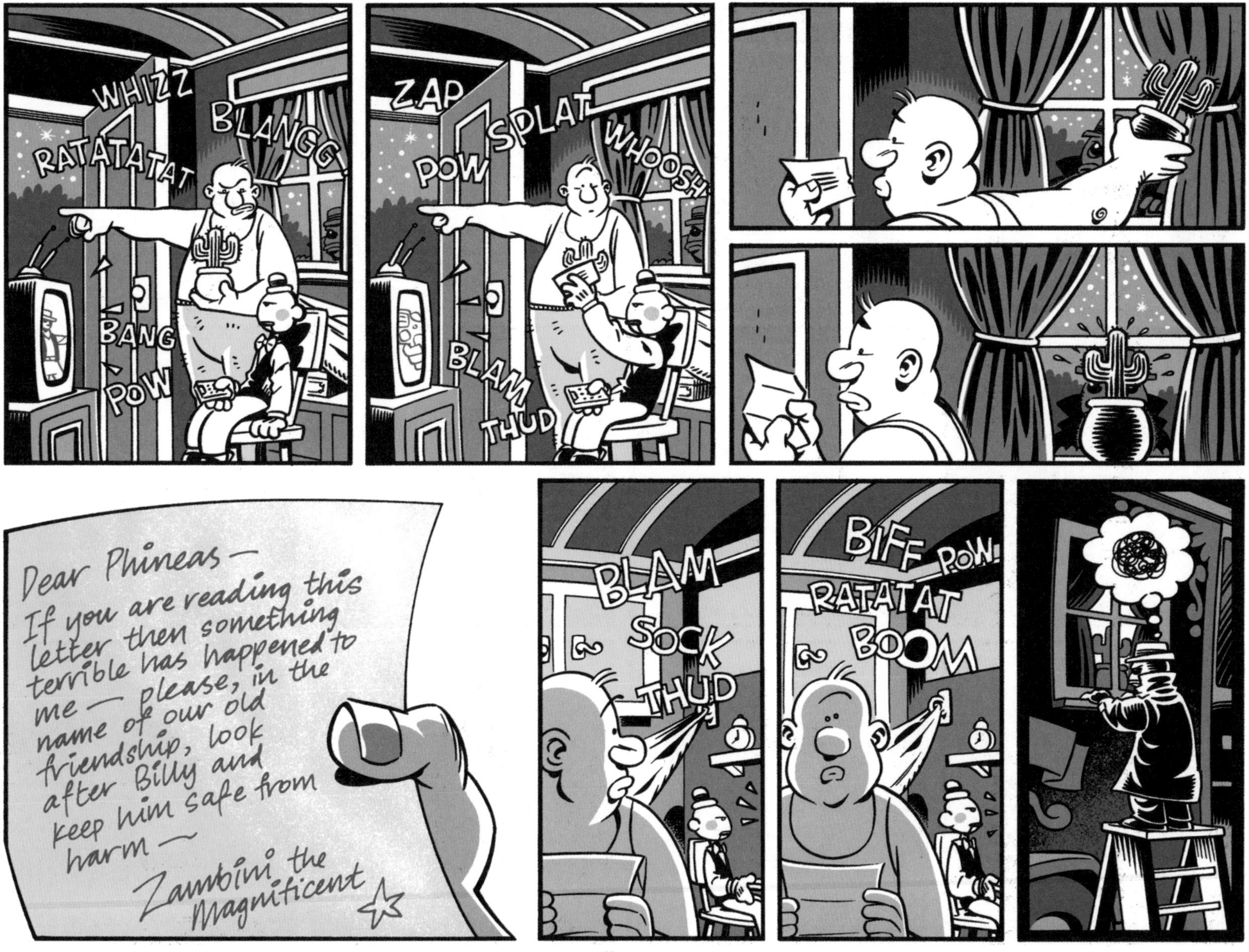
WHIZZ
RATATATATAT
BLANGG
BANG
POW
ZAP
POW
SPLAT
WHOOSH
BLAM
THUD
Dear Phineas—
If you are reading this letter then something terrible has happened to me—please, in the name of our old friendship, look after Billy and keep him safe from harm—
Zambini the Magnificent
BLAM
SOCK
THUD
BIFF
POW
RATATAT
BOOM

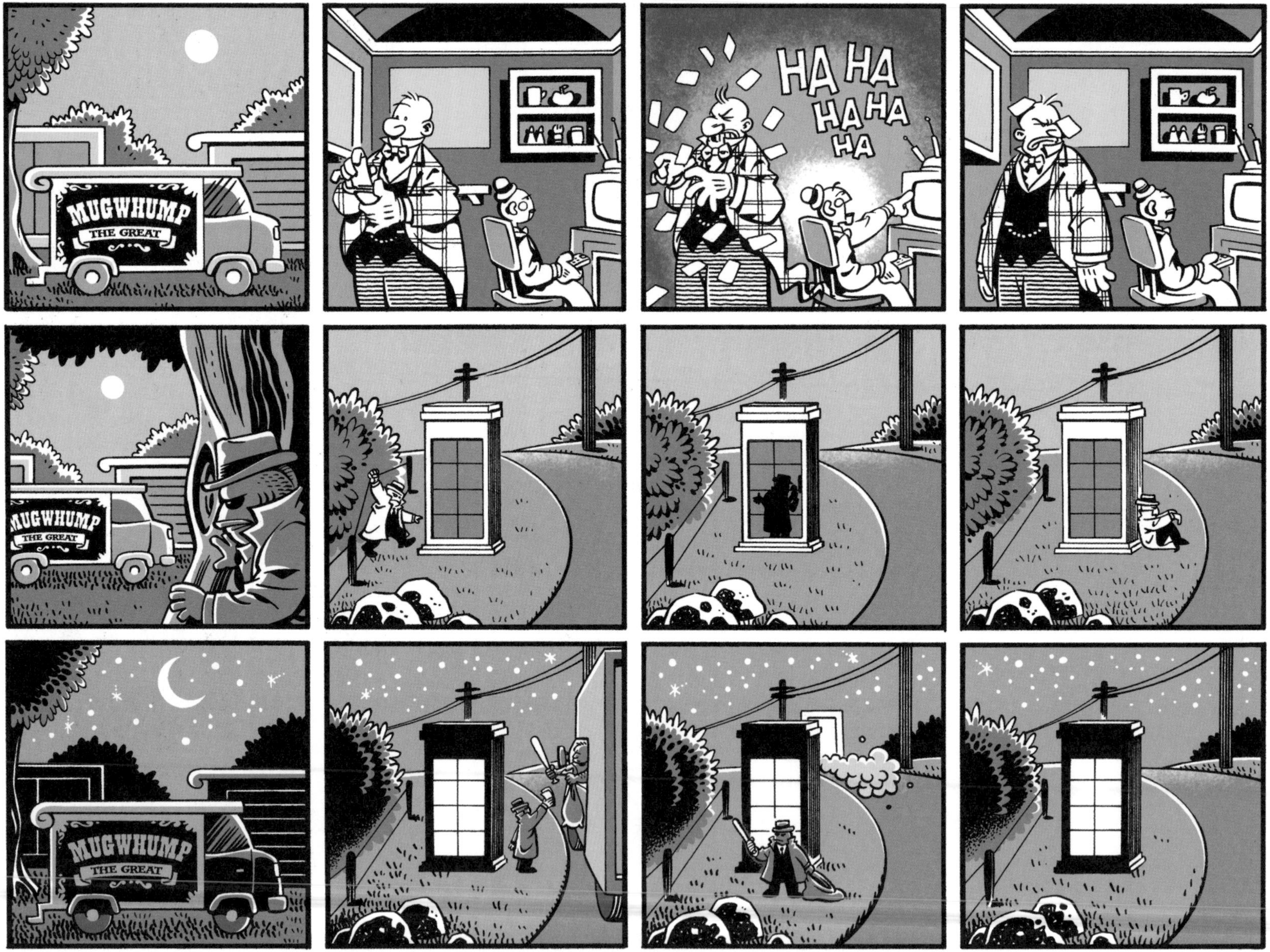
MUGWHUMP
THE GREAT
HA HA
HA HA
HA
MUGWHUMP
THE GREAT
MUGWHUMP
THE GREAT

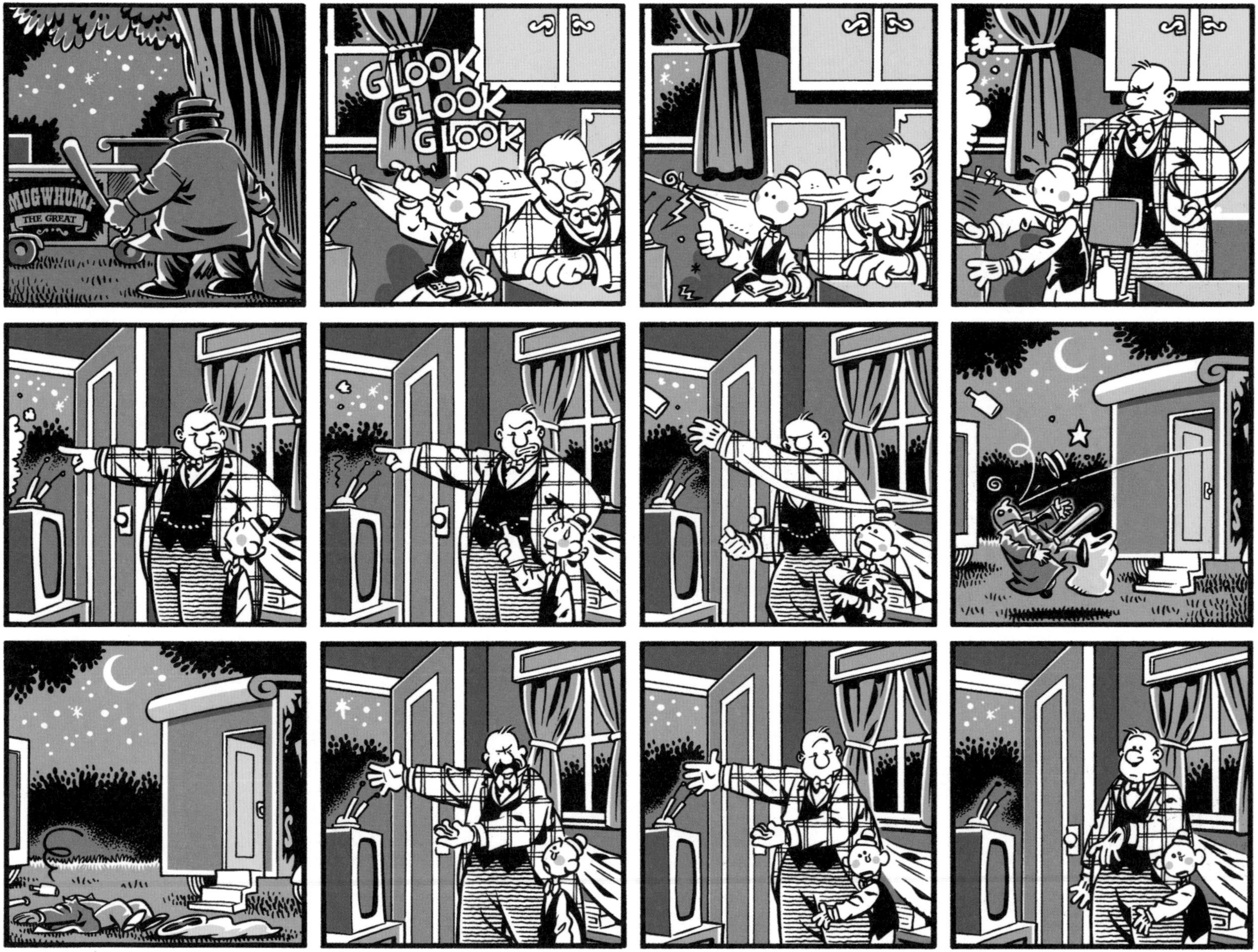
MUGWHUMP
THE GREAT
GLOOK
GLOOK
GLOOK

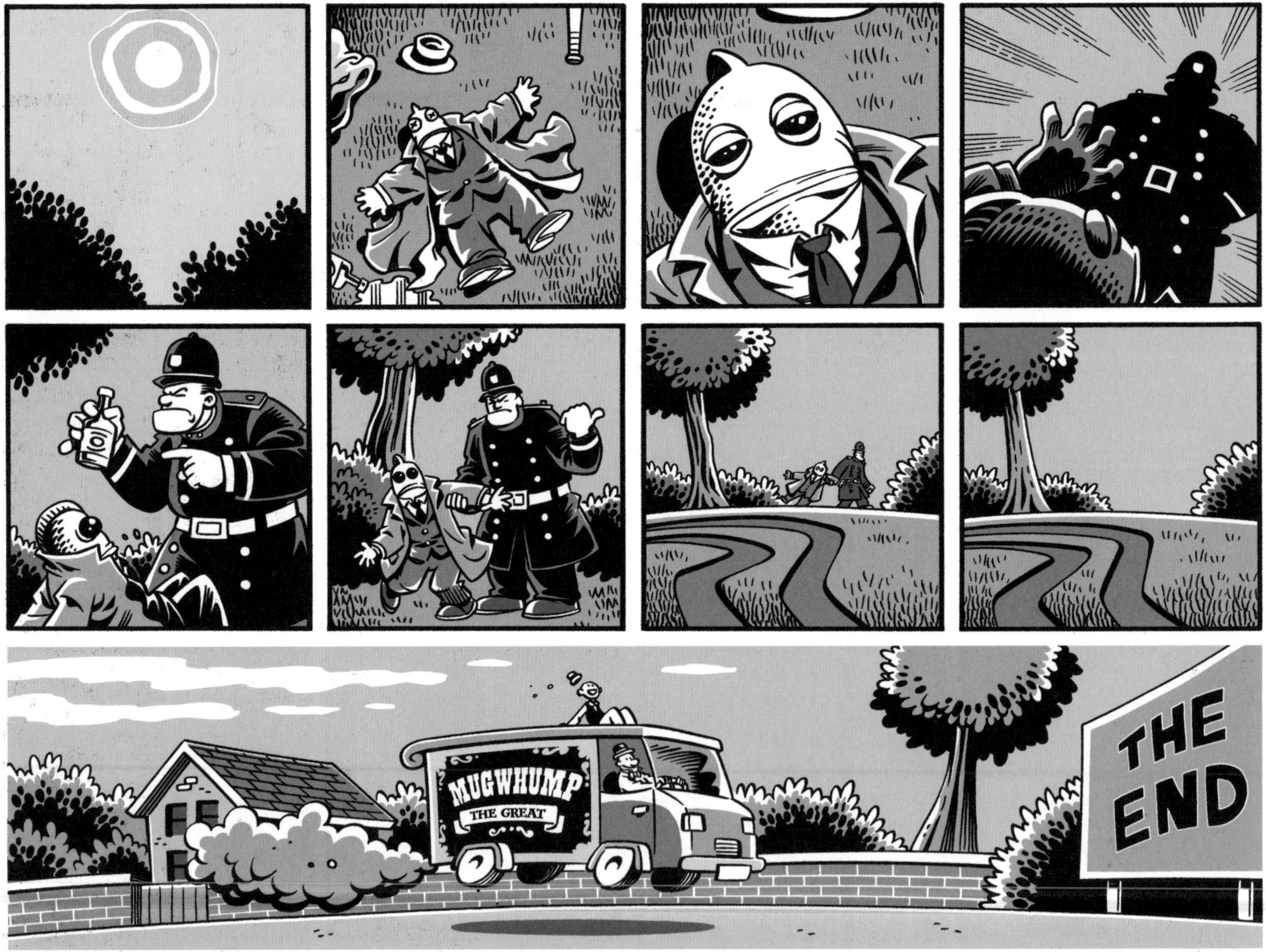
MUGWHUMP
THE GREAT
THE END

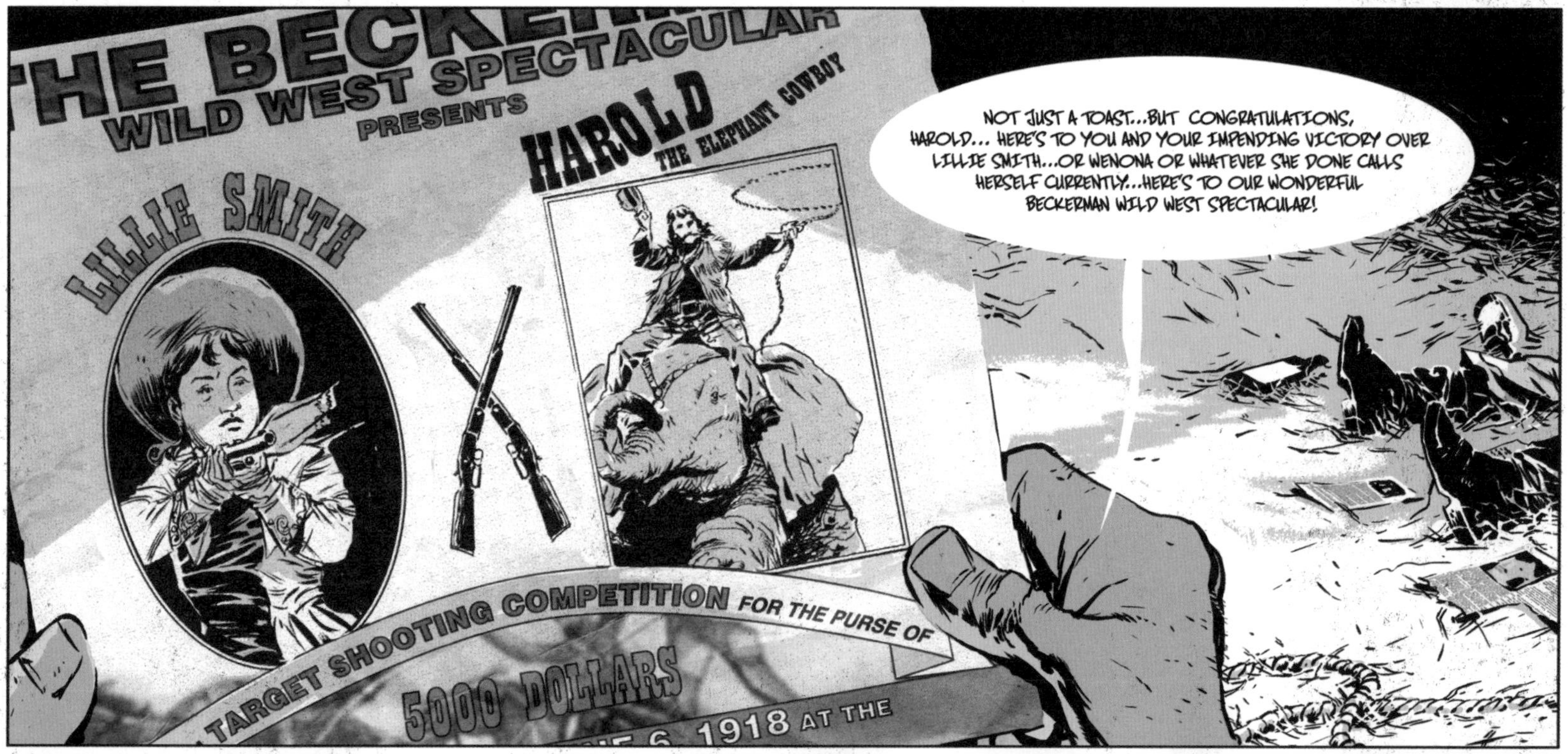
THE BECKE
WILD WEST SPECTACULAR
PRESENTS
LILLIE SMITH
HAROLD
THE ELEPHANT COWBOY
TARGET SHOOTING COMPETITION FOR THE PURSE OF
5000 DOLLARS
1918 AT THE
NOT JUST A TOAST...BUT CONGRATULATIONS, HAROLD... HERE'S TO YOU AND YOUR IMPENDING VICTORY OVER LILLIE SMITH...OR WENONA OR WHATEVER SHE DONE CALLS HERSELF CURRENTLY...HERE'S TO OUR WONDERFUL BECKERMAN WILD WEST SPECTACULAR!

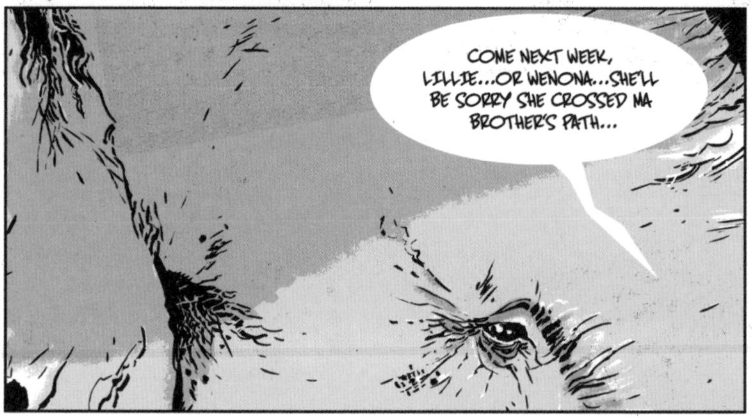
COME NEXT WEEK, LILLIE...OR WENONA...SHE'LL BE SORRY SHE CROSSED MA BROTHER'S PATH...

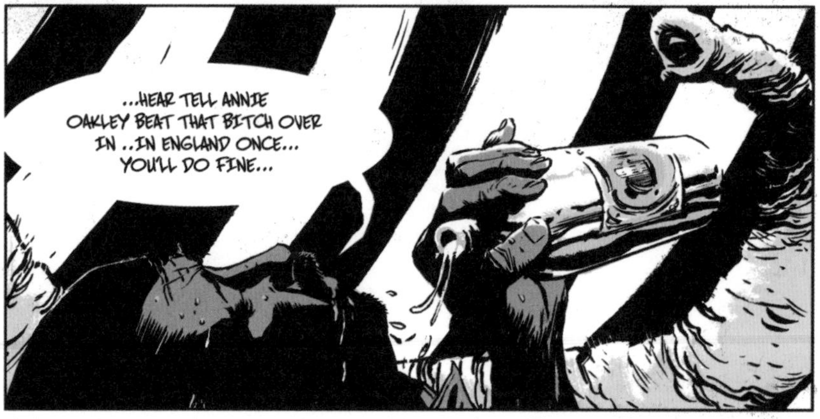
...HEAR TELL ANNIE OAKLEY BEAT THAT BITCH OVER IN ..IN ENGLAND ONCE... YOU'LL DO FINE...

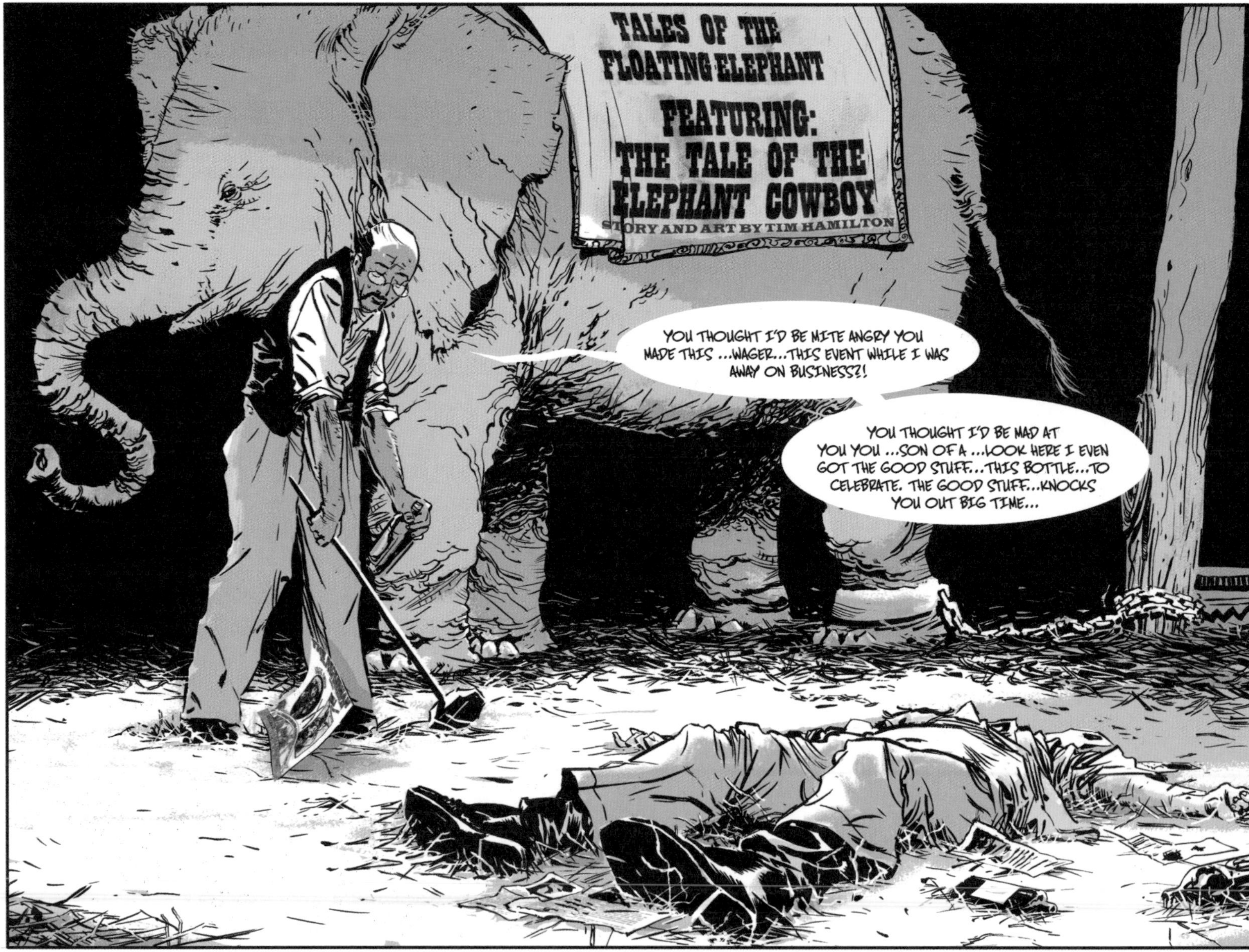
TALES OF THE FLOATING ELEPHANT
FEATURING: THE TALE OF THE ELEPHANT COWBOY
STORY AND ART BY TIM HAMILTON
YOU THOUGHT I'D BE MITE ANGRY YOU MADE THIS ...WAGER...THIS EVENT WHILE I WAS AWAY ON BUSINESS?!
YOU THOUGHT I'D BE MAD AT YOU YOU ...SON OF A ...LOOK HERE I EVEN GOT THE GOOD STUFF...THIS BOTTLE...TO CELEBRATE. THE GOOD STUFF...KNOCKS YOU OUT BIG TIME...

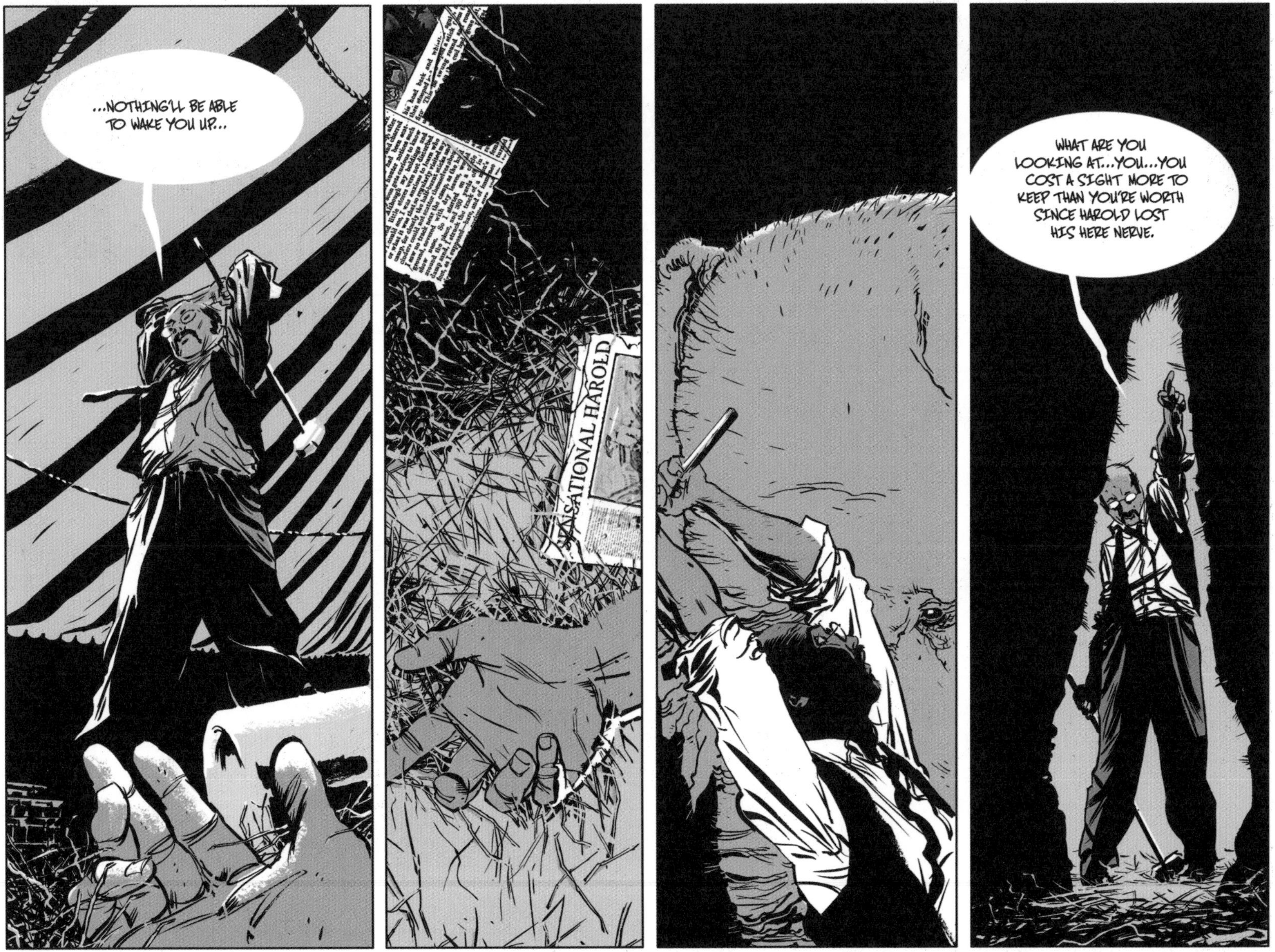
...NOTHING'LL BE ABLE TO WAKE YOU UP...
WHAT ARE YOU LOOKING AT...YOU...YOU COST A SIGHT MORE TO KEEP THAN YOU'RE WORTH SINCE HAROLD LOST HIS HERE NERVE.

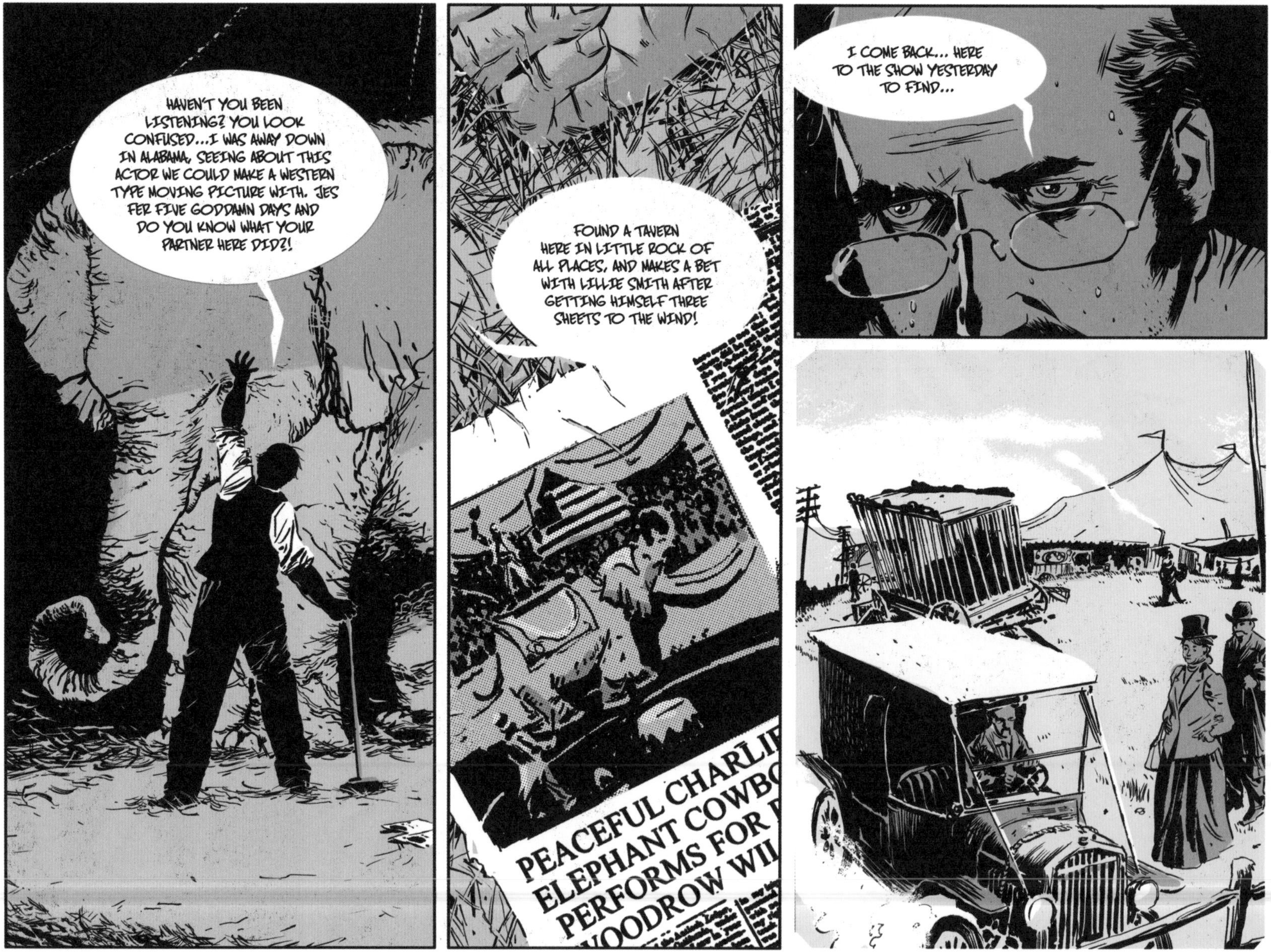
HAVEN'T YOU BEEN LISTENING? YOU LOOK CONFUSED...I WAS AWAY DOWN IN ALABAMA, SEEING ABOUT THIS ACTOR WE COULD MAKE A WESTERN TYPE MOVING PICTURE WITH. JES FER FIVE GODDAMN DAYS AND DO YOU KNOW WHAT YOUR PARTNER HERE DID?!
FOUND A TAVERN HERE IN LITTLE ROCK OF ALL PLACES, AND MAKES A BET WITH LILLIE SMITH AFTER GETTING HIMSELF THREE SHEETS TO THE WIND!
PEACEFUL CHARLI
ELEPHANT COWBO
PERFORMS FOR
WOODROW WI
I COME BACK... HERE TO THE SHOW YESTERDAY TO FIND...

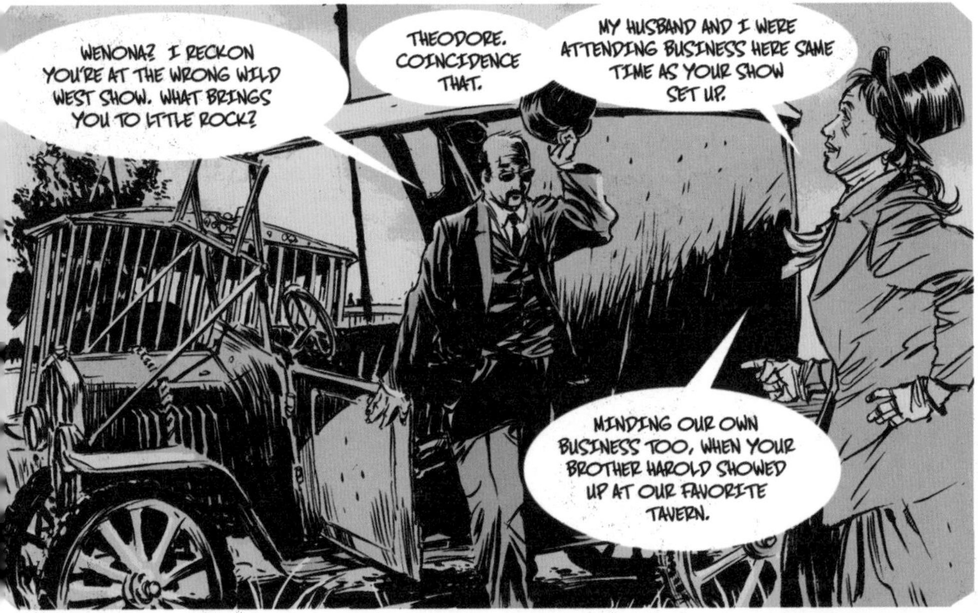
WENONA? I RECKON YOU'RE AT THE WRONG WILD WEST SHOW. WHAT BRINGS YOU TO LITTLE ROCK?
THEODORE. COINCIDENCE THAT.
MY HUSBAND AND I WERE ATTENDING BUSINESS HERE SAME TIME AS YOUR SHOW SET UP.
MINDING OUR OWN BUSINESS TOO, WHEN YOUR BROTHER HAROLD SHOWED UP AT OUR FAVORITE TAVERN.

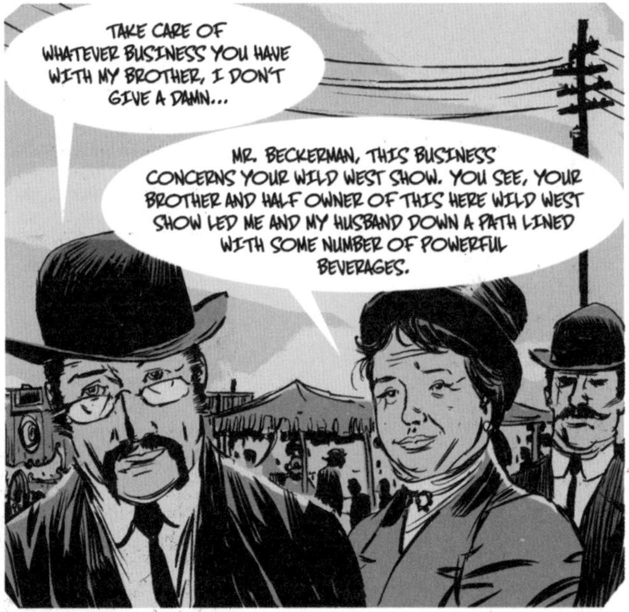
TAKE CARE OF WHATEVER BUSINESS YOU HAVE WITH MY BROTHER, I DON'T GIVE A DAMN...
MR. BECKERMAN, THIS BUSINESS CONCERNS YOUR WILD WEST SHOW. YOU SEE, YOUR BROTHER AND HALF OWNER OF THIS HERE WILD WEST SHOW LED ME AND MY HUSBAND DOWN A PATH LINED WITH SOME NUMBER OF POWERFUL BEVERAGES.

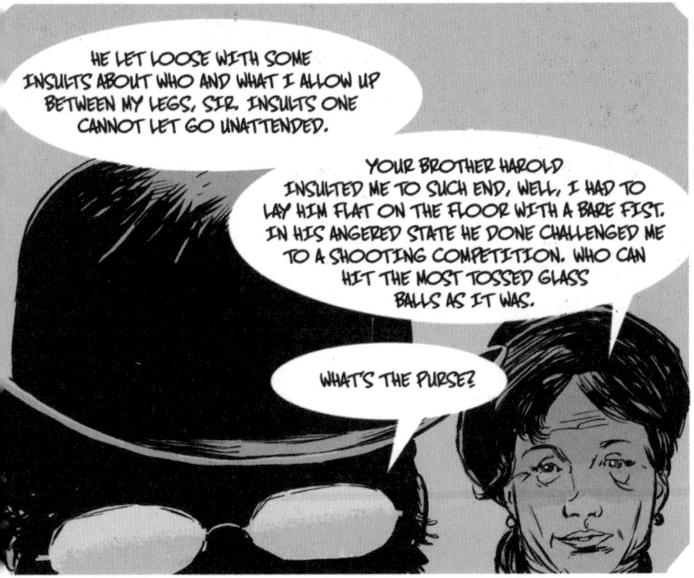
HE LET LOOSE WITH SOME INSULTS ABOUT WHO AND WHAT I ALLOW UP BETWEEN MY LEGS, SIR. INSULTS ONE CANNOT LET GO UNATTENDED.
YOUR BROTHER HAROLD INSULTED ME TO SUCH END, WELL, I HAD TO LAY HIM FLAT ON THE FLOOR WITH A BARE FIST. IN HIS ANGERED STATE HE DONE CHALLENGED ME TO A SHOOTING COMPETITION. WHO CAN HIT THE MOST TOSSED GLASS BALLS AS IT WAS.
WHAT'S THE PURSE?

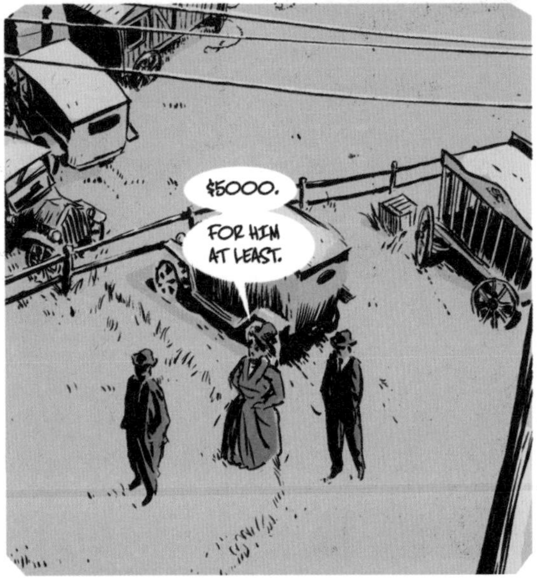
$5000.
FOR HIM AT LEAST.

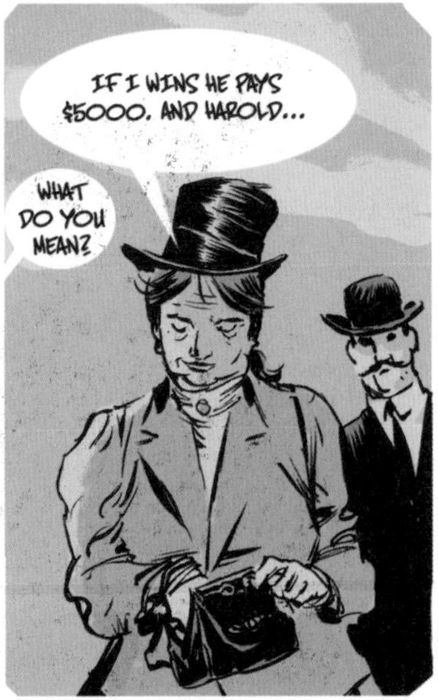
IF I WINS HE PAYS $5000. AND HAROLD...
WHAT DO YOU MEAN?

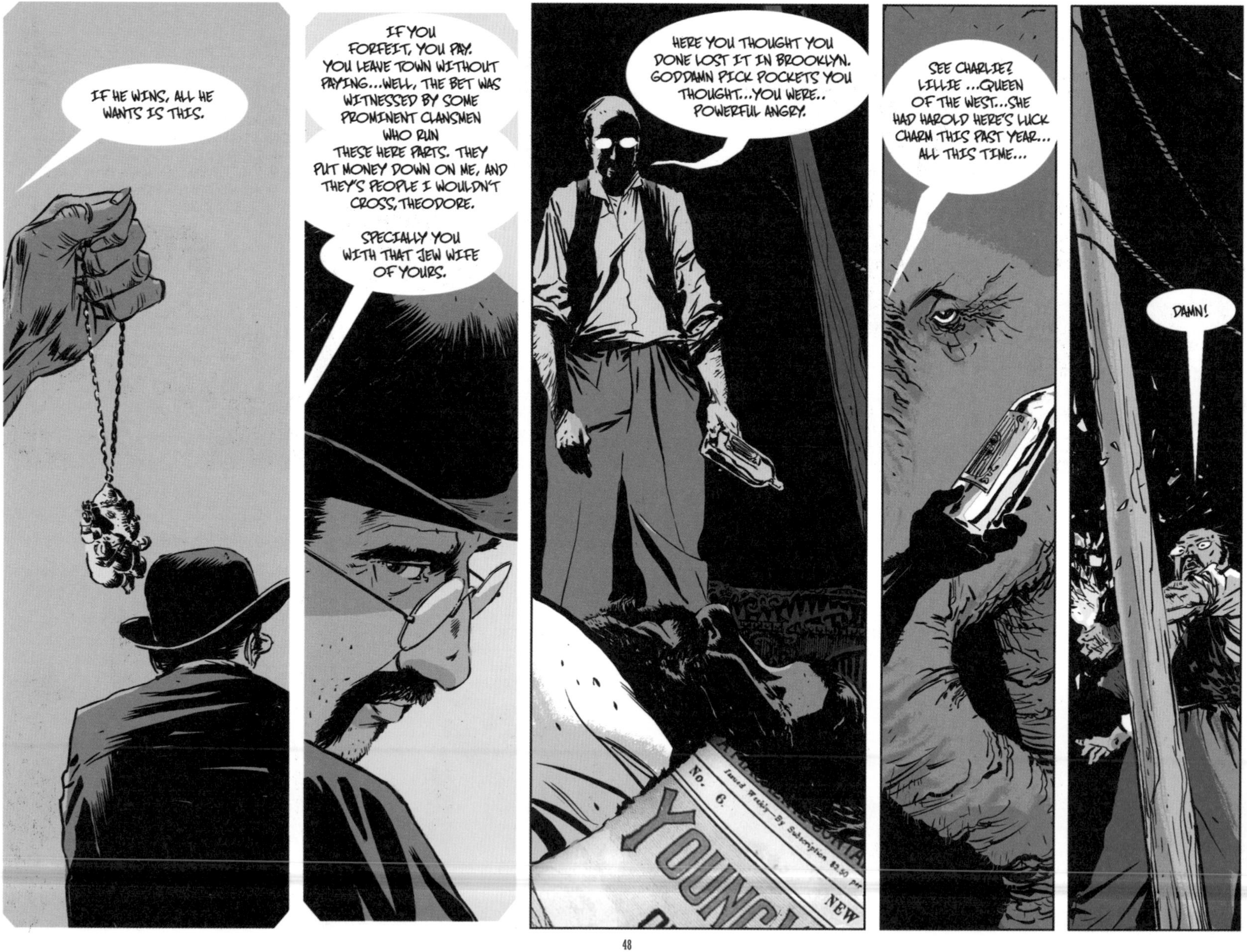
IF HE WINS, ALL HE WANTS IS THIS.
IF YOU FORFEIT, YOU PAY. YOU LEAVE TOWN WITHOUT PAYING...WELL, THE BET WAS WITNESSED BY SOME PROMINENT CLANSMEN WHO RUN THESE HERE PARTS. THEY PUT MONEY DOWN ON ME, AND THEY'S PEOPLE I WOULDN'T CROSS, THEODORE.
SPECIALLY YOU WITH THAT JEW WIFE OF YOURS.
HERE YOU THOUGHT YOU DONE LOST IT IN BROOKLYN. GODDAMN PICK POCKETS YOU THOUGHT...YOU WERE.. POWERFUL ANGRY.
No. 6.
YOUNG
NEW
SEE CHARLIE? LILLIE ...QUEEN OF THE WEST...SHE HAD HAROLD HERE'S LUCK CHARM THIS PAST YEAR... ALL THIS TIME...
DAMN!

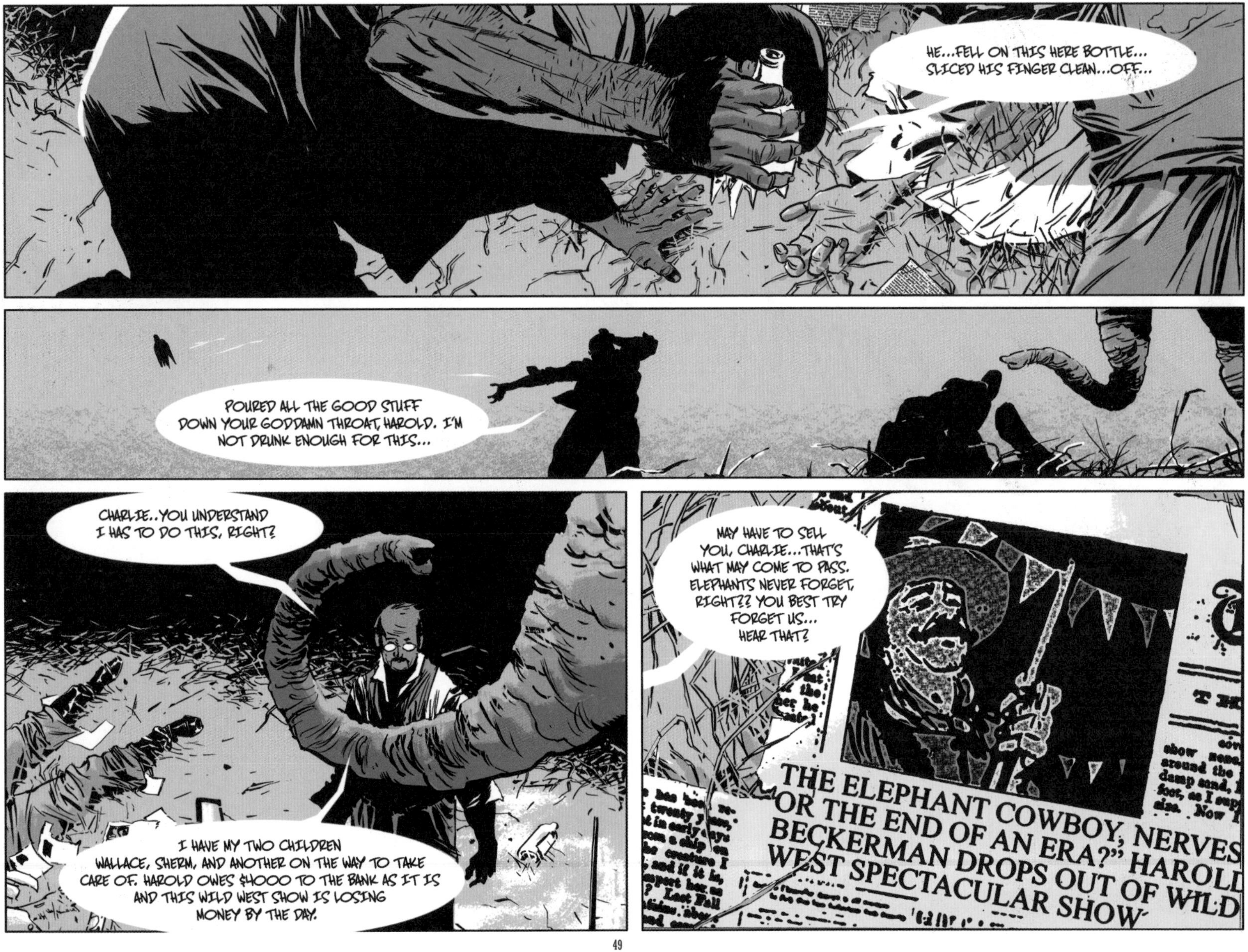
HE...FELL ON THIS HERE BOTTLE... SLICED HIS FINGER CLEAN...OFF...
POURED ALL THE GOOD STUFF DOWN YOUR GODDAMN THROAT, HAROLD. I'M NOT DRUNK ENOUGH FOR THIS...
CHARLIE..YOU UNDERSTAND I HAS TO DO THIS, RIGHT?
I HAVE MY TWO CHILDREN WALLACE, SHERM, AND ANOTHER ON THE WAY TO TAKE CARE OF. HAROLD OWES $4000 TO THE BANK AS IT IS AND THIS WILD WEST SHOW IS LOSING MONEY BY THE DAY.
MAY HAVE TO SELL YOU, CHARLIE...THAT'S WHAT MAY COME TO PASS. ELEPHANTS NEVER FORGET, RIGHT?? YOU BEST TRY FORGET US... HEAR THAT?
THE ELEPHANT COWBOY, NERVES OR THE END OF AN ERA?" HAROLD BECKERMAN DROPS OUT OF WILD WEST SPECTACULAR SHOW

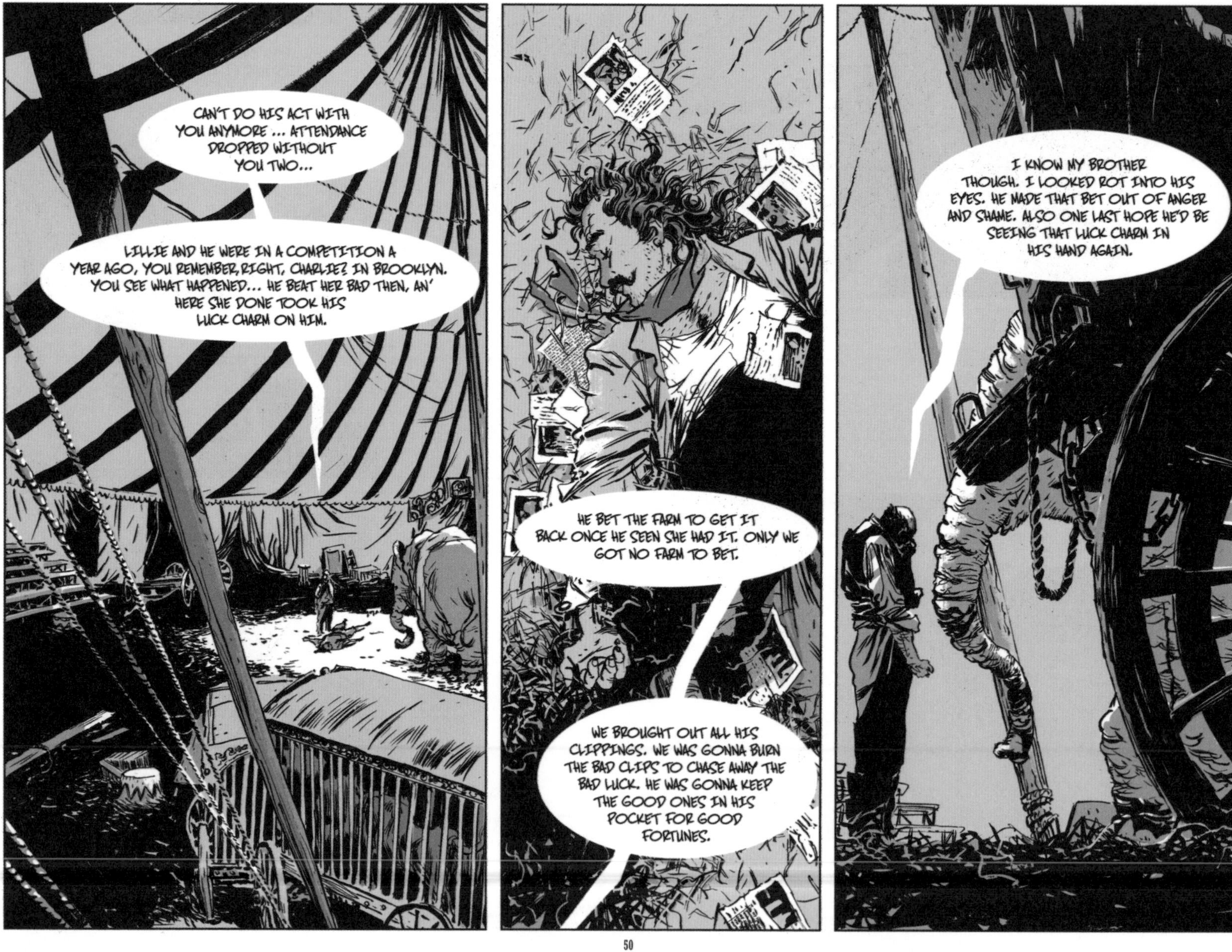
CAN'T DO HIS ACT WITH YOU ANYMORE ... ATTENDANCE DROPPED WITHOUT YOU TWO...
LILLIE AND HE WERE IN A COMPETITION A YEAR AGO, YOU REMEMBER, RIGHT, CHARLIE? IN BROOKLYN. YOU SEE WHAT HAPPENED... HE BEAT HER BAD THEN, AN' HERE SHE DONE TOOK HIS LUCK CHARM ON HIM.
HE BET THE FARM TO GET IT BACK ONCE HE SEEN SHE HAD IT. ONLY WE GOT NO FARM TO BET.
WE BROUGHT OUT ALL HIS CLIPPINGS. WE WAS GONNA BURN THE BAD CLIPS TO CHASE AWAY THE BAD LUCK. HE WAS GONNA KEEP THE GOOD ONES IN HIS POCKET FOR GOOD FORTUNES.
I KNOW MY BROTHER THOUGH. I LOOKED ROT INTO HIS EYES. HE MADE THAT BET OUT OF ANGER AND SHAME. ALSO ONE LAST HOPE HE'D BE SEEING THAT LUCK CHARM IN HIS HAND AGAIN.

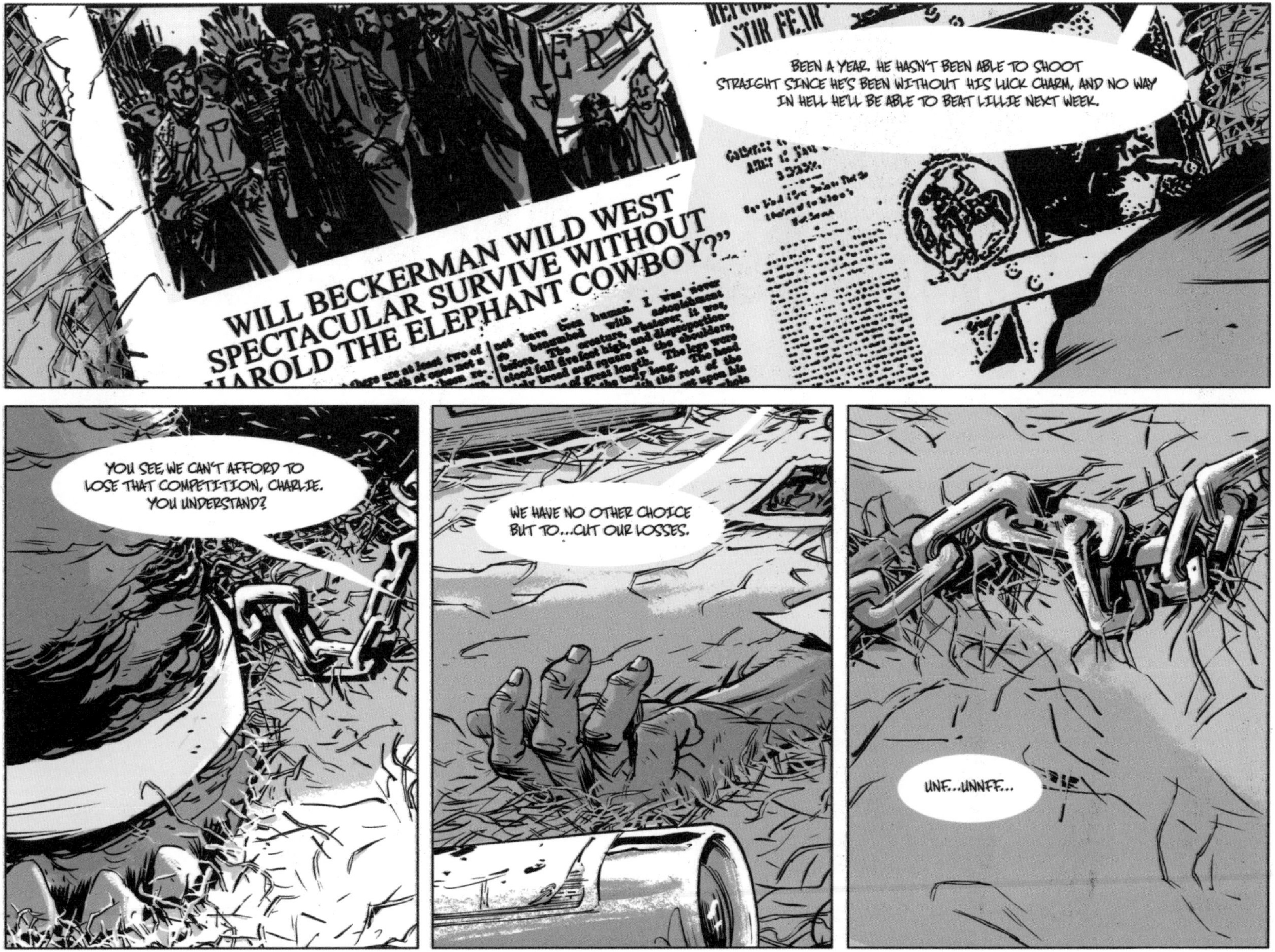
STIR FEAR
WILL BECKERMAN WILD WEST SPECTACULAR SURVIVE WITHOUT HAROLD THE ELEPHANT COWBOY?"
BEEN A YEAR. HE HASN'T BEEN ABLE TO SHOOT STRAIGHT SINCE HE'S BEEN WITHOUT HIS LUCK CHARM, AND NO WAY IN HELL HE'LL BE ABLE TO BEAT LILLIE NEXT WEEK.
YOU SEE, WE CAN'T AFFORD TO LOSE THAT COMPETITION, CHARLIE. YOU UNDERSTAND?
WE HAVE NO OTHER CHOICE BUT TO...CUT OUR LOSSES.
UNF...UNNFF...

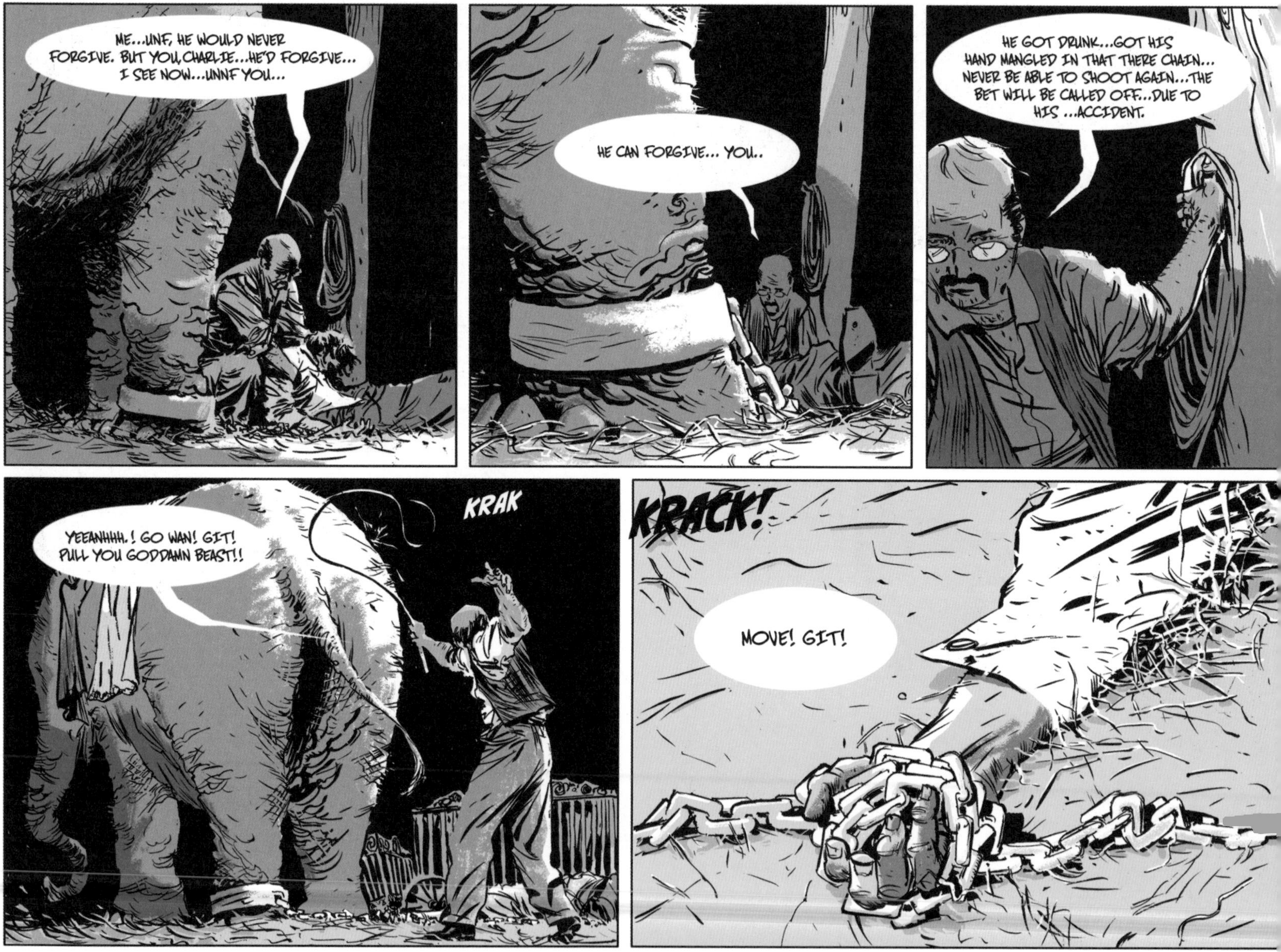
ME...UNF, HE WOULD NEVER FORGIVE. BUT YOU,CHARLIE...HE'D FORGIVE... I SEE NOW...UNNF YOU...
HE CAN FORGIVE... YOU..
HE GOT DRUNK...GOT HIS HAND MANGLED IN THAT THERE CHAIN... NEVER BE ABLE TO SHOOT AGAIN...THE BET WILL BE CALLED OFF...DUE TO HIS ...ACCIDENT.
KRAK
YEEANHHH.! GO WAN! GIT! PULL YOU GODDAMN BEAST!!
KRACK!
MOVE! GIT!

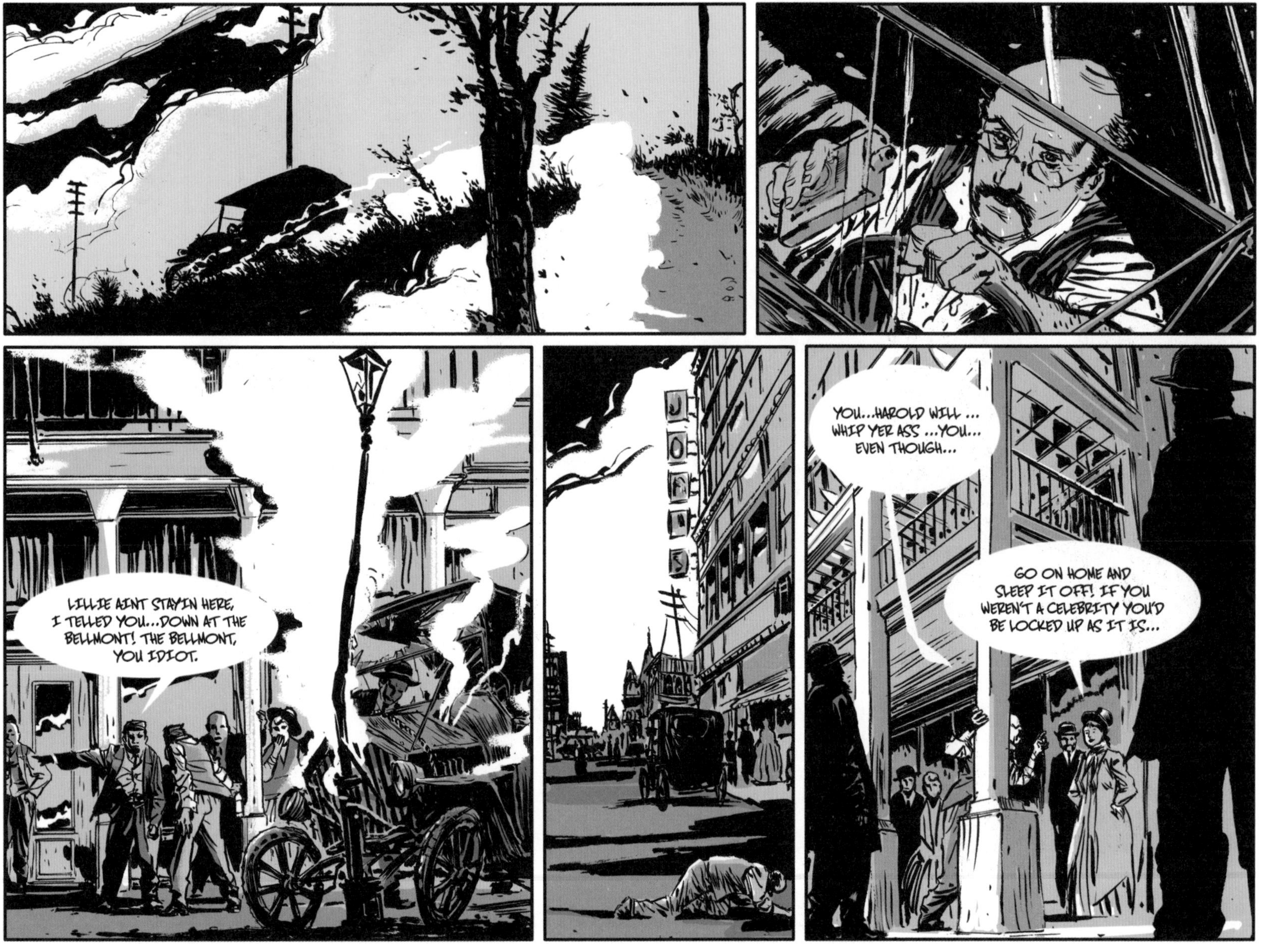
LILLIE AINT STAYIN HERE, I TELLED YOU...DOWN AT THE BELLMONT! THE BELLMONT, YOU IDIOT.
YOU...HAROLD WILL ... WHIP YER ASS ...YOU... EVEN THOUGH...
GO ON HOME AND SLEEP IT OFF! IF YOU WEREN'T A CELEBRITY YOU'D BE LOCKED UP AS IT IS...

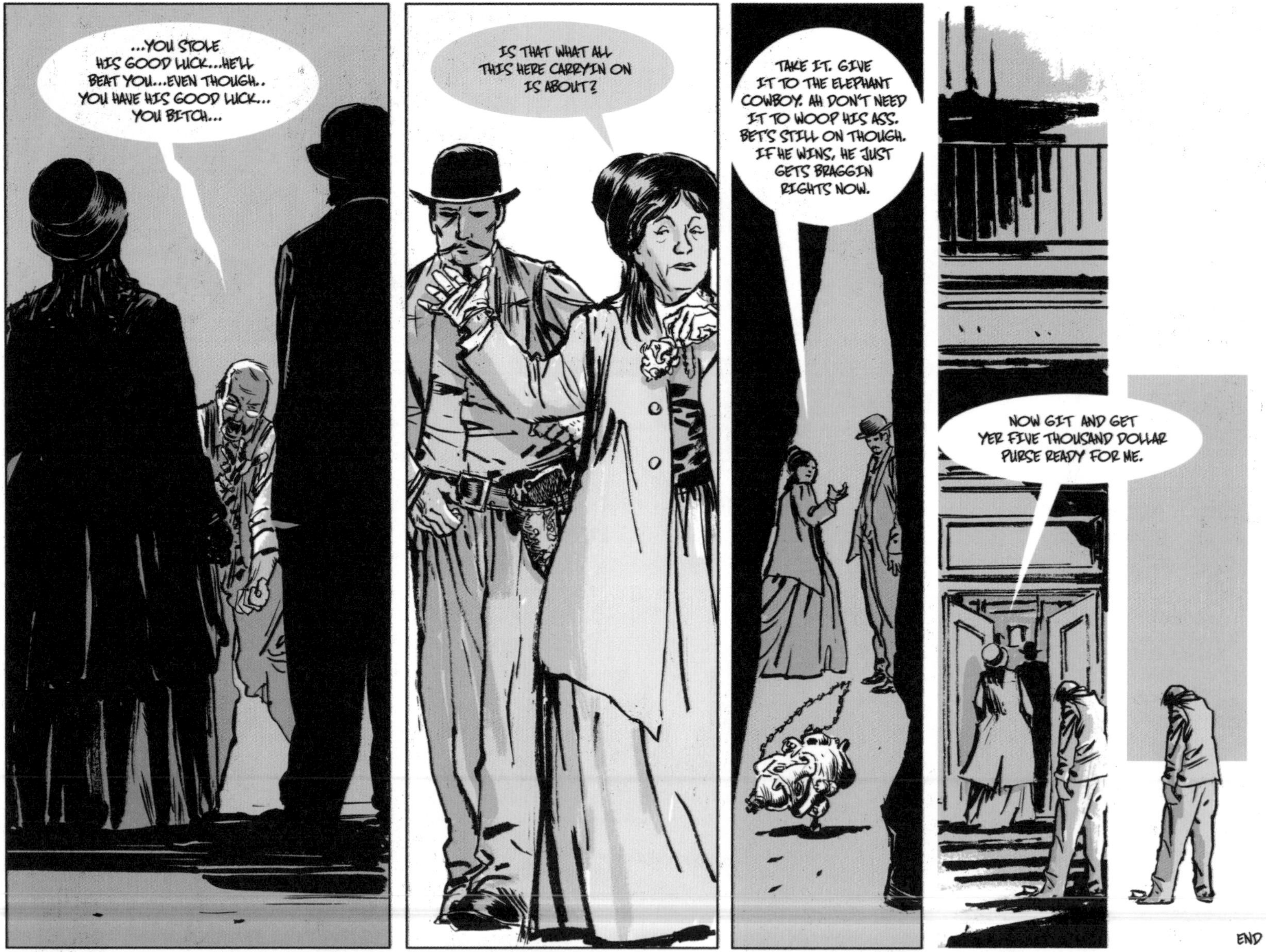
...YOU STOLE HIS GOOD LUCK...HE'LL BEAT YOU...EVEN THOUGH.. YOU HAVE HIS GOOD LUCK... YOU BITCH...
IS THAT WHAT ALL THIS HERE CARRY'IN ON IS ABOUT?
TAKE IT. GIVE IT TO THE ELEPHANT COWBOY. AH DON'T NEED IT TO WOOP HIS ASS. BET'S STILL ON THOUGH. IF HE WINS, HE JUST GETS BRAGGIN RIGHTS NOW.
NOW GIT AND GET YER FIVE THOUSAND DOLLAR PURSE READY FOR ME.
END

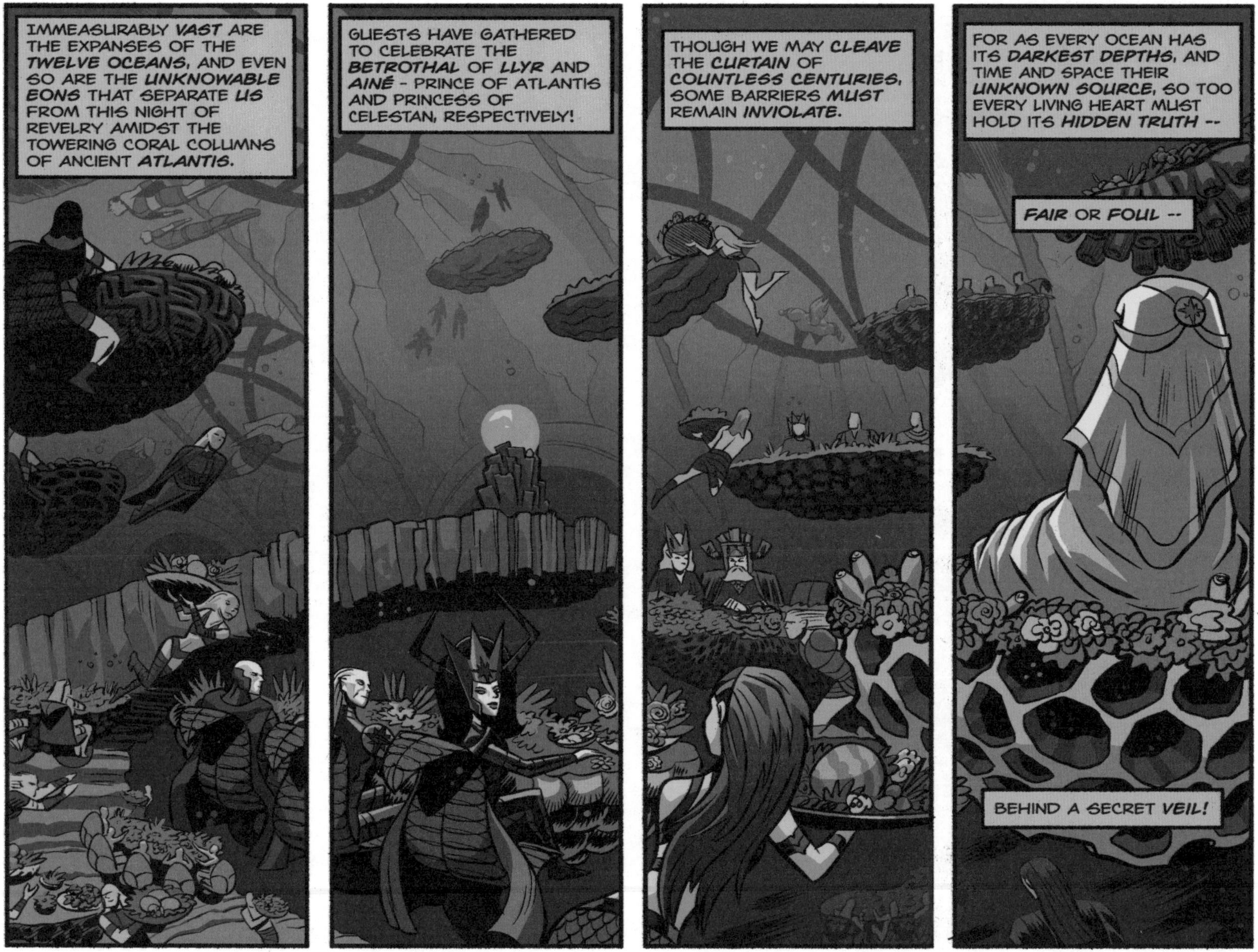
IMMEASURABLY VAST ARE THE EXPANSES OF THE TWELVE OCEANS, AND EVEN SO ARE THE UNKNOWABLE EONS THAT SEPARATE US FROM THIS NIGHT OF REVELRY AMIDST THE TOWERING CORAL COLUMNS OF ANCIENT ATLANTIS.
GUESTS HAVE GATHERED TO CELEBRATE THE BETROTHAL OF LLYR AND AINÉ - PRINCE OF ATLANTIS AND PRINCESS OF CELESTAN, RESPECTIVELY!
THOUGH WE MAY CLEAVE THE CURTAIN OF COUNTLESS CENTURIES, SOME BARRIERS MUST REMAIN INVIOLATE.
FOR AS EVERY OCEAN HAS ITS DARKEST DEPTHS, AND TIME AND SPACE THEIR UNKNOWN SOURCE, SO TOO EVERY LIVING HEART MUST HOLD ITS HIDDEN TRUTH --
FAIR OR FOUL --
BEHIND A SECRET VEIL!

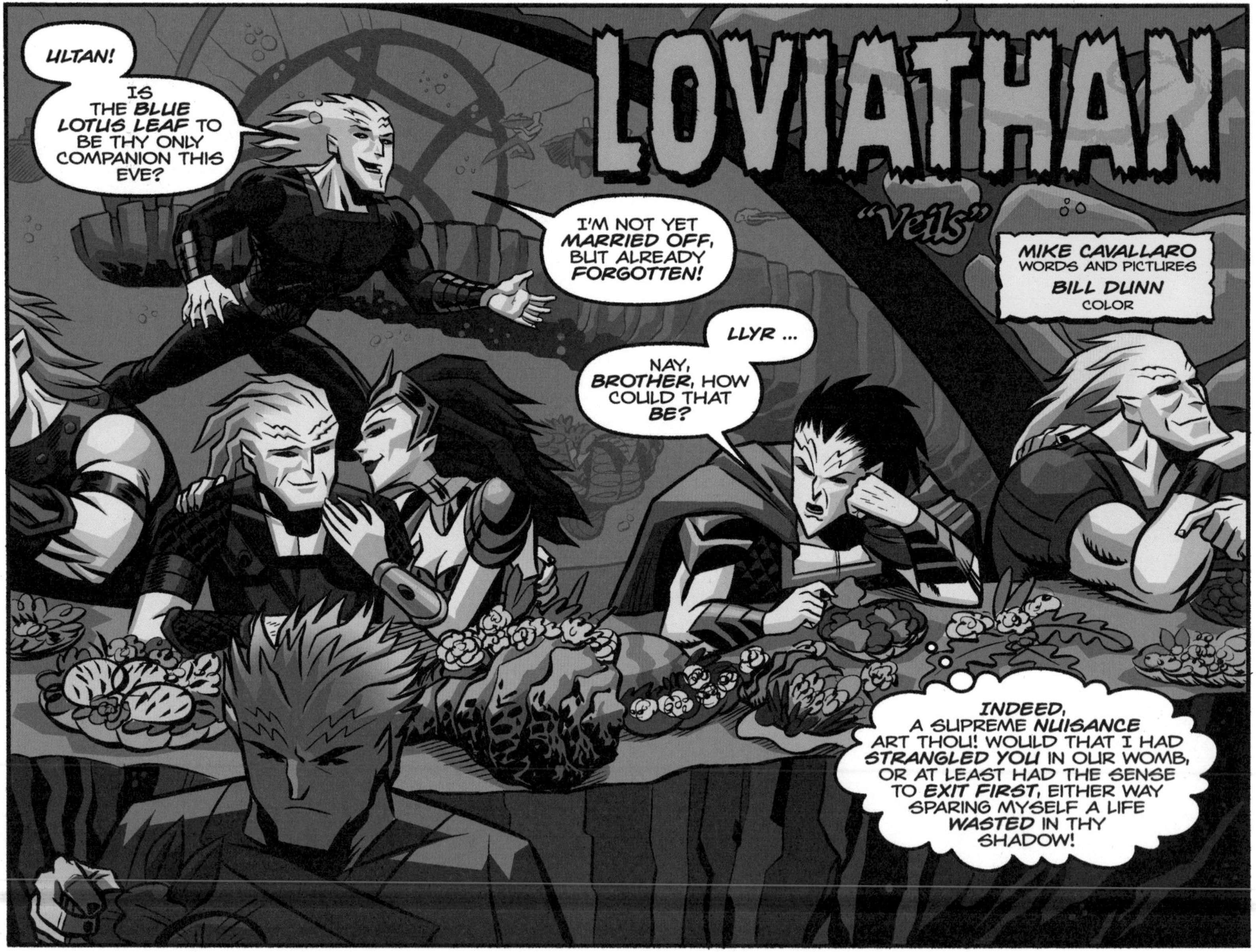
LOVIATHAN
"Veils"
MIKE CAVALLARO
WORDS AND PICTURES
BILL DUNN
COLOR
ULTAN!
IS THE BLUE LOTUS LEAF TO BE THY ONLY COMPANION THIS EVE?
I'M NOT YET MARRIED OFF, BUT ALREADY FORGOTTEN!
LLYR ...
NAY, BROTHER, HOW COULD THAT BE?
INDEED, A SUPREME NUISANCE ART THOU! WOULD THAT I HAD STRANGLED YOU IN OUR WOMB, OR AT LEAST HAD THE SENSE TO EXIT FIRST, EITHER WAY SPARING MYSELF A LIFE WASTED IN THY SHADOW!

TOO MUCH LEAF ADDLES THE MIND! REMEMBER --
AFTER THE GREAT SEER'S BLESSING, TRADITION DEMANDS YOU ADDRESS THE ASSEMBLAGE!
IT WILL BE MY HONOR.
WERE IT TO EVER HAPPEN, THAT IS! FOR THIS NIGHT SHALL BRING AN END TO TRADITION!
A TALE, NO DOUBT, TO AMUSE ALL AT MY OWN EXPENSE? PERHAPS AN ADVENTURE FROM OUR MISSPENT YOUTH, OUR YEARS OF MISCHIEF?
THAT TIME, MAYHAP, WHEN WE WERE TRAPPED IN THE ICE EEL'S CAVE?
AH, I REMEMBER IT WELL...
ANOTHER MISSED OPPORTUNITY! YOU SHOULD HAVE PERISHED THERE, BUT AGAIN I WAS CHEATED, AS EVER...
I MISS THOSE BYGONE DAYS, BROTHER. RESPONSIBILITY DRAWS ABOUT ME -- TIGHT AS THE SIX ARMS OF THE KRAKEN!
WHEN I'M KING, I MUST DEFEND THE FREEDOM OF OTHERS AT THE EXPENSE OF MY OWN. SOMETIMES I ENVY YOU...
WHAT WOULD OUR KINGLY FATHER SAY TO HEAR YOU SPEAK SO? YOU, WHO ART EVER HIS FAVORITE. THE WORLD IS YOURS, AS IS NOW THE PRINCESS OF CELESTAN.
LOUT. KINGSHIP IS WASTED ON THEE. TONIGHT, MY PLANS SHALL AVERT THAT INJUSTICE!
AYE, THE PRINCESS. A WOMAN I'VE NEVER SEEN NOR MET BEFORE. IF SHE IS MY FUTURE, THEN MY FUTURE IS HIDDEN.
TIME REVEALS ALL, BROTHER.
AS YOU SHALL LEARN. I HAVE FORMED A PACT WITH THY ARCH-FOE, THE DEMON OROLUS! EVEN NOW, HIS TALISMAN INFECTS YON MYSTIC GLOBE, AND GUARANTEES THY DOOM!

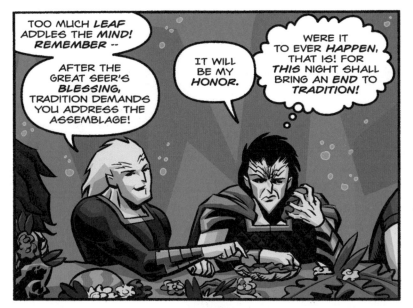

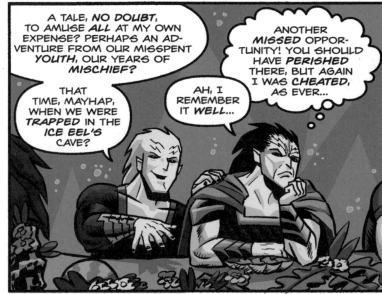

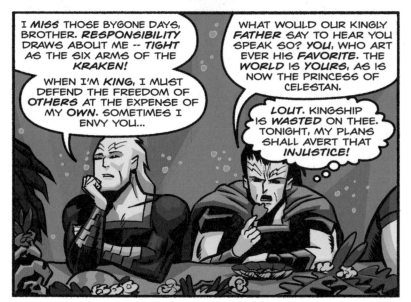

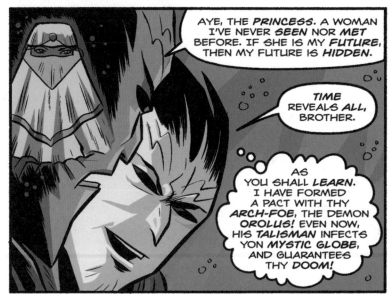

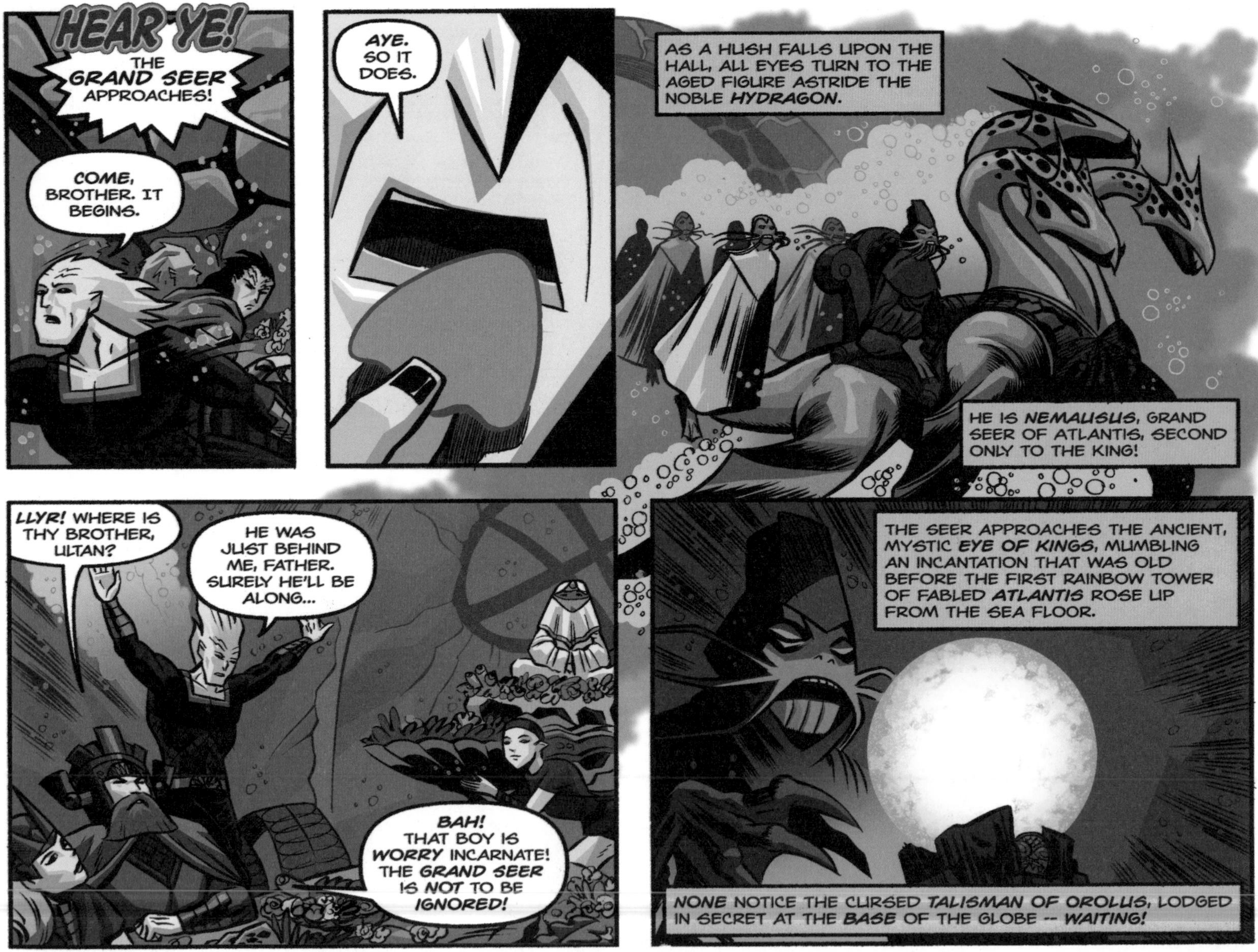
HEAR YE! THE GRAND SEER APPROACHES!
COME, BROTHER. IT BEGINS.
AYE. SO IT DOES.
AS A HUSH FALLS UPON THE HALL, ALL EYES TURN TO THE AGED FIGURE ASTRIDE THE NOBLE HYDRAGON.
HE IS NEMAUSUS, GRAND SEER OF ATLANTIS, SECOND ONLY TO THE KING!
LLYR! WHERE IS THY BROTHER, ULTAN?
HE WAS JUST BEHIND ME, FATHER. SURELY HE'LL BE ALONG...
BAH! THAT BOY IS WORRY INCARNATE! THE GRAND SEER IS NOT TO BE IGNORED!
THE SEER APPROACHES THE ANCIENT, MYSTIC EYE OF KINGS, MUMBLING AN INCANTATION THAT WAS OLD BEFORE THE FIRST RAINBOW TOWER OF FABLED ATLANTIS ROSE UP FROM THE SEA FLOOR.
NONE NOTICE THE CURSED TALISMAN OF OROLUS, LODGED IN SECRET AT THE BASE OF THE GLOBE -- WAITING!

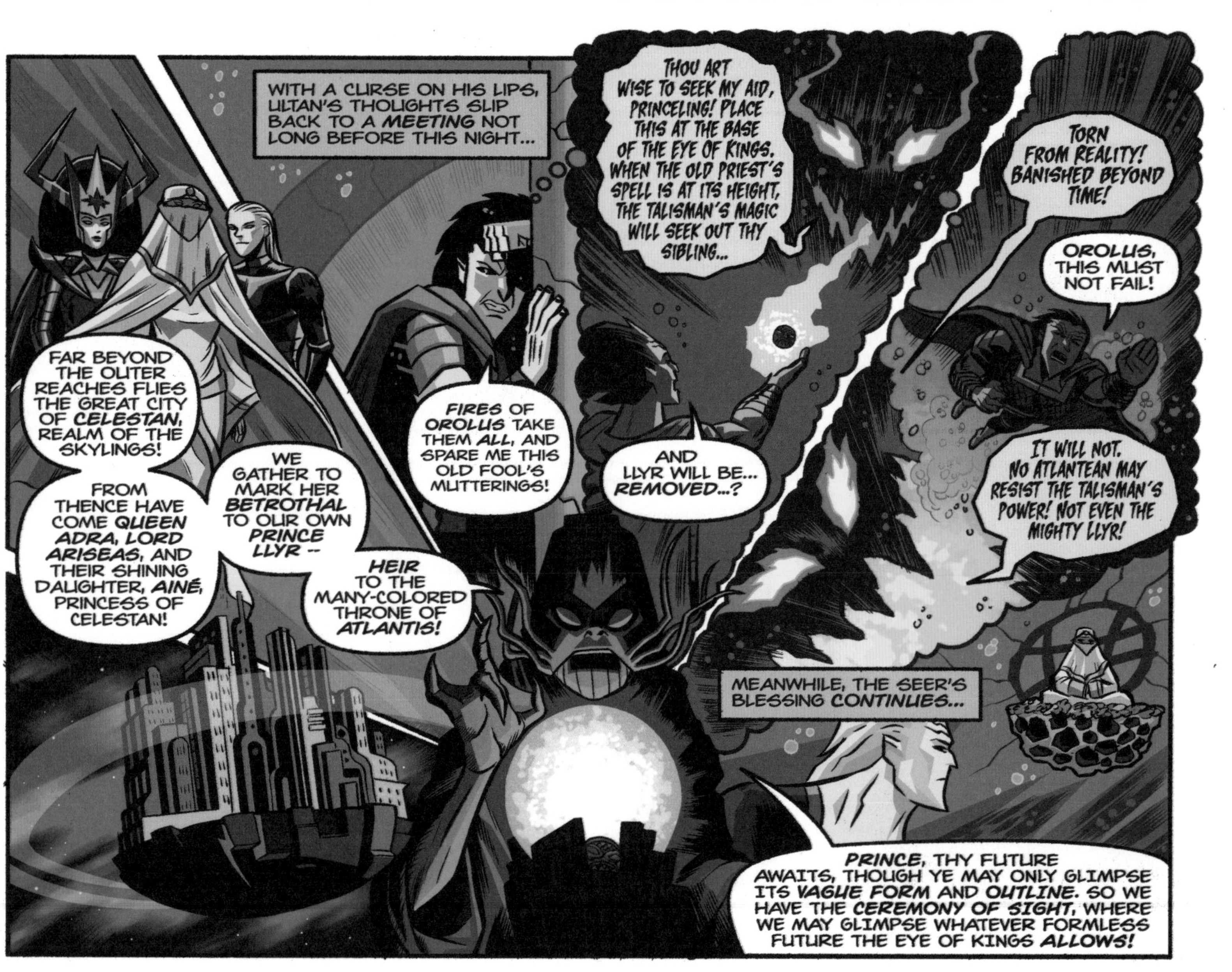
WITH A CURSE ON HIS LIPS, ULTAN'S THOUGHTS SLIP BACK TO A MEETING NOT LONG BEFORE THIS NIGHT...
FAR BEYOND THE OUTER REACHES FLIES THE GREAT CITY OF CELESTAN, REALM OF THE SKYLINGS!
FROM THENCE HAVE COME QUEEN ADRA, LORD ARISEAS, AND THEIR SHINING DAUGHTER, AINÉ, PRINCESS OF CELESTAN!
WE GATHER TO MARK HER BETROTHAL TO OUR OWN PRINCE LLYR --
HEIR TO THE MANY-COLORED THRONE OF ATLANTIS!
FIRES OF OROLUS TAKE THEM ALL, AND SPARE ME THIS OLD FOOL'S MUTTERINGS!
THOU ART WISE TO SEEK MY AID, PRINCELING! PLACE THIS AT THE BASE OF THE EYE OF KINGS. WHEN THE OLD PRIEST'S SPELL IS AT ITS HEIGHT, THE TALISMAN'S MAGIC WILL SEEK OUT THY SIBLING...
AND LLYR WILL BE... REMOVED...?
TORN FROM REALITY! BANISHED BEYOND TIME!
OROLUS, THIS MUST NOT FAIL!
IT WILL NOT. NO ATLANTEAN MAY RESIST THE TALISMAN'S POWER! NOT EVEN THE MIGHTY LLYR!
MEANWHILE, THE SEER'S BLESSING CONTINUES...
PRINCE, THY FUTURE AWAITS, THOUGH YE MAY ONLY GLIMPSE ITS VAGUE FORM AND OUTLINE. SO WE HAVE THE CEREMONY OF SIGHT, WHERE WE MAY GLIMPSE WHATEVER FORMLESS FUTURE THE EYE OF KINGS ALLOWS!

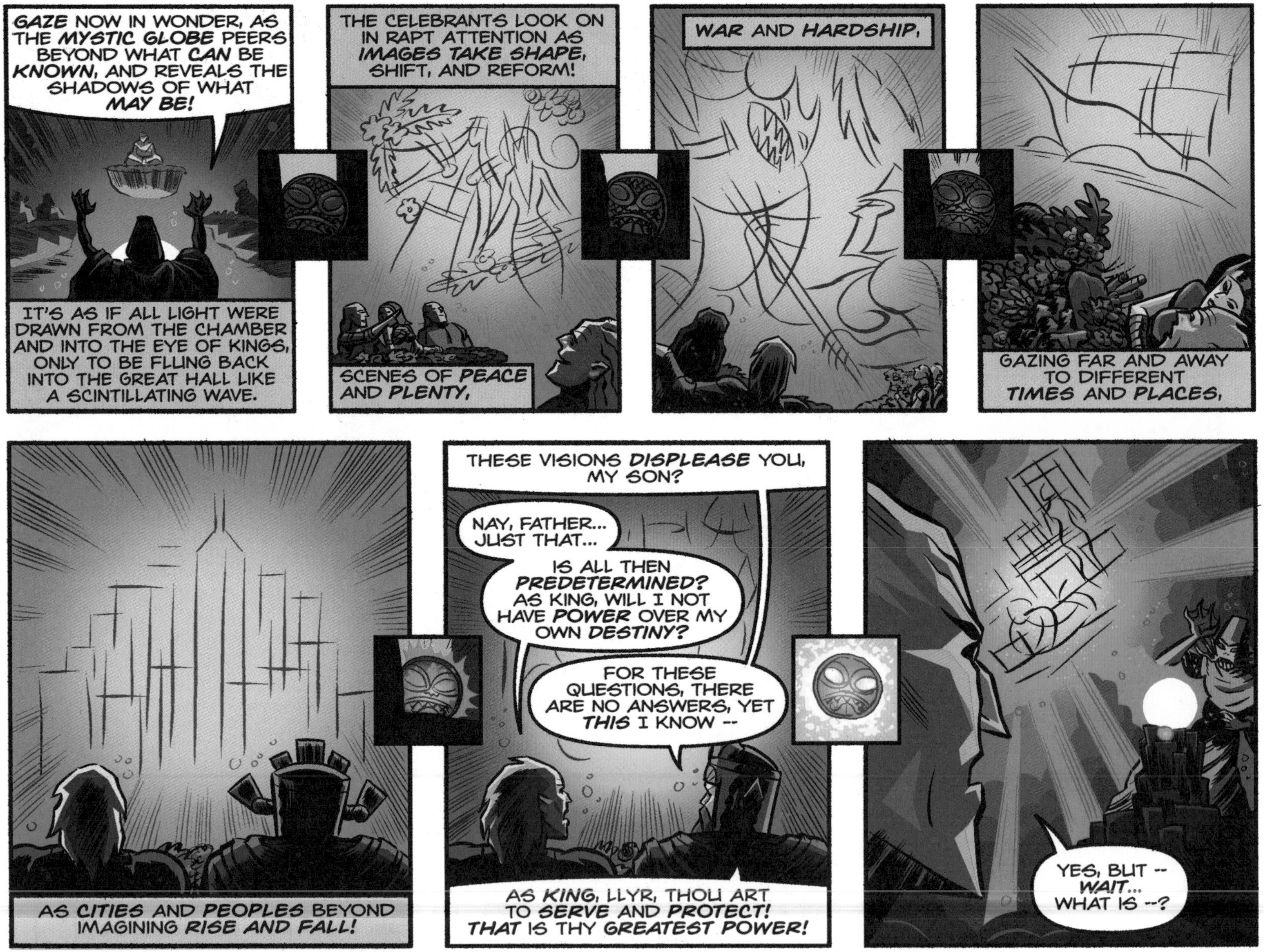

GAZE NOW IN WONDER, AS THE MYSTIC GLOBE PEERS BEYOND WHAT CAN BE KNOWN, AND REVEALS THE SHADOWS OF WHAT MAY BE!
IT'S AS IF ALL LIGHT WERE DRAWN FROM THE CHAMBER AND INTO THE EYE OF KINGS, ONLY TO BE FLUNG BACK INTO THE GREAT HALL LIKE A SCINTILLATING WAVE.
THE CELEBRANTS LOOK ON IN RAPT ATTENTION AS IMAGES TAKE SHAPE, SHIFT, AND REFORM!
SCENES OF PEACE AND PLENTY,
WAR AND HARDSHIP,
GAZING FAR AND AWAY TO DIFFERENT TIMES AND PLACES,
AS CITIES AND PEOPLES BEYOND IMAGINING RISE AND FALL!
THESE VISIONS DISPLEASE YOU, MY SON?
NAY, FATHER... JUST THAT...
IS ALL THEN PREDETERMINED? AS KING, WILL I NOT HAVE POWER OVER MY OWN DESTINY?
FOR THESE QUESTIONS, THERE ARE NO ANSWERS, YET THIS I KNOW --
AS KING, LLYR, THOU ART TO SERVE AND PROTECT! THAT IS THY GREATEST POWER!
YES, BUT -- WAIT... WHAT IS --?

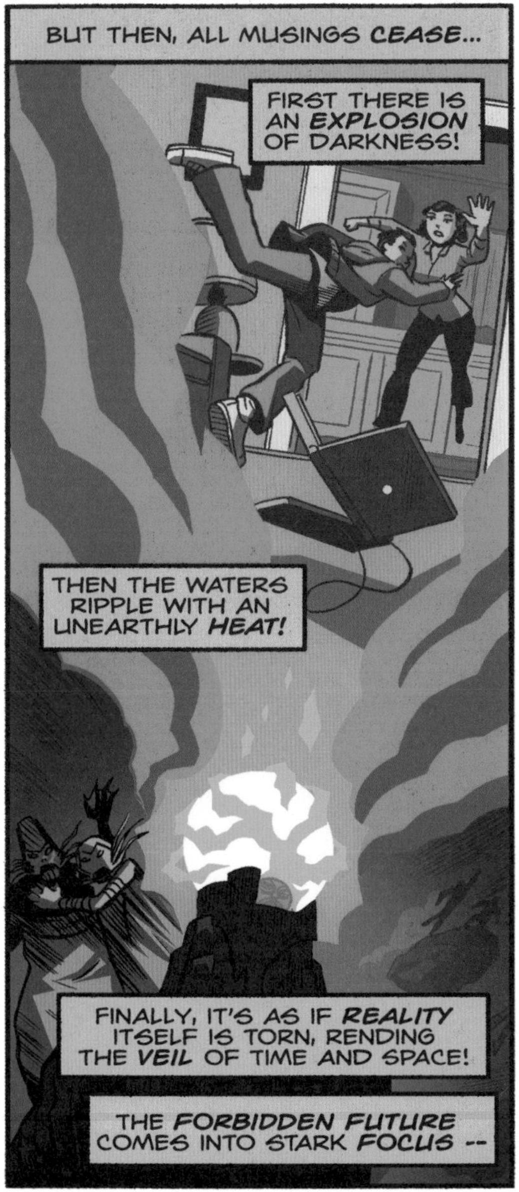

BUT THEN, ALL MUSINGS CEASE...
FIRST THERE IS AN EXPLOSION OF DARKNESS!
THEN THE WATERS RIPPLE WITH AN UNEARTHLY HEAT!
FINALLY, IT'S AS IF REALITY ITSELF IS TORN, RENDING THE VEIL OF TIME AND SPACE!
THE FORBIDDEN FUTURE COMES INTO STARK FOCUS --

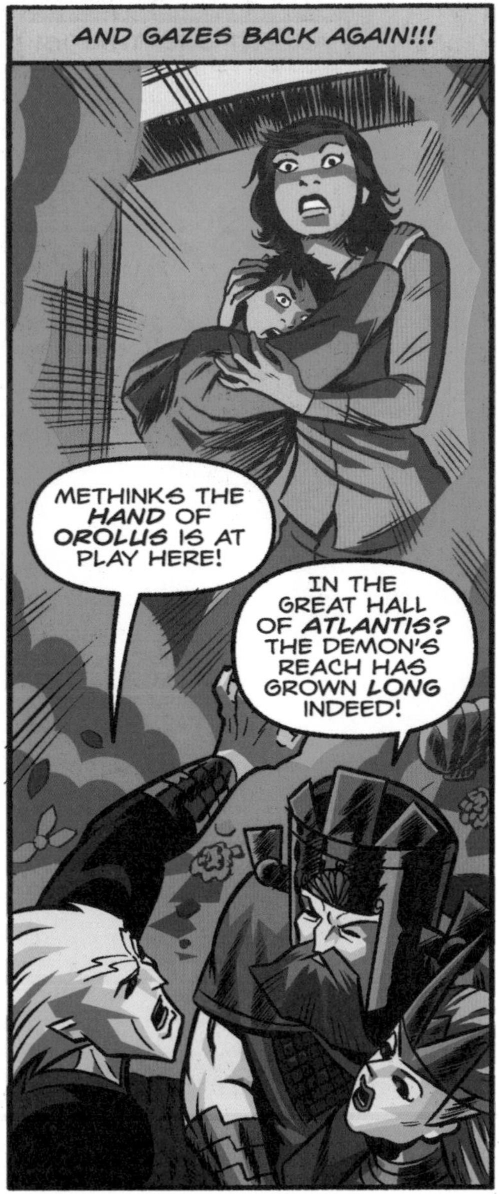

AND GAZES BACK AGAIN!!!
METHINKS THE HAND OF OROLUS IS AT PLAY HERE!
IN THE GREAT HALL OF ATLANTIS? THE DEMON'S REACH HAS GROWN LONG INDEED!

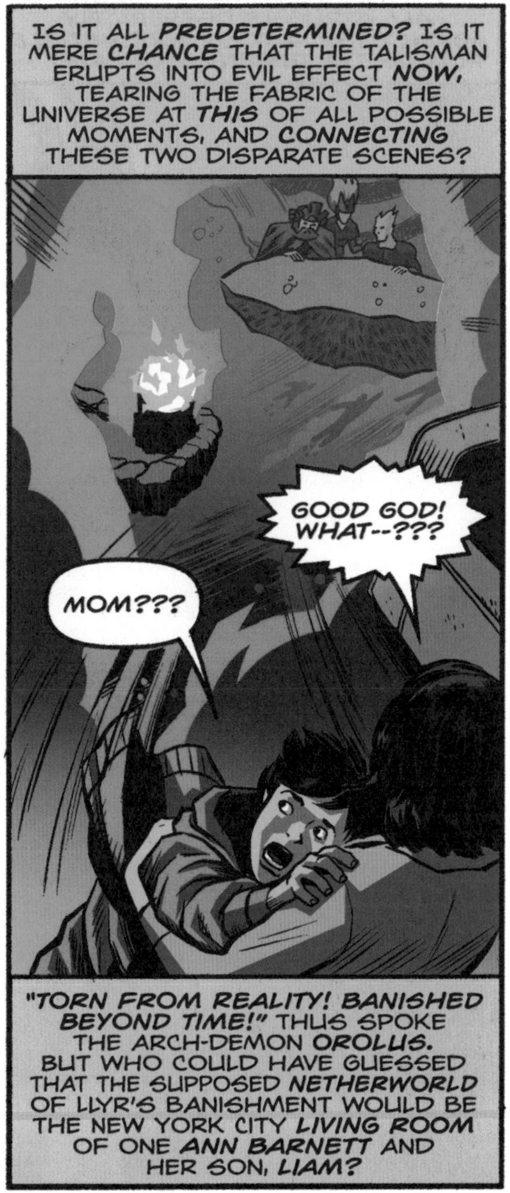

IS IT ALL PREDETERMINED? IS IT MERE CHANCE THAT THE TALISMAN ERUPTS INTO EVIL EFFECT NOW, TEARING THE FABRIC OF THE UNIVERSE AT THIS OF ALL POSSIBLE MOMENTS, AND CONNECTING THESE TWO DISPARATE SCENES?
GOOD GOD! WHAT--???
MOM???
"TORN FROM REALITY! BANISHED BEYOND TIME!" THUS SPOKE THE ARCH-DEMON OROLUS. BUT WHO COULD HAVE GUESSED THAT THE SUPPOSED NETHERWORLD OF LLYR'S BANISHMENT WOULD BE THE NEW YORK CITY LIVING ROOM OF ONE ANN BARNETT AND HER SON, LIAM?

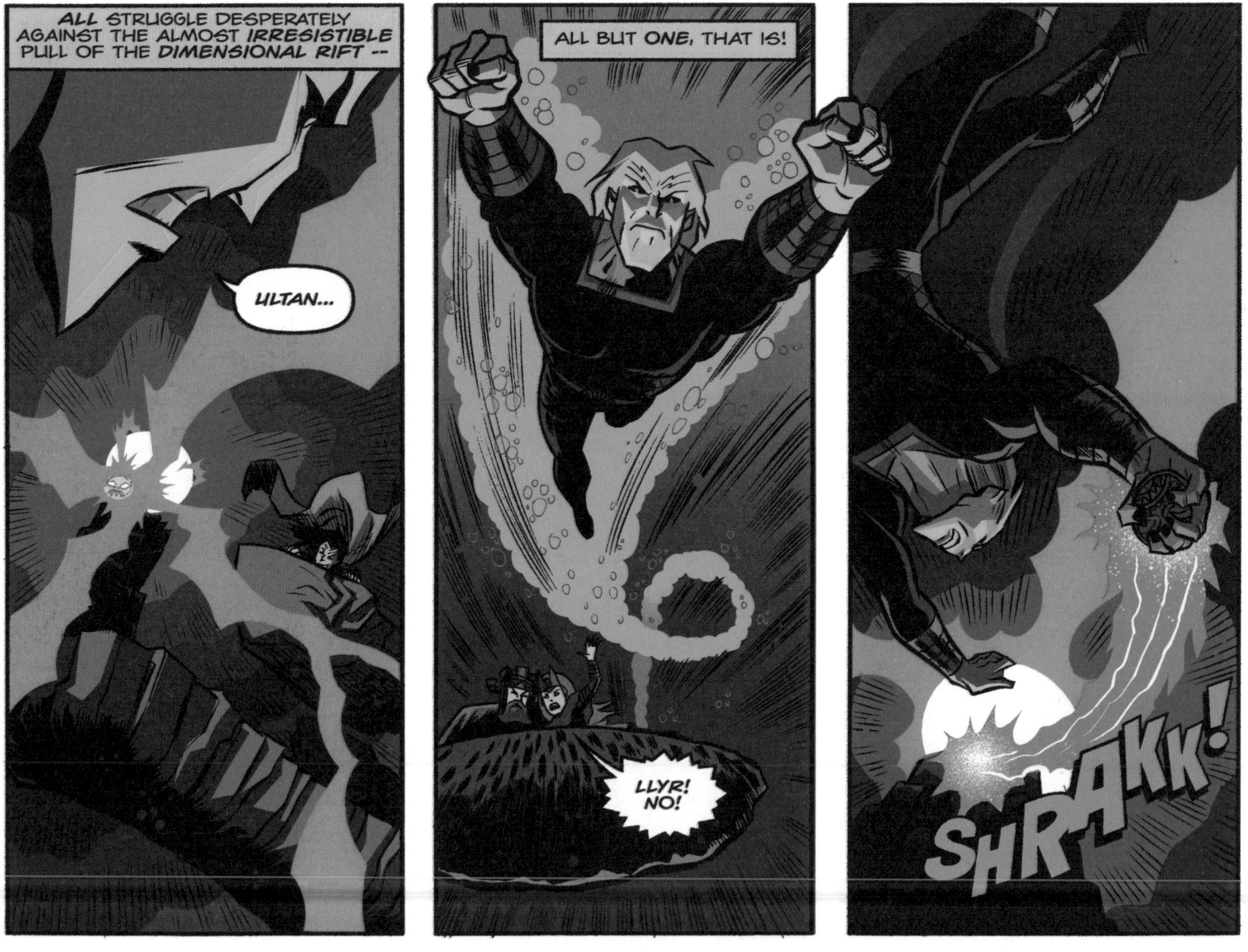
ALL STRUGGLE DESPERATELY AGAINST THE ALMOST IRRESISTIBLE PULL OF THE DIMENSIONAL RIFT --
ULTAN...
ALL BUT ONE, THAT IS!
LLYR! NO!
SHRAKK!

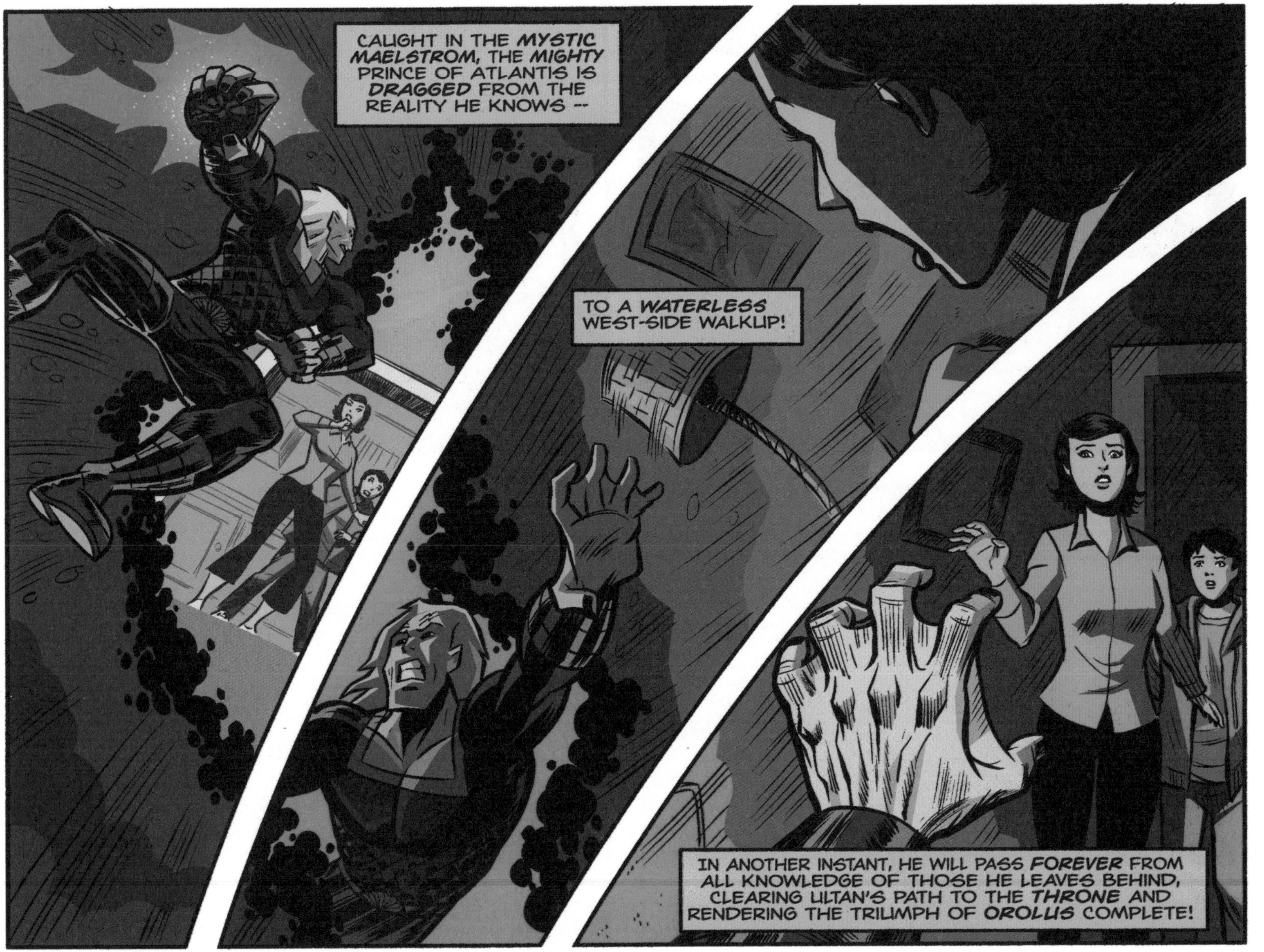
CAUGHT IN THE MYSTIC MAELSTROM, THE MIGHTY PRINCE OF ATLANTIS IS DRAGGED FROM THE REALITY HE KNOWS --
TO A WATERLESS WEST-SIDE WALKUP!
IN ANOTHER INSTANT, HE WILL PASS FOREVER FROM ALL KNOWLEDGE OF THOSE HE LEAVES BEHIND, CLEARING ULTAN'S PATH TO THE THRONE AND RENDERING THE TRIUMPH OF OROLUS COMPLETE!

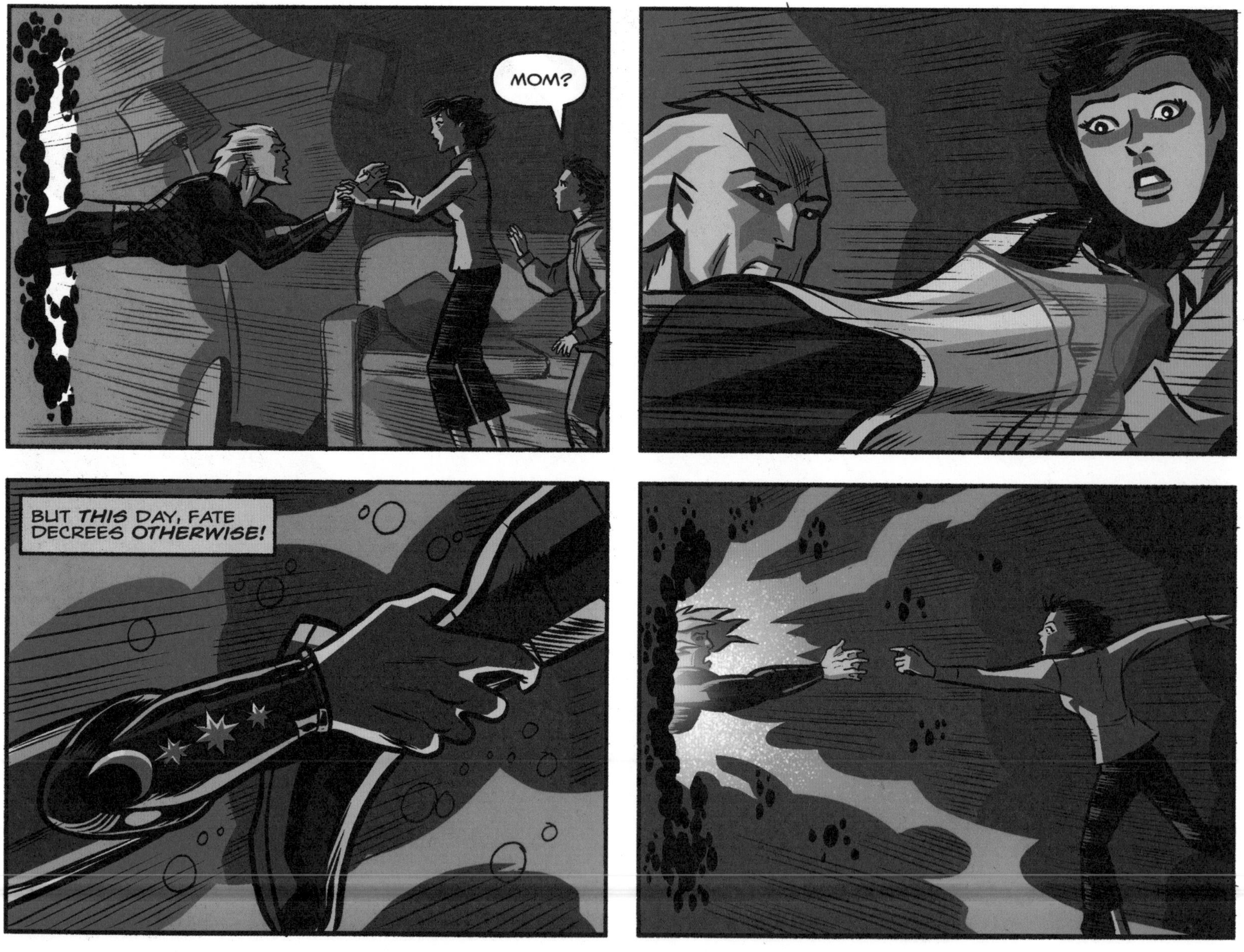
MOM?
BUT THIS DAY, FATE DECREES OTHERWISE!

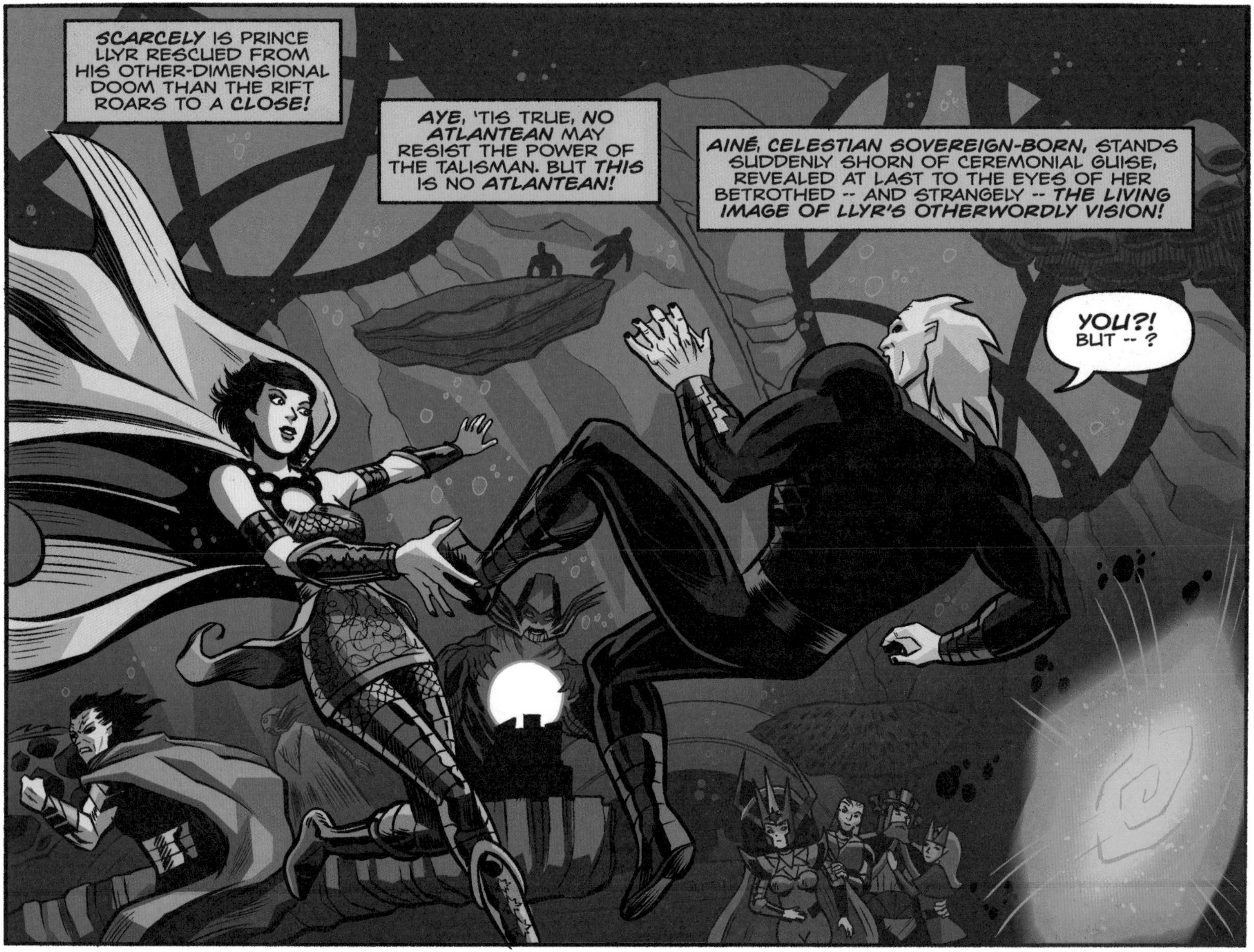
SCARCELY IS PRINCE LLYR RESCUED FROM HIS OTHER-DIMENSIONAL DOOM THAN THE RIFT ROARS TO A CLOSE!
AYE, 'TIS TRUE, NO ATLANTEAN MAY RESIST THE POWER OF THE TALISMAN. BUT THIS IS NO ATLANTEAN!
AINÉ, CELESTIAN SOVEREIGN-BORN, STANDS SUDDENLY SHORN OF CEREMONIAL GUISE, REVEALED AT LAST TO THE EYES OF HER BETROTHED -- AND STRANGELY -- THE LIVING IMAGE OF LLYR'S OTHERWORDLY VISION!
YOU?! BUT -- ?

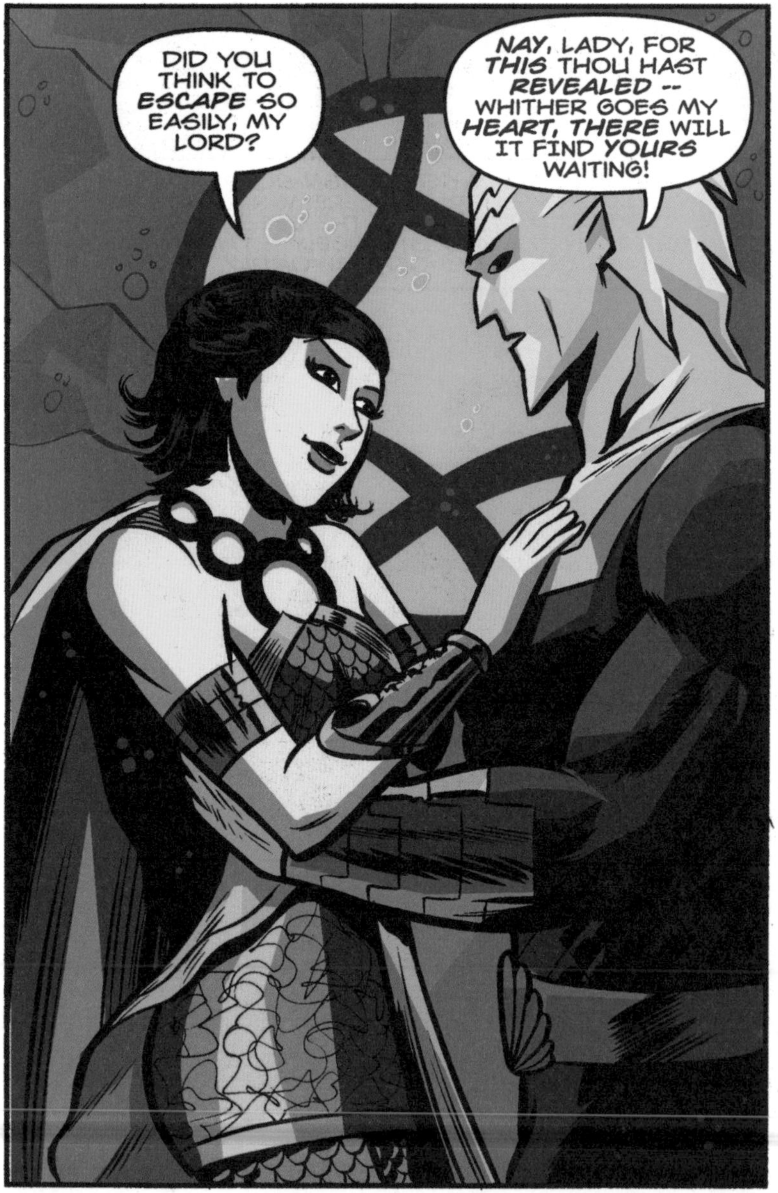
DID YOU THINK TO ***ESCAPE*** SO EASILY, MY LORD?
NAY, LADY, FOR ***THIS*** THOU HAST ***REVEALED*** -- WHITHER GOES MY ***HEART, THERE*** WILL IT FIND ***YOURS*** WAITING!

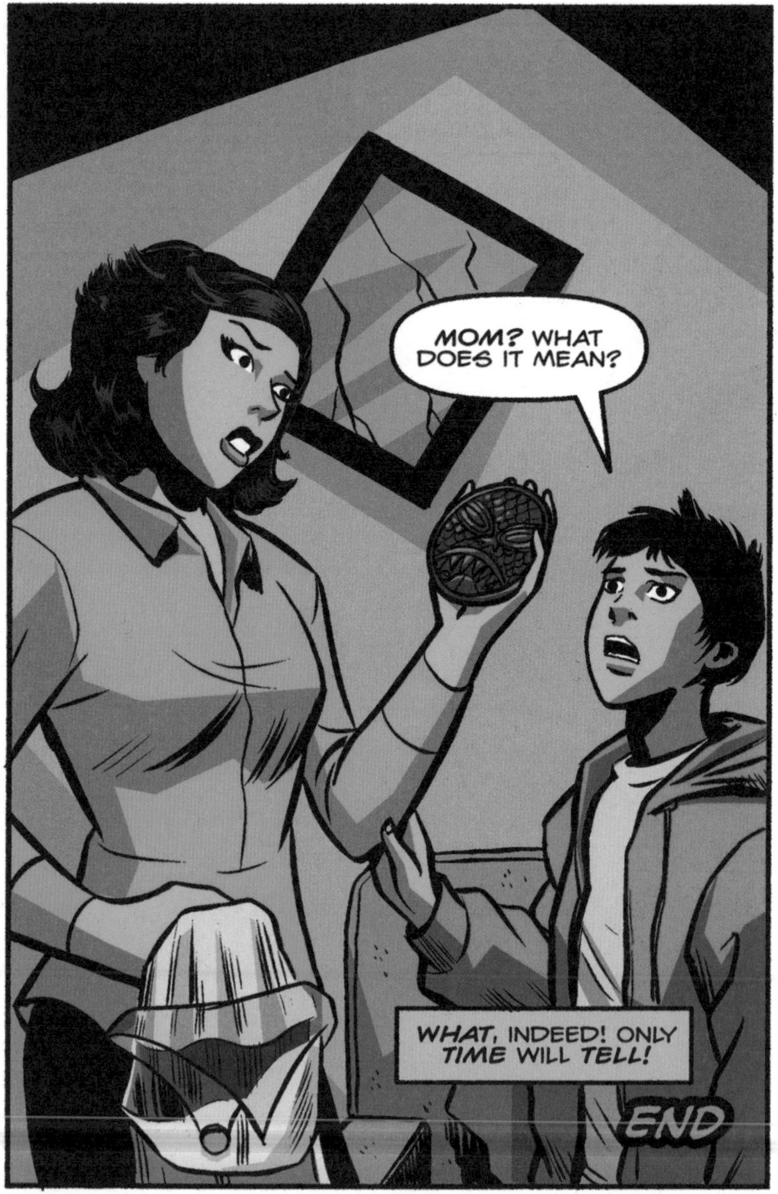
MOM? WHAT DOES IT MEAN?
WHAT, INDEED! ONLY ***TIME*** WILL ***TELL!***
END

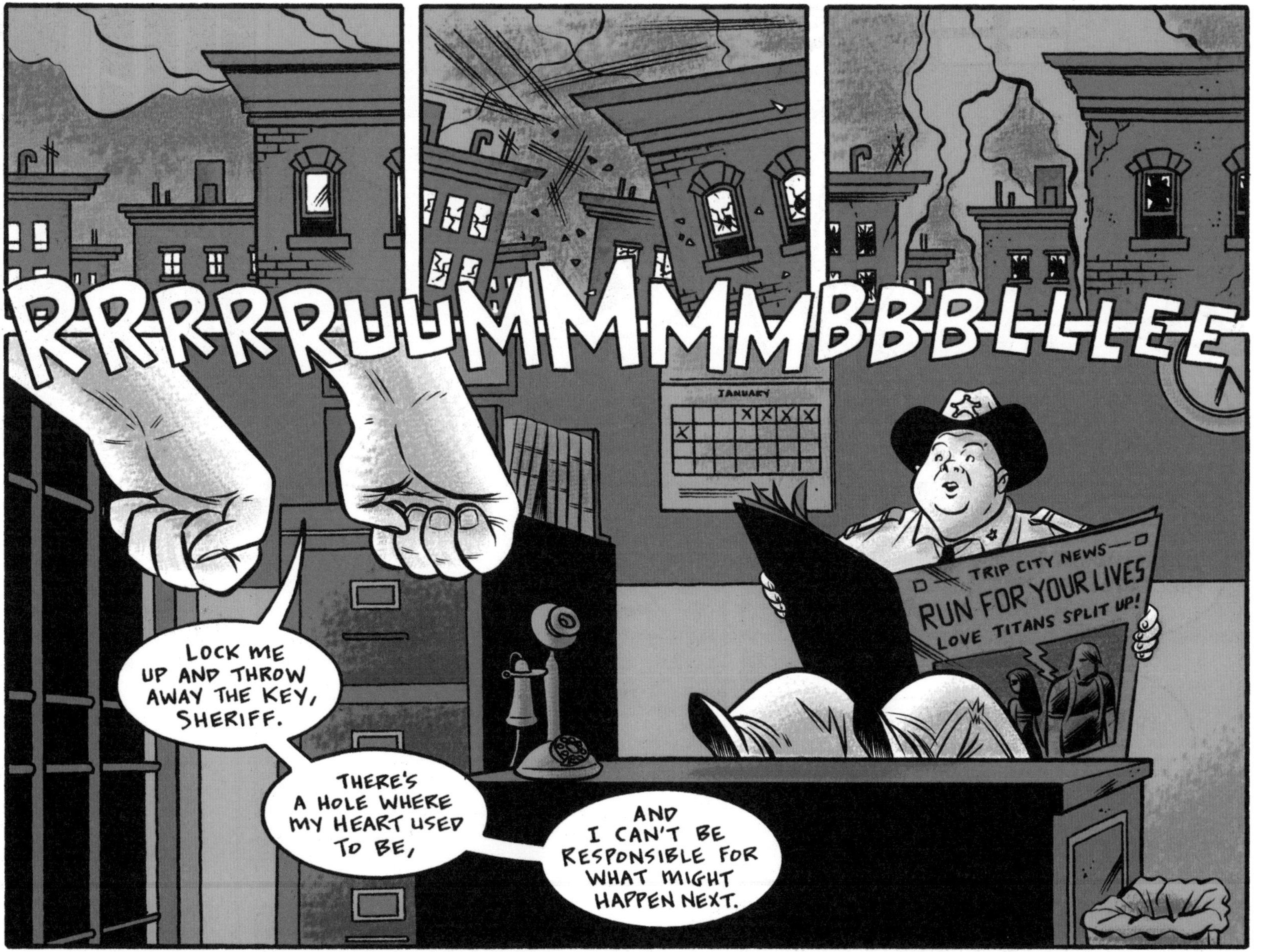

RRRRRUUMMMMMMBBBLLLEE
JANUARY
TRIP CITY NEWS
RUN FOR YOUR LIVES
LOVE TITANS SPLIT UP!
LOCK ME UP AND THROW AWAY THE KEY, SHERIFF.
THERE'S A HOLE WHERE MY HEART USED TO BE,
AND I CAN'T BE RESPONSIBLE FOR WHAT MIGHT HAPPEN NEXT.

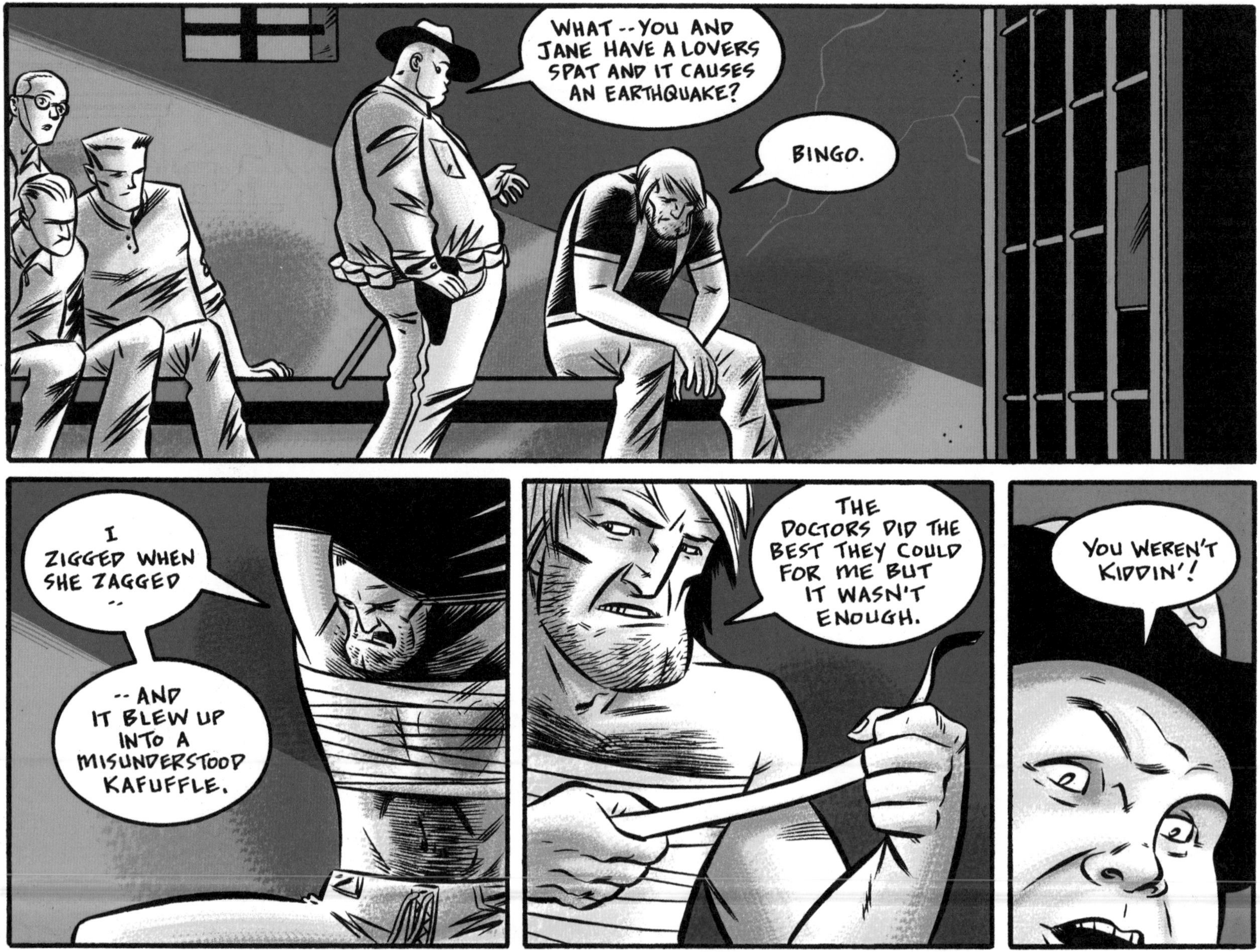
WHAT--YOU AND JANE HAVE A LOVERS SPAT AND IT CAUSES AN EARTHQUAKE?
BINGO.
I ZIGGED WHEN SHE ZAGGED--
--AND IT BLEW UP INTO A MISUNDERSTOOD KAFUFFLE.
THE DOCTORS DID THE BEST THEY COULD FOR ME BUT IT WASN'T ENOUGH.
YOU WEREN'T KIDDIN'!

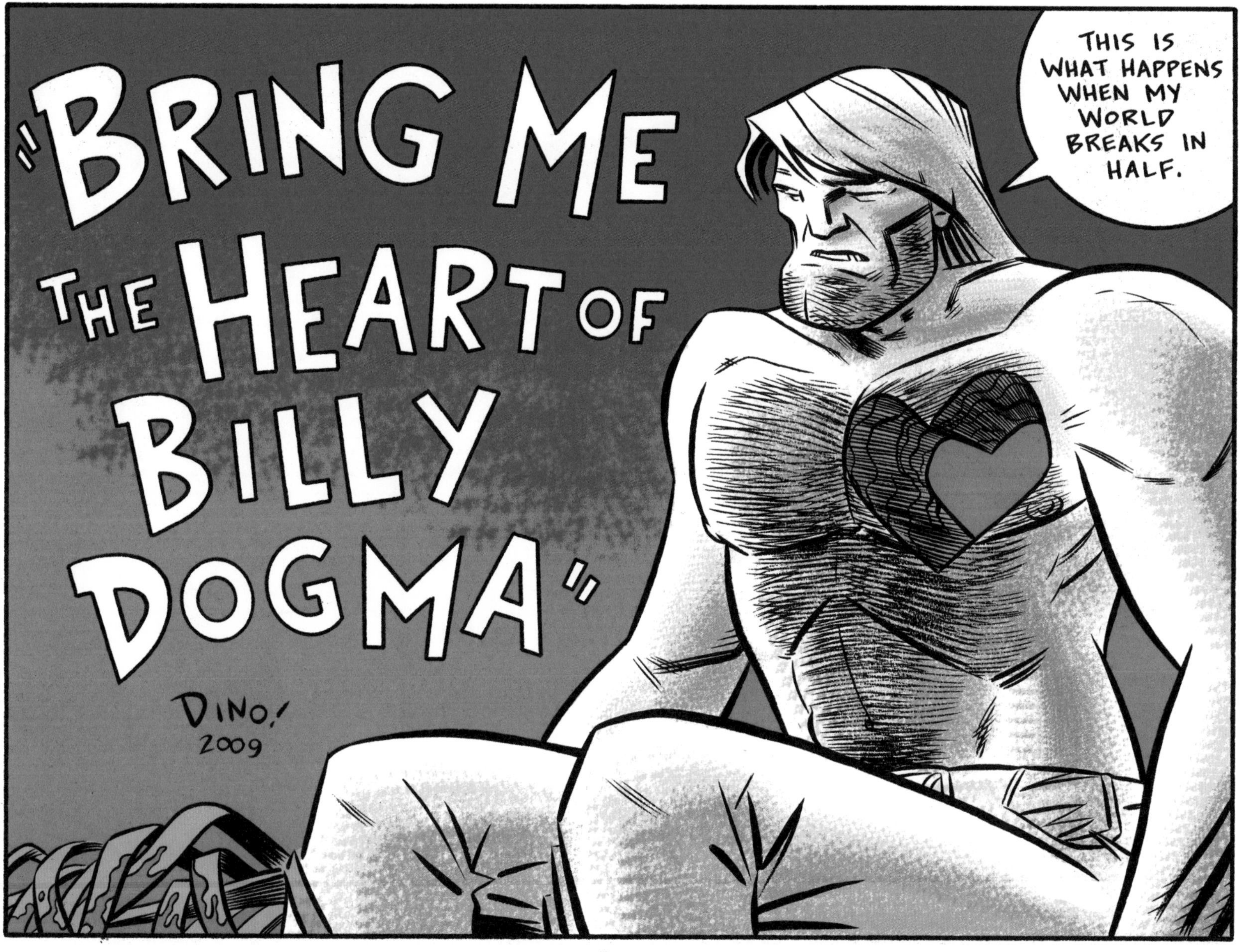
"BRING ME THE HEART OF BILLY DOGMA"
THIS IS WHAT HAPPENS WHEN MY WORLD BREAKS IN HALF.
DINO! 2009

THE UNEXPECTED BREAK-UP OF BILLY DOGMA AND JANE LEGIT HAS PUT TRIP CITY ON RED ALERT.
STOCKS CRASH TO A RECORD LOW WHILE OIL PRICES SKYROCKET. IS THIS TRIP CITY'S FIRST GREAT DEPRESSION?
IS THIS WHAT HAPPENS WHEN BILLY AND JANE ABSTAIN FROM THEIR ETERNAL LOVE FOR MORE THAN 24 HOURS?
SMASH
BILLY

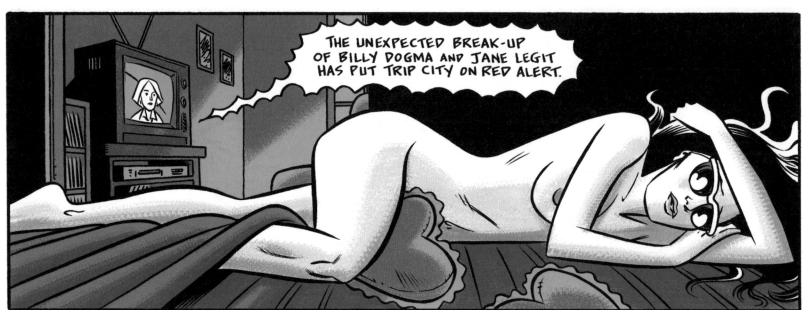

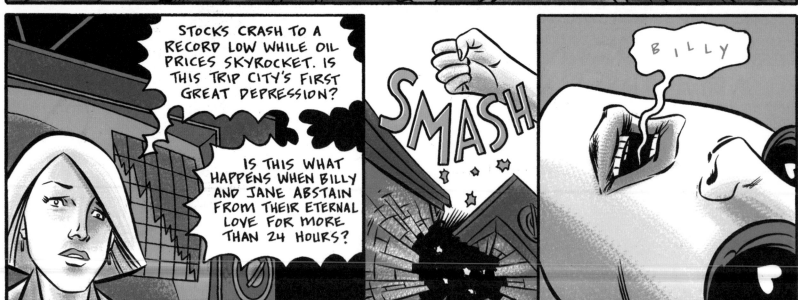

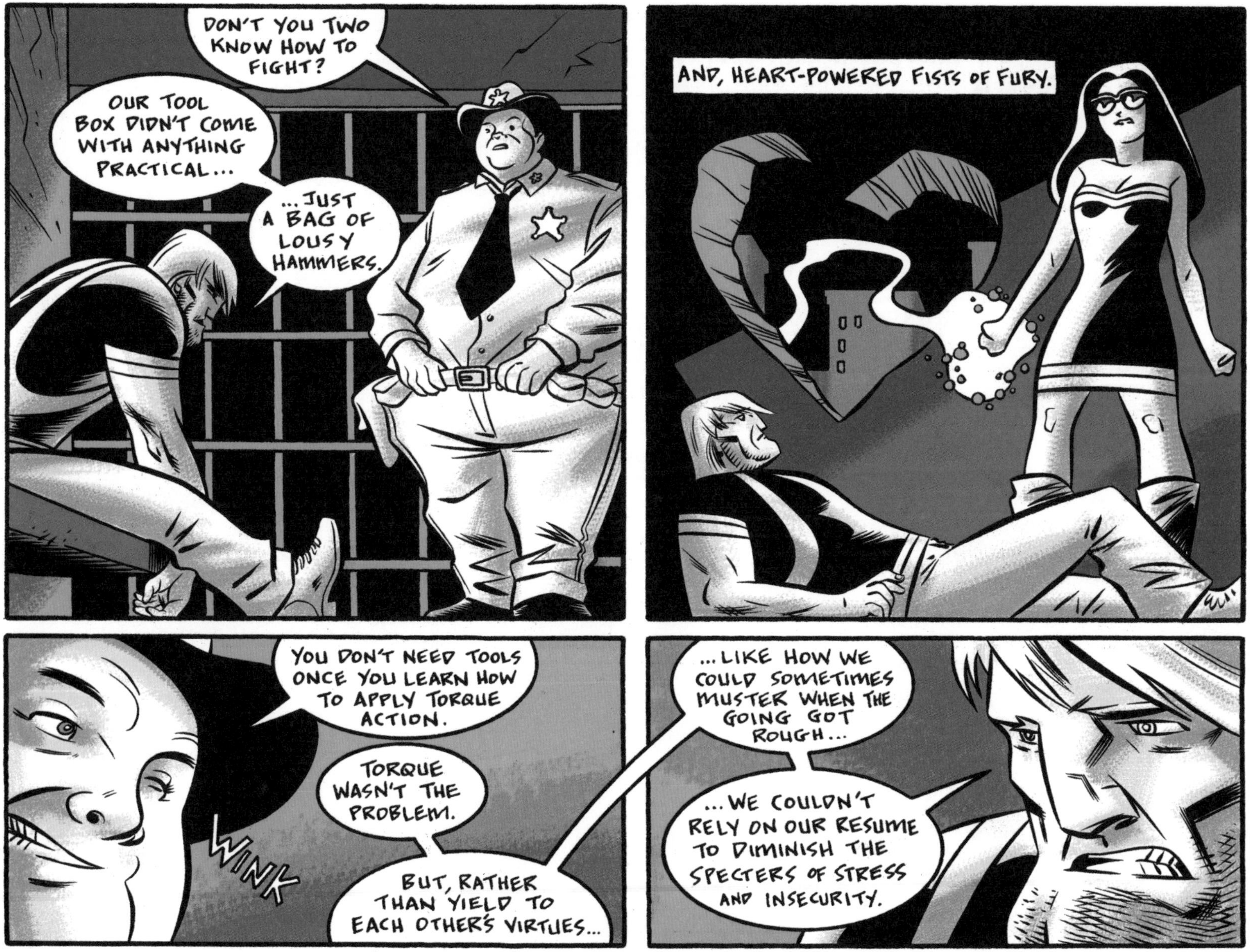
DON'T YOU TWO KNOW HOW TO FIGHT?
OUR TOOL BOX DIDN'T COME WITH ANYTHING PRACTICAL...
...JUST A BAG OF LOUSY HAMMERS.
AND, HEART-POWERED FISTS OF FURY.
YOU DON'T NEED TOOLS ONCE YOU LEARN HOW TO APPLY TORQUE ACTION.
WINK
TORQUE WASN'T THE PROBLEM.
BUT, RATHER THAN YIELD TO EACH OTHER'S VIRTUES...
...LIKE HOW WE COULD SOMETIMES MUSTER WHEN THE GOING GOT ROUGH...
...WE COULDN'T RELY ON OUR RESUME TO DIMINISH THE SPECTERS OF STRESS AND INSECURITY.

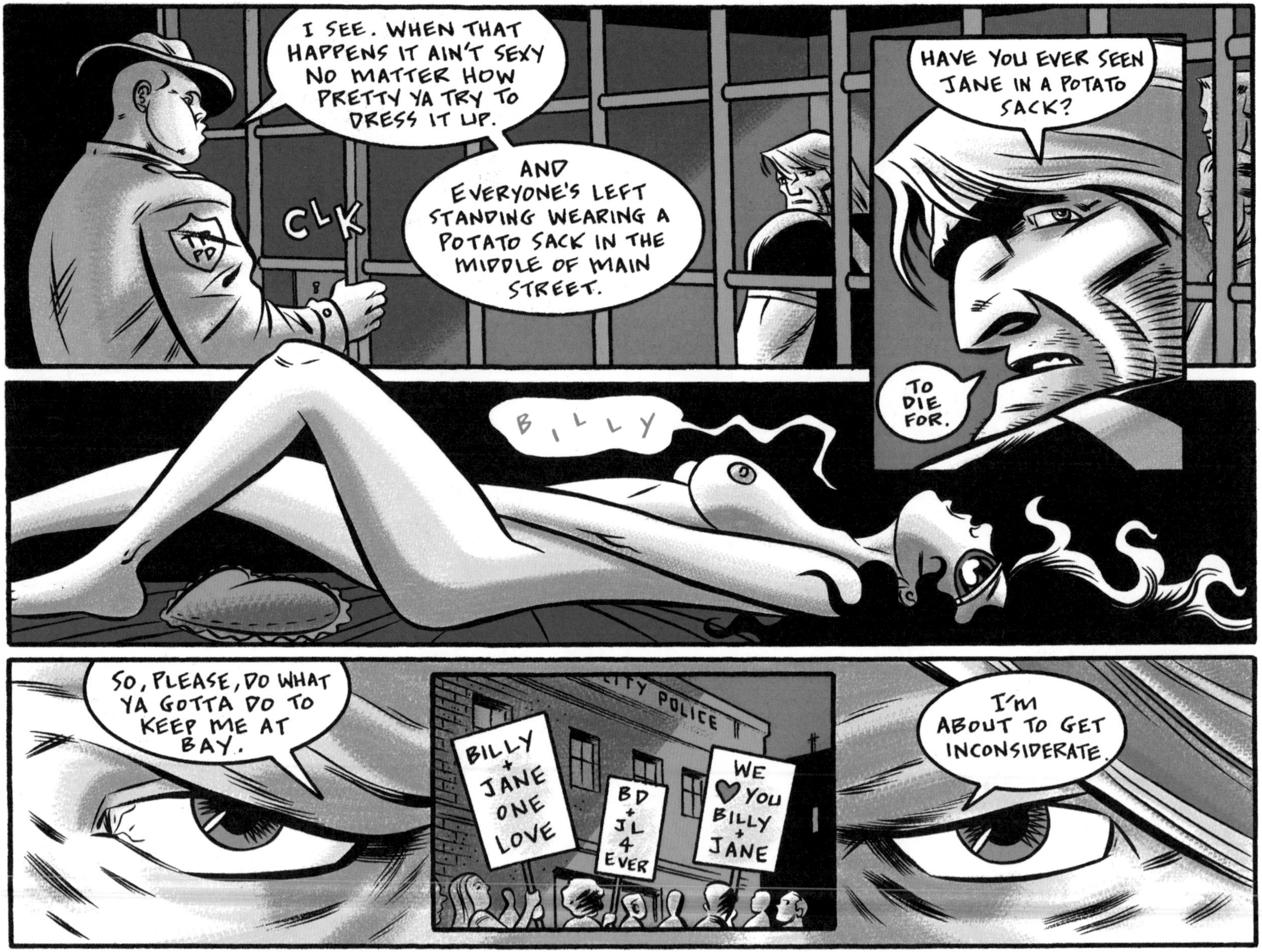
I SEE. WHEN THAT HAPPENS IT AIN'T SEXY NO MATTER HOW PRETTY YA TRY TO DRESS IT UP.
AND EVERYONE'S LEFT STANDING WEARING A POTATO SACK IN THE MIDDLE OF MAIN STREET.
CLK
HAVE YOU EVER SEEN JANE IN A POTATO SACK?
TO DIE FOR.
BILLY
SO, PLEASE, DO WHAT YA GOTTA DO TO KEEP ME AT BAY.
POLICE
BILLY + JANE ONE LOVE
BD + JL 4 EVER
WE ♥ YOU BILLY + JANE
I'M ABOUT TO GET INCONSIDERATE.

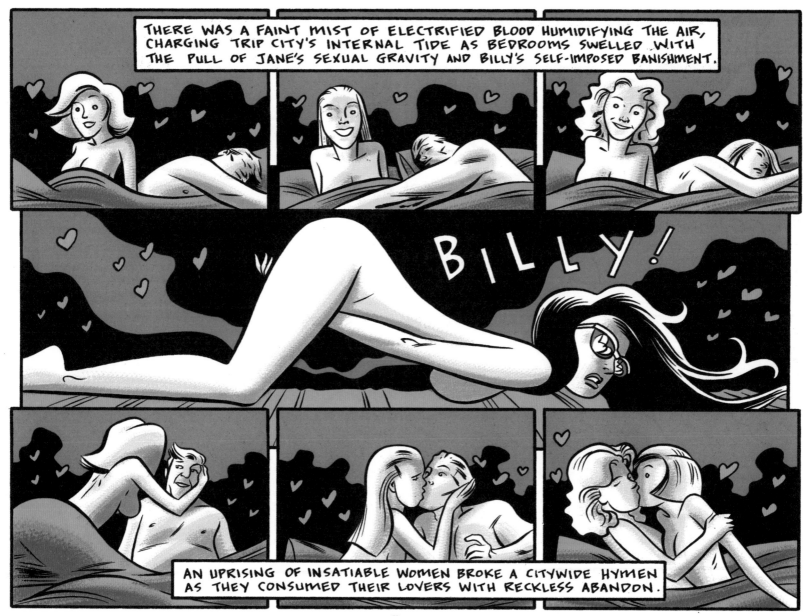

THERE WAS A FAINT MIST OF ELECTRIFIED BLOOD HUMIDIFYING THE AIR, CHARGING TRIP CITY'S INTERNAL TIDE AS BEDROOMS SWELLED WITH THE PULL OF JANE'S SEXUAL GRAVITY AND BILLY'S SELF-IMPOSED BANISHMENT.

BILLY!

AN UPRISING OF INSATIABLE WOMEN BROKE A CITYWIDE HYMEN AS THEY CONSUMED THEIR LOVERS WITH RECKLESS ABANDON.

BILLY AND JANE'S SEPARATION HAD MADE THEM EXTREMELY TOXIC.

THEIR COSMIC SATURATED PHEROMONES EMITTED PSYCHOSEXUAL EUPHORIA THAT UNLOCKED EROTIC AGGREGATORS IN THE LOINS OF TRIP CITY'S UNSUSPECTING CITIZENS.

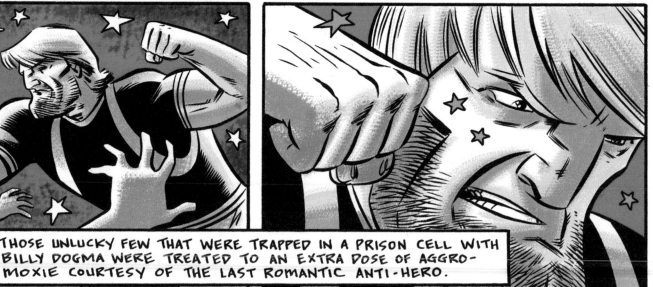

THOSE UNLUCKY FEW THAT WERE TRAPPED IN A PRISON CELL WITH BILLY DOGMA WERE TREATED TO AN EXTRA DOSE OF AGGRO-MOXIE COURTESY OF THE LAST ROMANTIC ANTI-HERO.

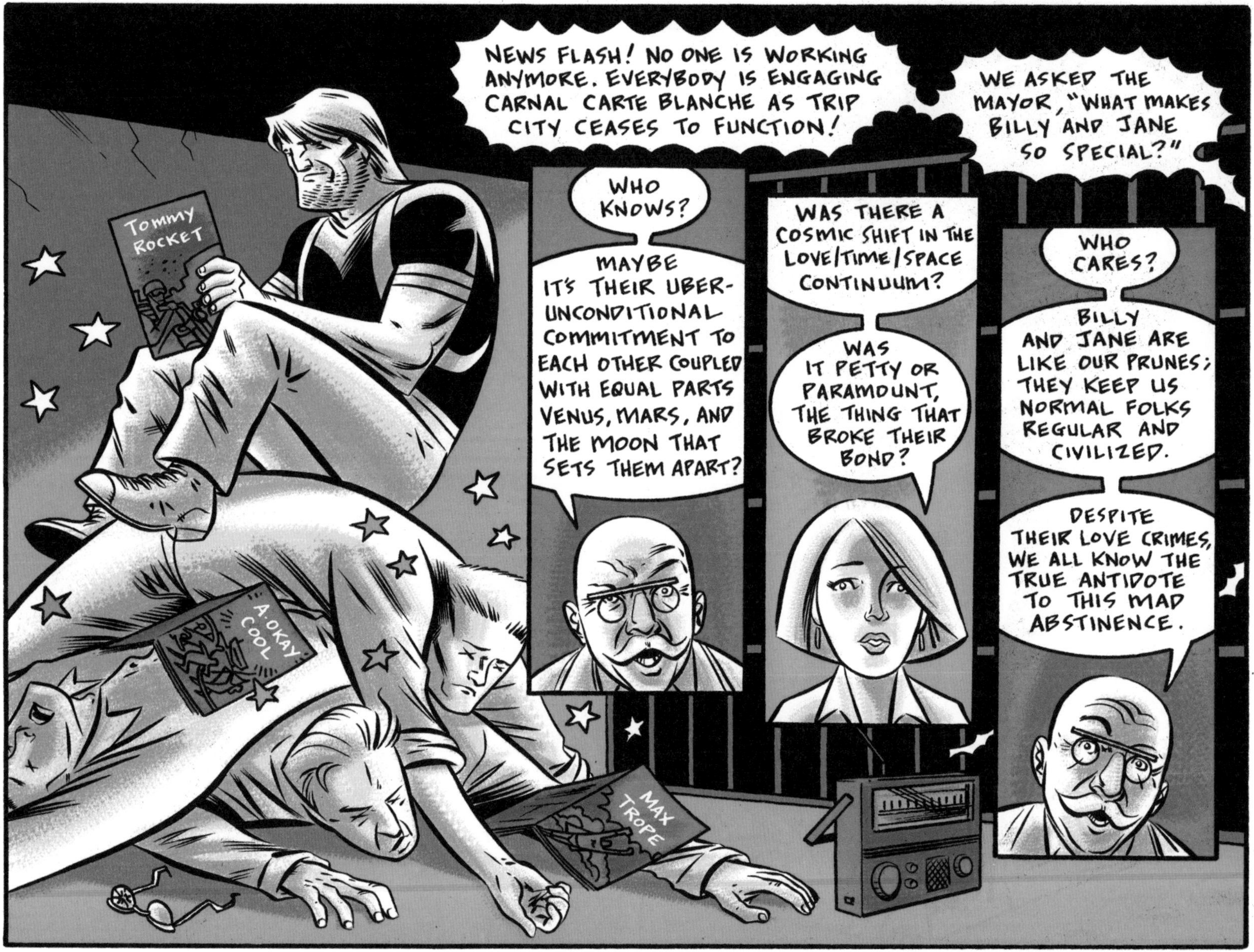
NEWS FLASH! NO ONE IS WORKING ANYMORE. EVERYBODY IS ENGAGING CARNAL CARTE BLANCHE AS TRIP CITY CEASES TO FUNCTION!
WE ASKED THE MAYOR, "WHAT MAKES BILLY AND JANE SO SPECIAL?"
TOMMY ROCKET
WHO KNOWS?
MAYBE IT'S THEIR UBER-UNCONDITIONAL COMMITMENT TO EACH OTHER COUPLED WITH EQUAL PARTS VENUS, MARS, AND THE MOON THAT SETS THEM APART?
WAS THERE A COSMIC SHIFT IN THE LOVE/TIME/SPACE CONTINUUM?
WAS IT PETTY OR PARAMOUNT, THE THING THAT BROKE THEIR BOND?
WHO CARES?
BILLY AND JANE ARE LIKE OUR PRUNES; THEY KEEP US NORMAL FOLKS REGULAR AND CIVILIZED.
DESPITE THEIR LOVE CRIMES, WE ALL KNOW THE TRUE ANTIDOTE TO THIS MAD ABSTINENCE.
A-OKAY COOL
MAX TROPE

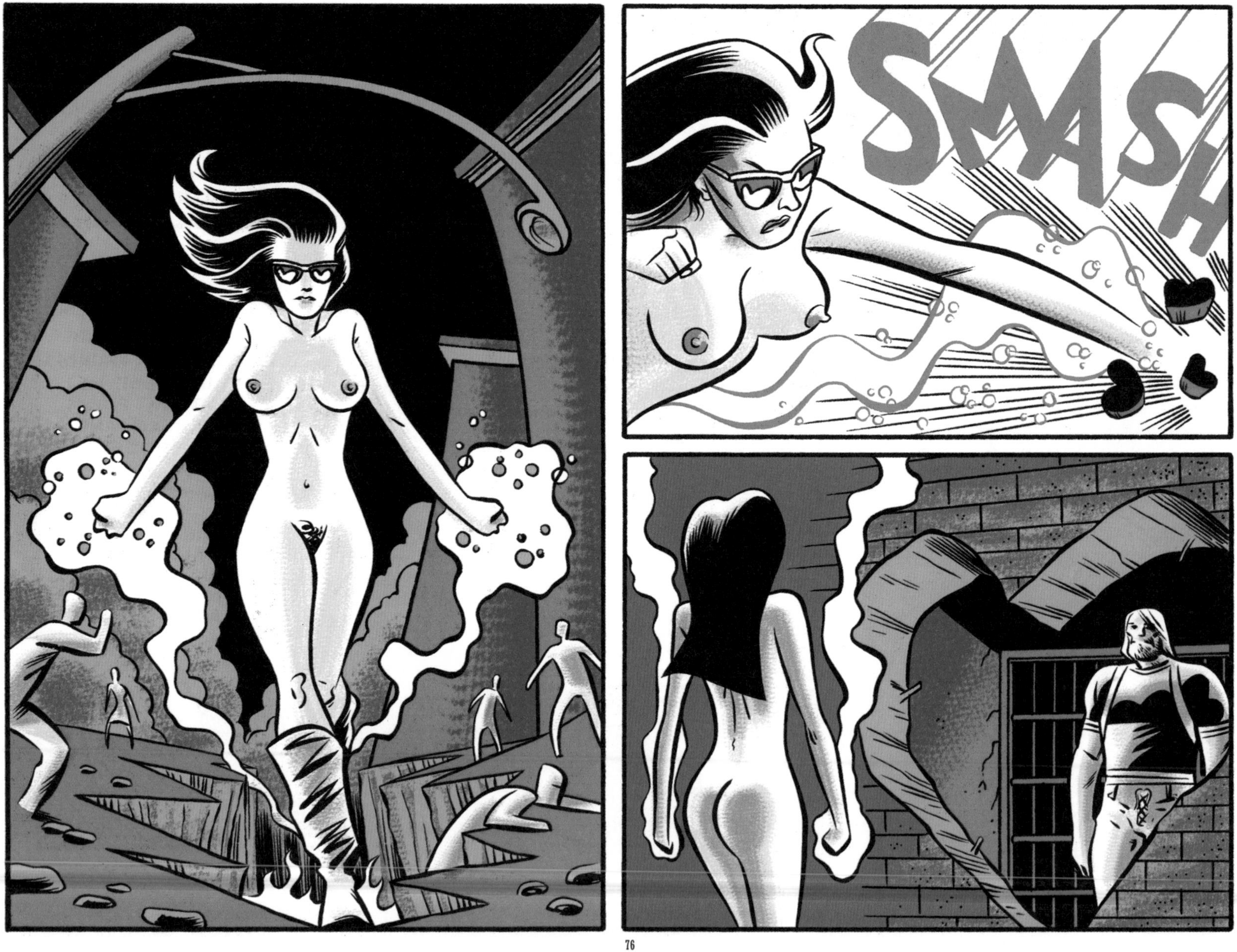
SMASH

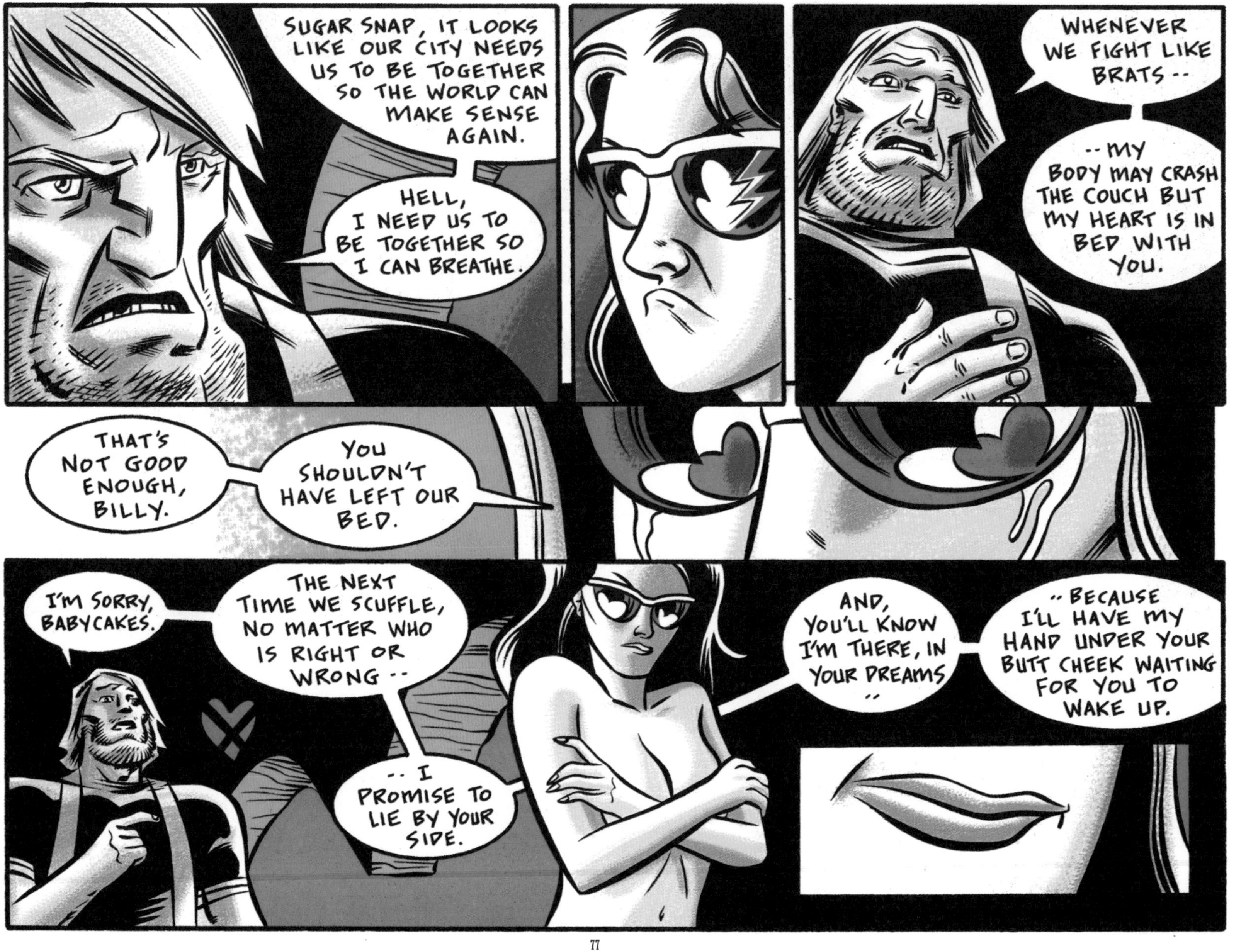
SUGAR SNAP, IT LOOKS LIKE OUR CITY NEEDS US TO BE TOGETHER SO THE WORLD CAN MAKE SENSE AGAIN.
HELL, I NEED US TO BE TOGETHER SO I CAN BREATHE.
WHENEVER WE FIGHT LIKE BRATS --
-- MY BODY MAY CRASH THE COUCH BUT MY HEART IS IN BED WITH YOU.
THAT'S NOT GOOD ENOUGH, BILLY.
YOU SHOULDN'T HAVE LEFT OUR BED.
I'M SORRY, BABYCAKES.
THE NEXT TIME WE SCUFFLE, NO MATTER WHO IS RIGHT OR WRONG --
-- I PROMISE TO LIE BY YOUR SIDE.
AND, YOU'LL KNOW I'M THERE, IN YOUR DREAMS --
-- BECAUSE I'LL HAVE MY HAND UNDER YOUR BUTT CHEEK WAITING FOR YOU TO WAKE UP.

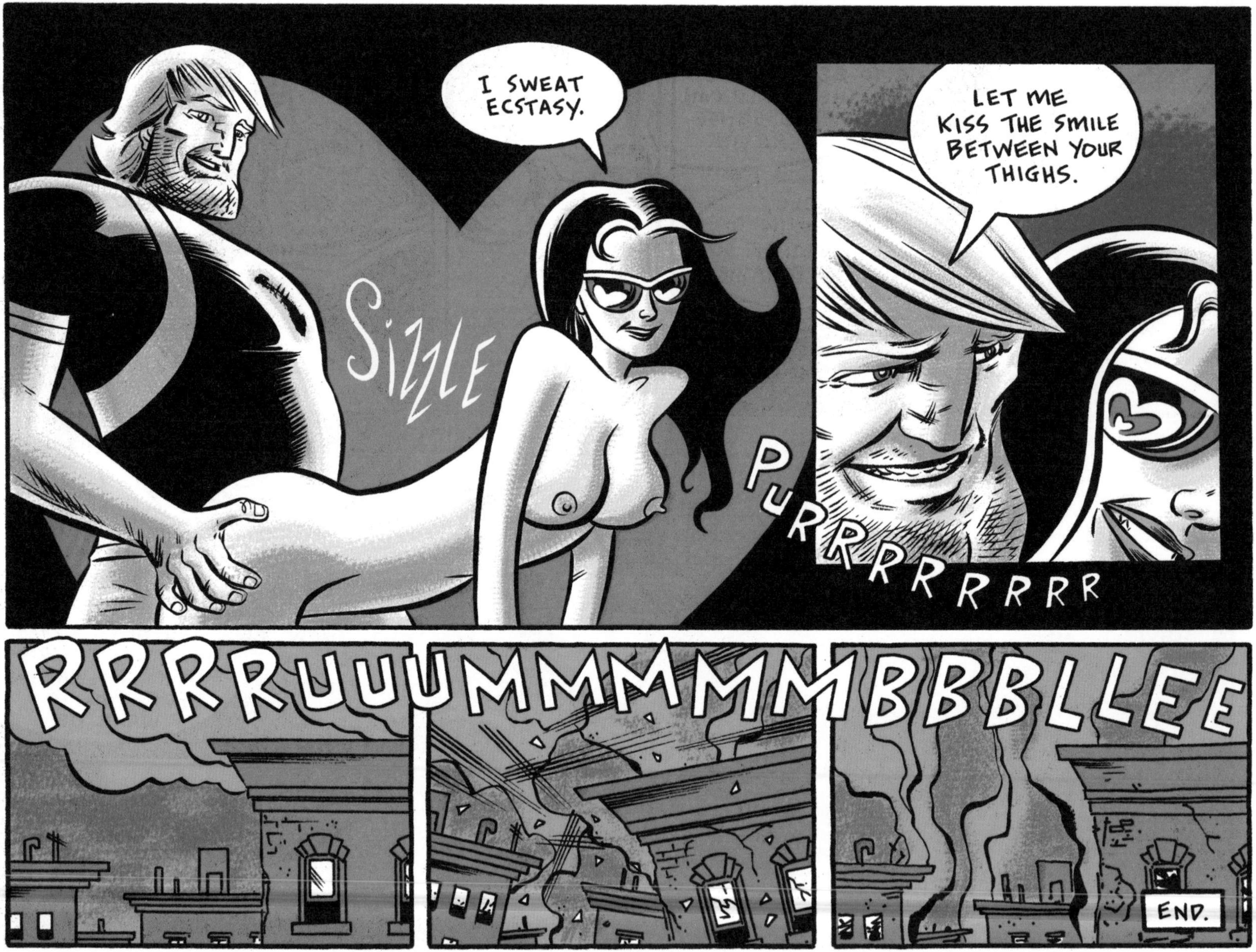
I SWEAT ECSTASY.
SIZZLE
LET ME KISS THE SMILE BETWEEN YOUR THIGHS.
PURRRRRRRRR
RRRRUUUMMMMMBBBLLEE
END.

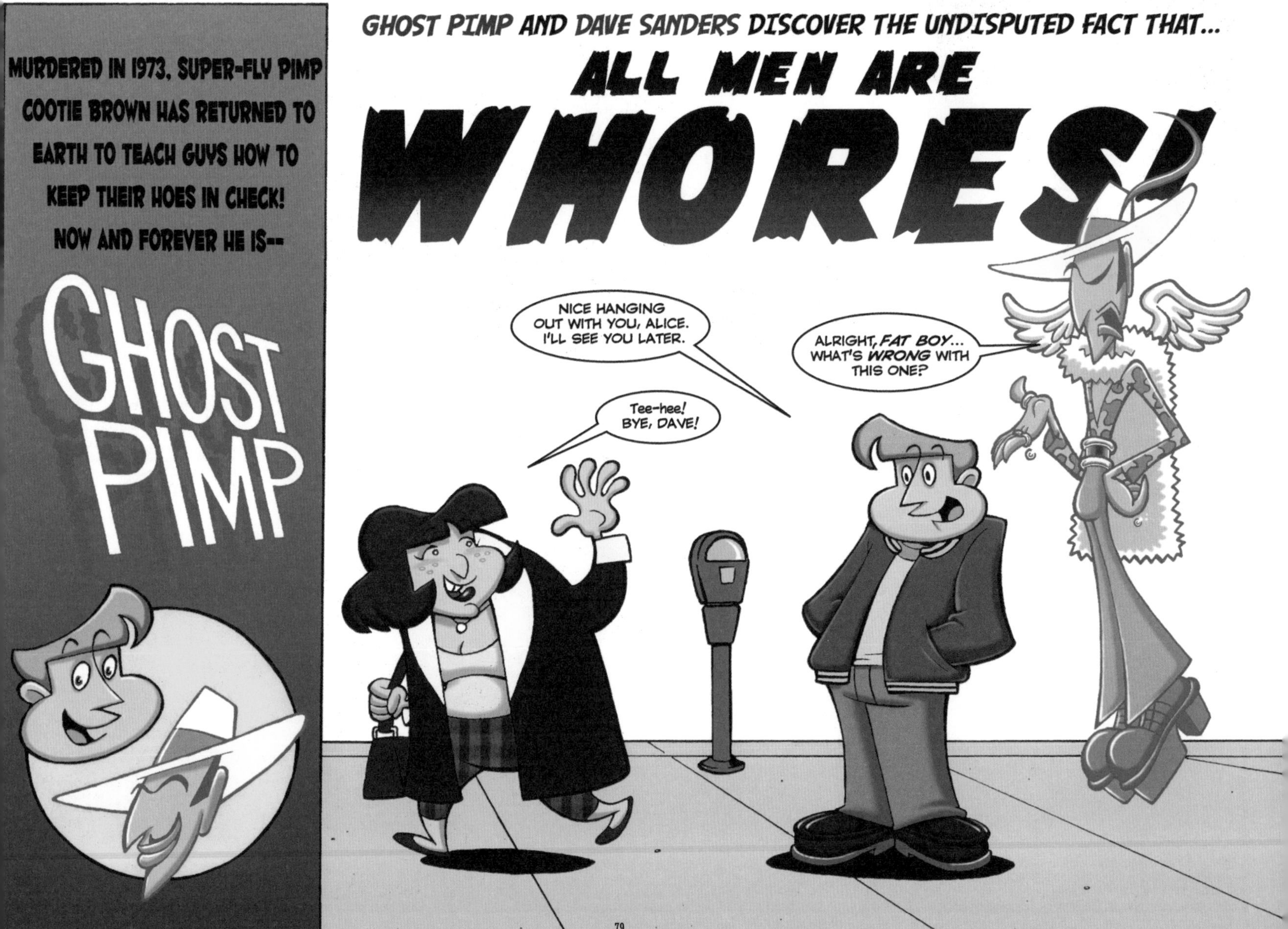
MURDERED IN 1973, SUPER-FLY PIMP COOTIE BROWN HAS RETURNED TO EARTH TO TEACH GUYS HOW TO KEEP THEIR HOES IN CHECK! NOW AND FOREVER HE IS--
GHOST PIMP
GHOST PIMP AND DAVE SANDERS DISCOVER THE UNDISPUTED FACT THAT...
ALL MEN ARE WHORES!
NICE HANGING OUT WITH YOU, ALICE. I'LL SEE YOU LATER.
Tee-hee! BYE, DAVE!
ALRIGHT, FAT BOY... WHAT'S WRONG WITH THIS ONE?

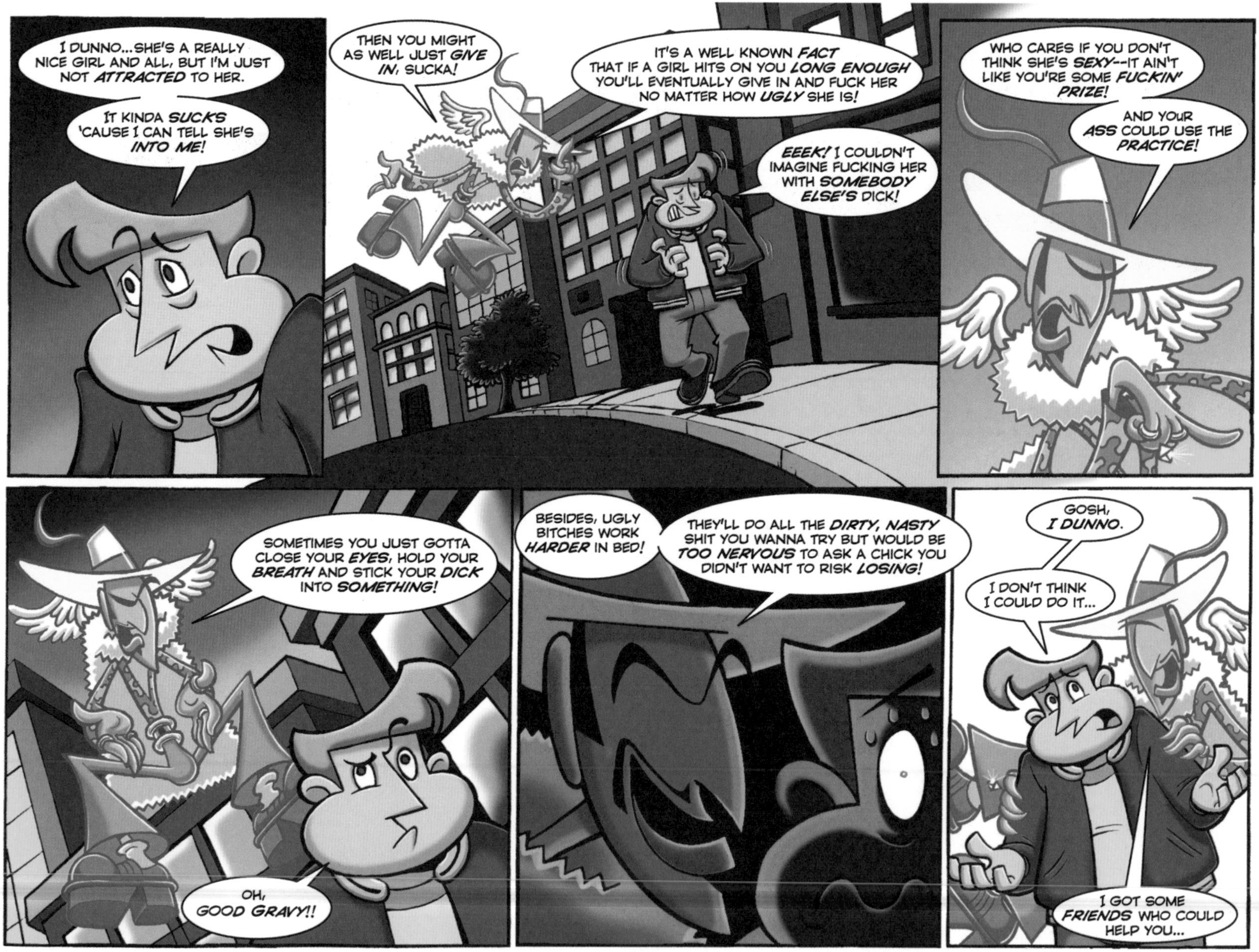
I DUNNO...SHE'S A REALLY NICE GIRL AND ALL, BUT I'M JUST NOT ATTRACTED TO HER.
IT KINDA SUCKS 'CAUSE I CAN TELL SHE'S INTO ME!
THEN YOU MIGHT AS WELL JUST GIVE IN, SUCKA!
IT'S A WELL KNOWN FACT THAT IF A GIRL HITS ON YOU LONG ENOUGH YOU'LL EVENTUALLY GIVE IN AND FUCK HER NO MATTER HOW UGLY SHE IS!
EEEK! I COULDN'T IMAGINE FUCKING HER WITH SOMEBODY ELSE'S DICK!
WHO CARES IF YOU DON'T THINK SHE'S SEXY--IT AIN'T LIKE YOU'RE SOME FUCKIN' PRIZE!
AND YOUR ASS COULD USE THE PRACTICE!
SOMETIMES YOU JUST GOTTA CLOSE YOUR EYES, HOLD YOUR BREATH AND STICK YOUR DICK INTO SOMETHING!
OH, GOOD GRAVY!!
BESIDES, UGLY BITCHES WORK HARDER IN BED!
THEY'LL DO ALL THE DIRTY, NASTY SHIT YOU WANNA TRY BUT WOULD BE TOO NERVOUS TO ASK A CHICK YOU DIDN'T WANT TO RISK LOSING!
GOSH, I DUNNO.
I DON'T THINK I COULD DO IT...
I GOT SOME FRIENDS WHO COULD HELP YOU...

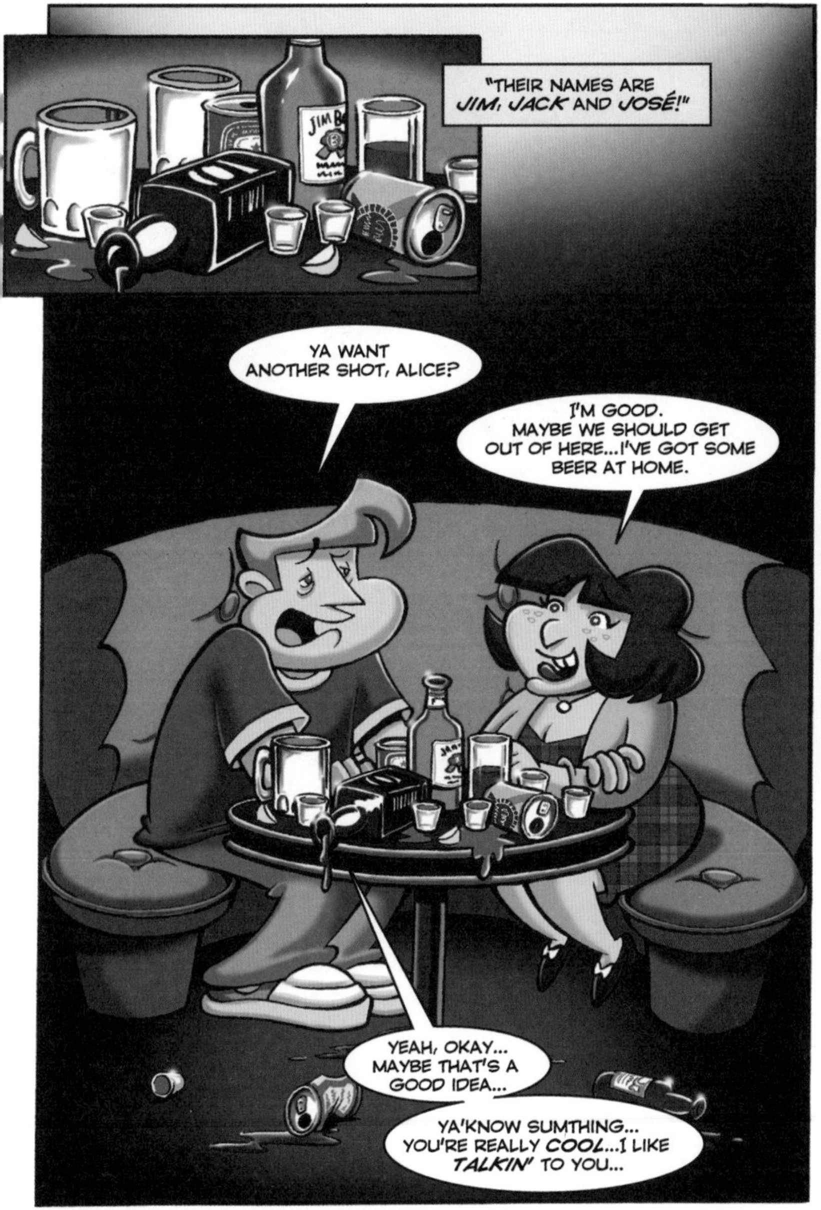
"THEIR NAMES ARE *JIM, JACK* AND *JOSÉ!*"
YA WANT ANOTHER SHOT, ALICE?
I'M GOOD. MAYBE WE SHOULD GET OUT OF HERE...I'VE GOT SOME BEER AT HOME.
YEAH, OKAY... MAYBE THAT'S A GOOD IDEA...
YA'KNOW SUMTHING... YOU'RE REALLY *COOL*...I LIKE *TALKIN'* TO YOU...

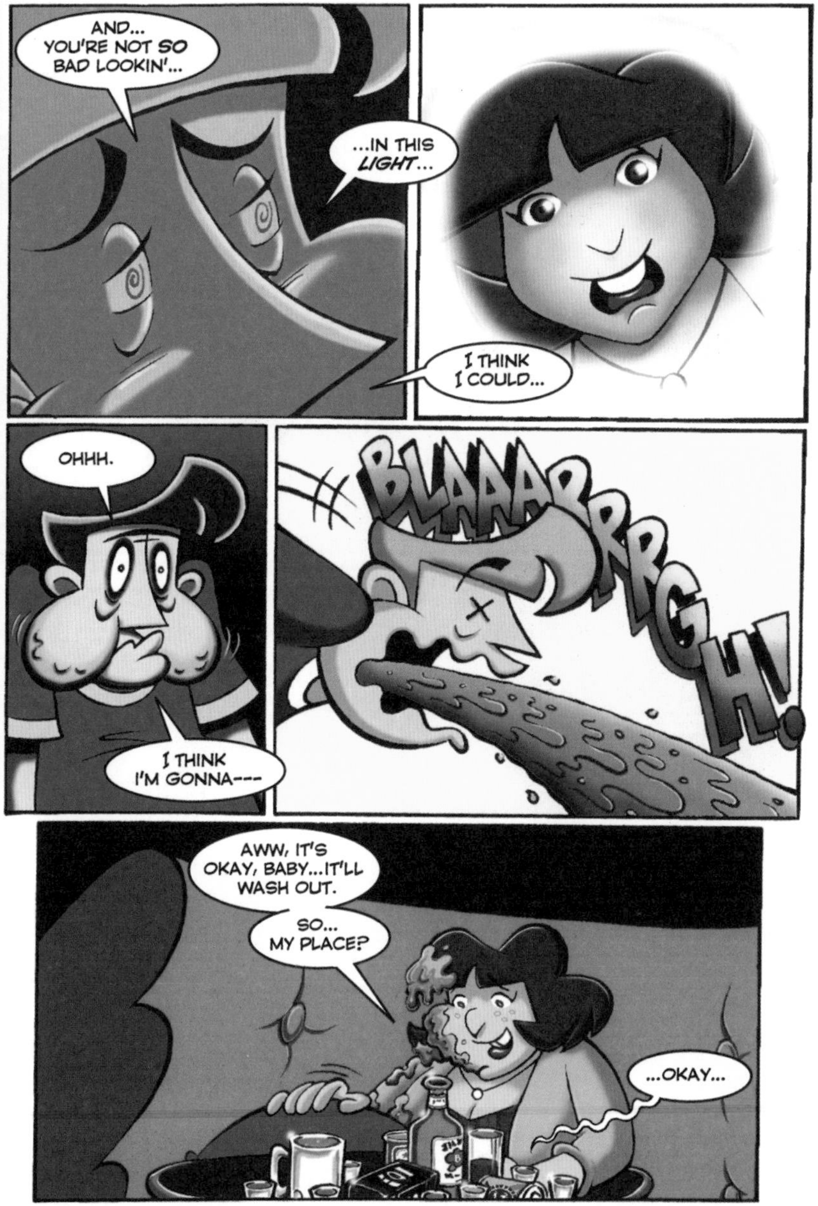
AND... YOU'RE NOT *SO* BAD LOOKIN'...
...IN THIS *LIGHT*...
I THINK I COULD...
OHHH.
I THINK I'M GONNA---
BLAAARRRGH!
AWW, IT'S OKAY, BABY...IT'LL WASH OUT.
SO... MY PLACE?
...OKAY...

...I'M COOTIE BROWN, AND I ENDORSE THIS MESSAGE...

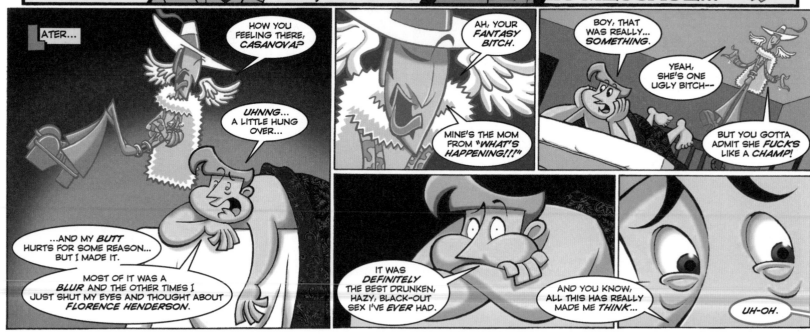

LATER...

HOW YOU FEELING THERE, CASANOVA?

UHNNG... A LITTLE HUNG OVER...

...AND MY *BUTT* HURTS FOR SOME REASON... BUT I MADE IT.

MOST OF IT WAS A *BLUR* AND THE OTHER TIMES I JUST SHUT MY EYES AND THOUGHT ABOUT *FLORENCE HENDERSON.*

AH, YOUR *FANTASY BITCH.*

MINE'S THE MOM FROM *"WHAT'S HAPPENING!!!"*

BOY, THAT WAS REALLY... *SOMETHING.*

YEAH, SHE'S ONE UGLY BITCH--

BUT YOU GOTTA ADMIT SHE *FUCKS* LIKE A *CHAMP!*

IT WAS *DEFINITELY* THE BEST DRUNKEN, HAZY, BLACK-OUT SEX I'VE *EVER* HAD.

AND YOU KNOW, ALL THIS HAS REALLY MADE ME *THINK*...

UH-OH.

82

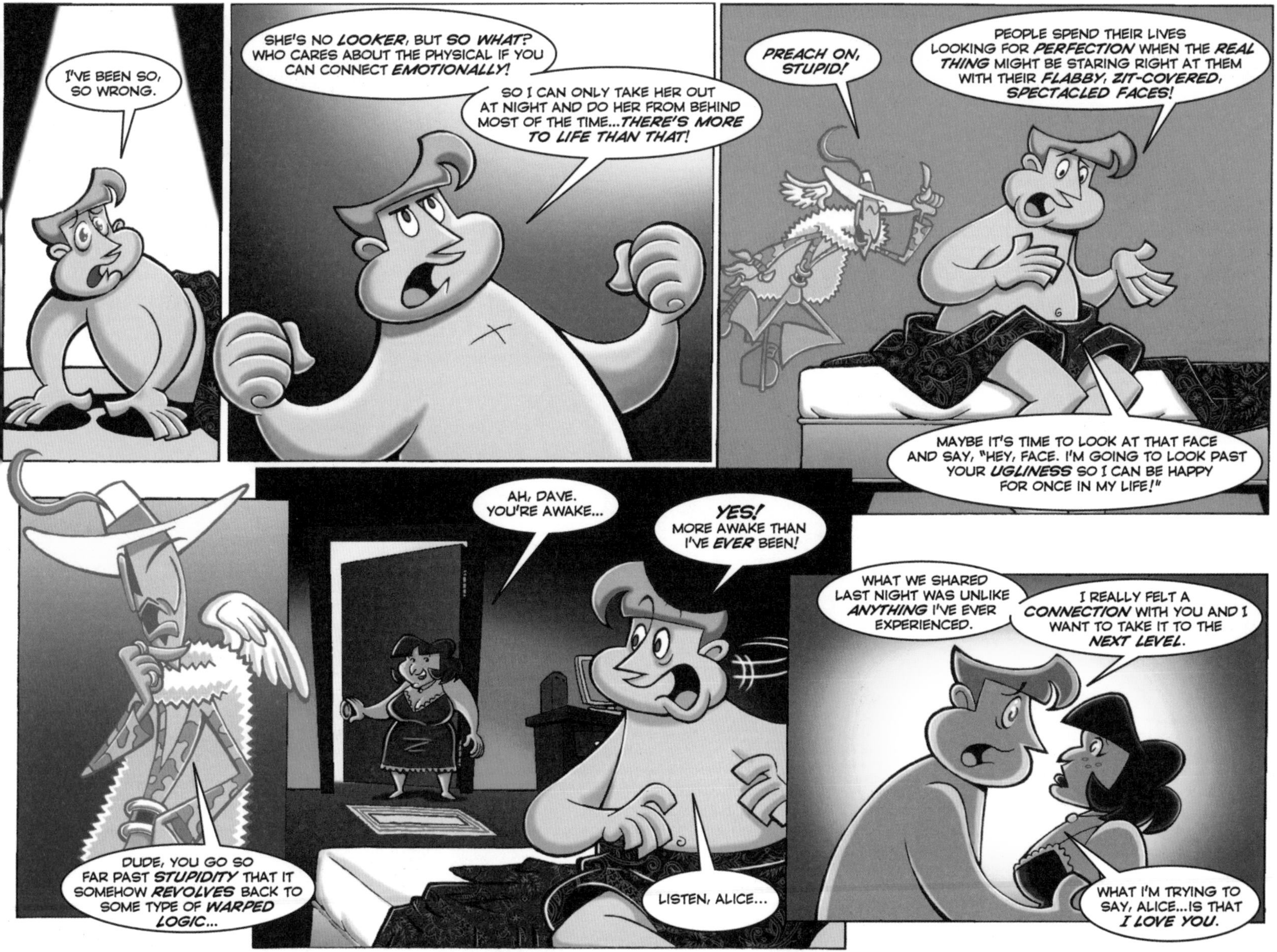
I'VE BEEN SO, SO WRONG.
SHE'S NO LOOKER, BUT SO WHAT? WHO CARES ABOUT THE PHYSICAL IF YOU CAN CONNECT EMOTIONALLY!
SO I CAN ONLY TAKE HER OUT AT NIGHT AND DO HER FROM BEHIND MOST OF THE TIME...THERE'S MORE TO LIFE THAN THAT!
PREACH ON, STUPID!
PEOPLE SPEND THEIR LIVES LOOKING FOR PERFECTION WHEN THE REAL THING MIGHT BE STARING RIGHT AT THEM WITH THEIR FLABBY, ZIT-COVERED, SPECTACLED FACES!
MAYBE IT'S TIME TO LOOK AT THAT FACE AND SAY, "HEY, FACE. I'M GOING TO LOOK PAST YOUR UGLINESS SO I CAN BE HAPPY FOR ONCE IN MY LIFE!"
DUDE, YOU GO SO FAR PAST STUPIDITY THAT IT SOMEHOW REVOLVES BACK TO SOME TYPE OF WARPED LOGIC...
AH, DAVE. YOU'RE AWAKE...
YES! MORE AWAKE THAN I'VE EVER BEEN!
LISTEN, ALICE...
WHAT WE SHARED LAST NIGHT WAS UNLIKE ANYTHING I'VE EVER EXPERIENCED.
I REALLY FELT A CONNECTION WITH YOU AND I WANT TO TAKE IT TO THE NEXT LEVEL.
WHAT I'M TRYING TO SAY, ALICE...IS THAT I LOVE YOU.

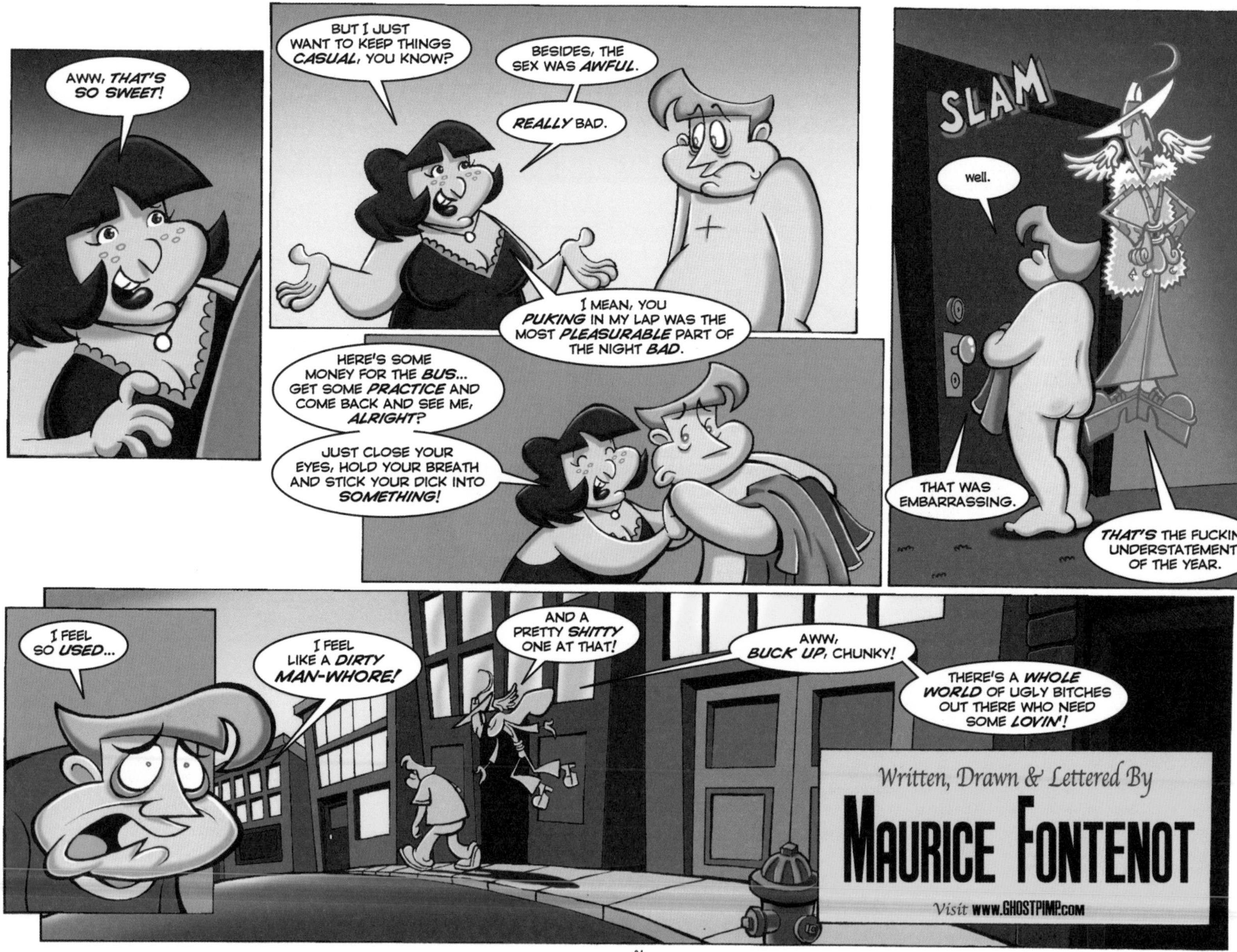
AWW, THAT'S SO SWEET!
BUT I JUST WANT TO KEEP THINGS CASUAL, YOU KNOW?
BESIDES, THE SEX WAS AWFUL.
REALLY BAD.
I MEAN, YOU PUKING IN MY LAP WAS THE MOST PLEASURABLE PART OF THE NIGHT BAD.
HERE'S SOME MONEY FOR THE BUS... GET SOME PRACTICE AND COME BACK AND SEE ME, ALRIGHT?
JUST CLOSE YOUR EYES, HOLD YOUR BREATH AND STICK YOUR DICK INTO SOMETHING!
SLAM
well.
THAT WAS EMBARRASSING.
THAT'S THE FUCKIN' UNDERSTATEMENT OF THE YEAR.
I FEEL SO USED...
I FEEL LIKE A DIRTY MAN-WHORE!
AND A PRETTY SHITTY ONE AT THAT!
AWW, BUCK UP, CHUNKY!
THERE'S A WHOLE WORLD OF UGLY BITCHES OUT THERE WHO NEED SOME LOVIN'!
Written, Drawn & Lettered By
MAURICE FONTENOT
Visit WWW.GHOSTPIMP.COM

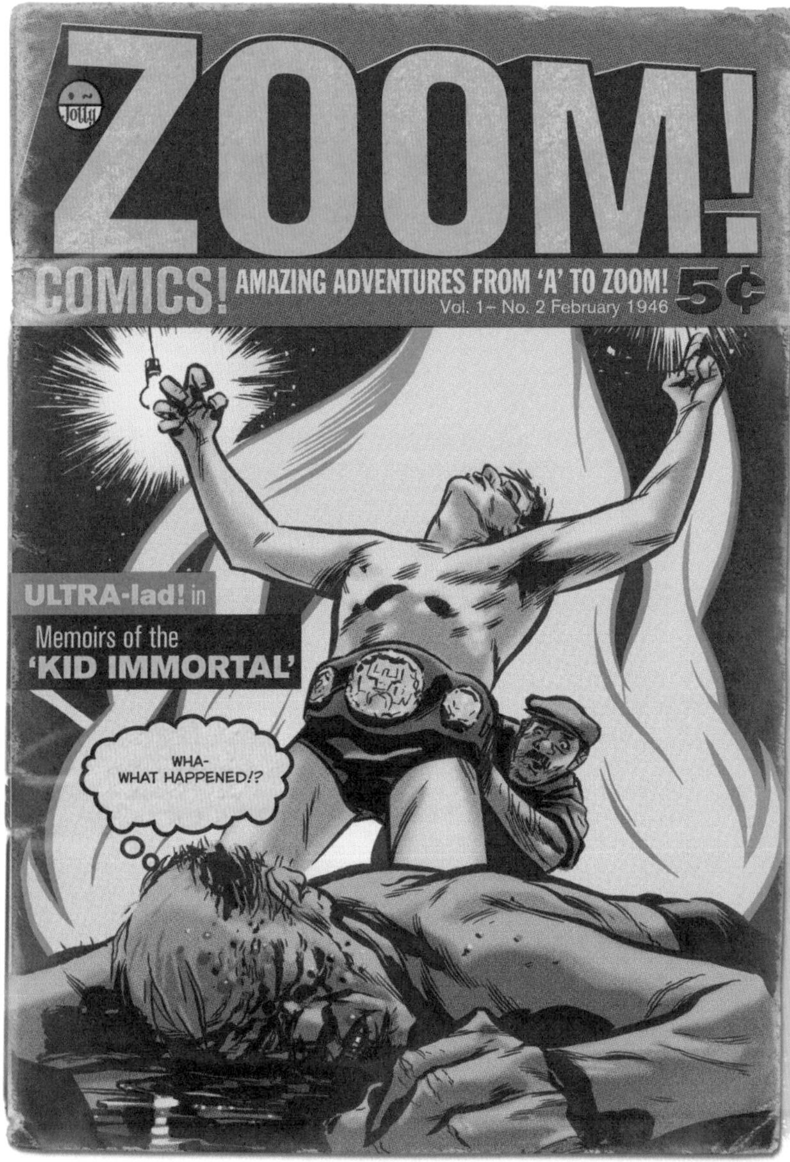
ZOOM!
COMICS! AMAZING ADVENTURES FROM 'A' TO ZOOM!
5¢
Vol. 1– No. 2 February 1946
ULTRA-lad! in
Memoirs of the
'KID IMMORTAL'
WHA- WHAT HAPPENED!?

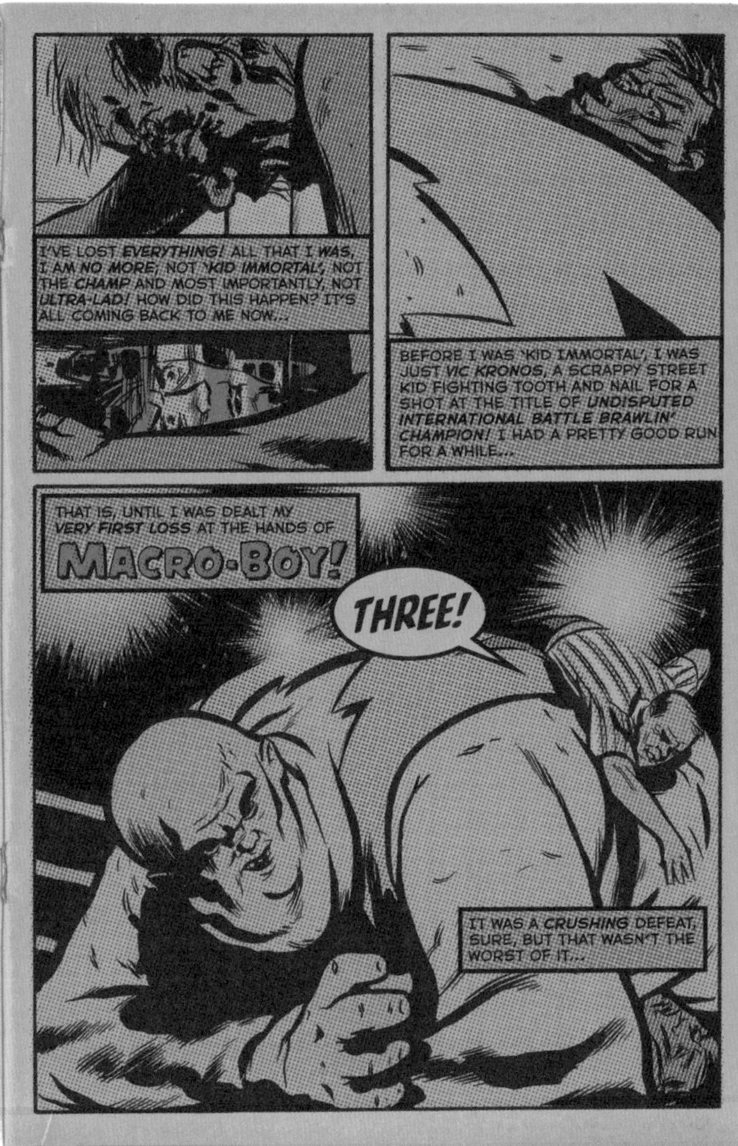
I'VE LOST EVERYTHING! ALL THAT I WAS, I AM NO MORE; NOT 'KID IMMORTAL', NOT THE CHAMP AND MOST IMPORTANTLY, NOT ULTRA-LAD! HOW DID THIS HAPPEN? IT'S ALL COMING BACK TO ME NOW...
BEFORE I WAS 'KID IMMORTAL', I WAS JUST VIC KRONOS, A SCRAPPY STREET KID FIGHTING TOOTH AND NAIL FOR A SHOT AT THE TITLE OF UNDISPUTED INTERNATIONAL BATTLE BRAWLIN' CHAMPION! I HAD A PRETTY GOOD RUN FOR A WHILE...
THAT IS, UNTIL I WAS DEALT MY VERY FIRST LOSS AT THE HANDS OF
MACRO-BOY!
THREE!
IT WAS A CRUSHING DEFEAT, SURE, BUT THAT WASN'T THE WORST OF IT...

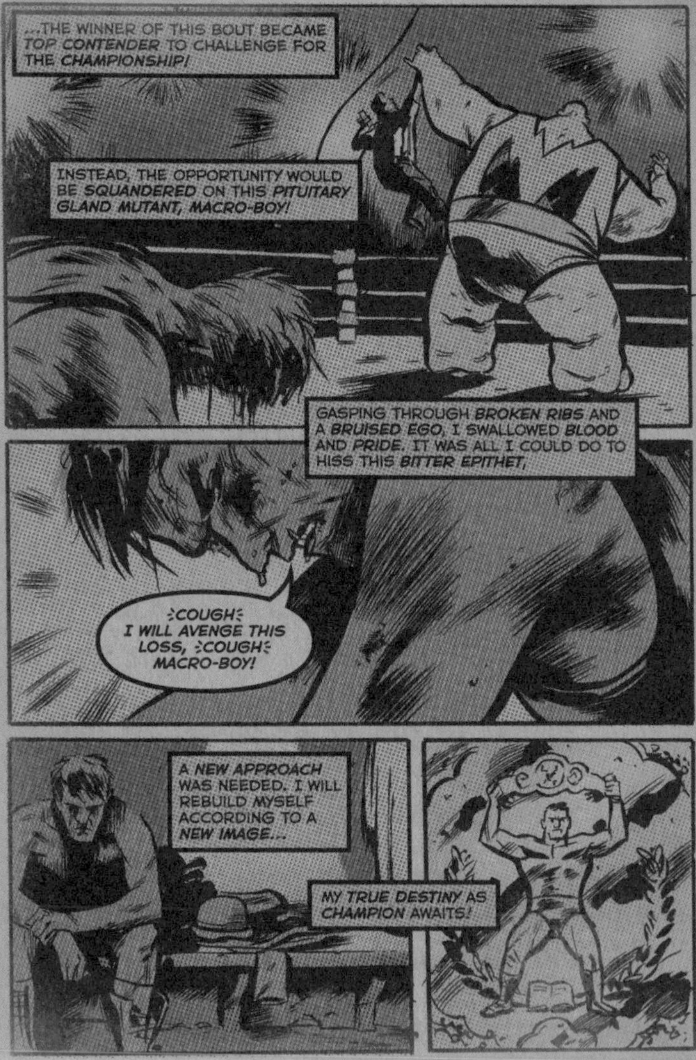
...THE WINNER OF THIS BOUT BECAME TOP CONTENDER TO CHALLENGE FOR THE CHAMPIONSHIP!
INSTEAD, THE OPPORTUNITY WOULD BE SQUANDERED ON THIS PITUITARY GLAND MUTANT, MACRO-BOY!
GASPING THROUGH BROKEN RIBS AND A BRUISED EGO, I SWALLOWED BLOOD AND PRIDE. IT WAS ALL I COULD DO TO HISS THIS BITTER EPITHET,
COUGH I WILL AVENGE THIS LOSS, COUGH MACRO-BOY!
A NEW APPROACH WAS NEEDED. I WILL REBUILD MYSELF ACCORDING TO A NEW IMAGE...
MY TRUE DESTINY AS CHAMPION AWAITS!

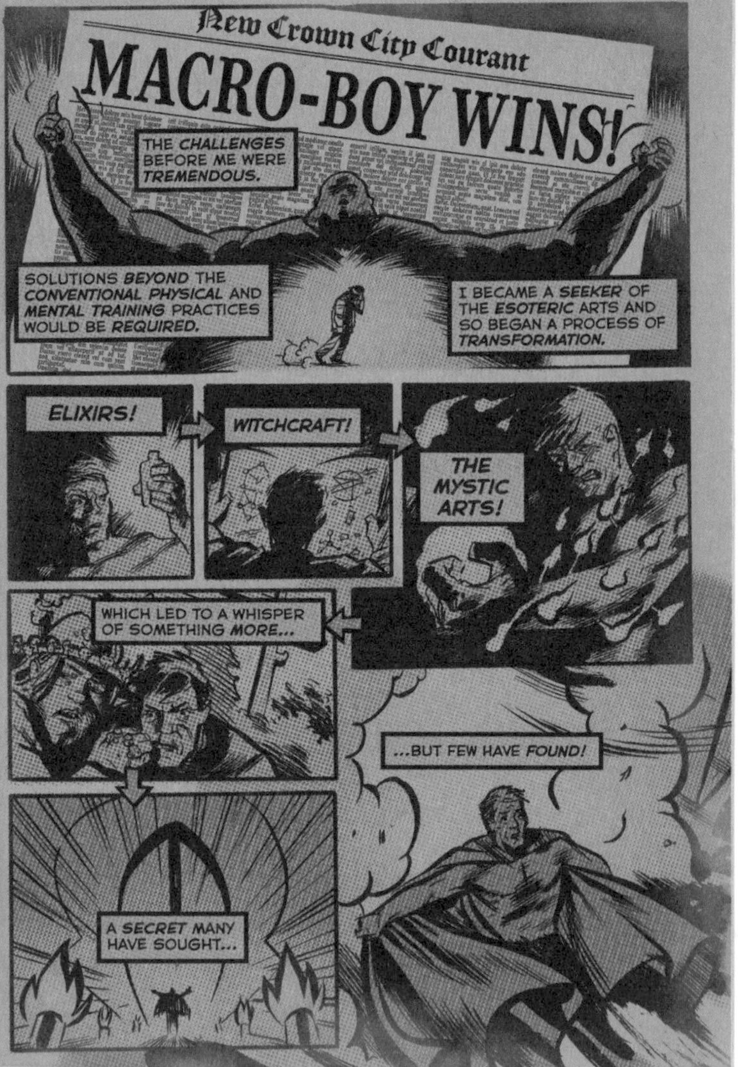
New Crown City Courant
MACRO-BOY WINS!
THE CHALLENGES BEFORE ME WERE TREMENDOUS.
SOLUTIONS BEYOND THE CONVENTIONAL PHYSICAL AND MENTAL TRAINING PRACTICES WOULD BE REQUIRED.
I BECAME A SEEKER OF THE ESOTERIC ARTS AND SO BEGAN A PROCESS OF TRANSFORMATION.
ELIXIRS!
WITCHCRAFT!
THE MYSTIC ARTS!
WHICH LED TO A WHISPER OF SOMETHING MORE...
A SECRET MANY HAVE SOUGHT...
...BUT FEW HAVE FOUND!

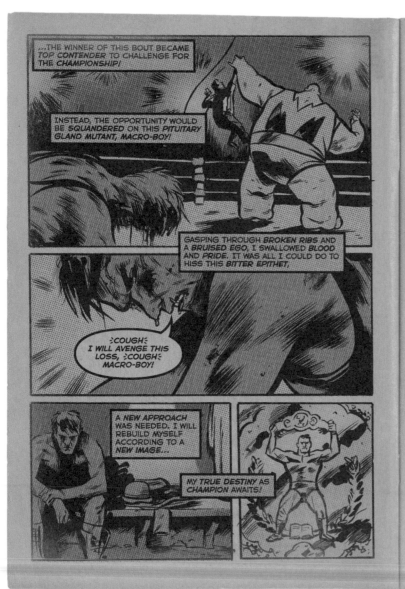

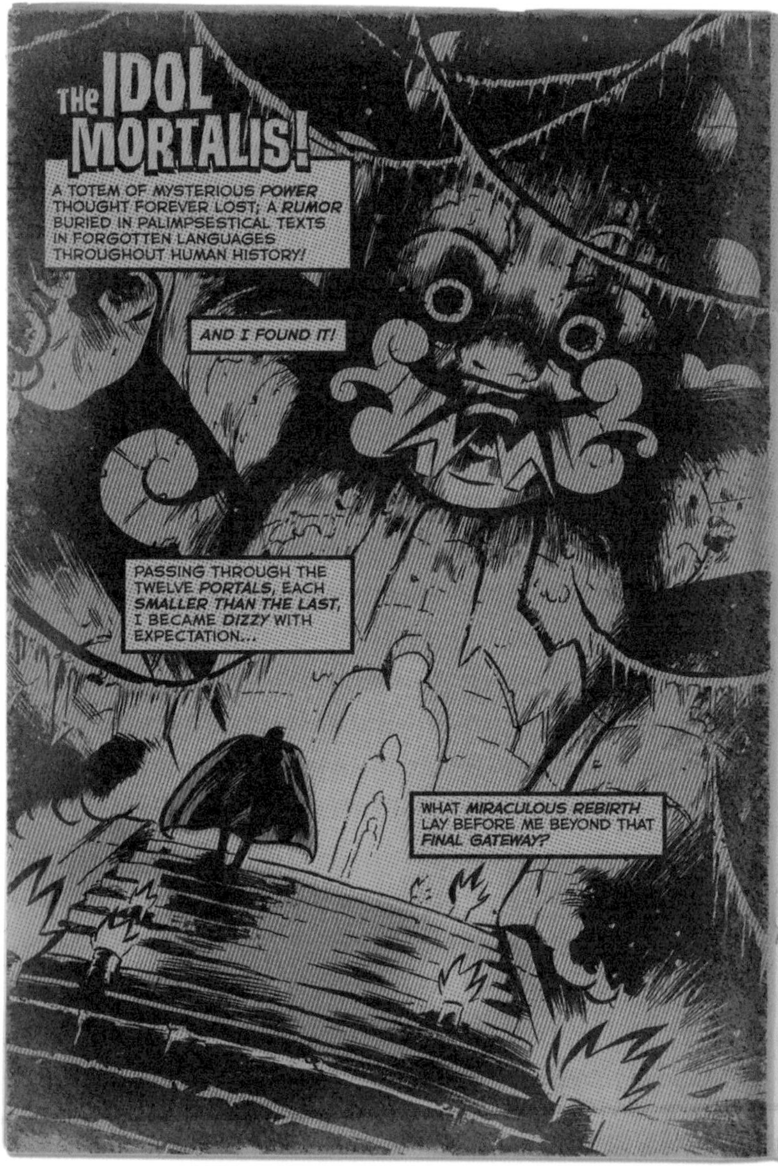
The IDOL MORTALIS!
A TOTEM OF MYSTERIOUS POWER THOUGHT FOREVER LOST; A RUMOR BURIED IN PALIMPSESTICAL TEXTS IN FORGOTTEN LANGUAGES THROUGHOUT HUMAN HISTORY!
AND I FOUND IT!
PASSING THROUGH THE TWELVE PORTALS, EACH SMALLER THAN THE LAST, I BECAME DIZZY WITH EXPECTATION...
WHAT MIRACULOUS REBIRTH LAY BEFORE ME BEYOND THAT FINAL GATEWAY?

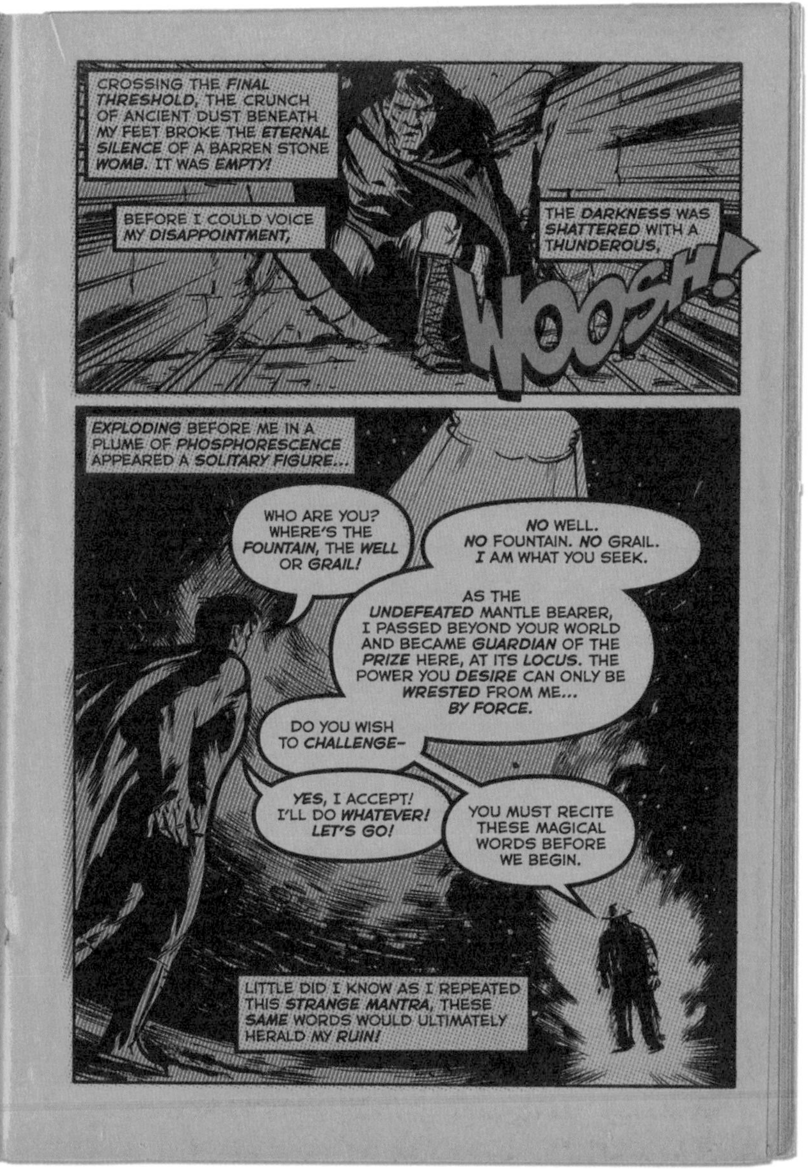
CROSSING THE FINAL THRESHOLD, THE CRUNCH OF ANCIENT DUST BENEATH MY FEET BROKE THE ETERNAL SILENCE OF A BARREN STONE WOMB. IT WAS EMPTY!
BEFORE I COULD VOICE MY DISAPPOINTMENT,
THE DARKNESS WAS SHATTERED WITH A THUNDEROUS,
WOOSH!
EXPLODING BEFORE ME IN A PLUME OF PHOSPHORESCENCE APPEARED A SOLITARY FIGURE...
WHO ARE YOU? WHERE'S THE FOUNTAIN, THE WELL OR GRAIL!
NO WELL. NO FOUNTAIN. NO GRAIL. I AM WHAT YOU SEEK.
AS THE UNDEFEATED MANTLE BEARER, I PASSED BEYOND YOUR WORLD AND BECAME GUARDIAN OF THE PRIZE HERE, AT ITS LOCUS. THE POWER YOU DESIRE CAN ONLY BE WRESTED FROM ME... BY FORCE.
DO YOU WISH TO CHALLENGE–
YES, I ACCEPT! I'LL DO WHATEVER! LET'S GO!
YOU MUST RECITE THESE MAGICAL WORDS BEFORE WE BEGIN.
LITTLE DID I KNOW AS I REPEATED THIS STRANGE MANTRA, THESE SAME WORDS WOULD ULTIMATELY HERALD MY RUIN!

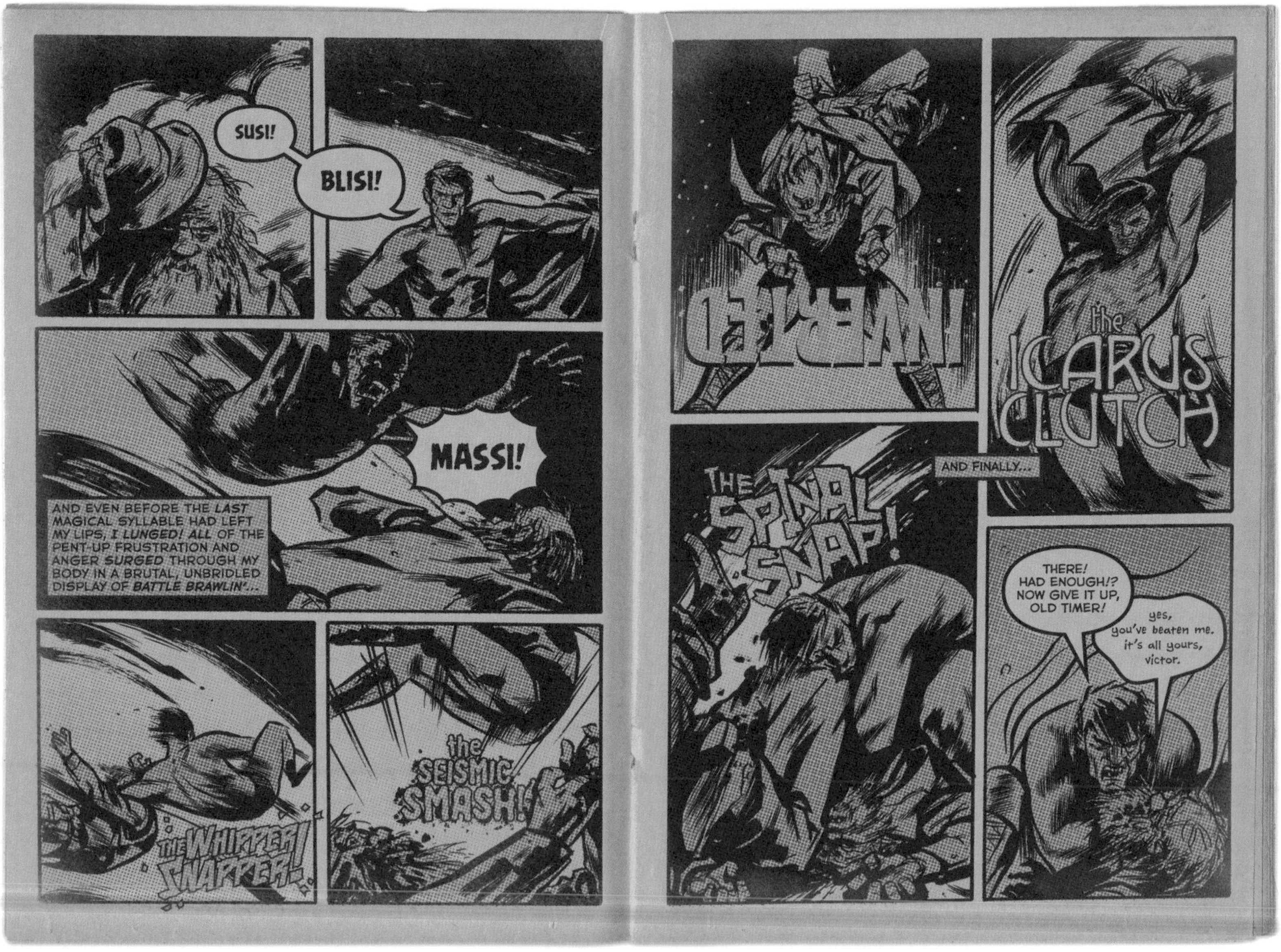
SUSI!
BLISI!
MASSI!
AND EVEN BEFORE THE *LAST* MAGICAL SYLLABLE HAD LEFT MY LIPS, *I LUNGED! ALL* OF THE PENT-UP FRUSTRATION AND ANGER *SURGED* THROUGH MY BODY IN A BRUTAL, UNBRIDLED DISPLAY OF *BATTLE BRAWLIN'*...
THE WHIPPER SNAPPER!
the SEISMIC SMASH!
the ICARUS CLUTCH
AND FINALLY...
THE SPINAL SNAP!
THERE! HAD ENOUGH!? NOW GIVE IT UP, OLD TIMER!
yes, you've beaten me. it's all yours, victor.

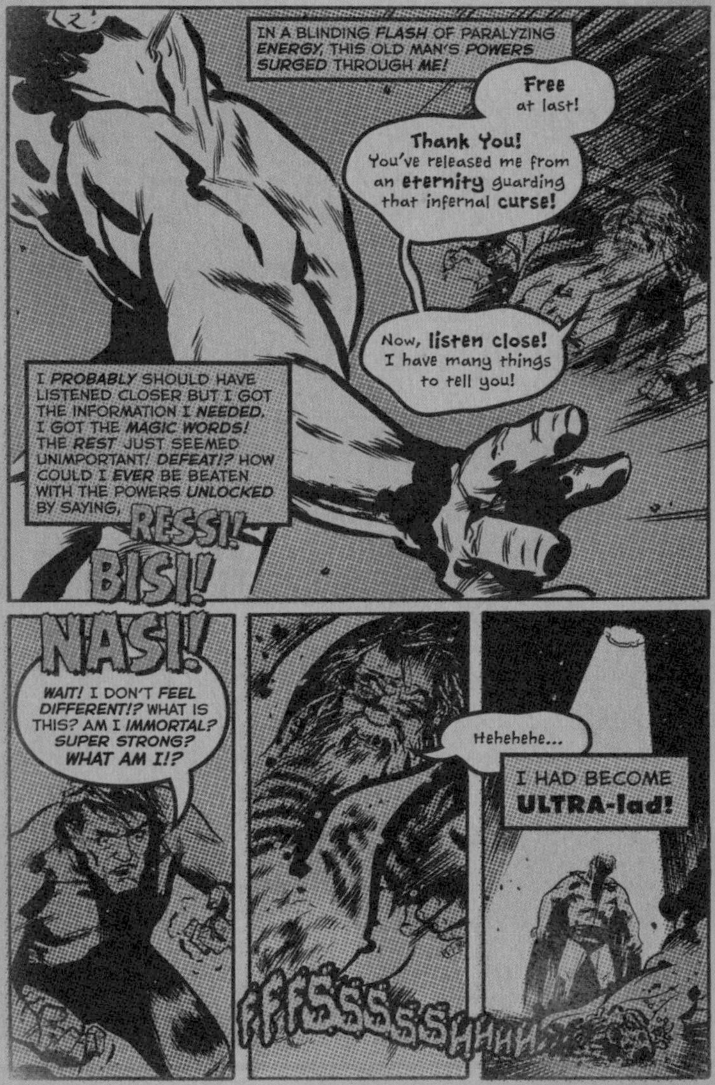

IN A BLINDING FLASH OF PARALYZING ENERGY, THIS OLD MAN'S POWERS SURGED THROUGH ME!
Free at last!
Thank You! You've released me from an eternity guarding that infernal curse!
Now, listen close! I have many things to tell you!
I PROBABLY SHOULD HAVE LISTENED CLOSER BUT I GOT THE INFORMATION I NEEDED. I GOT THE MAGIC WORDS! THE REST JUST SEEMED UNIMPORTANT! DEFEAT!? HOW COULD I EVER BE BEATEN WITH THE POWERS UNLOCKED BY SAYING,
RESSI! BISI! NASI!
WAIT! I DON'T FEEL DIFFERENT!? WHAT IS THIS? AM I IMMORTAL? SUPER STRONG? WHAT AM I!?
Hehehehe...
FFFSSSSSSHHHH
I HAD BECOME ULTRA-lad!

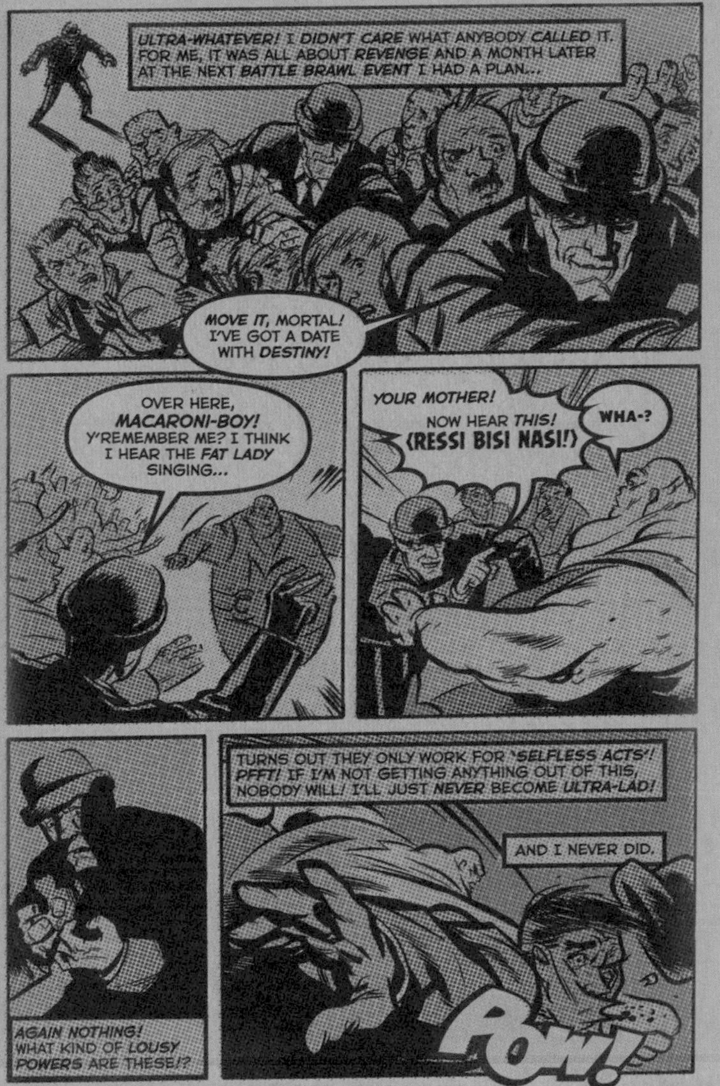

ULTRA-WHATEVER! I DIDN'T CARE WHAT ANYBODY CALLED IT. FOR ME, IT WAS ALL ABOUT REVENGE AND A MONTH LATER AT THE NEXT BATTLE BRAWL EVENT I HAD A PLAN...
MOVE IT, MORTAL! I'VE GOT A DATE WITH DESTINY!
OVER HERE, MACARONI-BOY! Y'REMEMBER ME? I THINK I HEAR THE FAT LADY SINGING...
YOUR MOTHER! NOW HEAR THIS! (RESSI BISI NASI!)
WHA-?
AGAIN NOTHING! WHAT KIND OF LOUSY POWERS ARE THESE!?
TURNS OUT THEY ONLY WORK FOR 'SELFLESS ACTS'! PFFT! IF I'M NOT GETTING ANYTHING OUT OF THIS, NOBODY WILL! I'LL JUST NEVER BECOME ULTRA-LAD!
AND I NEVER DID.
POW!

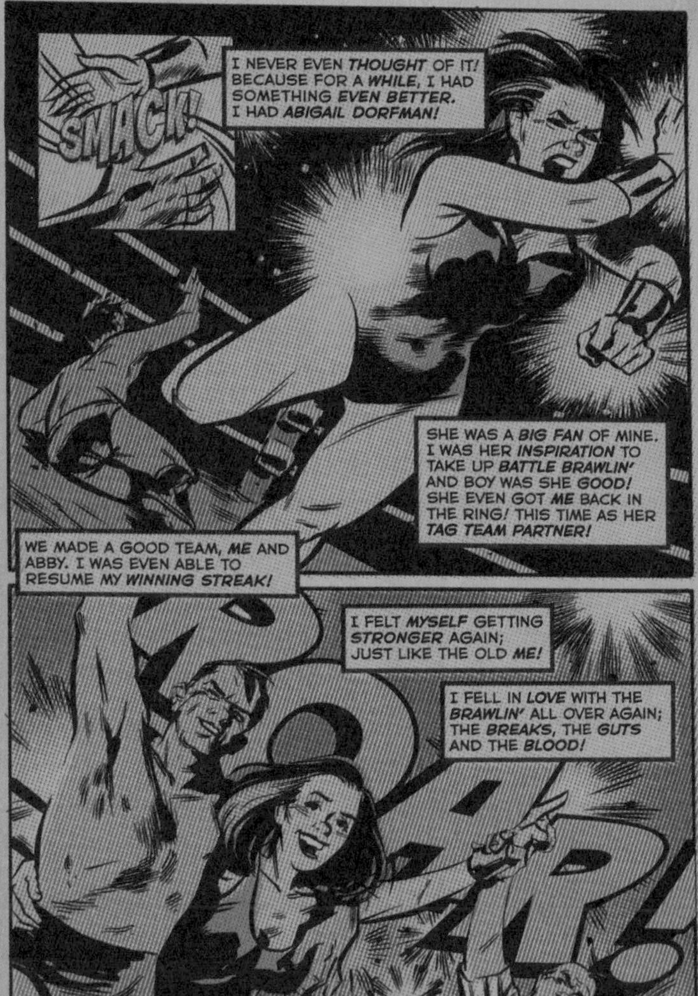
SMACK!
I NEVER EVEN THOUGHT OF IT! BECAUSE FOR A WHILE, I HAD SOMETHING EVEN BETTER. I HAD ABIGAIL DORFMAN!
SHE WAS A BIG FAN OF MINE. I WAS HER INSPIRATION TO TAKE UP BATTLE BRAWLIN' AND BOY WAS SHE GOOD! SHE EVEN GOT ME BACK IN THE RING! THIS TIME AS HER TAG TEAM PARTNER!
WE MADE A GOOD TEAM, ME AND ABBY. I WAS EVEN ABLE TO RESUME MY WINNING STREAK!
I FELT MYSELF GETTING STRONGER AGAIN; JUST LIKE THE OLD ME!
I FELL IN LOVE WITH THE BRAWLIN' ALL OVER AGAIN; THE BREAKS, THE GUTS AND THE BLOOD!

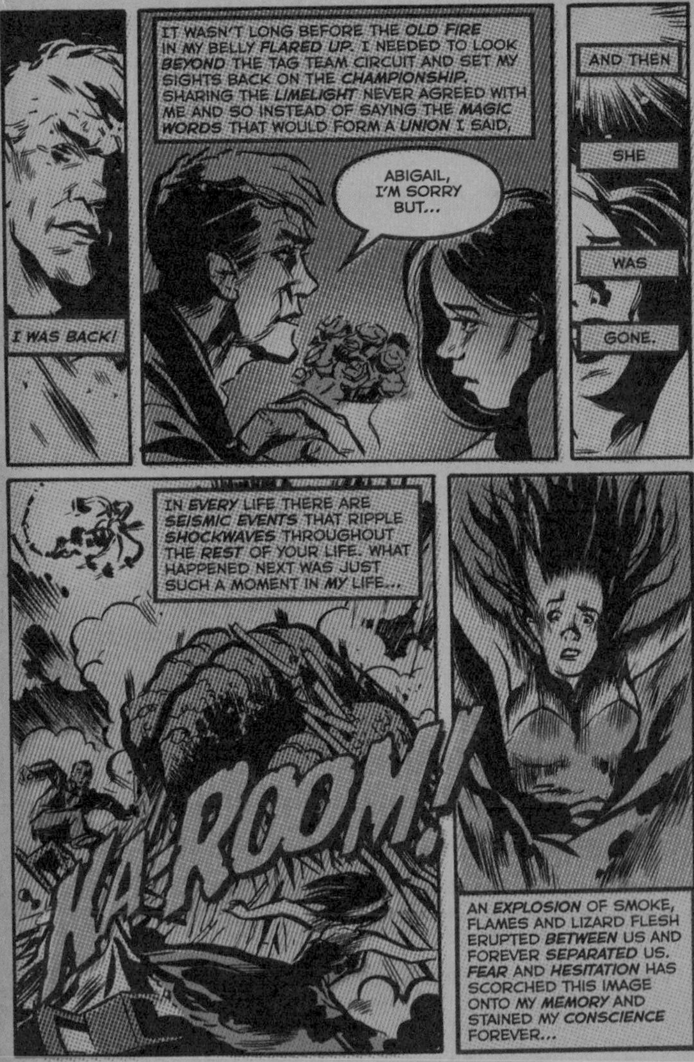
I WAS BACK!
IT WASN'T LONG BEFORE THE OLD FIRE IN MY BELLY FLARED UP. I NEEDED TO LOOK BEYOND THE TAG TEAM CIRCUIT AND SET MY SIGHTS BACK ON THE CHAMPIONSHIP. SHARING THE LIMELIGHT NEVER AGREED WITH ME AND SO INSTEAD OF SAYING THE MAGIC WORDS THAT WOULD FORM A UNION I SAID,
ABIGAIL, I'M SORRY BUT...
AND THEN
SHE
WAS
GONE.
IN EVERY LIFE THERE ARE SEISMIC EVENTS THAT RIPPLE SHOCKWAVES THROUGHOUT THE REST OF YOUR LIFE. WHAT HAPPENED NEXT WAS JUST SUCH A MOMENT IN MY LIFE...
KA-ROOM!
AN EXPLOSION OF SMOKE, FLAMES AND LIZARD FLESH ERUPTED BETWEEN US AND FOREVER SEPARATED US. FEAR AND HESITATION HAS SCORCHED THIS IMAGE ONTO MY MEMORY AND STAINED MY CONSCIENCE FOREVER...

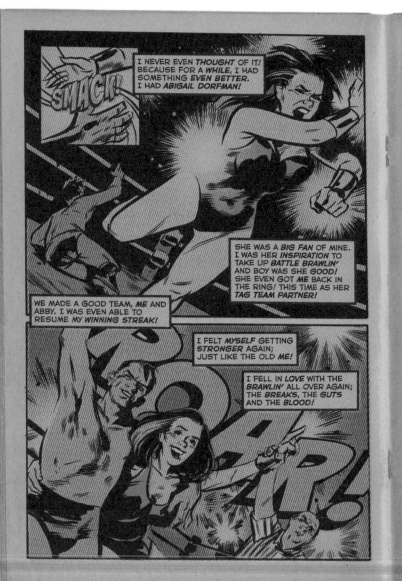

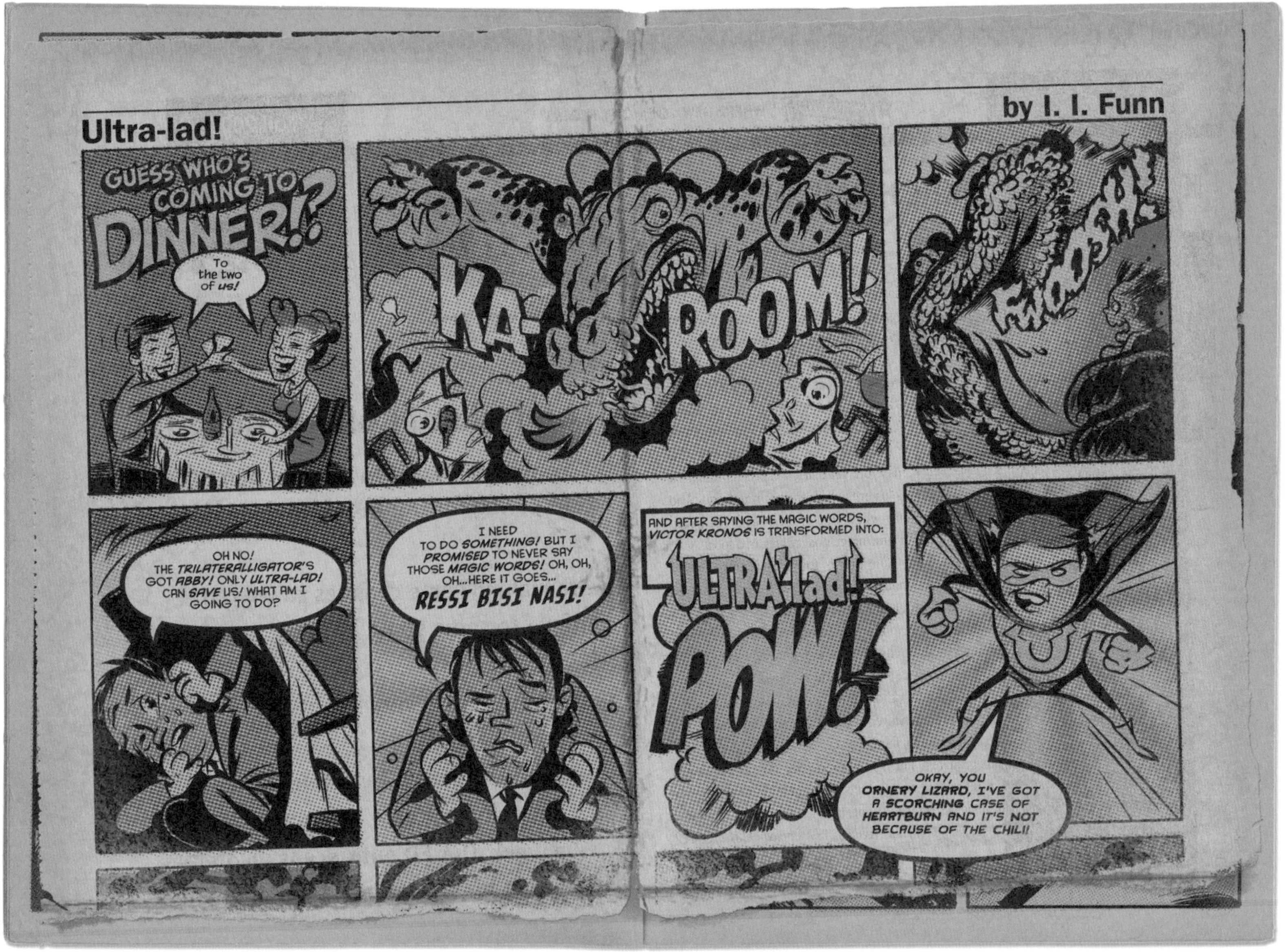
Ultra-lad!
by I. I. Funn
GUESS WHO'S COMING TO DINNER!?
To the two of us!
KA-ROOM!
FWOOSH!
OH NO! THE TRILATERALLIGATOR'S GOT ABBY! ONLY ULTRA-LAD! CAN SAVE US! WHAT AM I GOING TO DO?
I NEED TO DO SOMETHING! BUT I PROMISED TO NEVER SAY THOSE MAGIC WORDS! OH, OH, OH... HERE IT GOES... RESSI BISI NASI!
AND AFTER SAYING THE MAGIC WORDS, VICTOR KRONOS IS TRANSFORMED INTO:
ULTRA-lad!
POW!
OKAY, YOU ORNERY LIZARD, I'VE GOT A SCORCHING CASE OF HEARTBURN AND IT'S NOT BECAUSE OF THE CHILI!

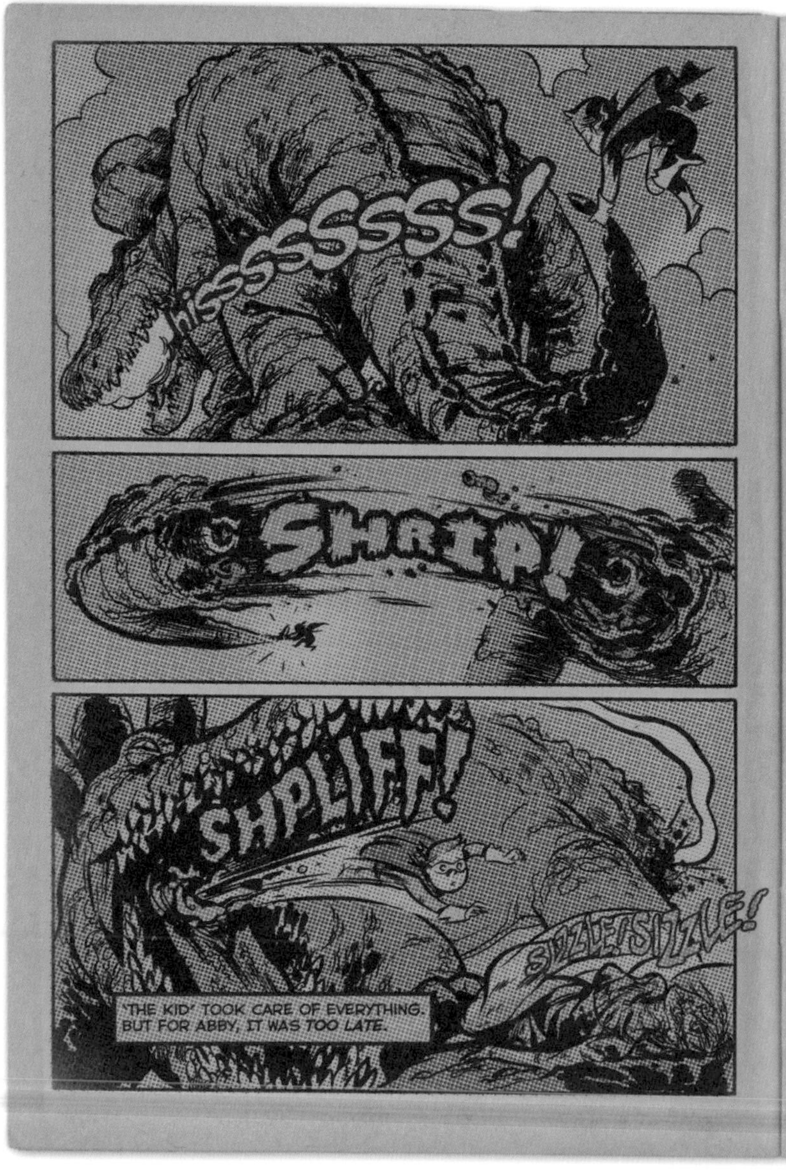
hiSSSSSSS!
SHRIP!
SHPLIFF!
SIZZLE!SIZZLE!
'THE KID' TOOK CARE OF EVERYTHING. BUT FOR ABBY, IT WAS TOO LATE.

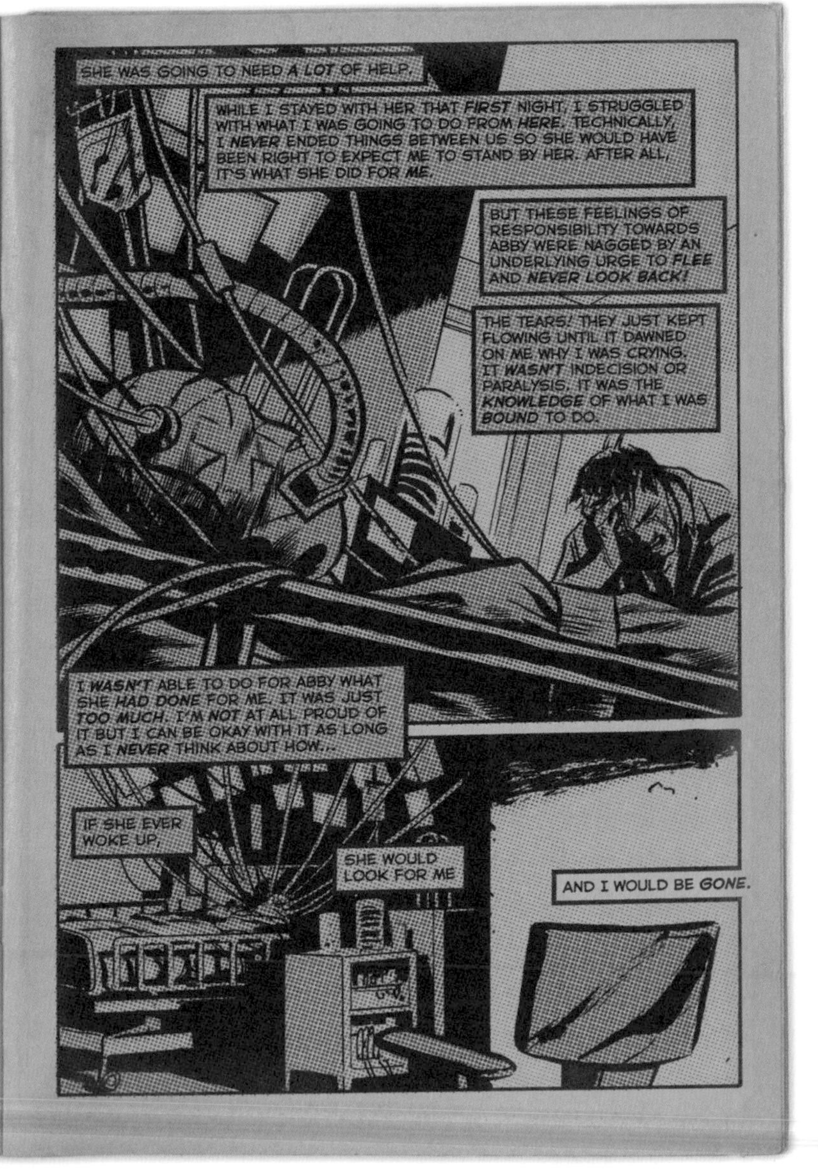
SHE WAS GOING TO NEED A LOT OF HELP.
WHILE I STAYED WITH HER THAT FIRST NIGHT, I STRUGGLED WITH WHAT I WAS GOING TO DO FROM HERE. TECHNICALLY, I NEVER ENDED THINGS BETWEEN US SO SHE WOULD HAVE BEEN RIGHT TO EXPECT ME TO STAND BY HER. AFTER ALL, IT'S WHAT SHE DID FOR ME.
BUT THESE FEELINGS OF RESPONSIBILITY TOWARDS ABBY WERE NAGGED BY AN UNDERLYING URGE TO FLEE AND NEVER LOOK BACK!
THE TEARS! THEY JUST KEPT FLOWING UNTIL IT DAWNED ON ME WHY I WAS CRYING. IT WASN'T INDECISION OR PARALYSIS. IT WAS THE KNOWLEDGE OF WHAT I WAS BOUND TO DO.
I WASN'T ABLE TO DO FOR ABBY WHAT SHE HAD DONE FOR ME. IT WAS JUST TOO MUCH. I'M NOT AT ALL PROUD OF IT BUT I CAN BE OKAY WITH IT AS LONG AS I NEVER THINK ABOUT HOW...
IF SHE EVER WOKE UP,
SHE WOULD LOOK FOR ME
AND I WOULD BE GONE.

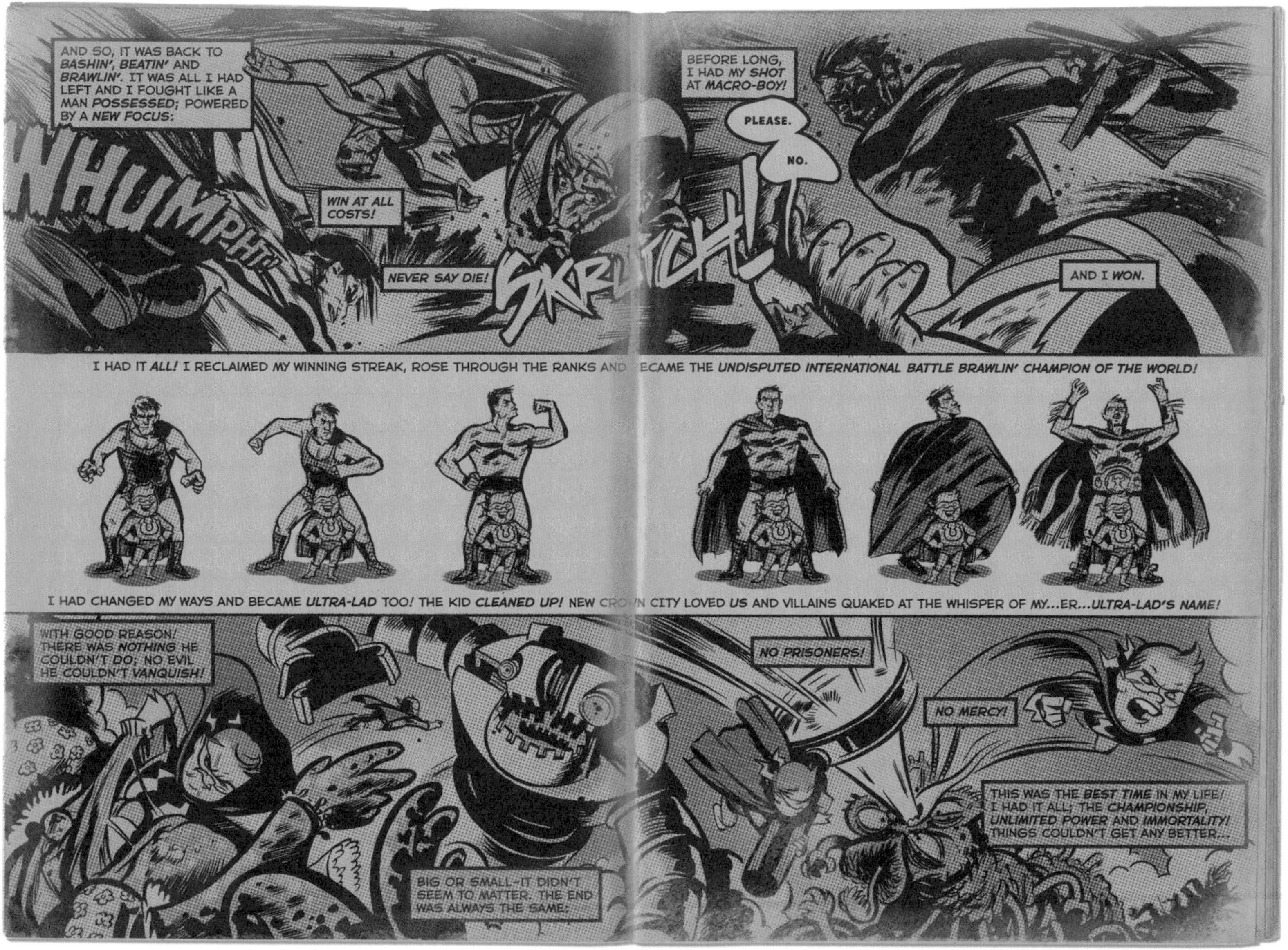
AND SO, IT WAS BACK TO BASHIN', BEATIN' AND BRAWLIN'. IT WAS ALL I HAD LEFT AND I FOUGHT LIKE A MAN POSSESSED; POWERED BY A NEW FOCUS:
WIN AT ALL COSTS!
NEVER SAY DIE!
BEFORE LONG, I HAD MY SHOT AT MACRO-BOY!
PLEASE.
NO.
AND I WON.
I HAD IT ALL! I RECLAIMED MY WINNING STREAK, ROSE THROUGH THE RANKS AND BECAME THE UNDISPUTED INTERNATIONAL BATTLE BRAWLIN' CHAMPION OF THE WORLD!
I HAD CHANGED MY WAYS AND BECAME ULTRA-LAD TOO! THE KID CLEANED UP! NEW CROWN CITY LOVED US AND VILLAINS QUAKED AT THE WHISPER OF MY...ER...ULTRA-LAD'S NAME!
WITH GOOD REASON! THERE WAS NOTHING HE COULDN'T DO; NO EVIL HE COULDN'T VANQUISH!
BIG OR SMALL-IT DIDN'T SEEM TO MATTER. THE END WAS ALWAYS THE SAME:
NO PRISONERS!
NO MERCY!
THIS WAS THE BEST TIME IN MY LIFE! I HAD IT ALL; THE CHAMPIONSHIP, UNLIMITED POWER AND IMMORTALITY! THINGS COULDN'T GET ANY BETTER...

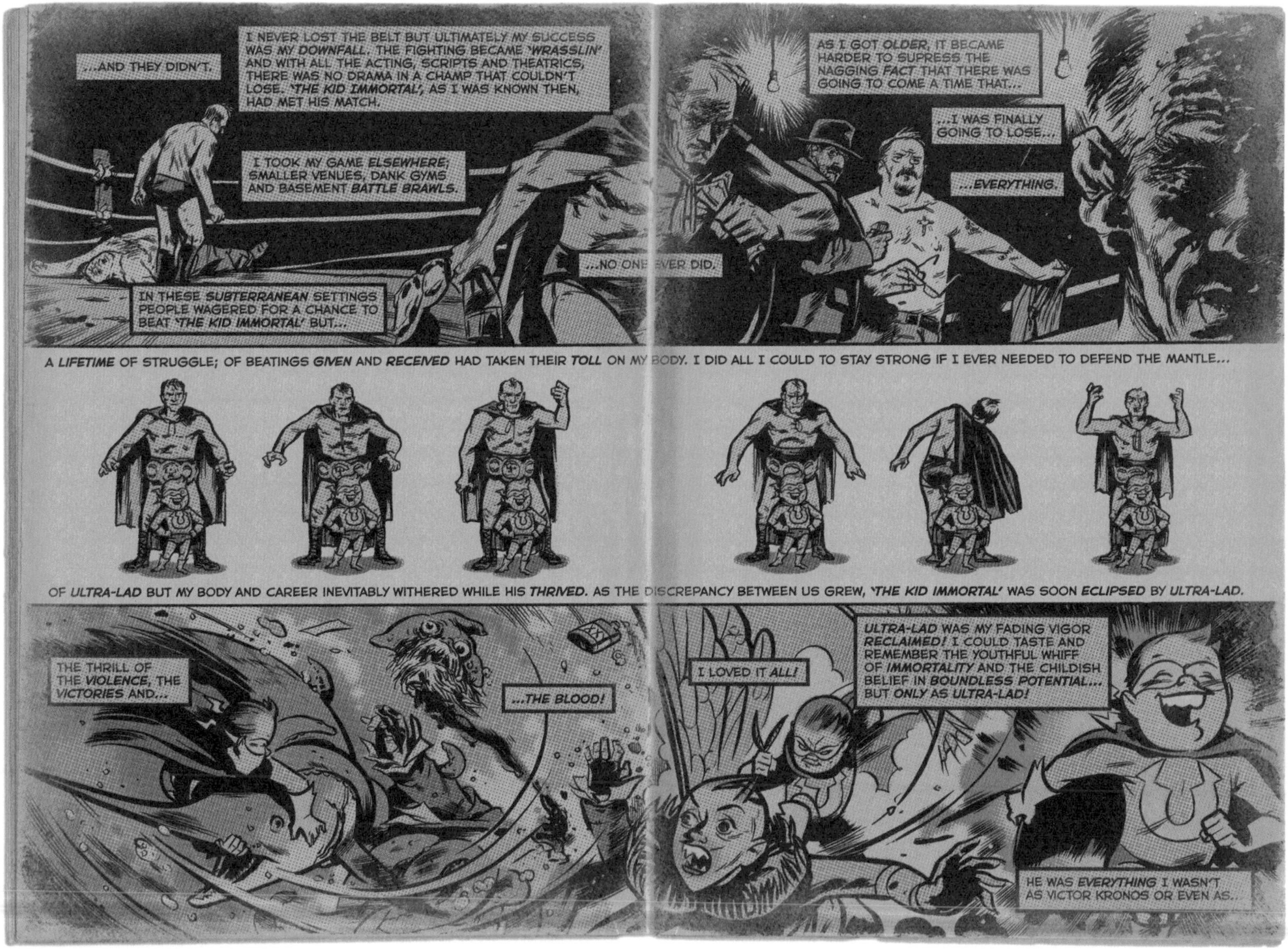
...AND THEY DIDN'T.
I NEVER LOST THE BELT BUT ULTIMATELY MY SUCCESS WAS MY DOWNFALL. THE FIGHTING BECAME 'WRASSLIN' AND WITH ALL THE ACTING, SCRIPTS AND THEATRICS, THERE WAS NO DRAMA IN A CHAMP THAT COULDN'T LOSE. 'THE KID IMMORTAL', AS I WAS KNOWN THEN, HAD MET HIS MATCH.
I TOOK MY GAME ELSEWHERE; SMALLER VENUES, DANK GYMS AND BASEMENT BATTLE BRAWLS.
IN THESE SUBTERRANEAN SETTINGS PEOPLE WAGERED FOR A CHANCE TO BEAT 'THE KID IMMORTAL' BUT...
...NO ONE EVER DID.
AS I GOT OLDER, IT BECAME HARDER TO SUPRESS THE NAGGING FACT THAT THERE WAS GOING TO COME A TIME THAT...
...I WAS FINALLY GOING TO LOSE...
...EVERYTHING.
A LIFETIME OF STRUGGLE; OF BEATINGS GIVEN AND RECEIVED HAD TAKEN THEIR TOLL ON MY BODY. I DID ALL I COULD TO STAY STRONG IF I EVER NEEDED TO DEFEND THE MANTLE...
OF ULTRA-LAD BUT MY BODY AND CAREER INEVITABLY WITHERED WHILE HIS THRIVED. AS THE DISCREPANCY BETWEEN US GREW, 'THE KID IMMORTAL' WAS SOON ECLIPSED BY ULTRA-LAD.
THE THRILL OF THE VIOLENCE, THE VICTORIES AND...
...THE BLOOD!
I LOVED IT ALL!
ULTRA-LAD WAS MY FADING VIGOR RECLAIMED! I COULD TASTE AND REMEMBER THE YOUTHFUL WHIFF OF IMMORTALITY AND THE CHILDISH BELIEF IN BOUNDLESS POTENTIAL... BUT ONLY AS ULTRA-LAD!
HE WAS EVERYTHING I WASN'T AS VICTOR KRONOS OR EVEN AS...

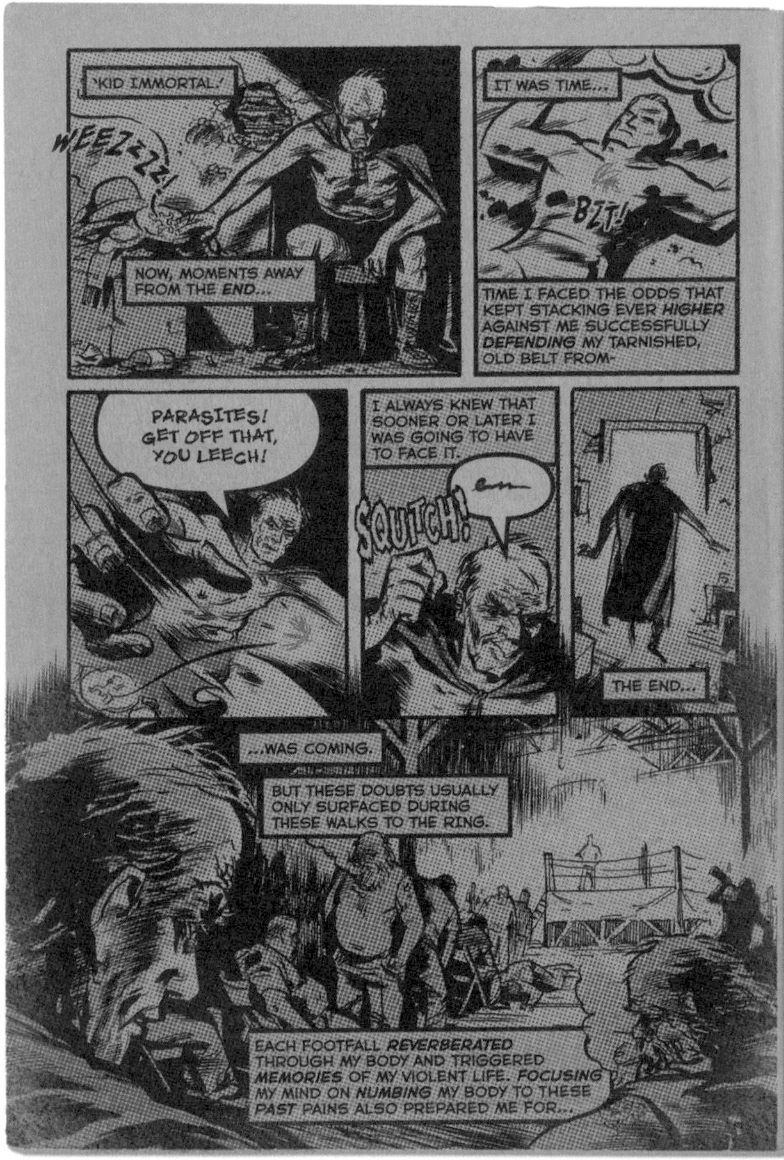
'KID IMMORTAL.'
WEEZ-ZZZ!
NOW, MOMENTS AWAY FROM THE END...
IT WAS TIME...
BZT!
TIME I FACED THE ODDS THAT KEPT STACKING EVER HIGHER AGAINST ME SUCCESSFULLY DEFENDING MY TARNISHED, OLD BELT FROM-
PARASITES! GET OFF THAT, YOU LEECH!
I ALWAYS KNEW THAT SOONER OR LATER I WAS GOING TO HAVE TO FACE IT.
SQUTCH!
THE END...
...WAS COMING.
BUT THESE DOUBTS USUALLY ONLY SURFACED DURING THESE WALKS TO THE RING.
EACH FOOTFALL REVERBERATED THROUGH MY BODY AND TRIGGERED MEMORIES OF MY VIOLENT LIFE. FOCUSING MY MIND ON NUMBING MY BODY TO THESE PAST PAINS ALSO PREPARED ME FOR...

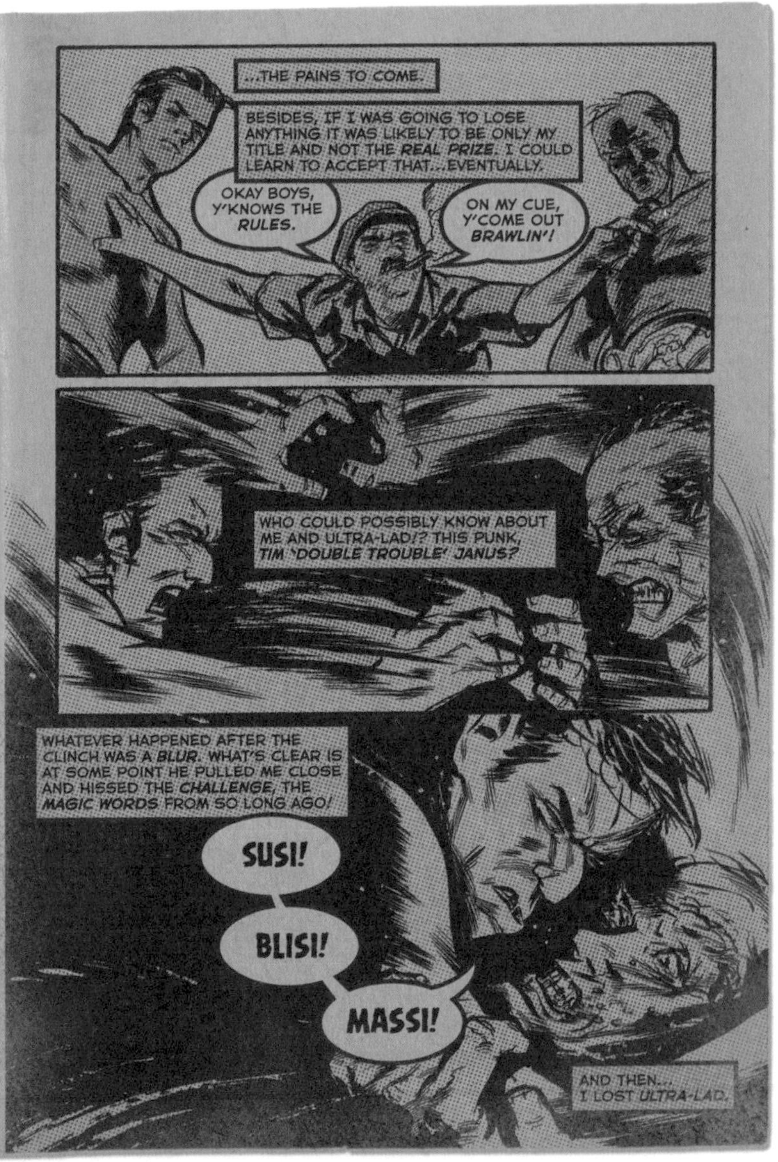
...THE PAINS TO COME.
BESIDES, IF I WAS GOING TO LOSE ANYTHING IT WAS LIKELY TO BE ONLY MY TITLE AND NOT THE REAL PRIZE. I COULD LEARN TO ACCEPT THAT...EVENTUALLY.
OKAY BOYS, Y'KNOWS THE RULES.
ON MY CUE, Y'COME OUT BRAWLIN'!
WHO COULD POSSIBLY KNOW ABOUT ME AND ULTRA-LAD!? THIS PUNK, TIM 'DOUBLE TROUBLE' JANUS?
WHATEVER HAPPENED AFTER THE CLINCH WAS A BLUR. WHAT'S CLEAR IS AT SOME POINT HE PULLED ME CLOSE AND HISSED THE CHALLENGE, THE MAGIC WORDS FROM SO LONG AGO!
SUSI!
BLISI!
MASSI!
AND THEN... I LOST ULTRA-LAD.

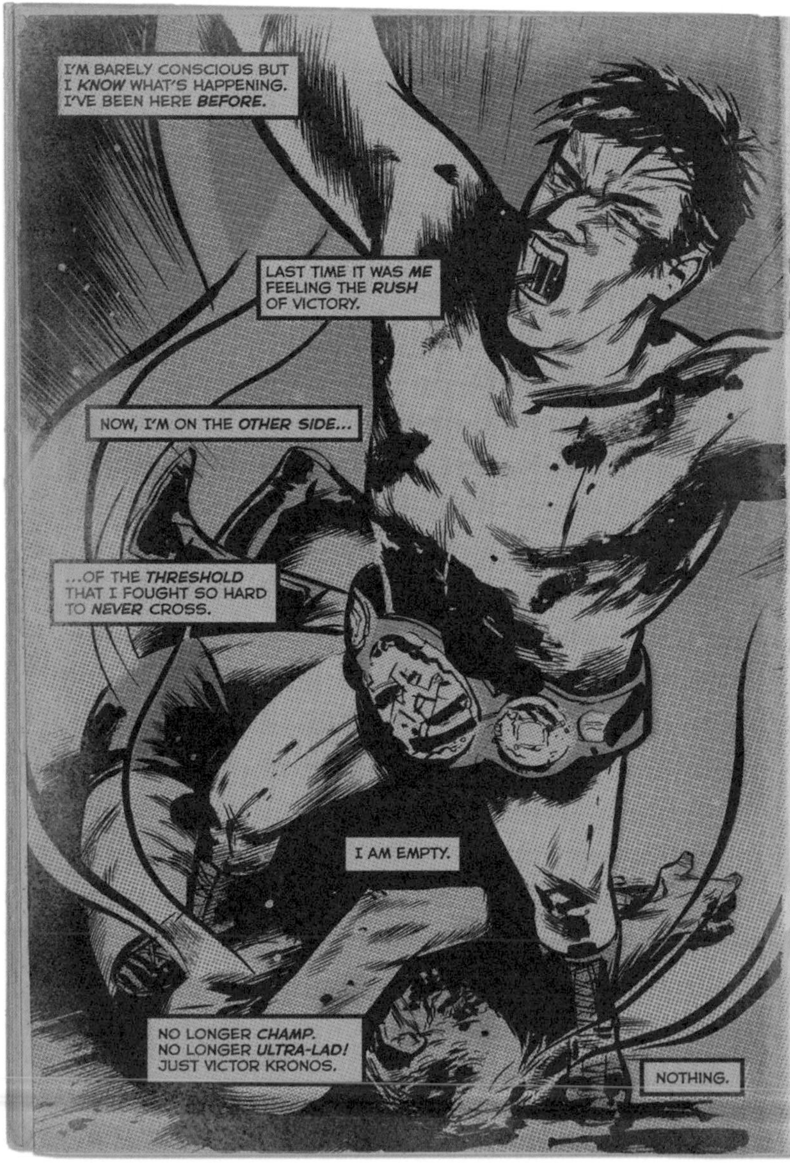
I'M BARELY CONSCIOUS BUT I KNOW WHAT'S HAPPENING. I'VE BEEN HERE BEFORE.
LAST TIME IT WAS ME FEELING THE RUSH OF VICTORY.
NOW, I'M ON THE OTHER SIDE...
...OF THE THRESHOLD THAT I FOUGHT SO HARD TO NEVER CROSS.
I AM EMPTY.
NO LONGER CHAMP. NO LONGER ULTRA-LAD! JUST VICTOR KRONOS.
NOTHING.

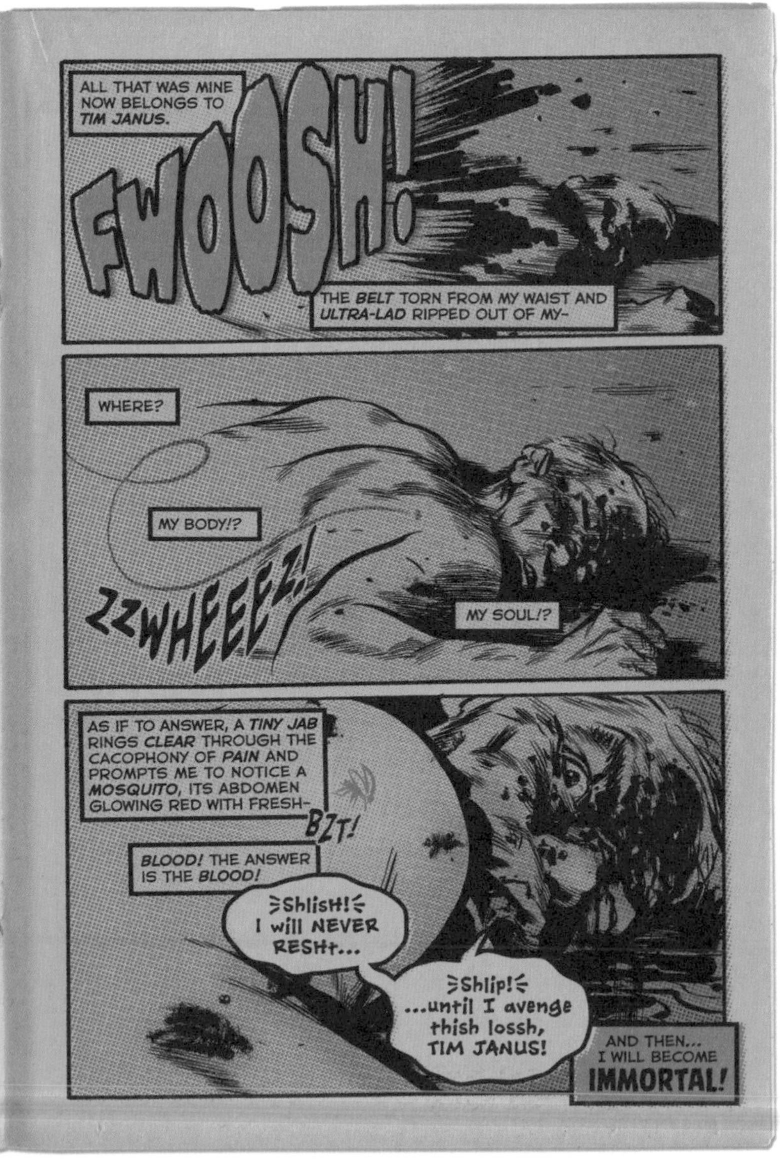
ALL THAT WAS MINE NOW BELONGS TO TIM JANUS.
FWOOSH!
THE BELT TORN FROM MY WAIST AND ULTRA-LAD RIPPED OUT OF MY-
WHERE?
MY BODY!?
ZZWHEEEZ!
MY SOUL!?
AS IF TO ANSWER, A TINY JAB RINGS CLEAR THROUGH THE CACOPHONY OF PAIN AND PROMPTS ME TO NOTICE A MOSQUITO, ITS ABDOMEN GLOWING RED WITH FRESH-
BZT!
BLOOD! THE ANSWER IS THE BLOOD!
Shlish! I will NEVER RESHt...
Shlip! ...until I avenge thish lossh, TIM JANUS!
AND THEN... I WILL BECOME IMMORTAL!

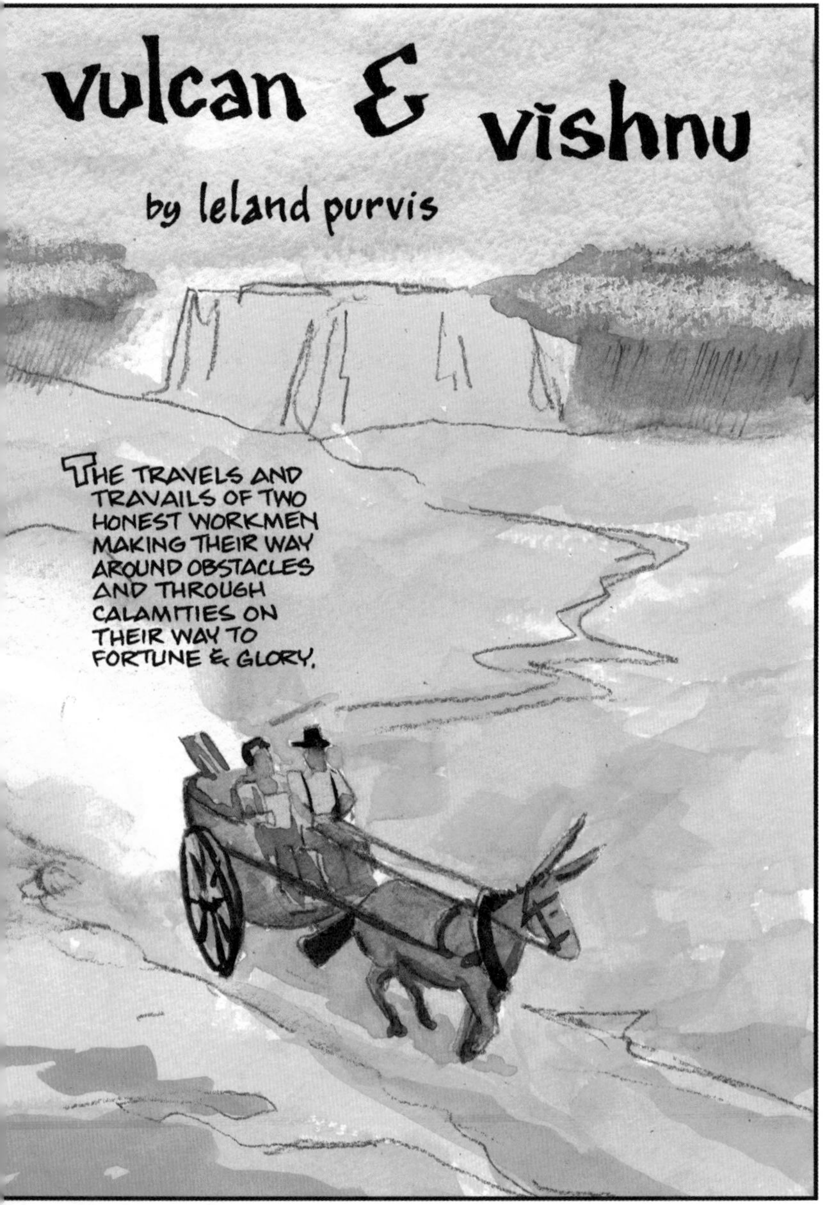
vulcan & vishnu
by leland purvis
THE TRAVELS AND TRAVAILS OF TWO HONEST WORKMEN MAKING THEIR WAY AROUND OBSTACLES AND THROUGH CALAMITIES ON THEIR WAY TO FORTUNE & GLORY.

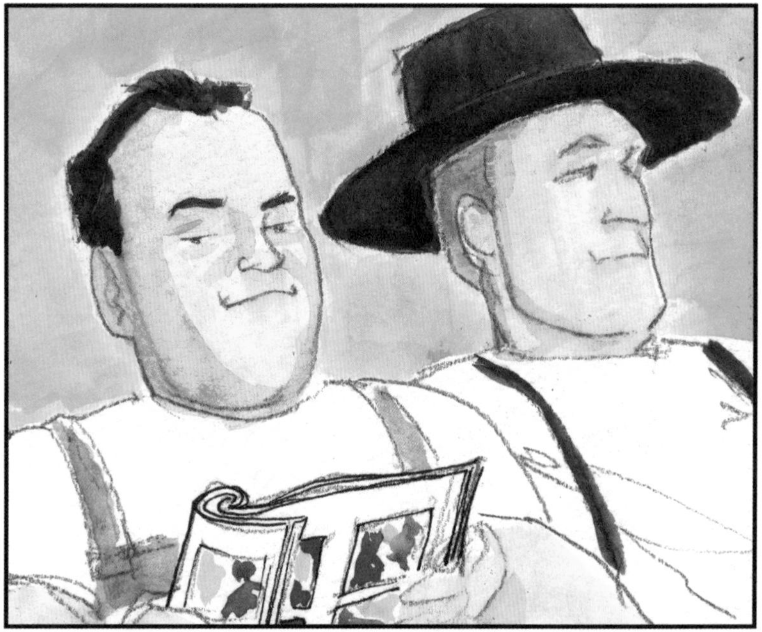

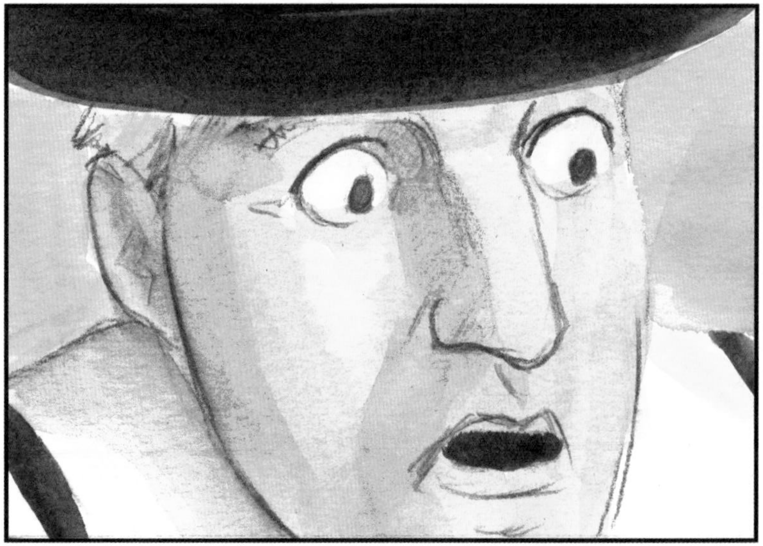

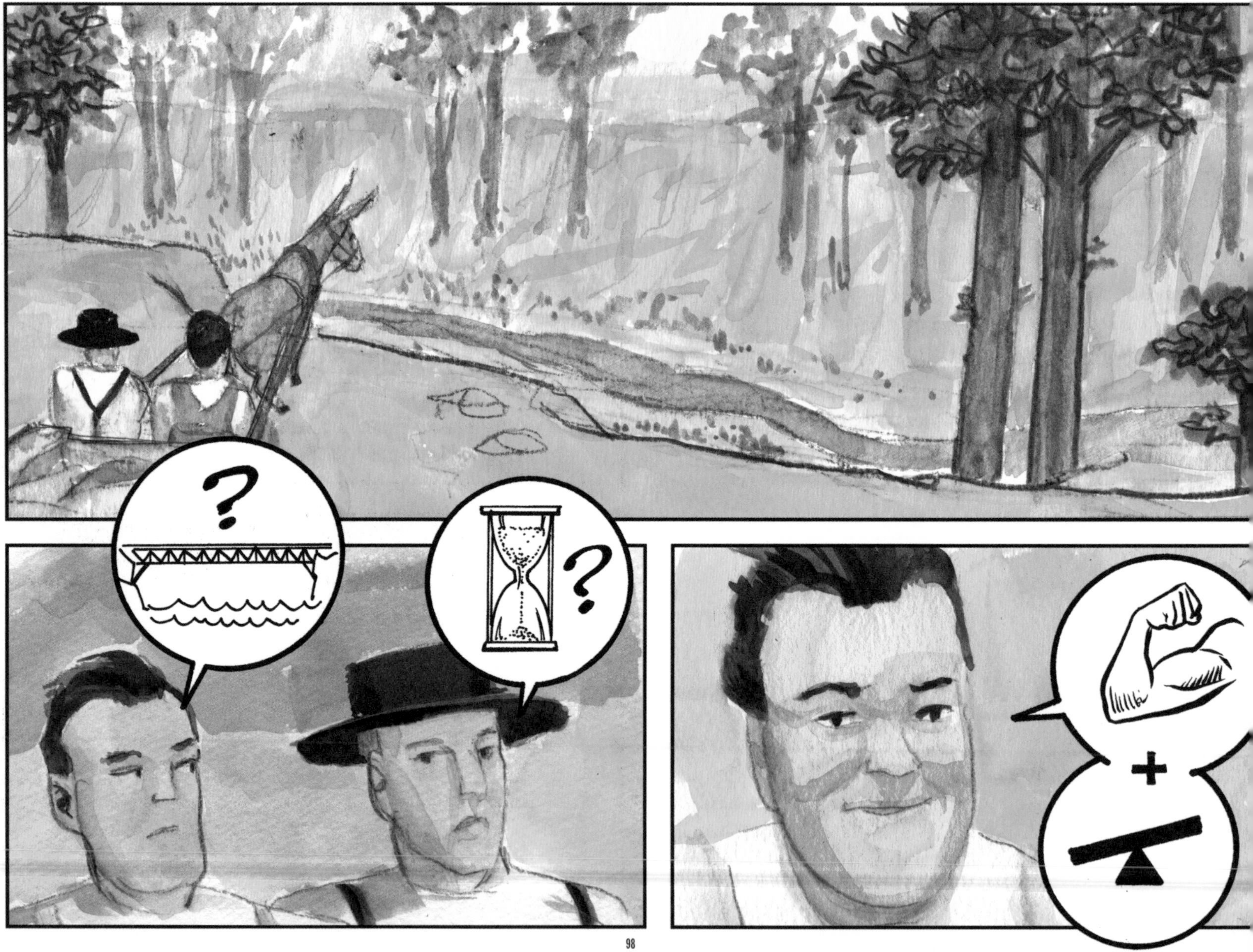
?
?
+

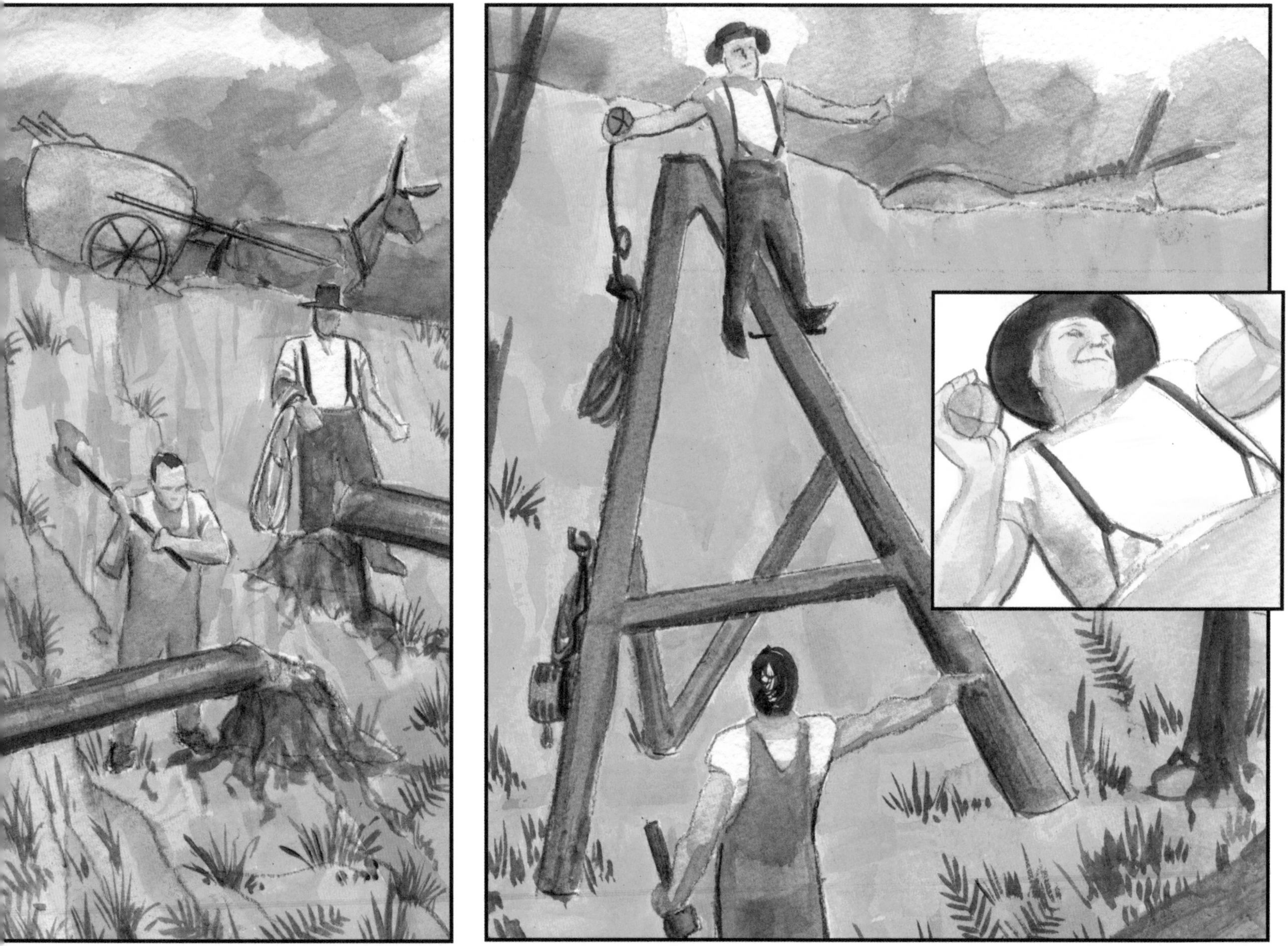

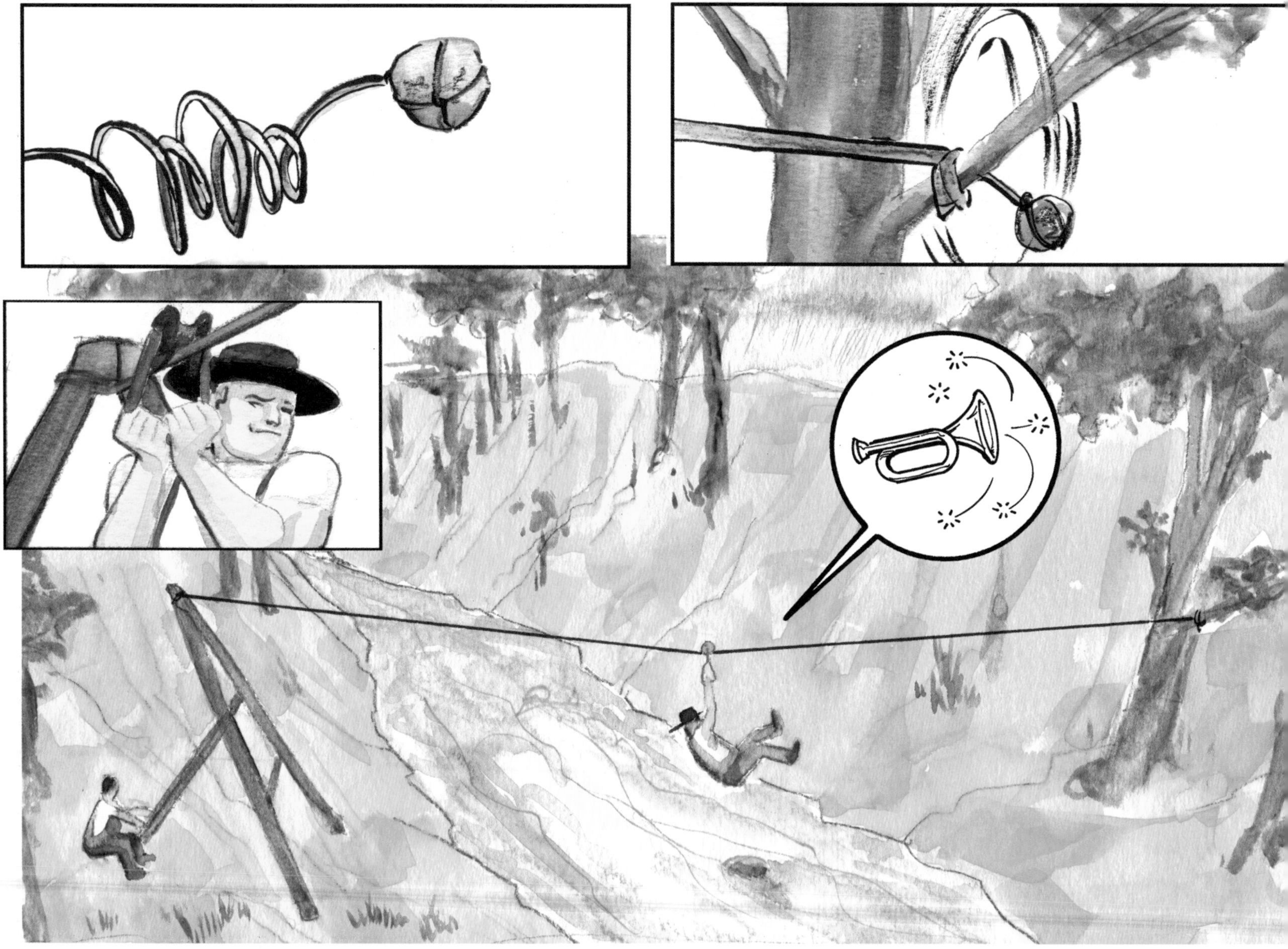

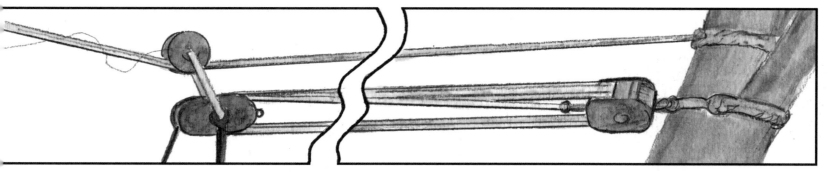

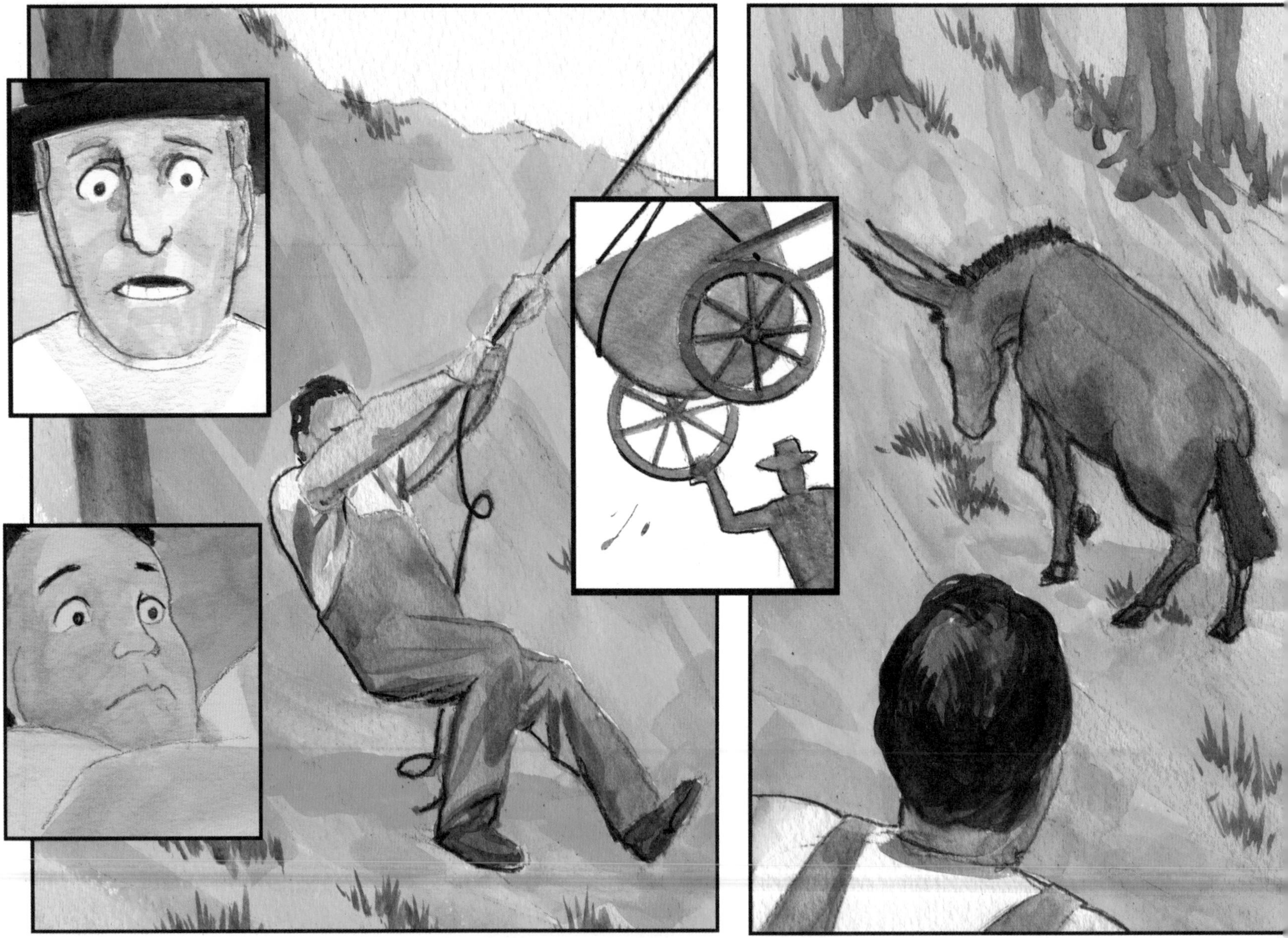

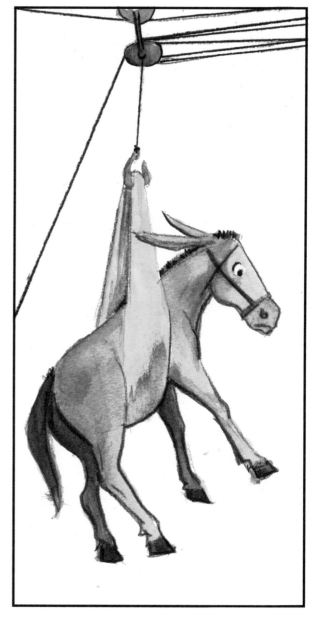

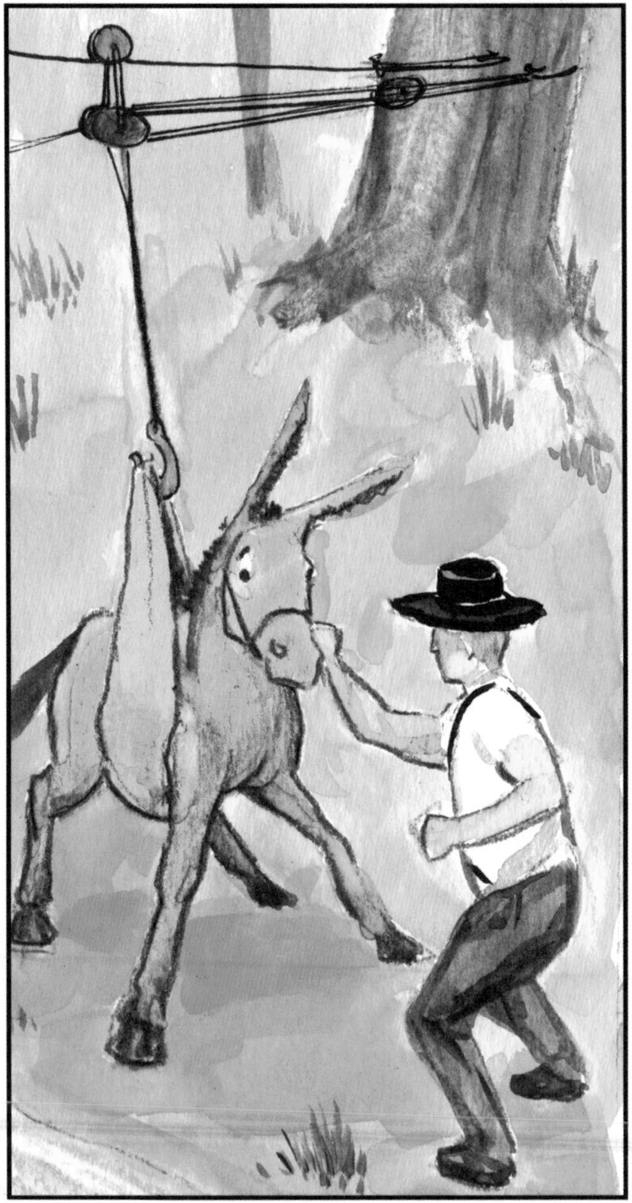

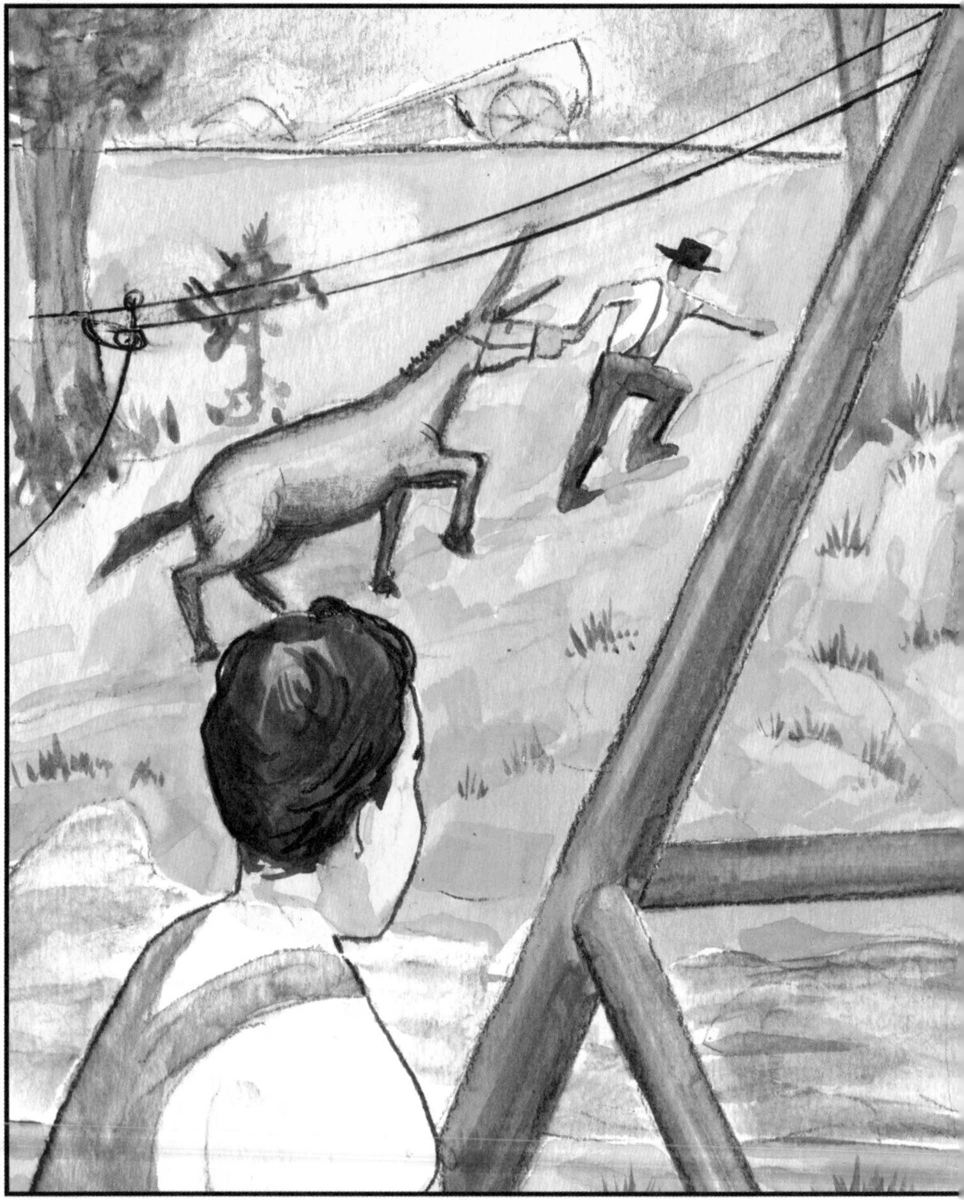

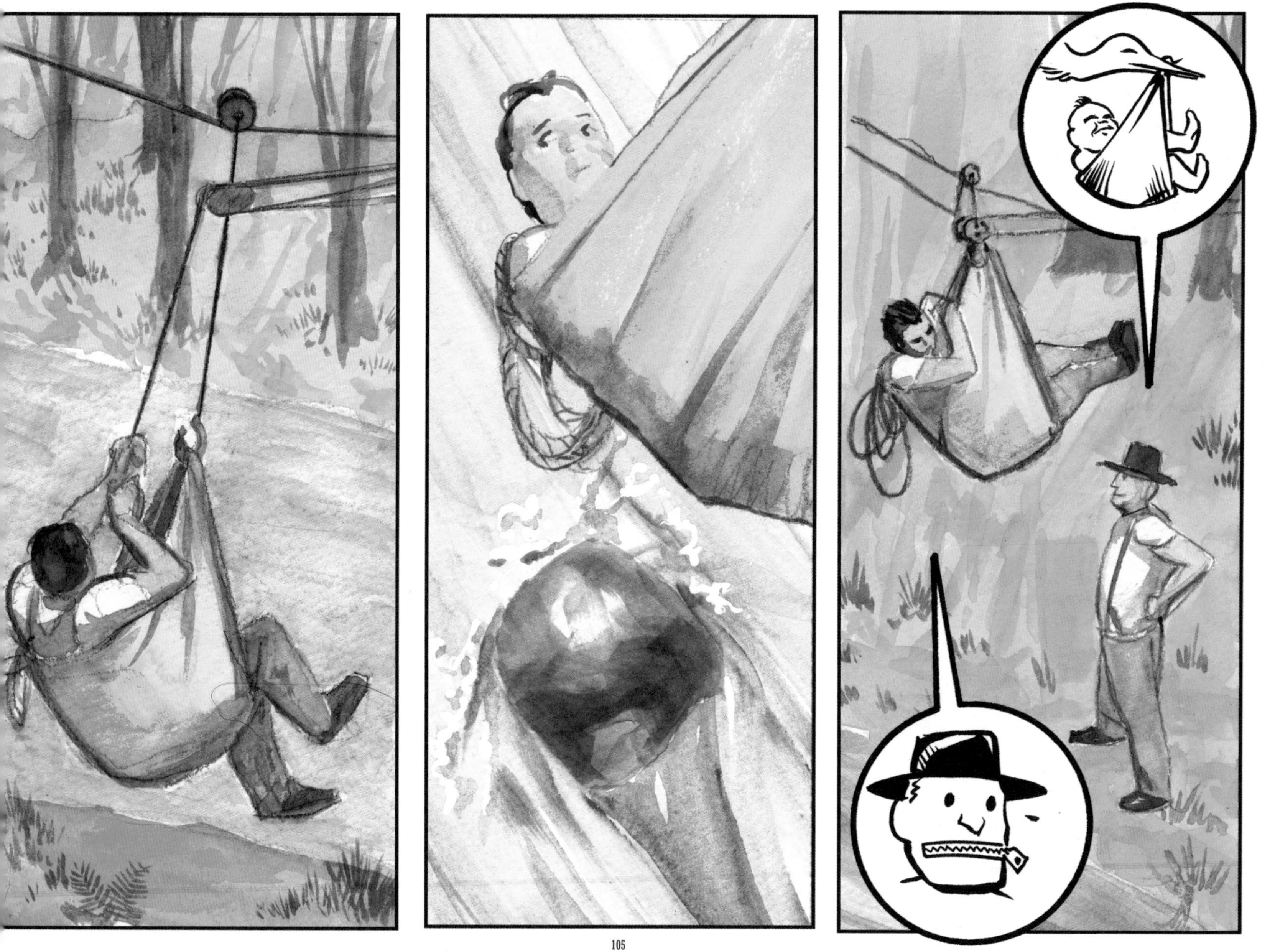

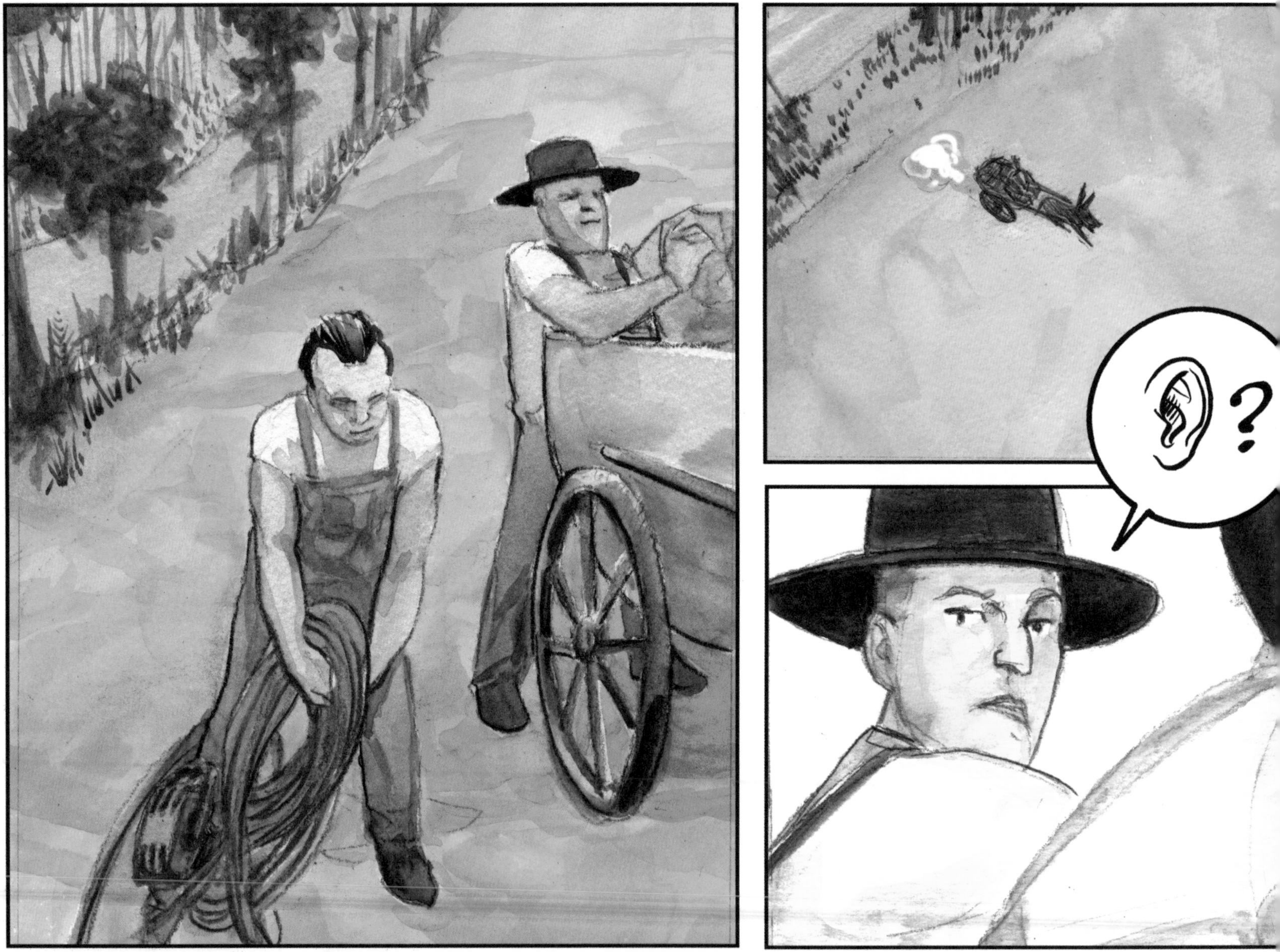
?

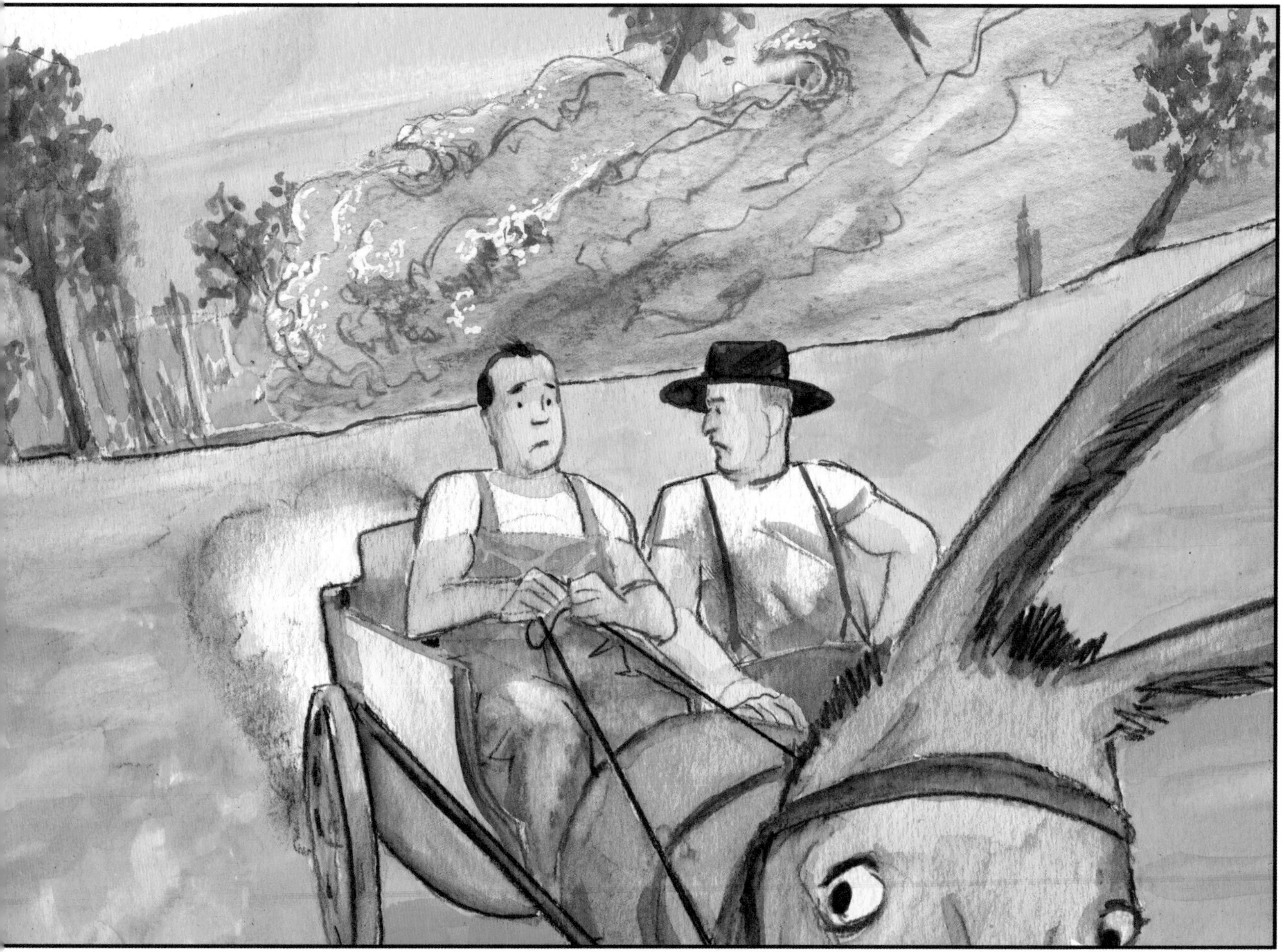

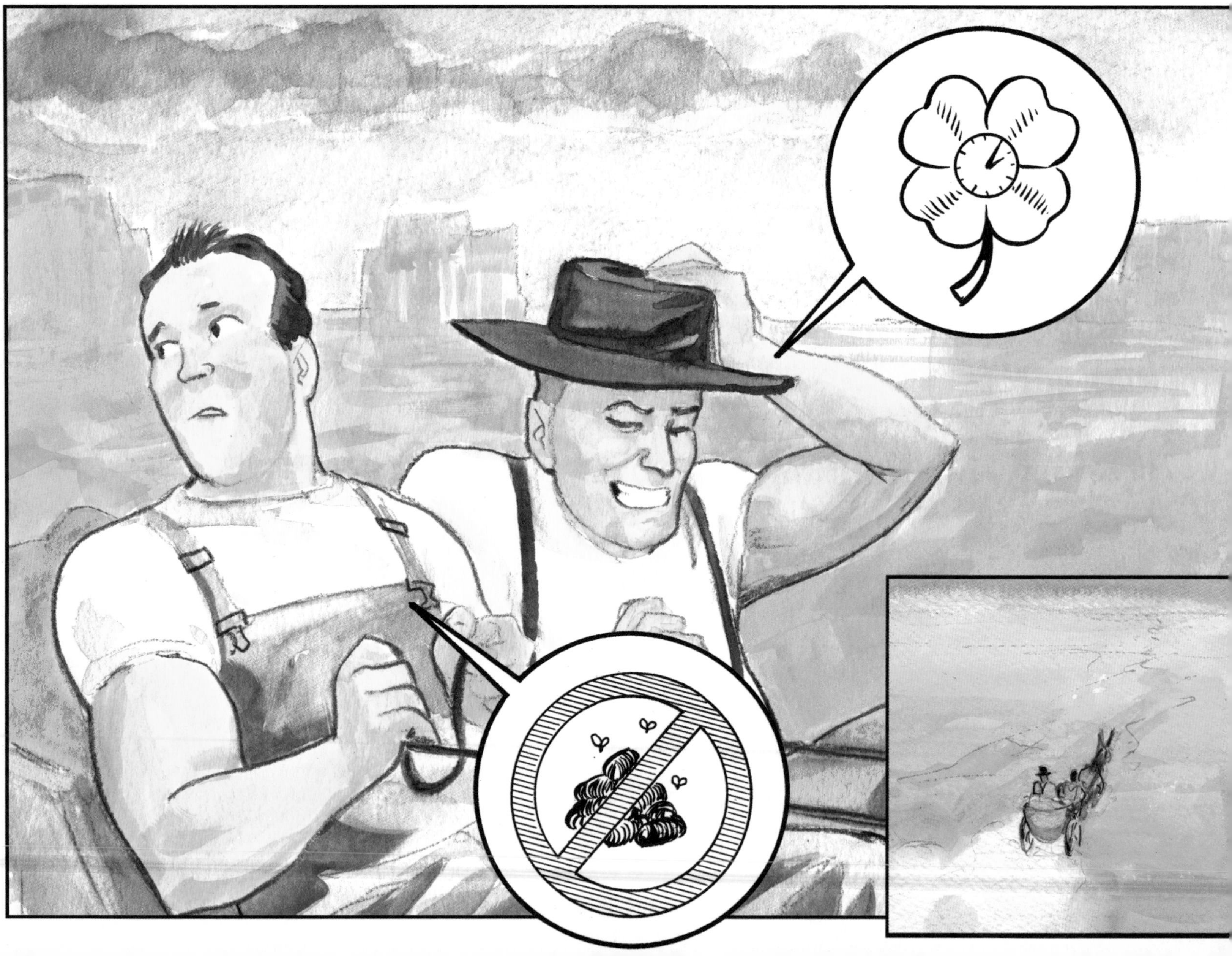

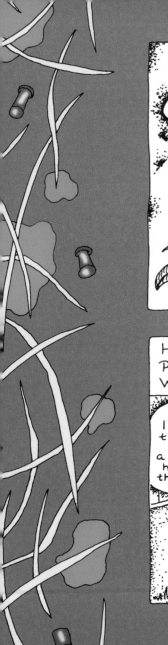

RAT-CHICKEN

BY: jennifer hayden

2009

ONCE AN OLD MAN CAME TO THE DOOR.

HE SAID HE KNEW THIS PLACE FROM WHEN HE WAS A KID.

No, I lived down the street. Spent a lot of time here, though.

HE WAITED FOR SOMETHING. (WHAT?) THEN HE SAID —

If it was all right with you, I'd be much obliged if I could see the house.

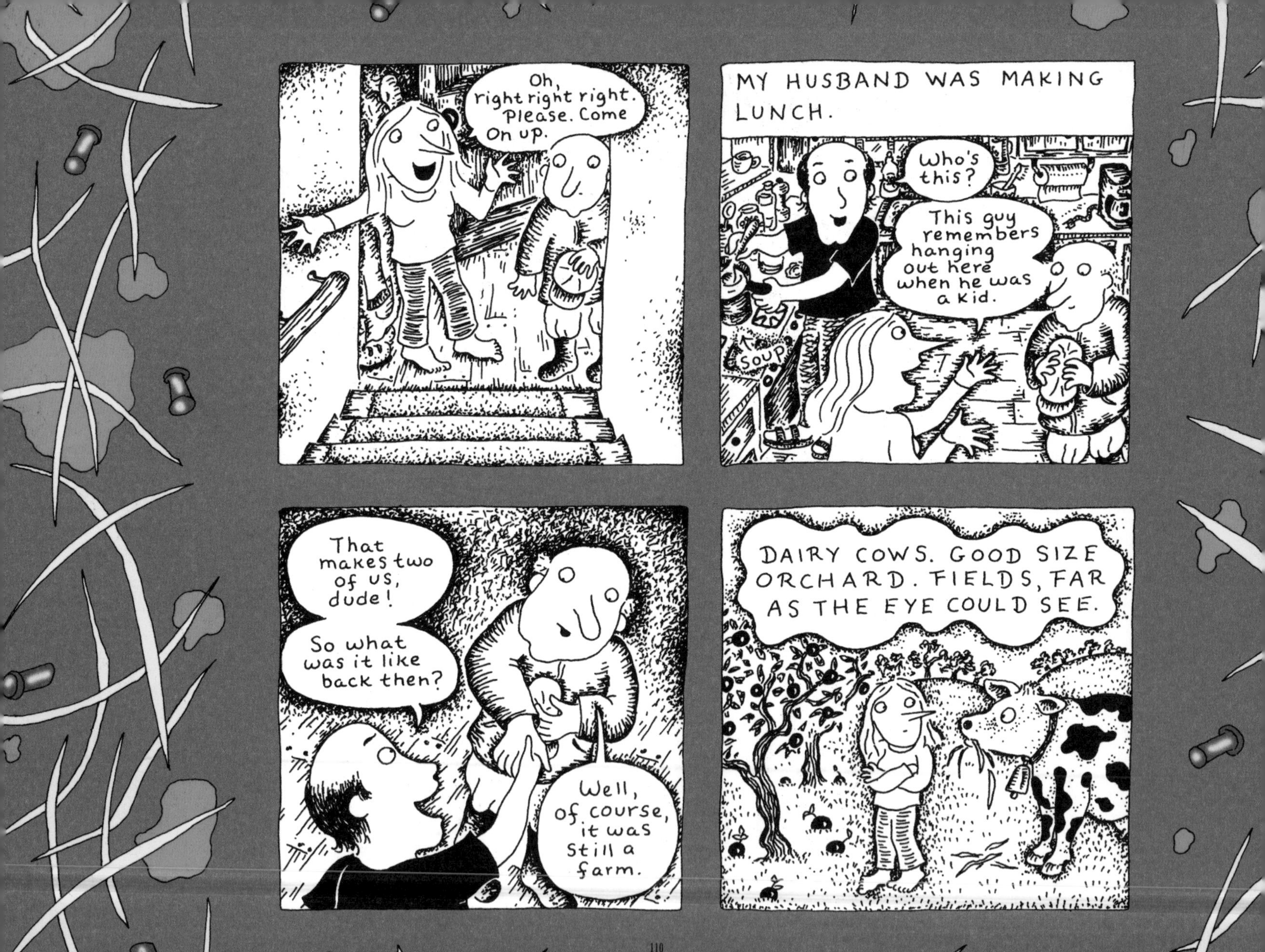
Oh, right right right. Please. Come on up.
MY HUSBAND WAS MAKING LUNCH.
Who's this?
This guy remembers hanging out here when he was a kid.
SOUP
That makes two of us, dude!
So what was it like back then?
Well, of course, it was still a farm.
DAIRY COWS. GOOD SIZE ORCHARD. FIELDS, FAR AS THE EYE COULD SEE.

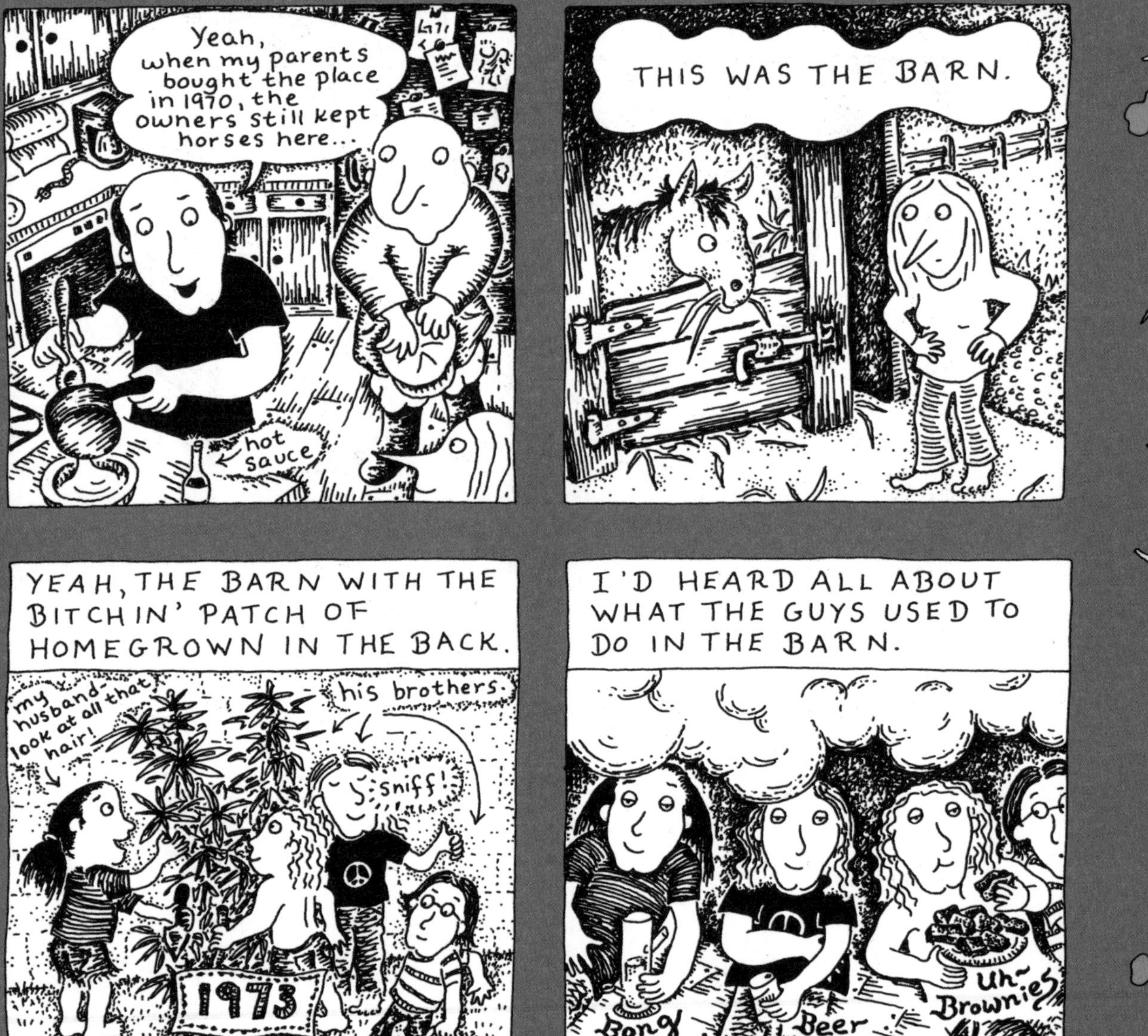

Yeah, when my parents bought the place in 1970, the owners still kept horses here...
hot sauce
THIS WAS THE BARN.
YEAH, THE BARN WITH THE BITCHIN' PATCH OF HOMEGROWN IN THE BACK.
my husband- look at all that hair!
his brothers.
sniff!
1973
I'D HEARD ALL ABOUT WHAT THE GUYS USED TO DO IN THE BARN.
Bong
Beer
Uh- Brownies

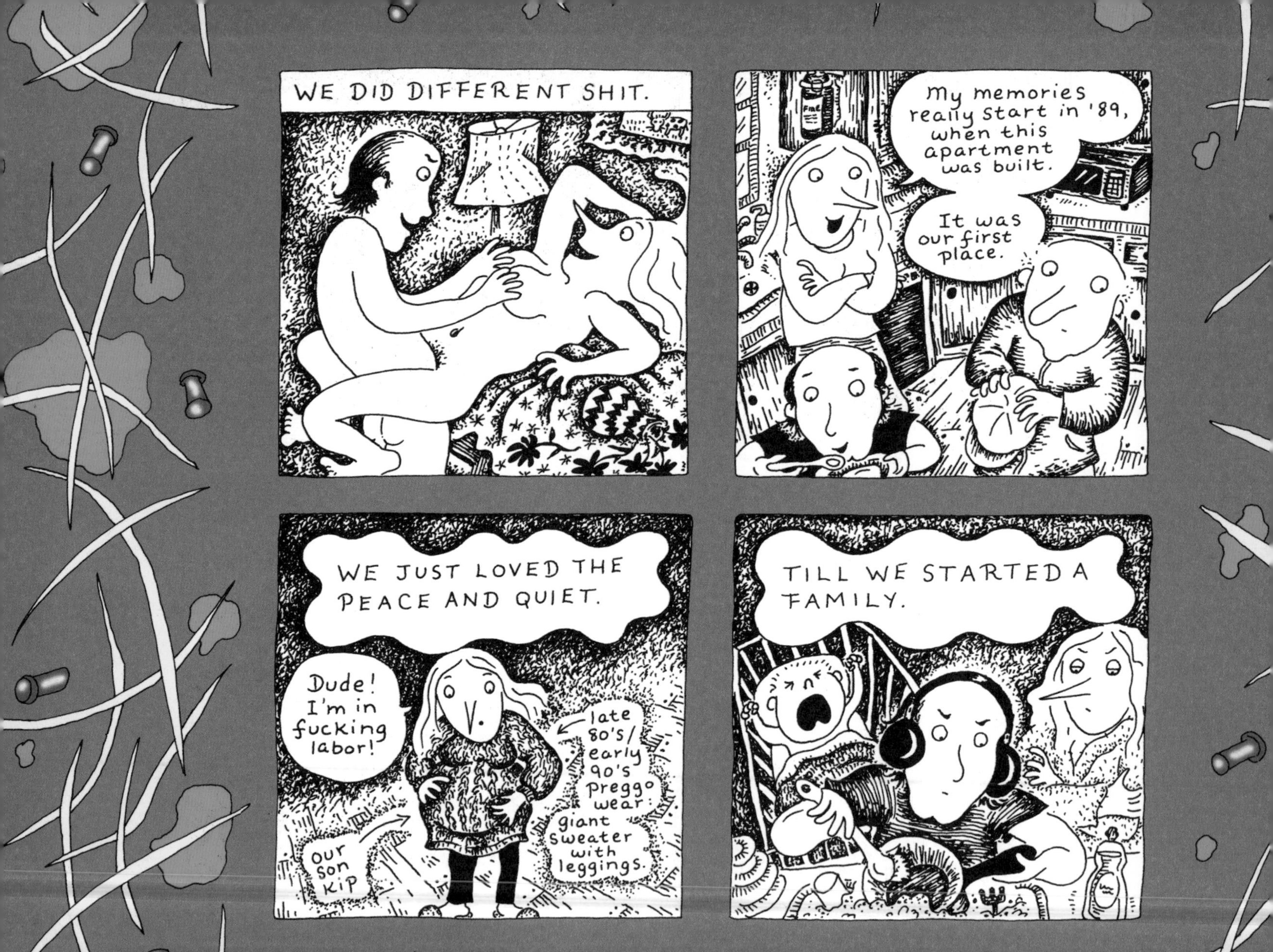
WE DID DIFFERENT SHIT.
My memories really start in '89, when this apartment was built.
It was our first place.
WE JUST LOVED THE PEACE AND QUIET.
Dude! I'm in fucking labor!
late 80's/ early 90's preggo wear:
giant sweater with leggings.
our son Kip
TILL WE STARTED A FAMILY.

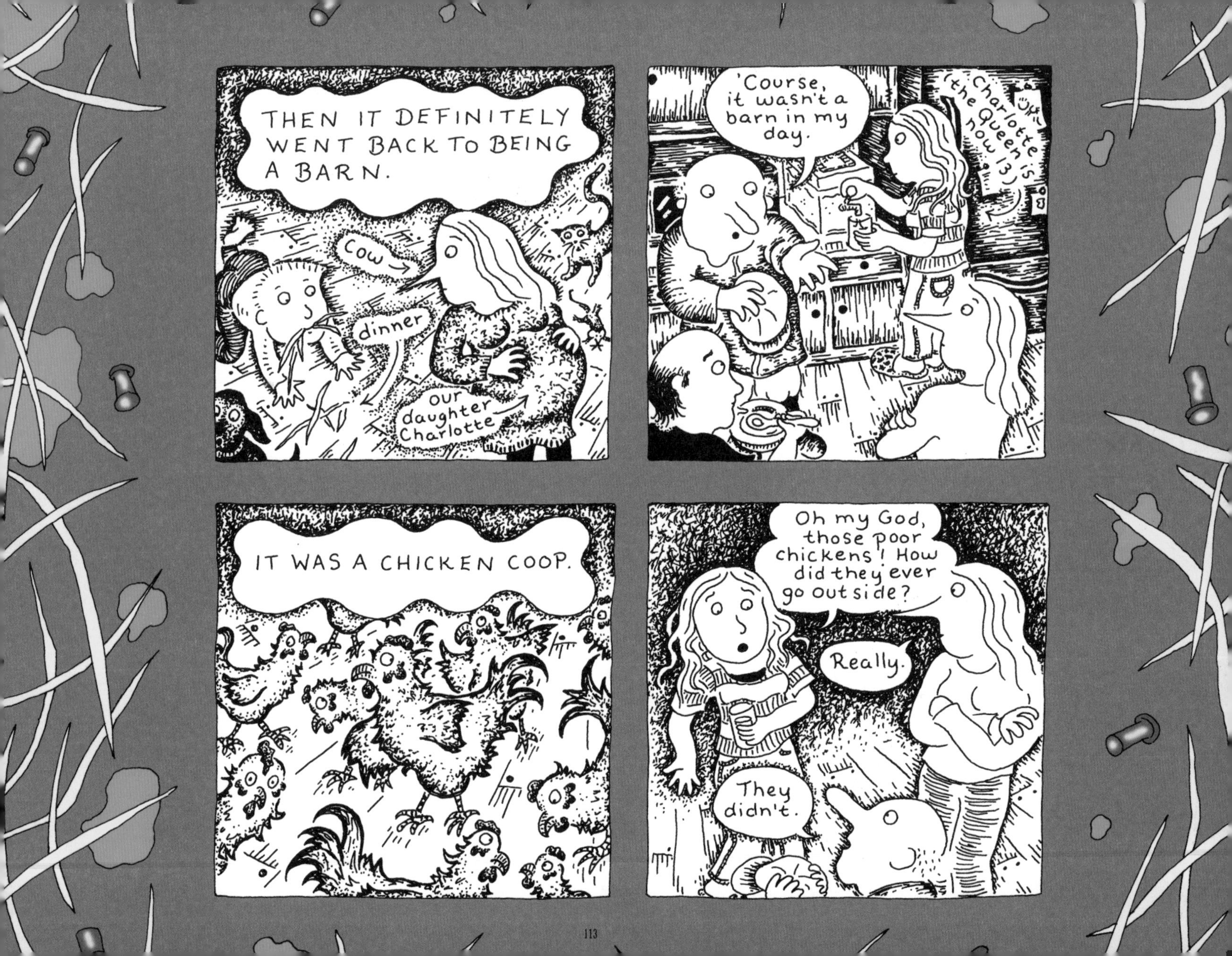
THEN IT DEFINITELY WENT BACK TO BEING A BARN.
Cow
dinner
our daughter Charlotte
'Course, it wasn't a barn in my day.
Charlotte is the Queen now
IT WAS A CHICKEN COOP.
Oh my God, those poor chickens! How did they ever go outside?
Really.
They didn't.

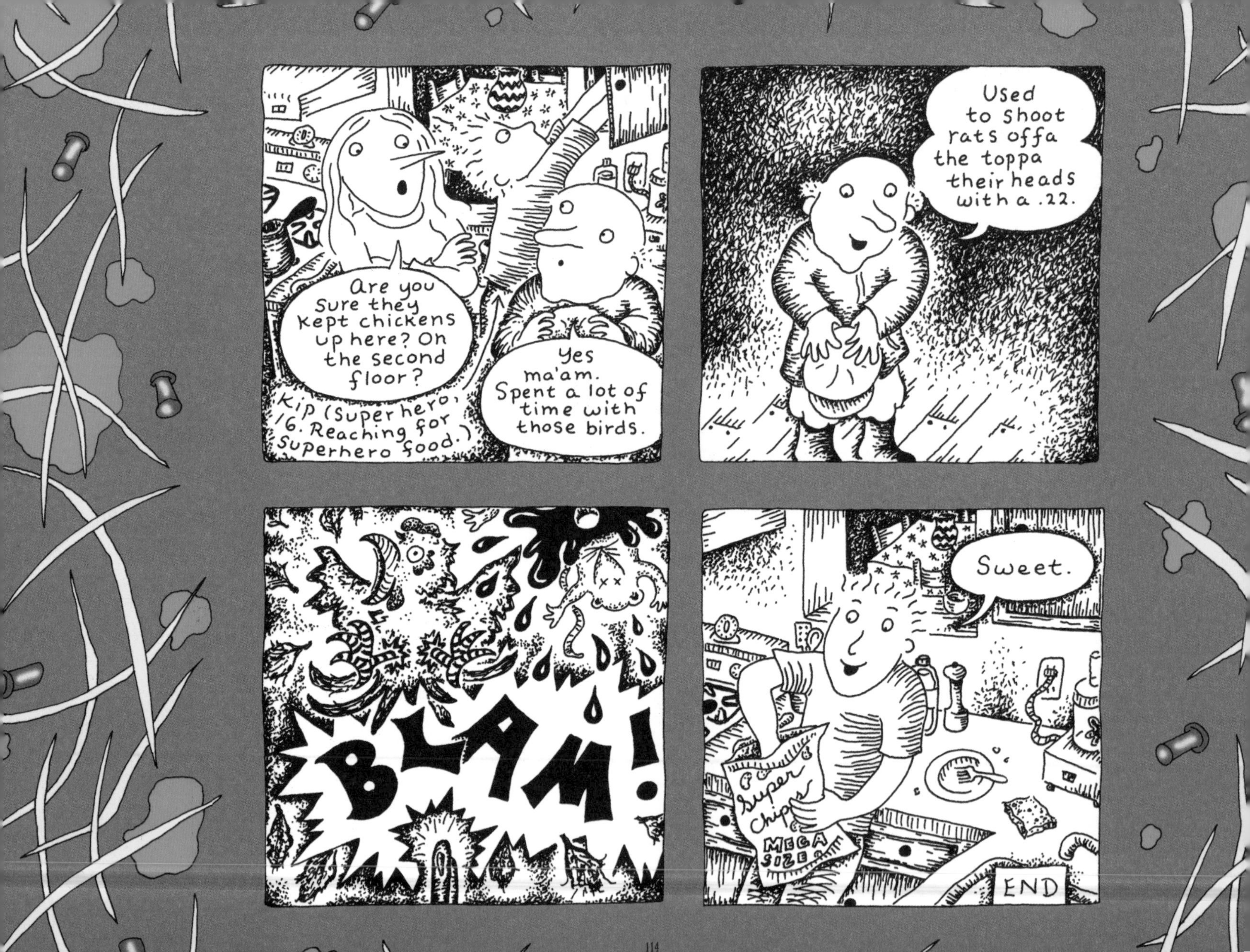
Are you sure they kept chickens up here? On the second floor?
Yes ma'am. Spent a lot of time with those birds.
Kip (Superhero, 16. Reaching for Superhero food.)
Used to shoot rats offa the toppa their heads with a .22.
BLAM!
Sweet.
Super Chips
MEGA SIZE
END

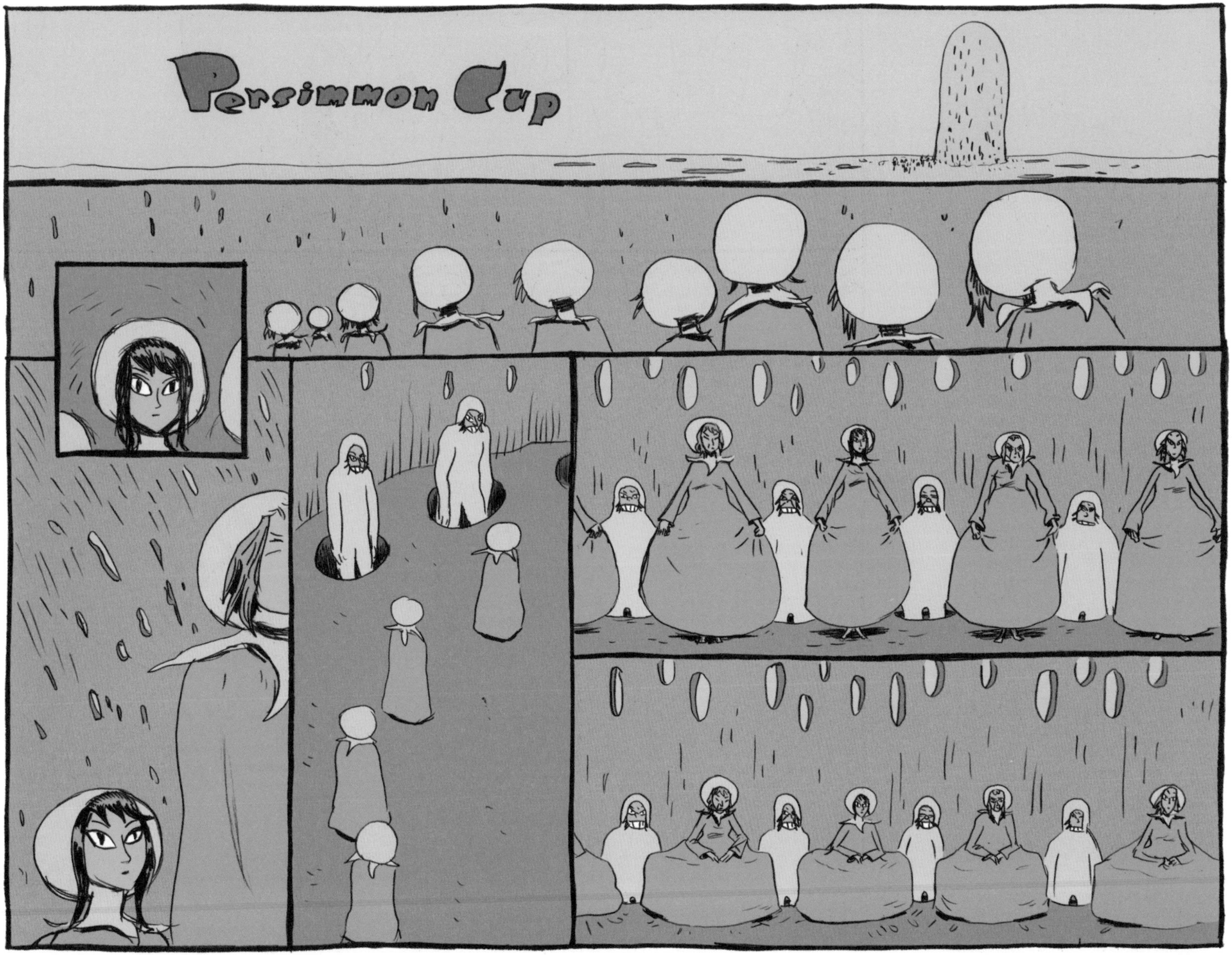
Persimmon Cup

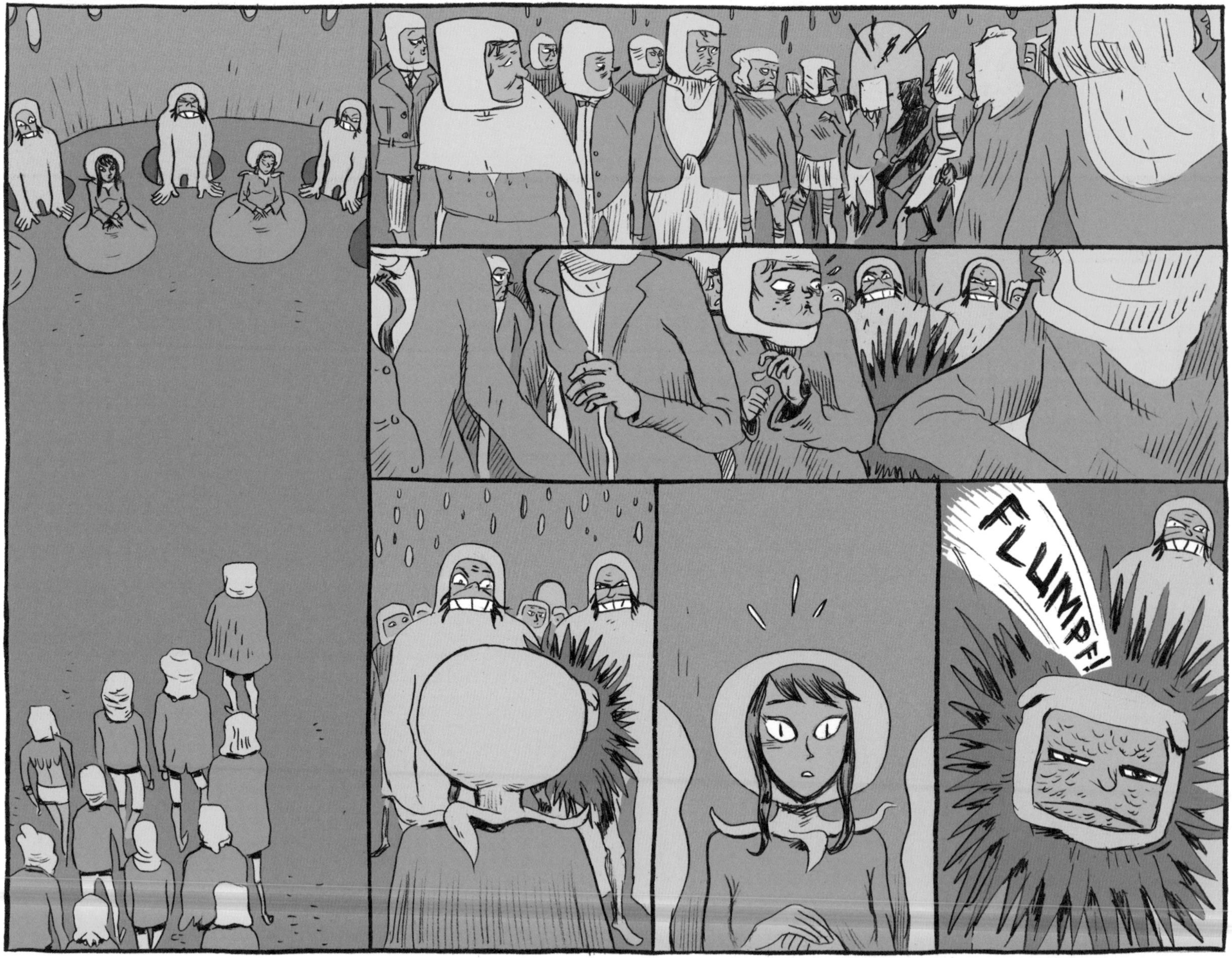
FLUMPF!

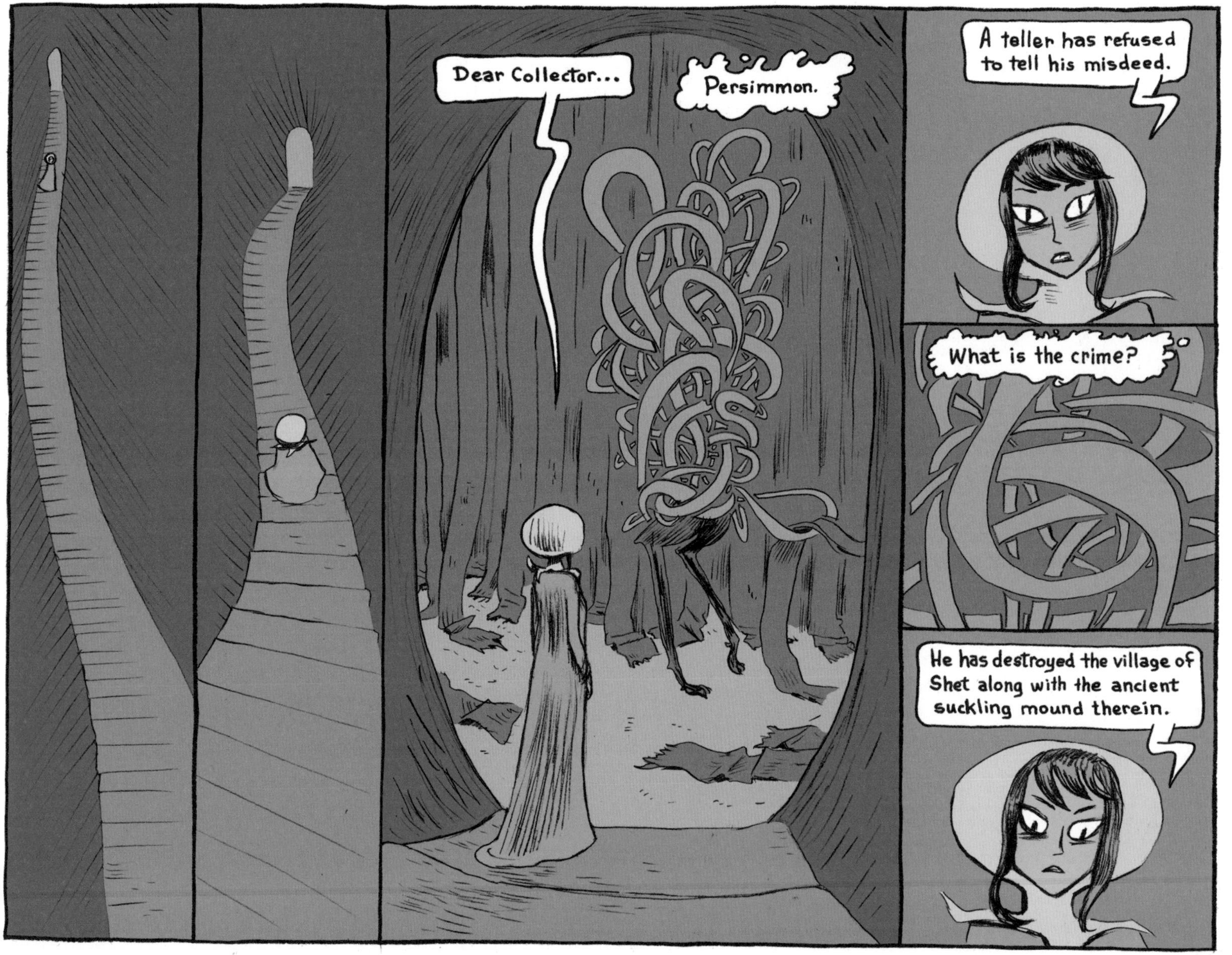
Dear Collector...
Persimmon.
A teller has refused to tell his misdeed.
What is the crime?
He has destroyed the village of Shet along with the ancient suckling mound therein.

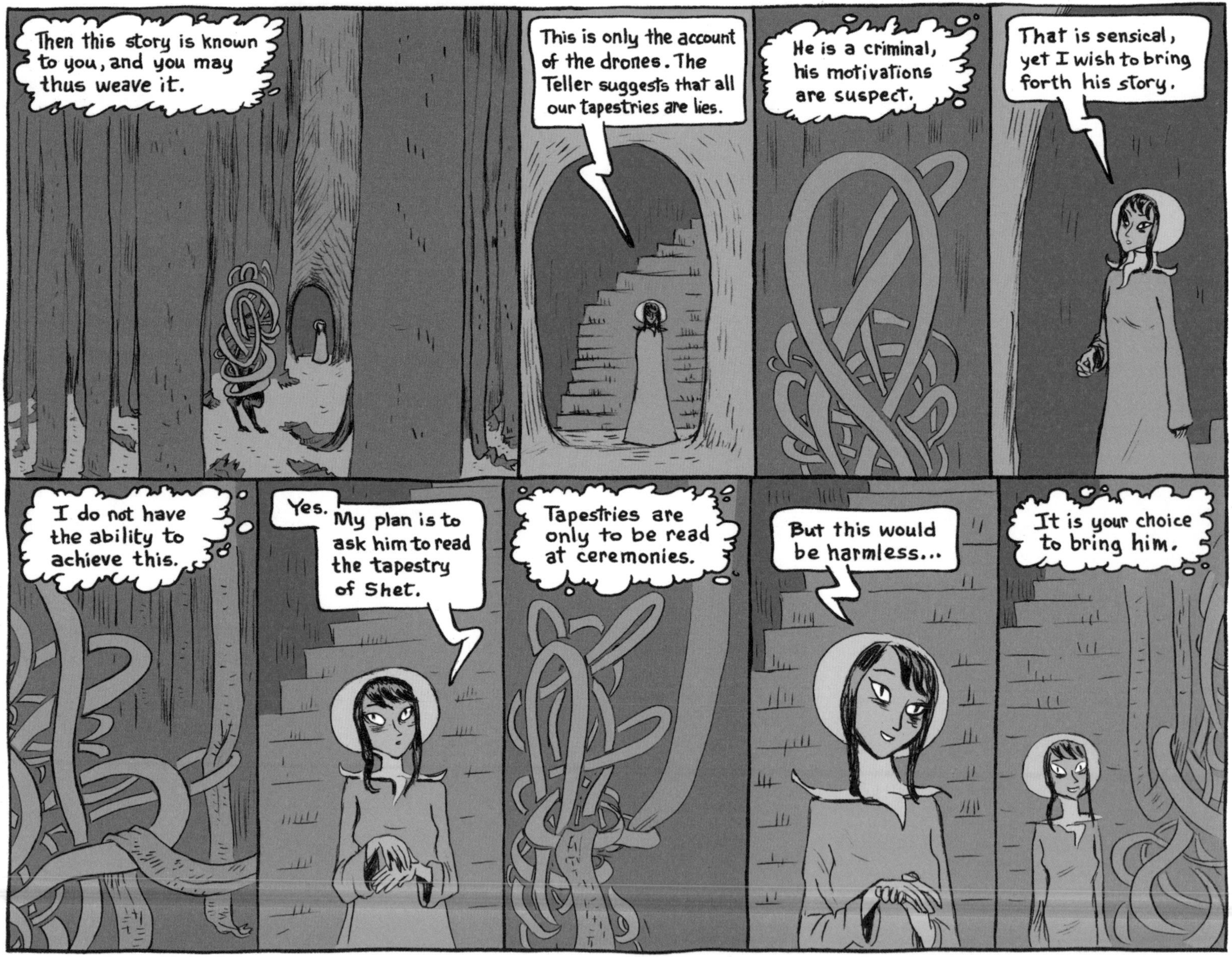
Then this story is known to you, and you may thus weave it.
This is only the account of the drones. The Teller suggests that all our tapestries are lies.
He is a criminal, his motivations are suspect.
That is sensical, yet I wish to bring forth his story.
I do not have the ability to achieve this.
Yes.
My plan is to ask him to read the tapestry of Shet.
Tapestries are only to be read at ceremonies.
But this would be harmless...
It is your choice to bring him.

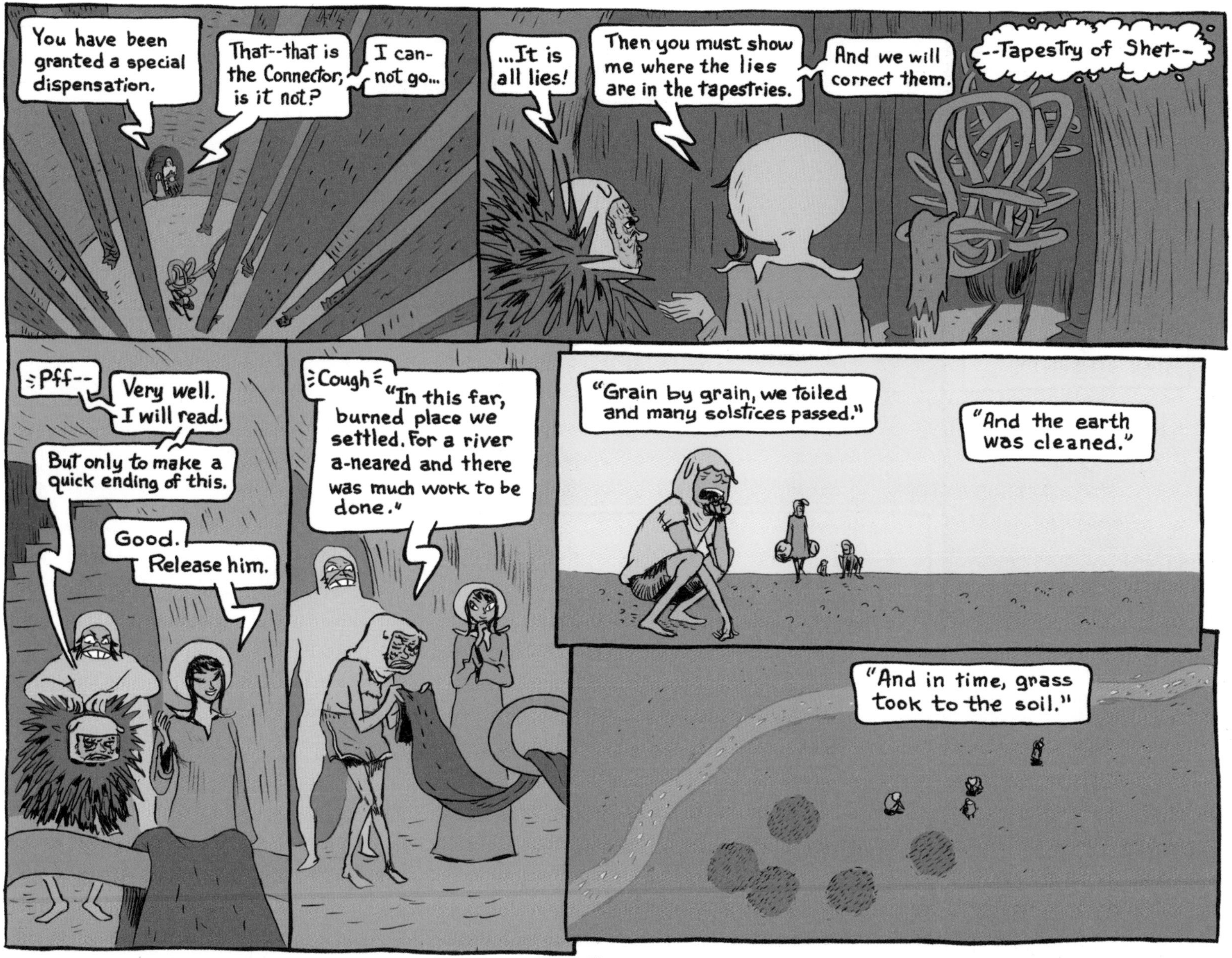
You have been granted a special dispensation.
That--that is the Connector, is it not?
I can-not go...
...It is all lies!
Then you must show me where the lies are in the tapestries.
And we will correct them.
--Tapestry of Shet--
Pff--
Very well. I will read.
But only to make a quick ending of this.
Good. Release him.
Cough
"In this far, burned place we settled. For a river a-neared and there was much work to be done."
"Grain by grain, we toiled and many solstices passed."
"And the earth was cleaned."
"And in time, grass took to the soil."

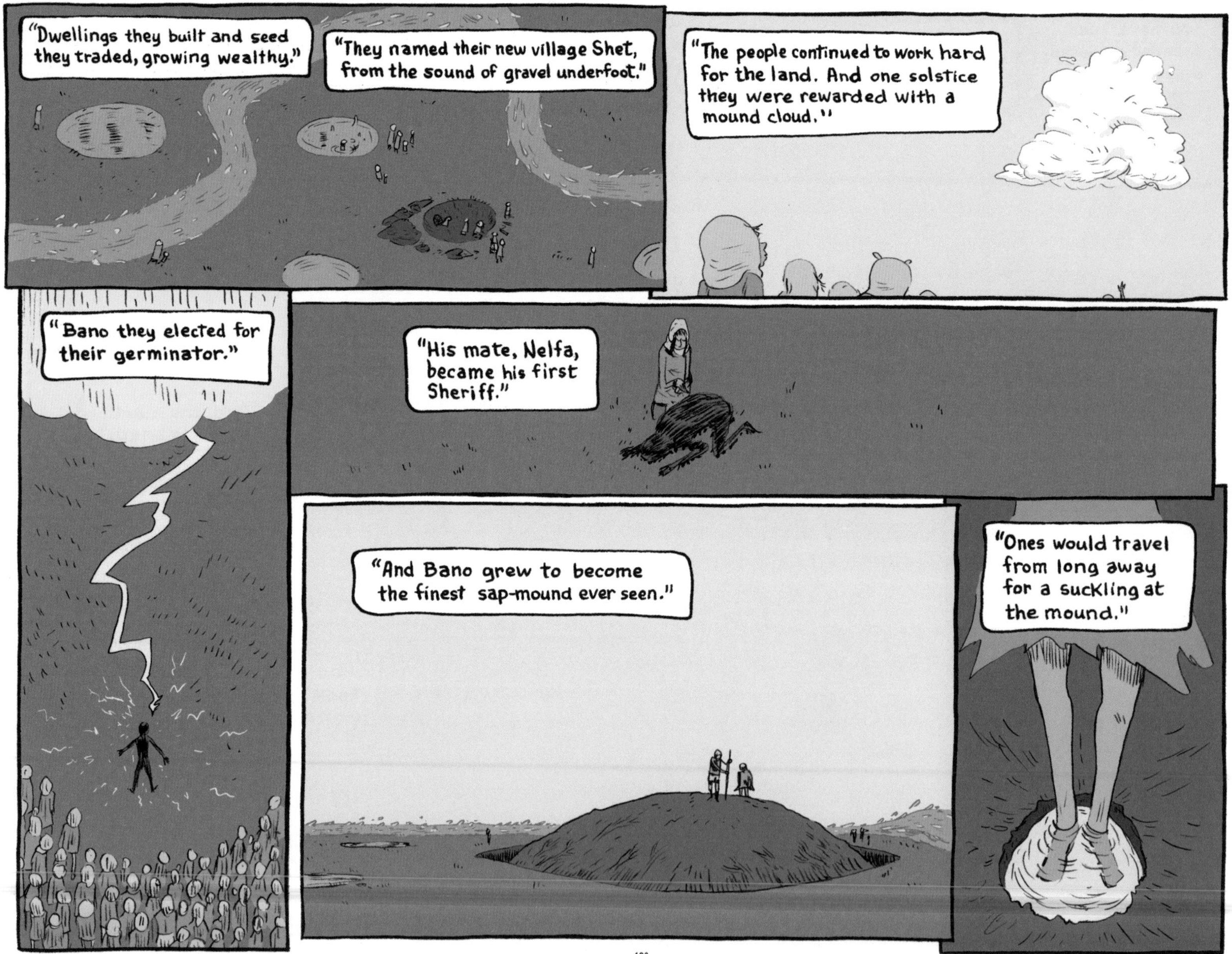
"Dwellings they built and seed they traded, growing wealthy."
"They named their new village Shet, from the sound of gravel underfoot."
"The people continued to work hard for the land. And one solstice they were rewarded with a mound cloud."
"Bano they elected for their germinator."
"His mate, Nelfa, became his first Sheriff."
"And Bano grew to become the finest sap-mound ever seen."
"Ones would travel from long away for a suckling at the mound."

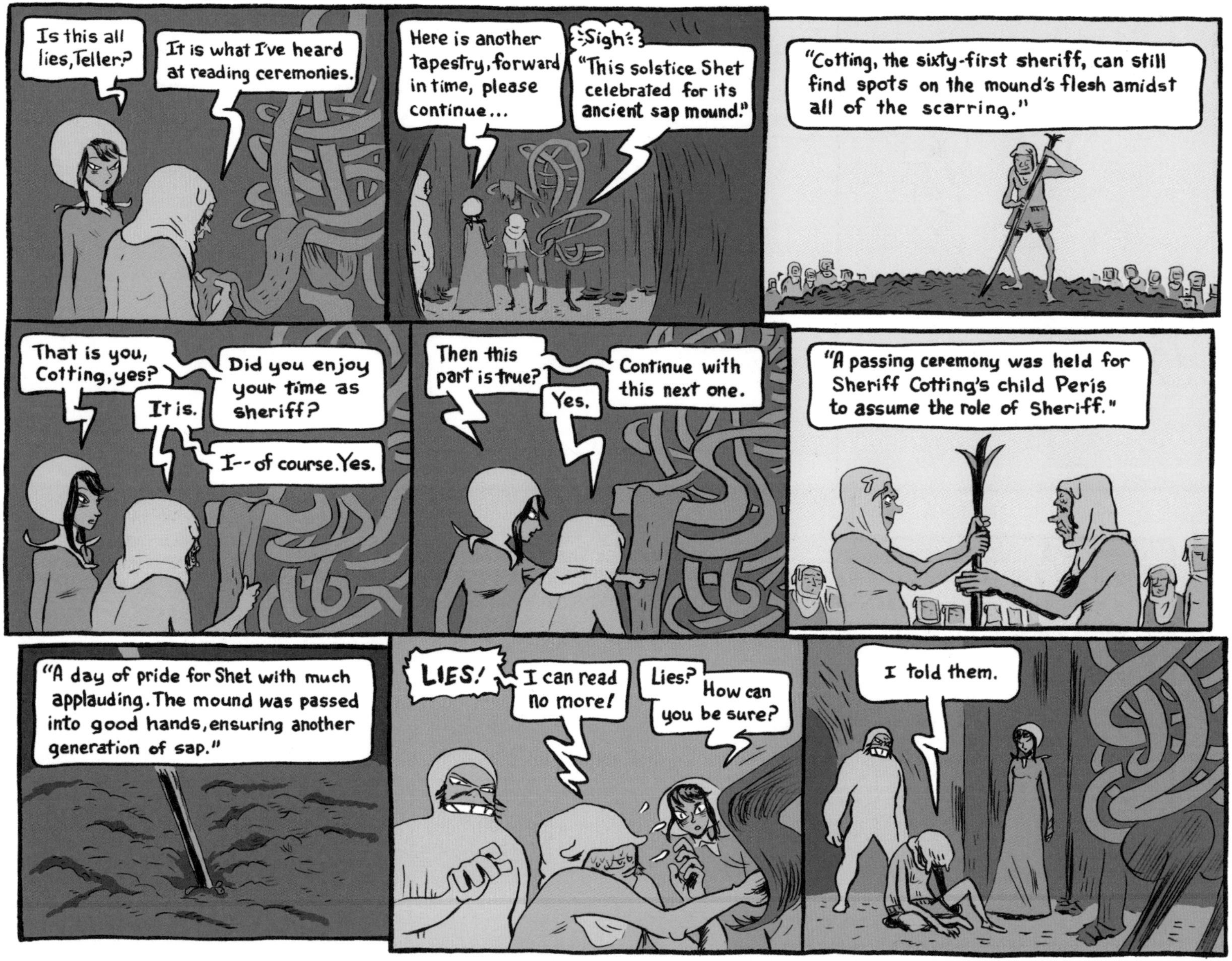

Is this all lies, Teller?
It is what I've heard at reading ceremonies.
Here is another tapestry, forward in time, please continue...
Sigh
"This solstice Shet celebrated for its ancient sap mound."
"Cotting, the sixty-first sheriff, can still find spots on the mound's flesh amidst all of the scarring."
That is you, Cotting, yes?
It is.
Did you enjoy your time as sheriff?
I-- of course. Yes.
Then this part is true?
Yes.
Continue with this next one.
"A passing ceremony was held for Sheriff Cotting's child Peris to assume the role of Sheriff."
"A day of pride for Shet with much applauding. The mound was passed into good hands, ensuring another generation of sap."
LIES!
I can read no more!
Lies? How can you be sure?
I told them.

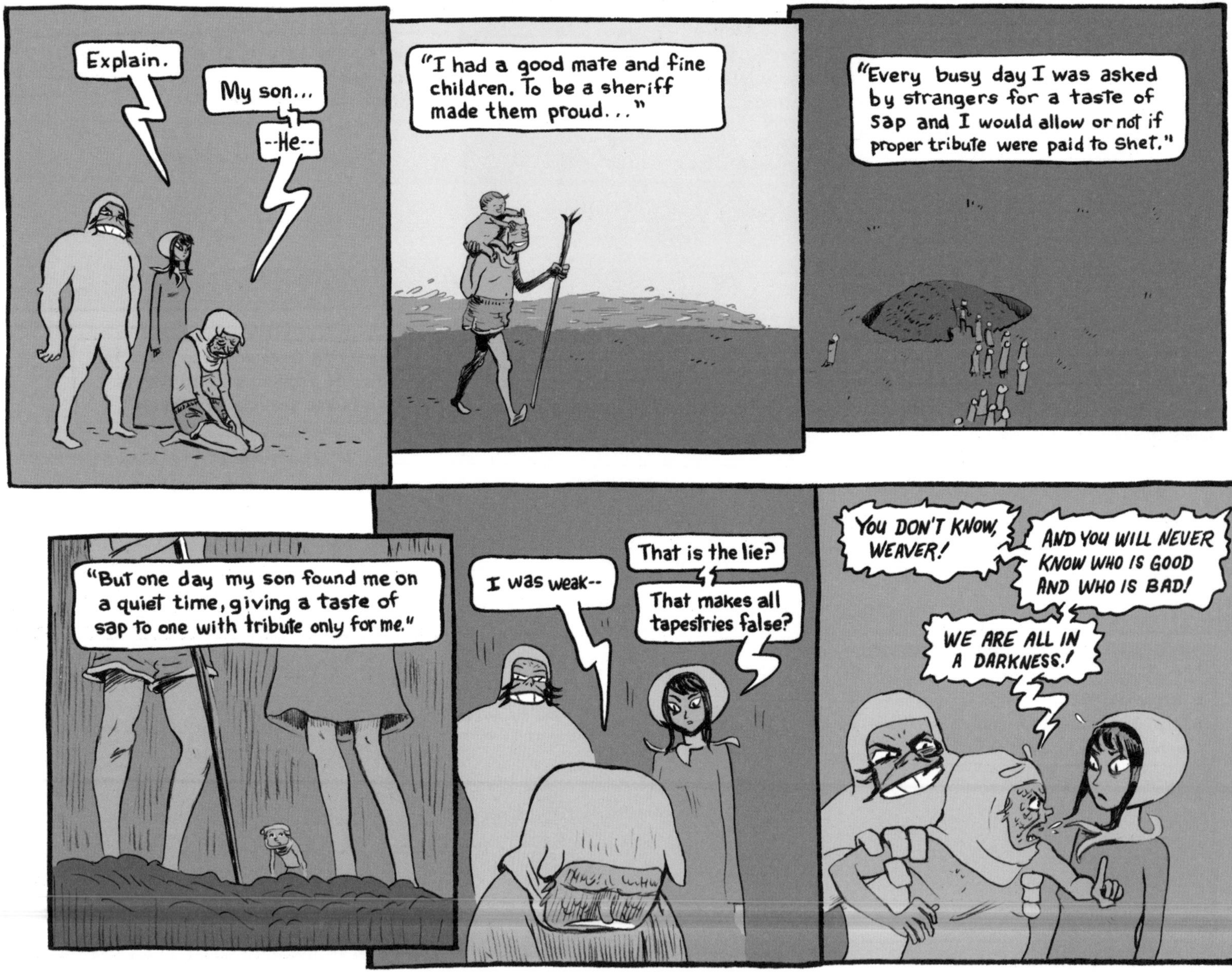
Explain.
My son...
--He--
"I had a good mate and fine children. To be a sheriff made them proud..."
"Every busy day I was asked by strangers for a taste of sap and I would allow or not if proper tribute were paid to Shet."
"But one day my son found me on a quiet time, giving a taste of sap to one with tribute only for me."
I was weak--
That is the lie?
That makes all tapestries false?
YOU DON'T KNOW, WEAVER!
AND YOU WILL NEVER KNOW WHO IS GOOD AND WHO IS BAD!
WE ARE ALL IN A DARKNESS!

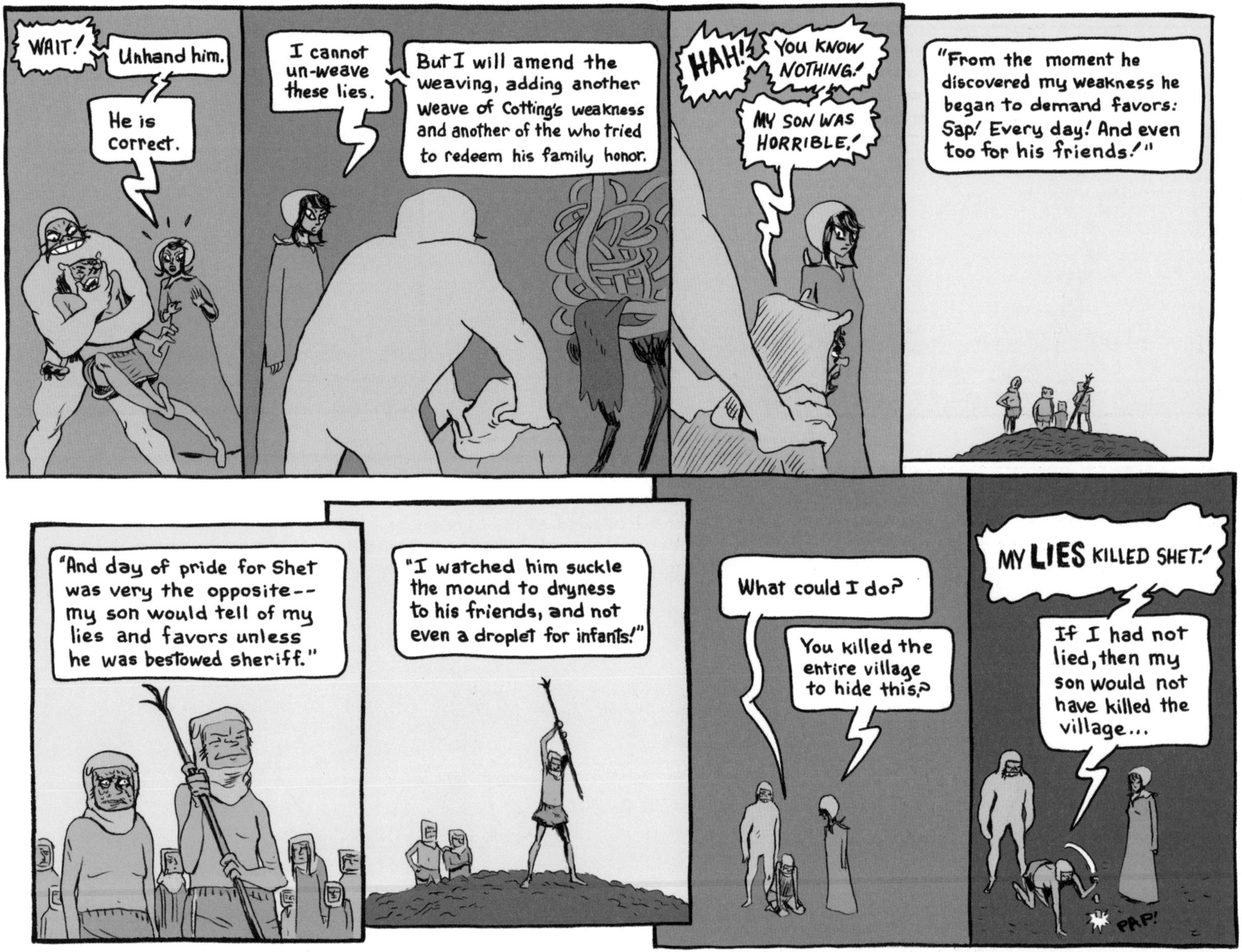
WAIT!
Unhand him.
He is correct.
I cannot un-weave these lies.
But I will amend the weaving, adding another weave of Cotting's weakness and another of the who tried to redeem his family honor.
HAH!
YOU KNOW NOTHING!
MY SON WAS HORRIBLE!
"From the moment he discovered my weakness he began to demand favors: Sap! Every day! And even too for his friends!"
"And day of pride for Shet was very the opposite-- my son would tell of my lies and favors unless he was bestowed sheriff."
"I watched him suckle the mound to dryness to his friends, and not even a droplet for infants!"
What could I do?
You killed the entire village to hide this?
MY LIES KILLED SHET!
If I had not lied, then my son would not have killed the village...
PAP!

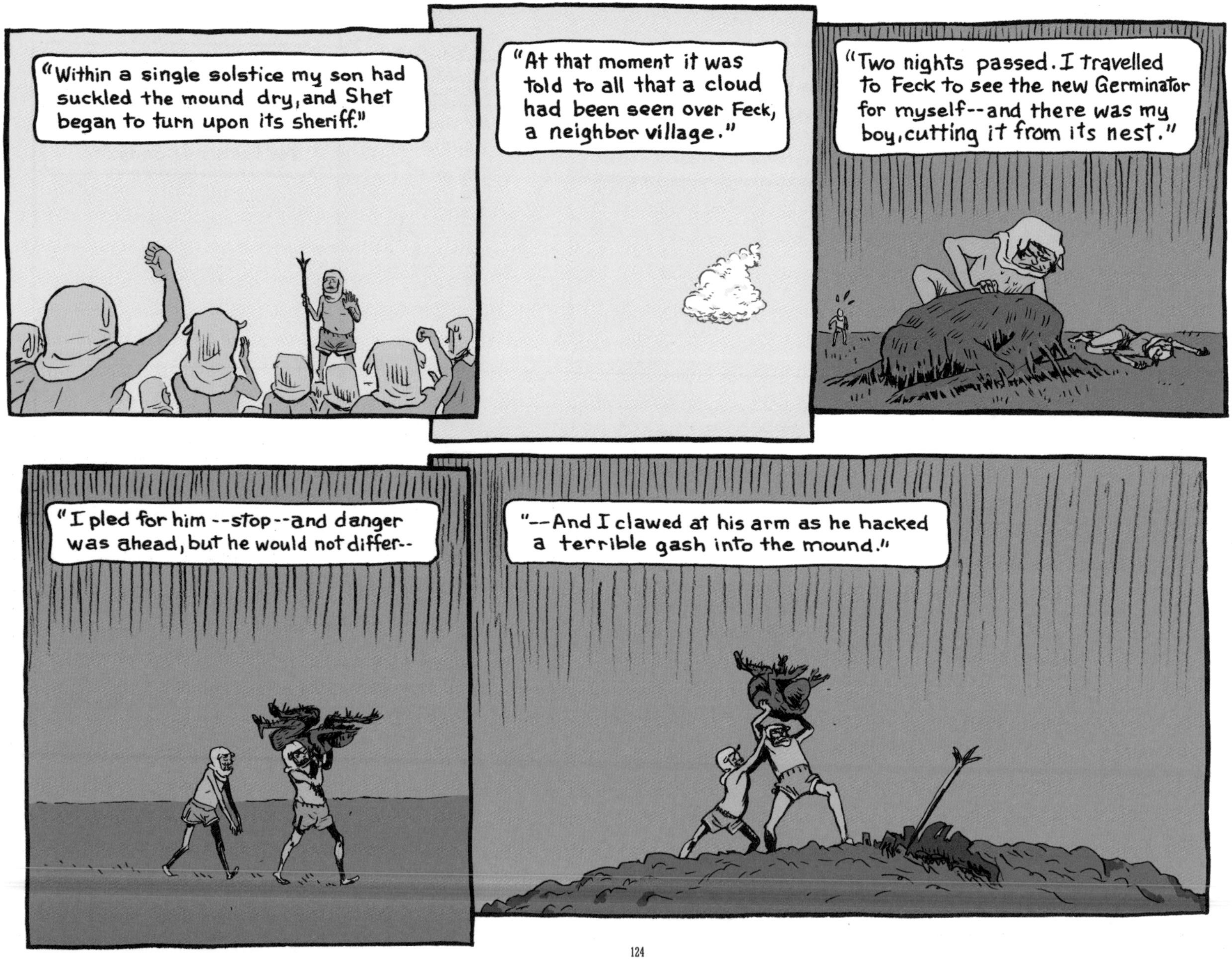
"Within a single solstice my son had suckled the mound dry, and Shet began to turn upon its sheriff."
"At that moment it was told to all that a cloud had been seen over Feck, a neighbor village."
"Two nights passed. I travelled to Feck to see the new Germinator for myself--and there was my boy, cutting it from its nest."
"I pled for him --stop--and danger was ahead, but he would not differ--
"--And I clawed at his arm as he hacked a terrible gash into the mound."

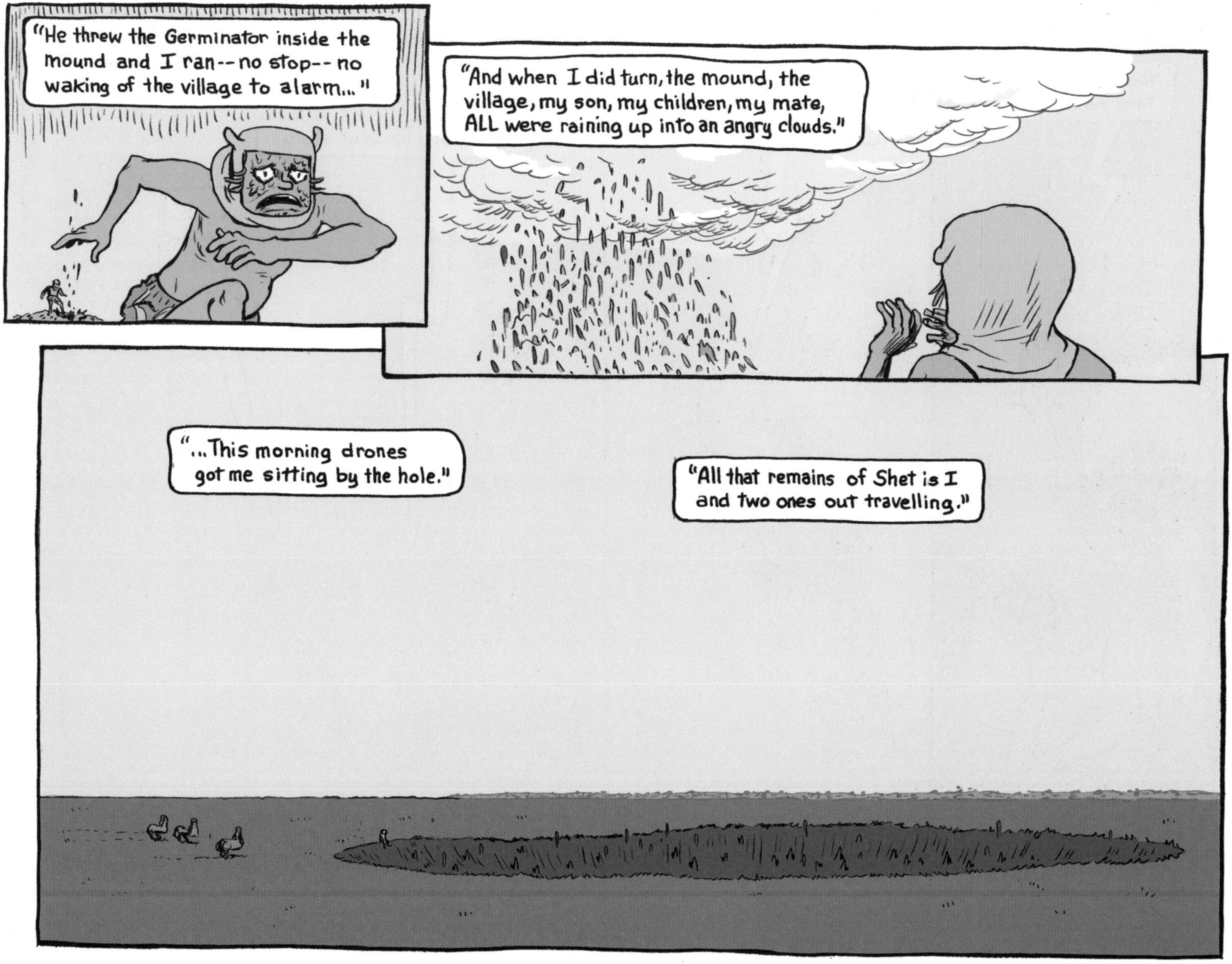
"He threw the Germinator inside the mound and I ran-- no stop-- no waking of the village to alarm..."
"And when I did turn, the mound, the village, my son, my children, my mate, ALL were raining up into an angry clouds."
"...This morning drones got me sitting by the hole."
"All that remains of Shet is I and two ones out travelling."

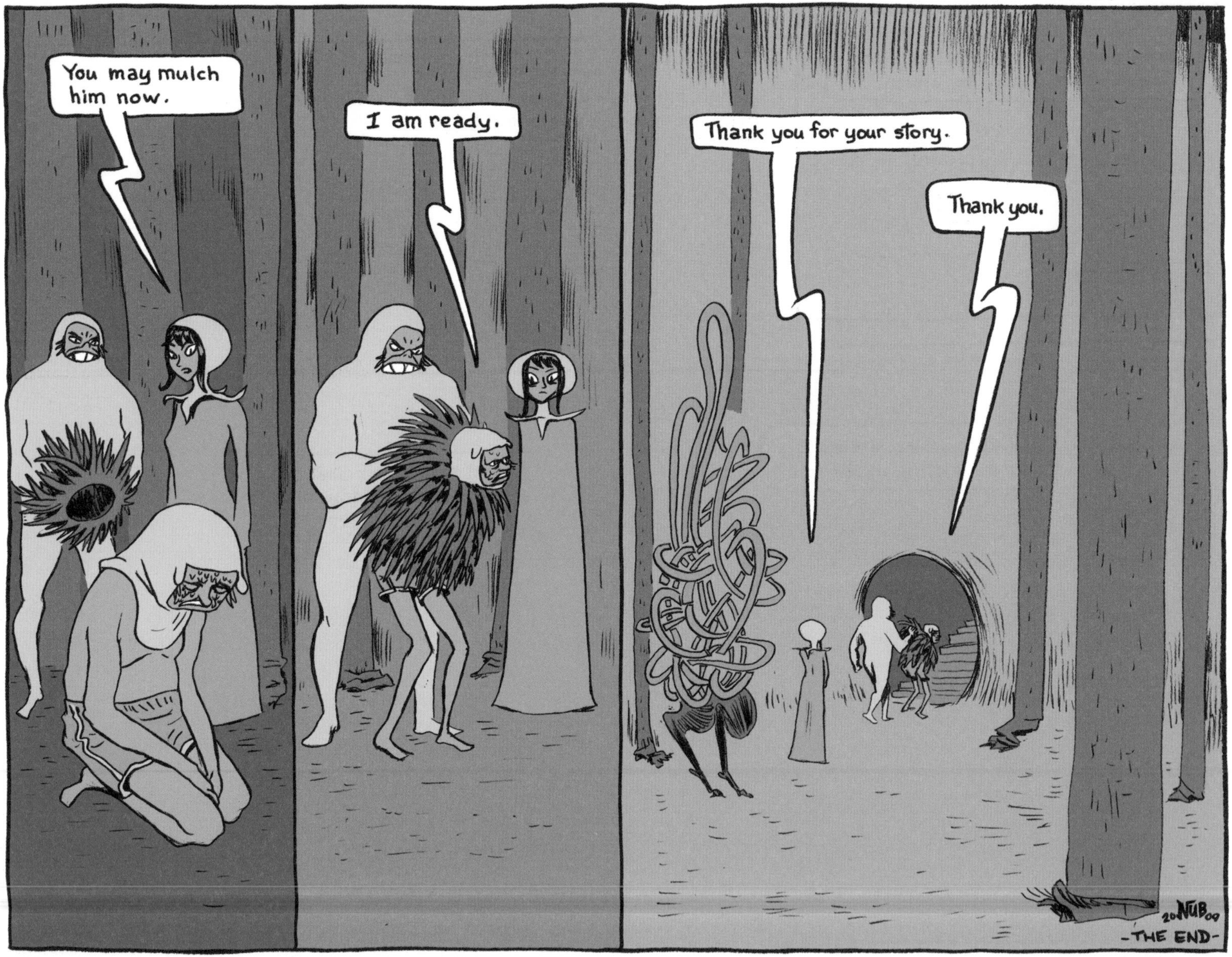
You may mulch him now.
I am ready.
Thank you for your story.
Thank you.
20 NUB 09
-THE END-

colored by Chris Sinderson sinderson.com

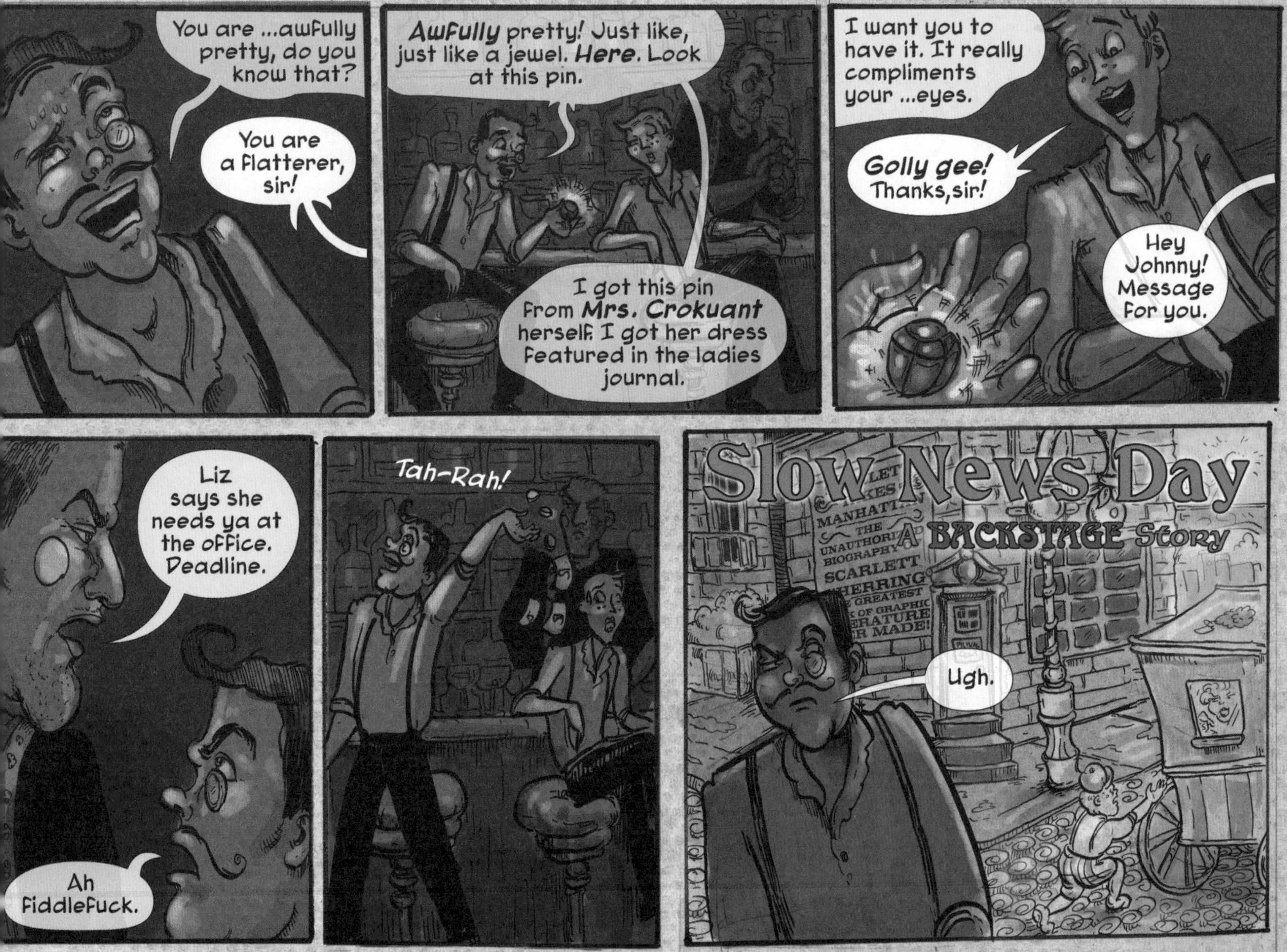
You are ...awfully pretty, do you know that?
You are a flatterer, sir!
Awfully pretty! Just like, just like a jewel. Here. Look at this pin.
I got this pin from Mrs. Crokuant herself. I got her dress featured in the ladies journal.
I want you to have it. It really compliments your ...eyes.
Golly gee! Thanks, sir!
Hey Johnny! Message for you.
Liz says she needs ya at the office. Deadline.
Ah Fiddlefuck.
Tah-Rah!
Slow News Day
A BACKSTAGE Story
Ugh.

Written by John Leavitt - Art by Molly Crabapple - Lettering by Chris Lowrance

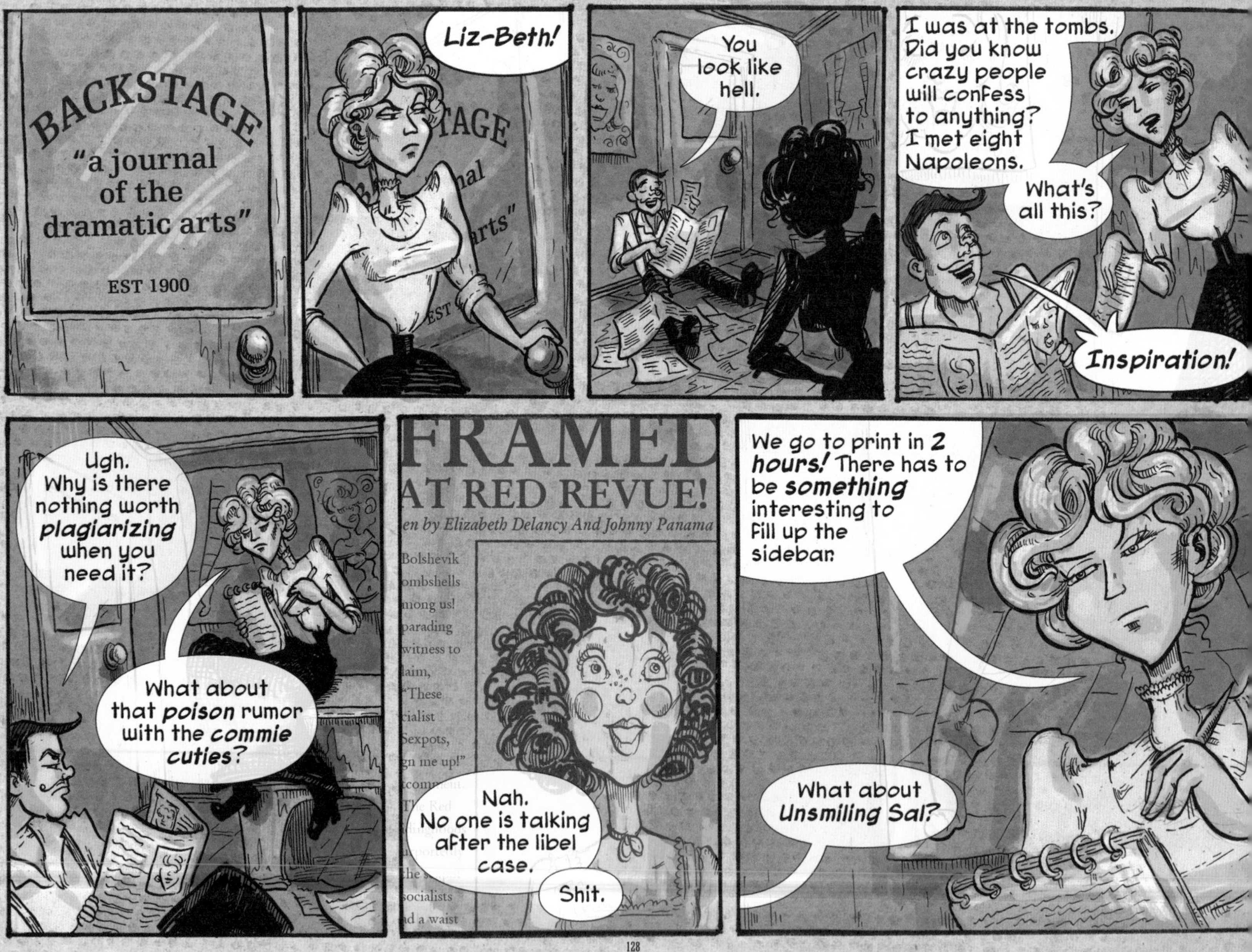

BACKSTAGE
"a journal of the dramatic arts"
EST 1900
Liz-Beth!
You look like hell.
I was at the tombs. Did you know crazy people will confess to anything? I met eight Napoleons.
What's all this?
Inspiration!
Ugh. Why is there nothing worth plagiarizing when you need it?
What about that poison rumor with the commie cuties?
FRAMED AT RED REVUE!
en by Elizabeth Delancy And Johnny Panama
Bolshevik
ombshells
mong us!
parading
witness to
laim,
"These
cialist
Sexpots,
gn me up!"
Nah. No one is talking after the libel case.
Shit.
We go to print in 2 hours! There has to be something interesting to fill up the sidebar.
What about Unsmiling Sal?

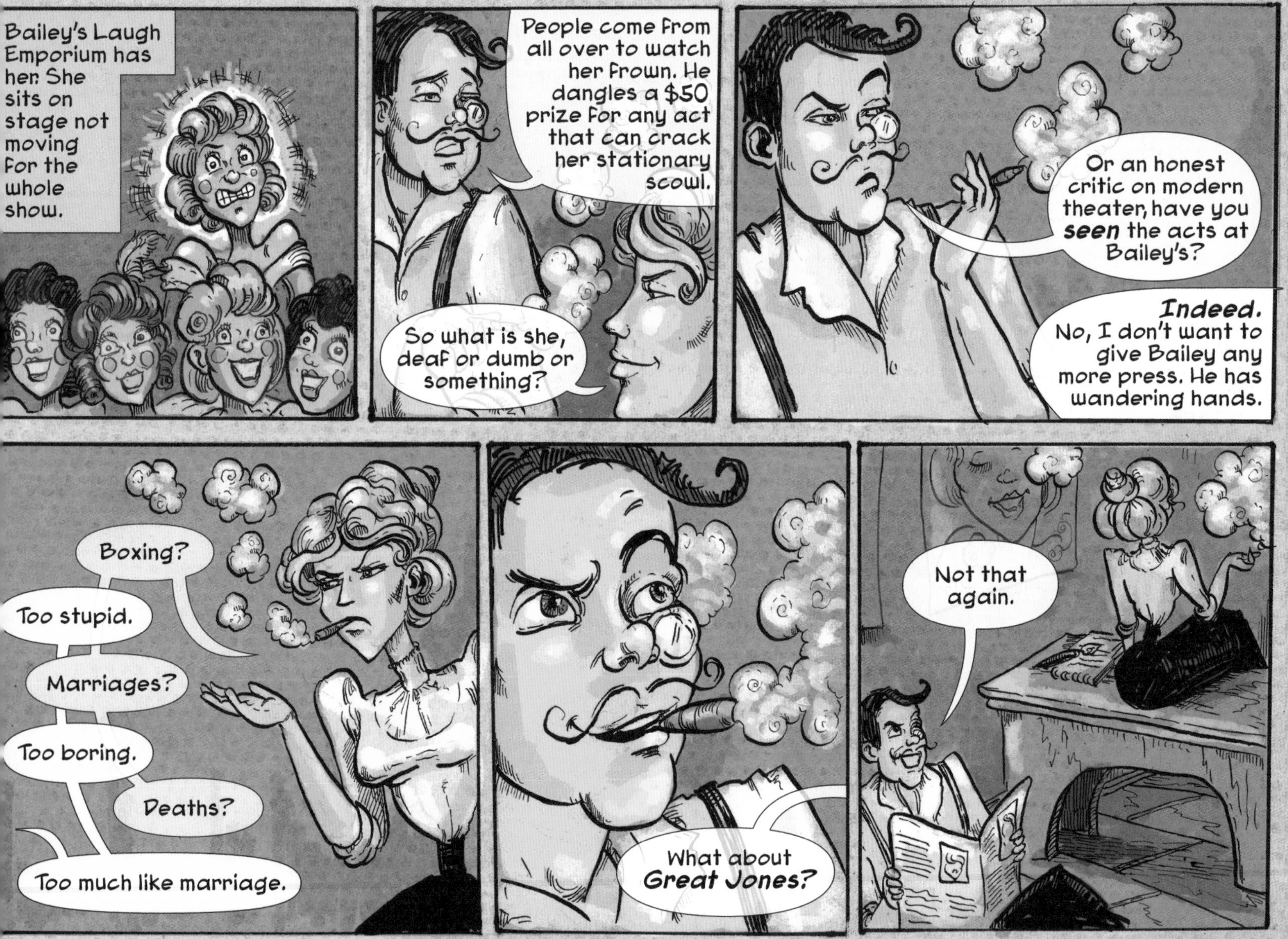
Bailey's Laugh Emporium has her. She sits on stage not moving for the whole show.
People come from all over to watch her frown. He dangles a $50 prize for any act that can crack her stationary scowl.
So what is she, deaf or dumb or something?
Or an honest critic on modern theater, have you *seen* the acts at Bailey's?
Indeed. No, I don't want to give Bailey any more press. He has wandering hands.
Boxing?
Too stupid.
Marriages?
Too boring.
Deaths?
Too much like marriage.
What about *Great Jones?*
Not that again.

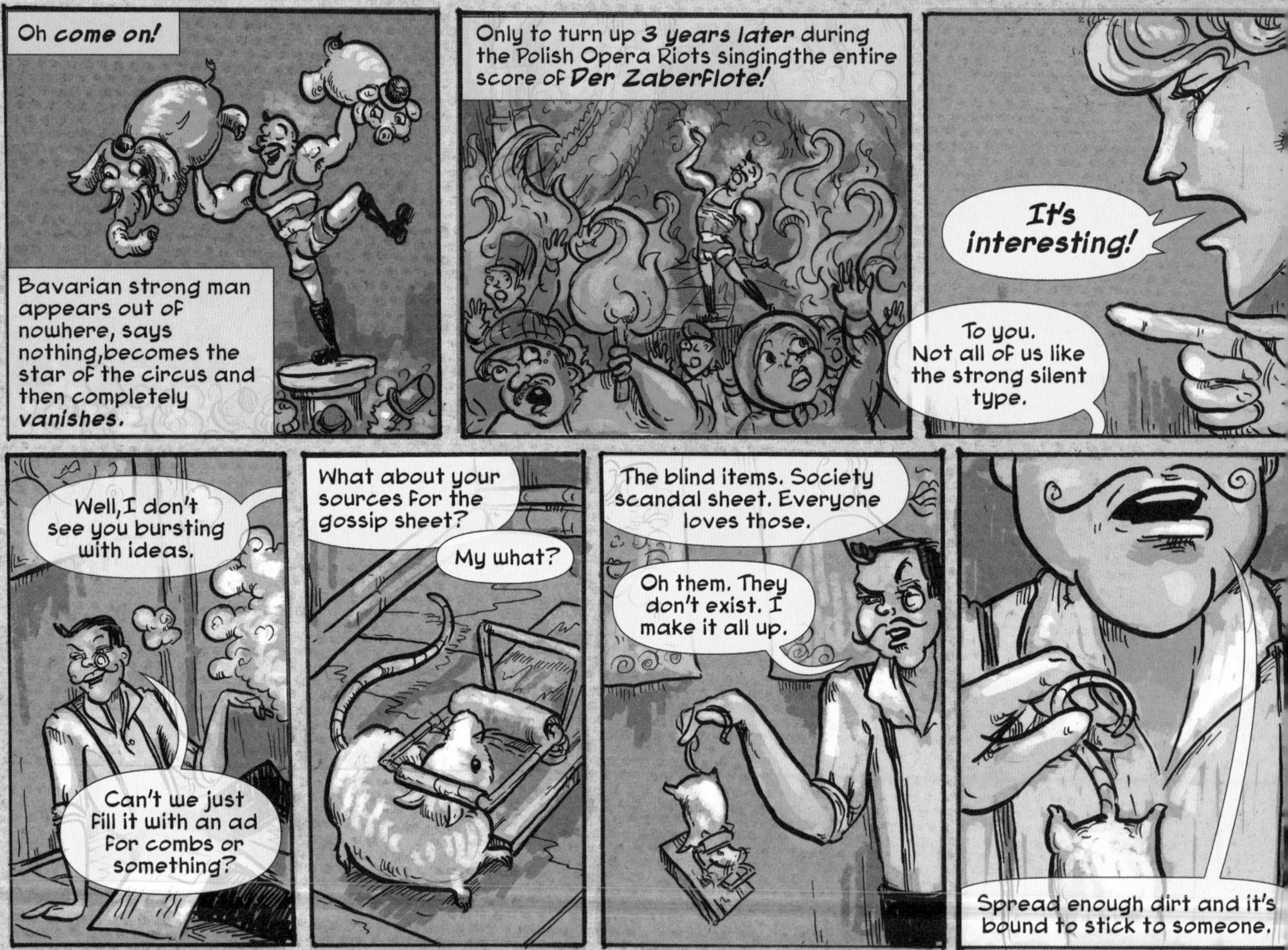
Oh come on!
Bavarian strong man appears out of nowhere, says nothing,becomes the star of the circus and then completely vanishes.
Only to turn up 3 years later during the Polish Opera Riots singingthe entire score of Der Zaberflote!
It's interesting!
To you. Not all of us like the strong silent type.
Well,I don't see you bursting with ideas.
Can't we just fill it with an ad for combs or something?
What about your sources for the gossip sheet?
My what?
The blind items. Society scandal sheet. Everyone loves those.
Oh them. They don't exist. I make it all up.
Spread enough dirt and it's bound to stick to someone.

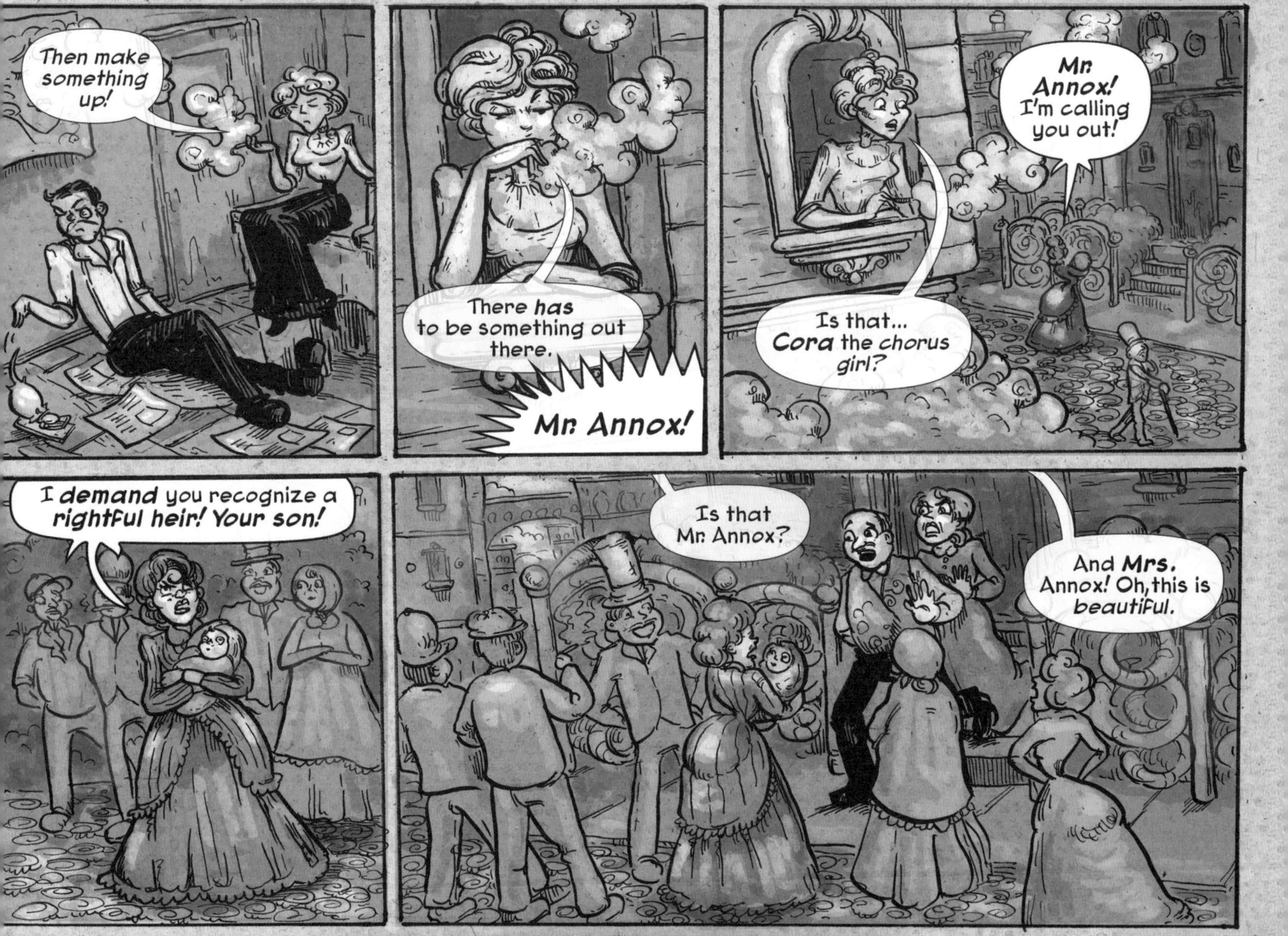
Then make something up!
There has to be something out there.
Mr. Annox!
Is that... Cora the chorus girl?
Mr. Annox! I'm calling you out!
I demand you recognize a rightful heir! Your son!
Is that Mr. Annox?
And Mrs. Annox! Oh, this is beautiful.

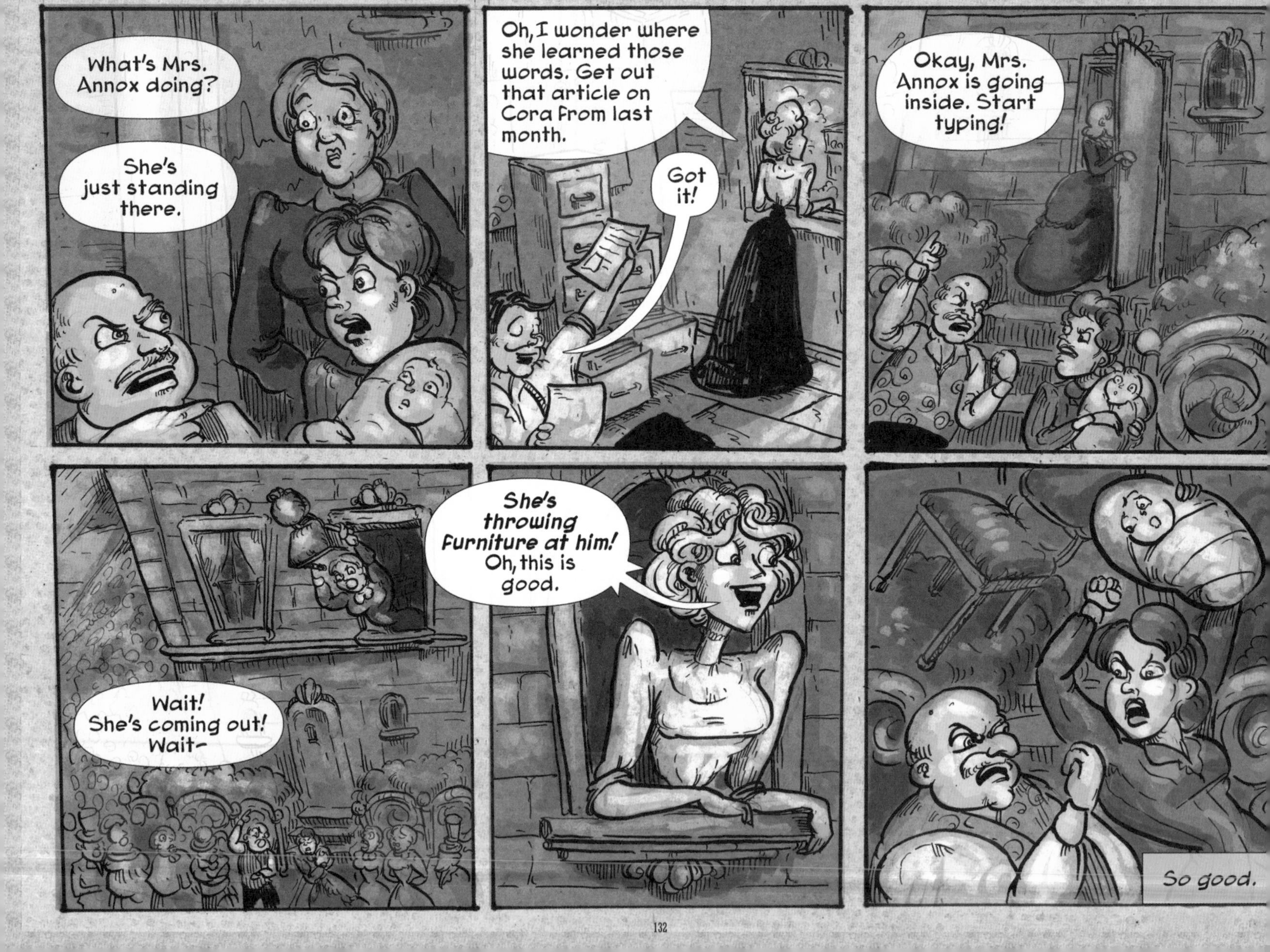
What's Mrs. Annox doing?
She's just standing there.
Oh, I wonder where she learned those words. Get out that article on Cora from last month.
Got it!
Okay, Mrs. Annox is going inside. Start typing!
Wait! She's coming out! Wait-
She's throwing furniture at him! Oh, this is good.
So good.

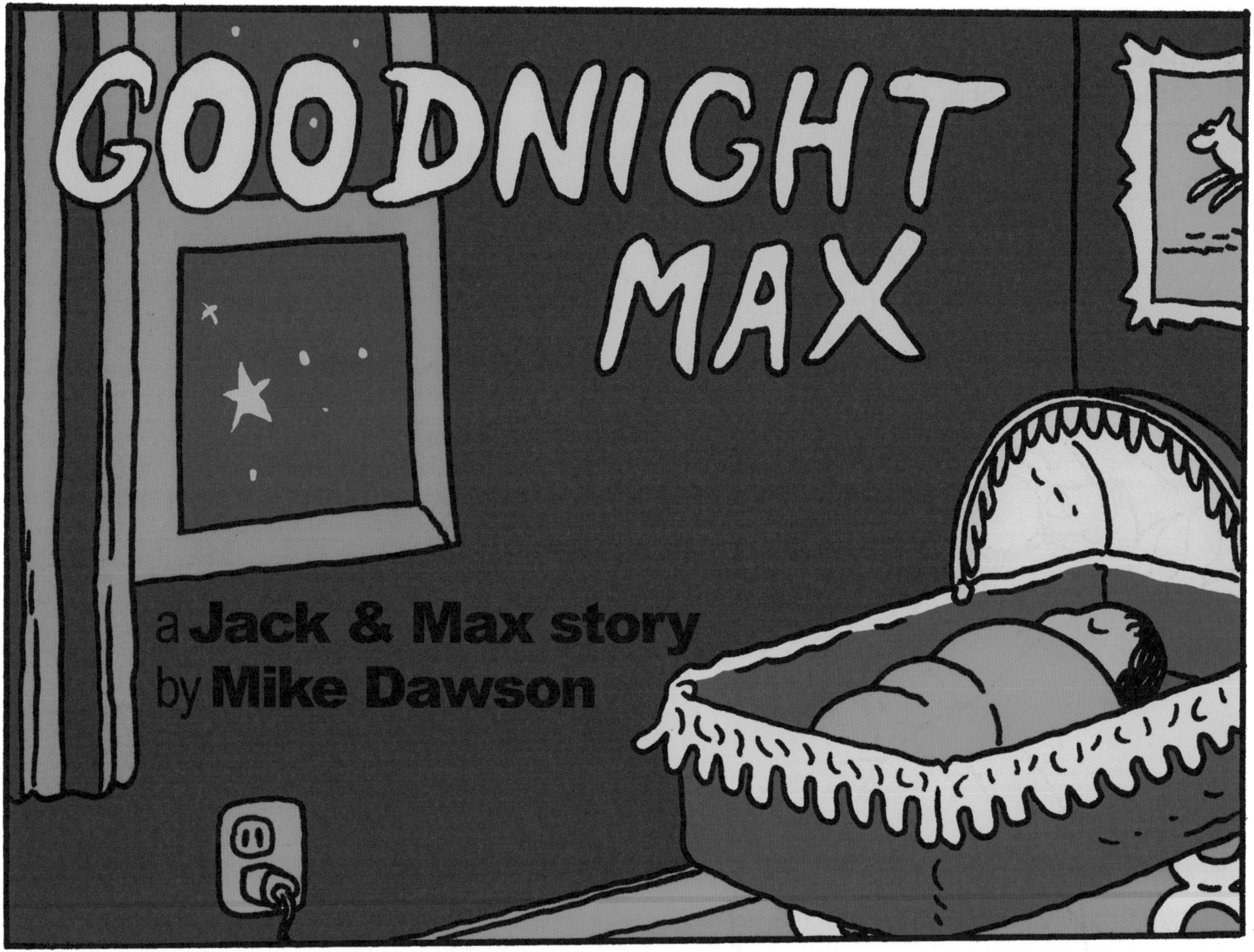
GOODNIGHT
MAX
a Jack & Max story
by Mike Dawson

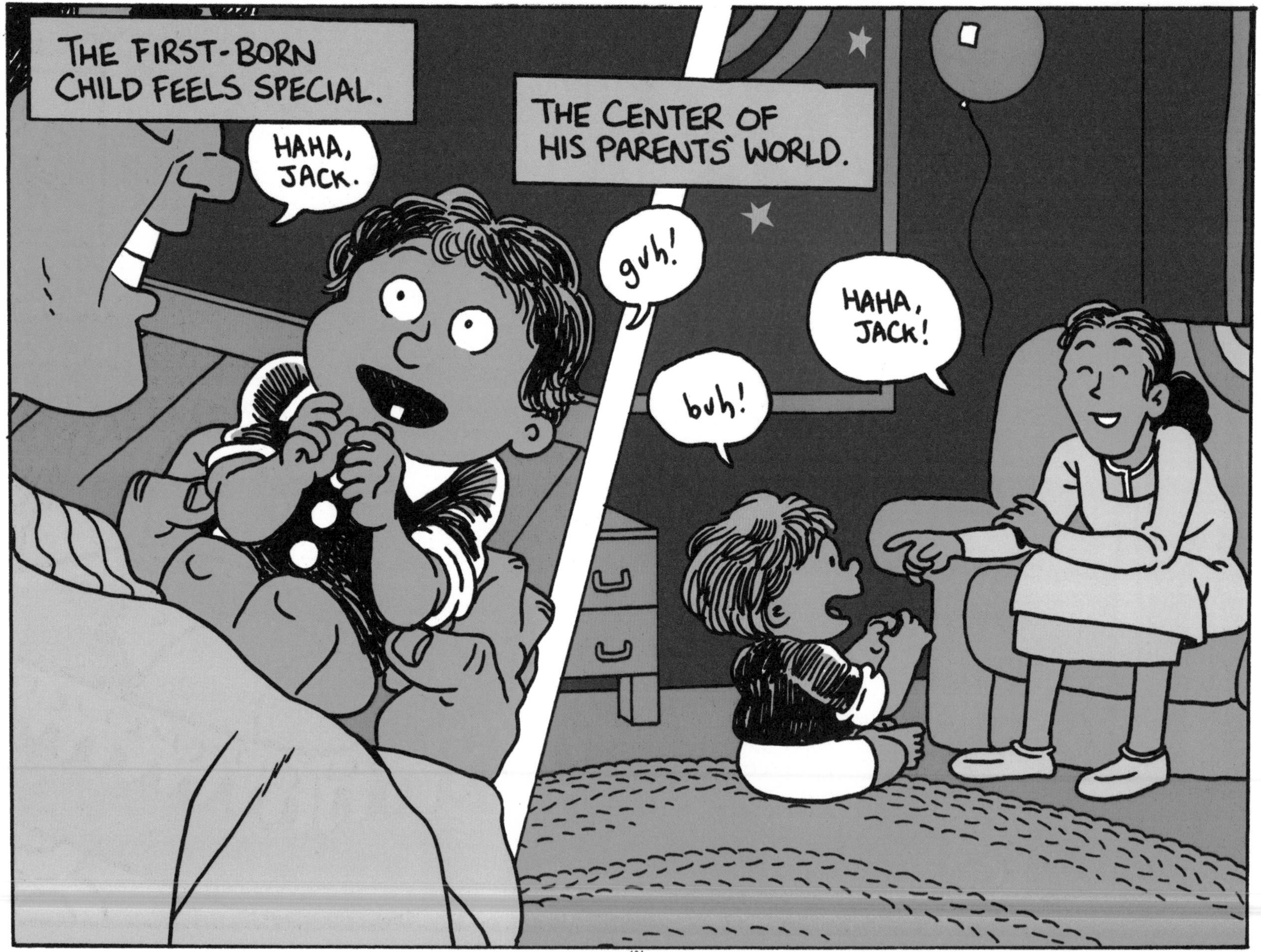
THE FIRST-BORN CHILD FEELS SPECIAL.
HAHA, JACK.
THE CENTER OF HIS PARENTS' WORLD.
guh!
buh!
HAHA, JACK!

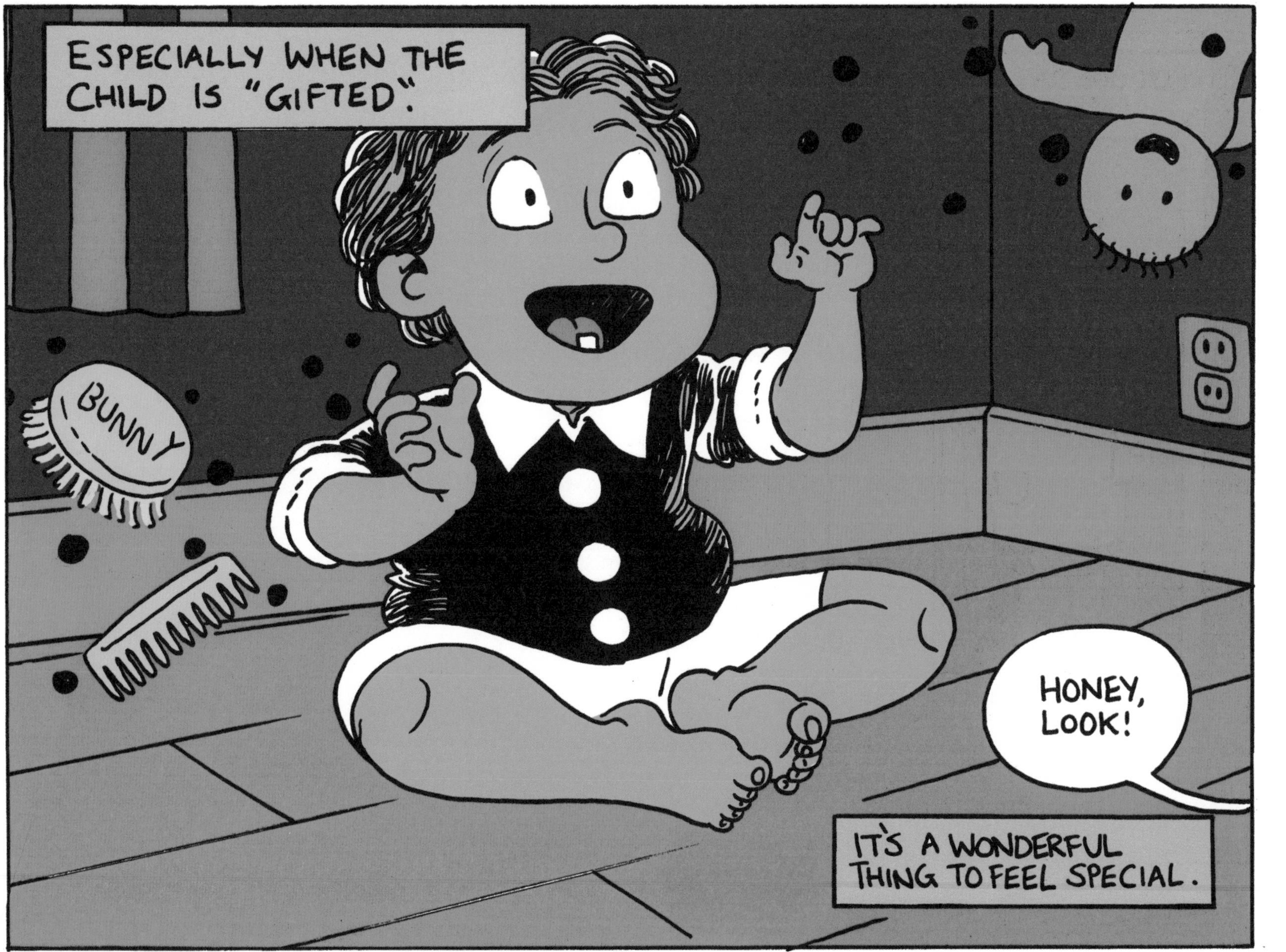
ESPECIALLY WHEN THE CHILD IS "GIFTED".
BUNNY
HONEY, LOOK!
IT'S A WONDERFUL THING TO FEEL SPECIAL.

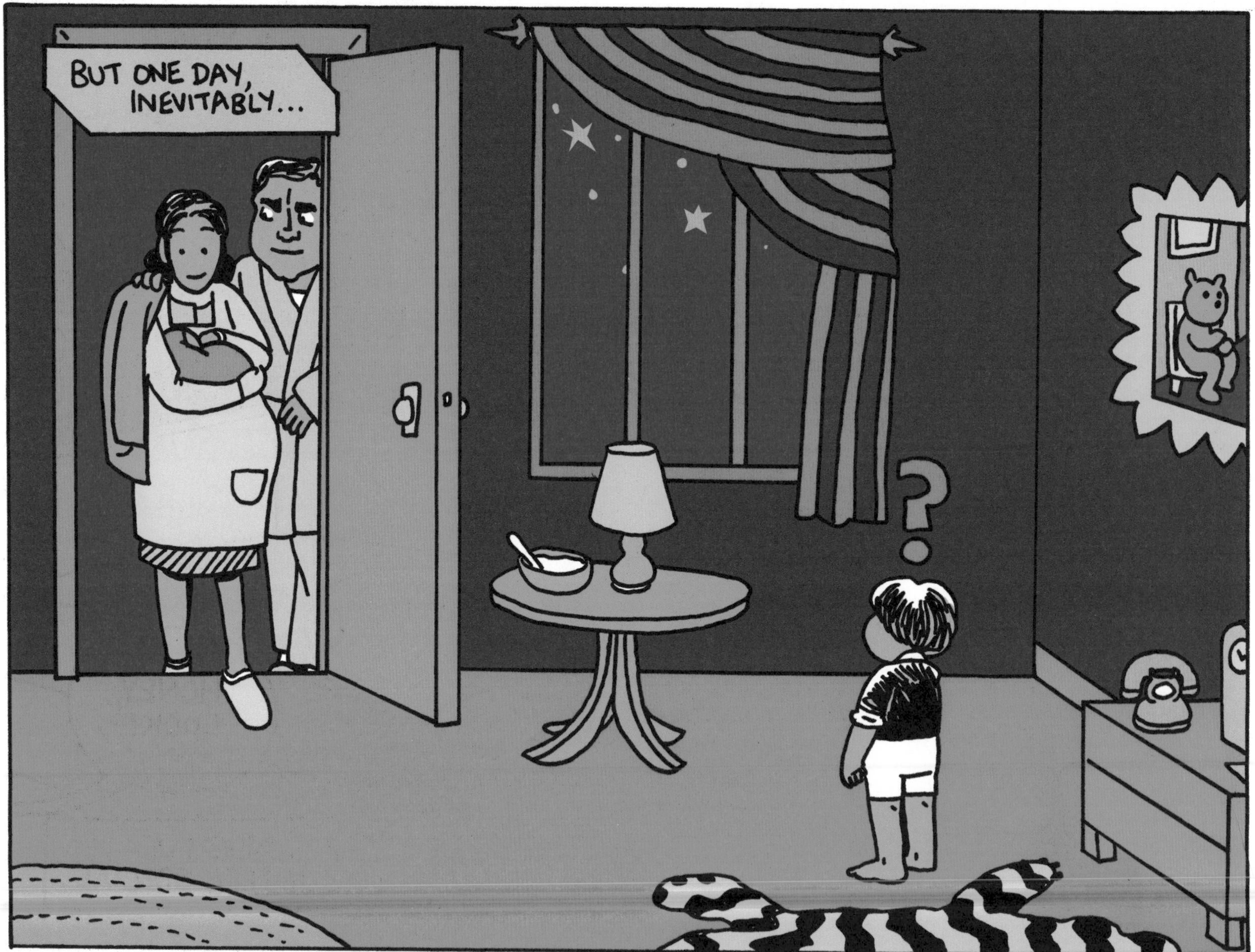
BUT ONE DAY, INEVITABLY...
?

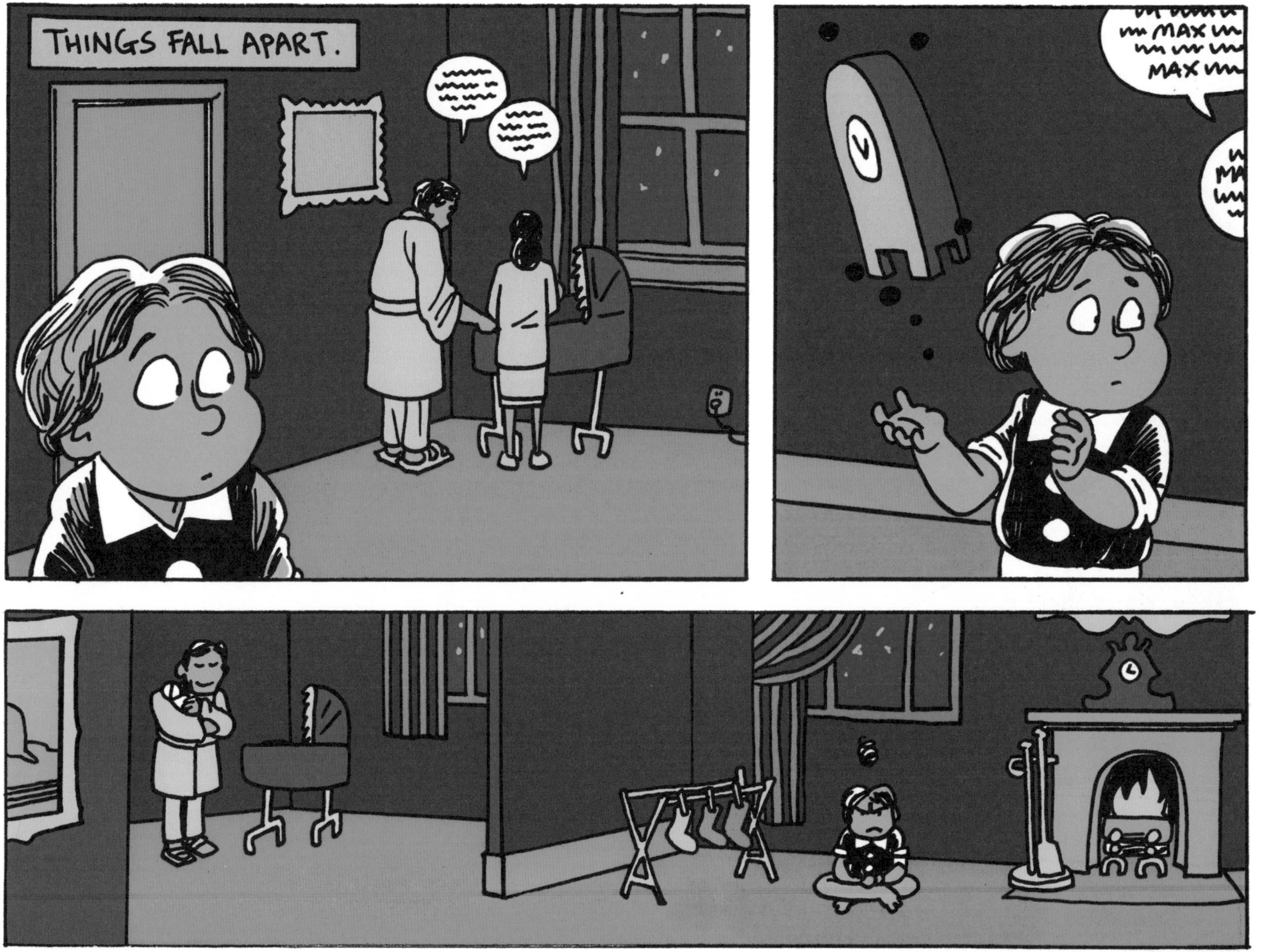
THINGS FALL APART.
MAX
MAX

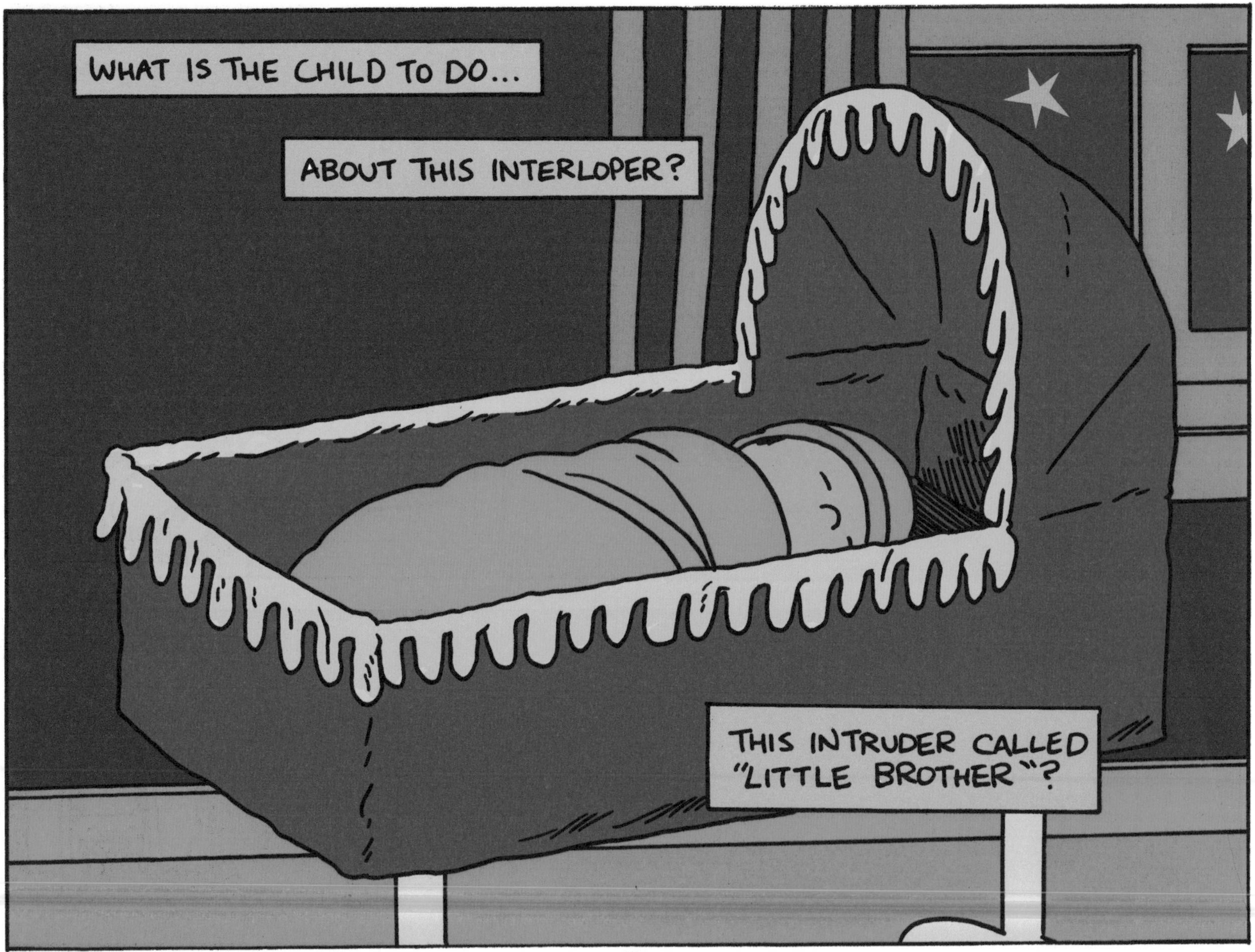
WHAT IS THE CHILD TO DO...
ABOUT THIS INTERLOPER?
THIS INTRUDER CALLED "LITTLE BROTHER"?

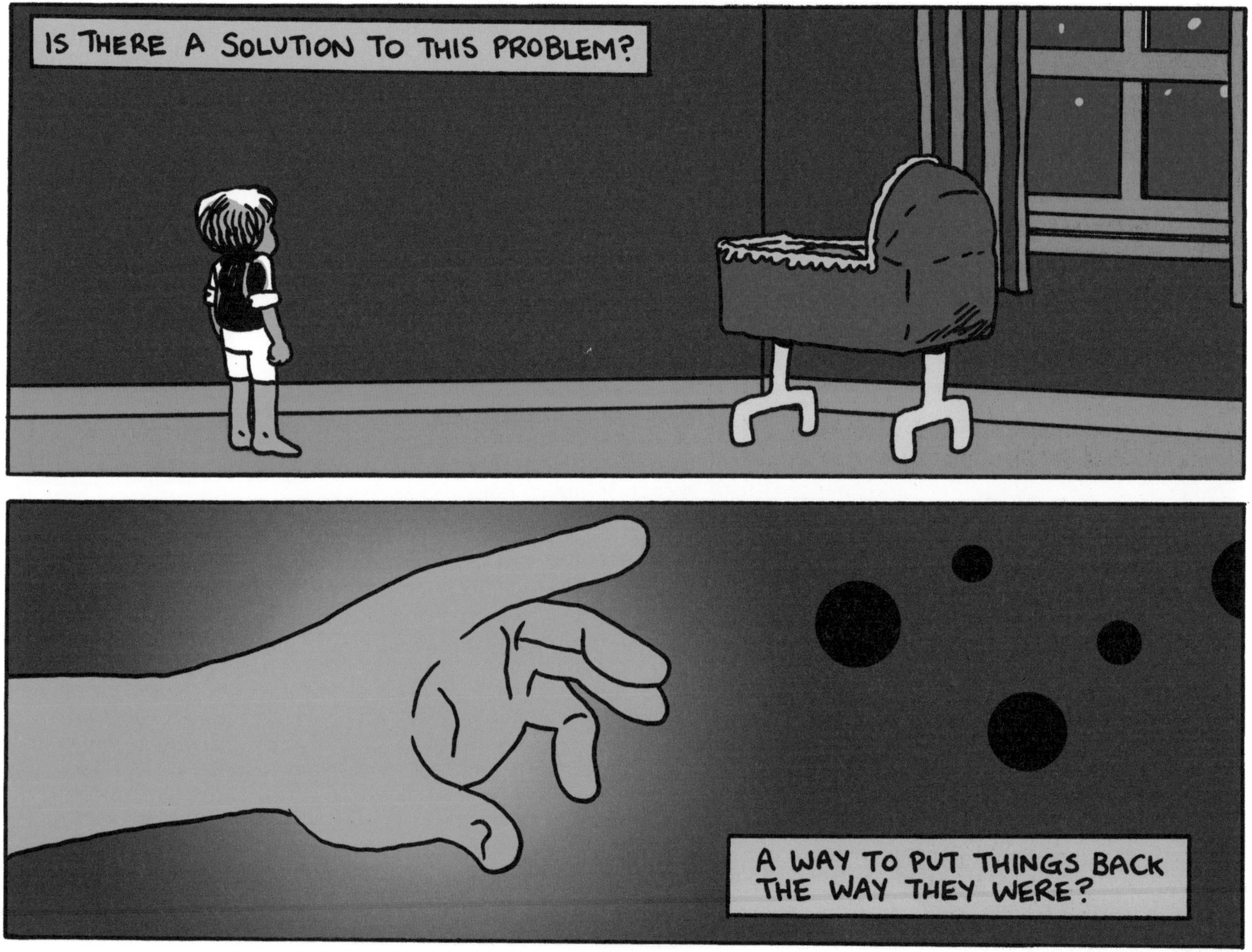
IS THERE A SOLUTION TO THIS PROBLEM?
A WAY TO PUT THINGS BACK THE WAY THEY WERE?

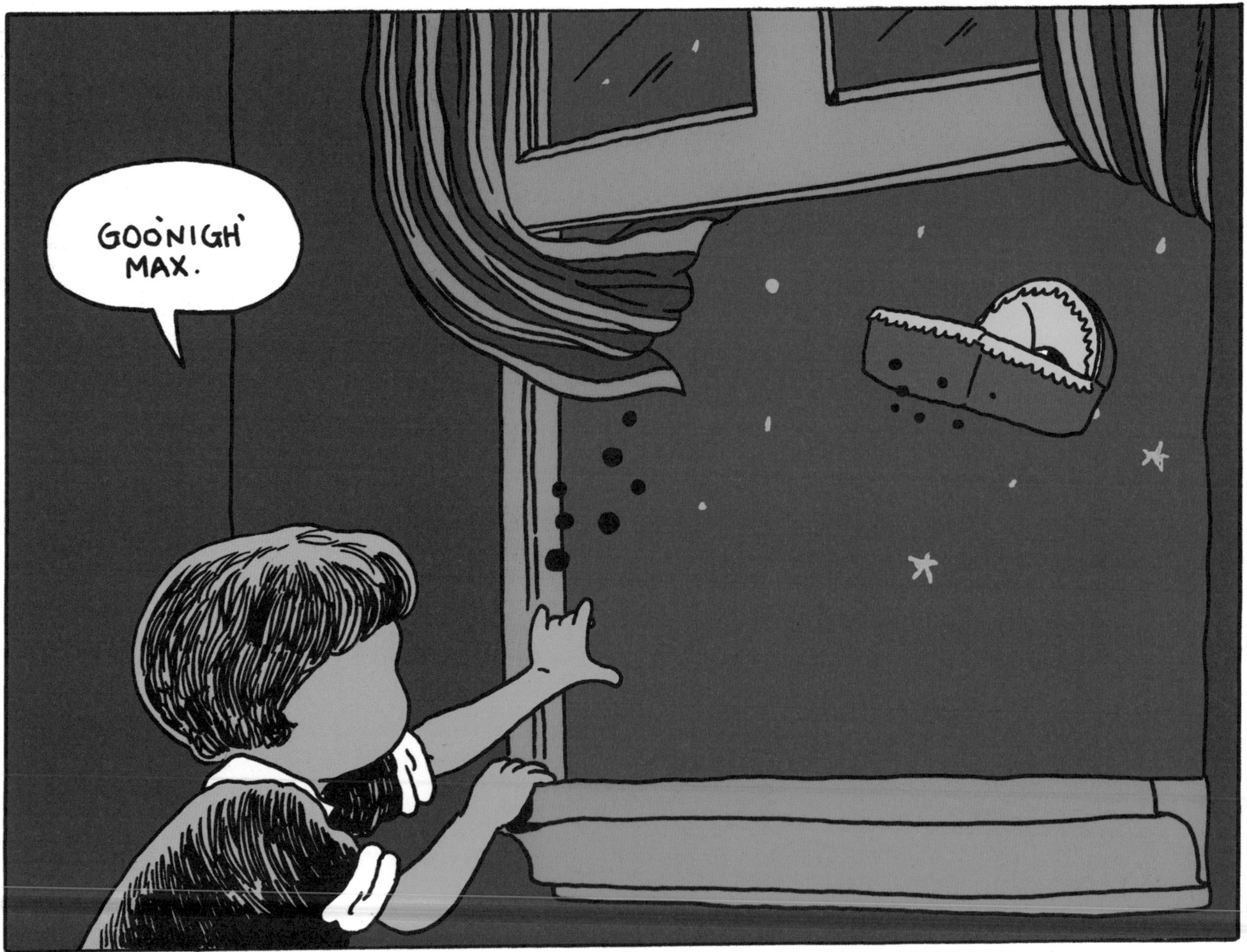
GOO'NIGH' MAX.

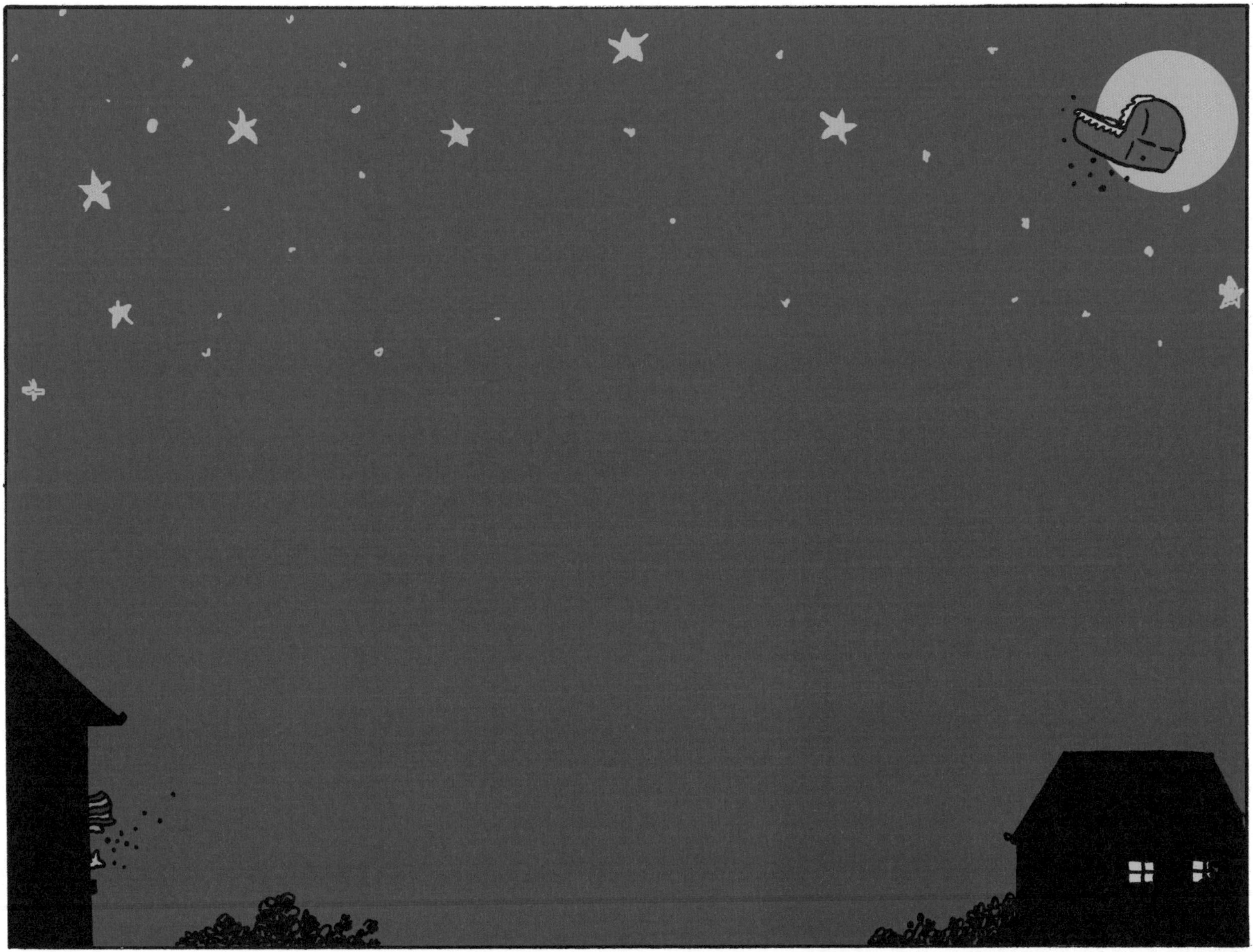

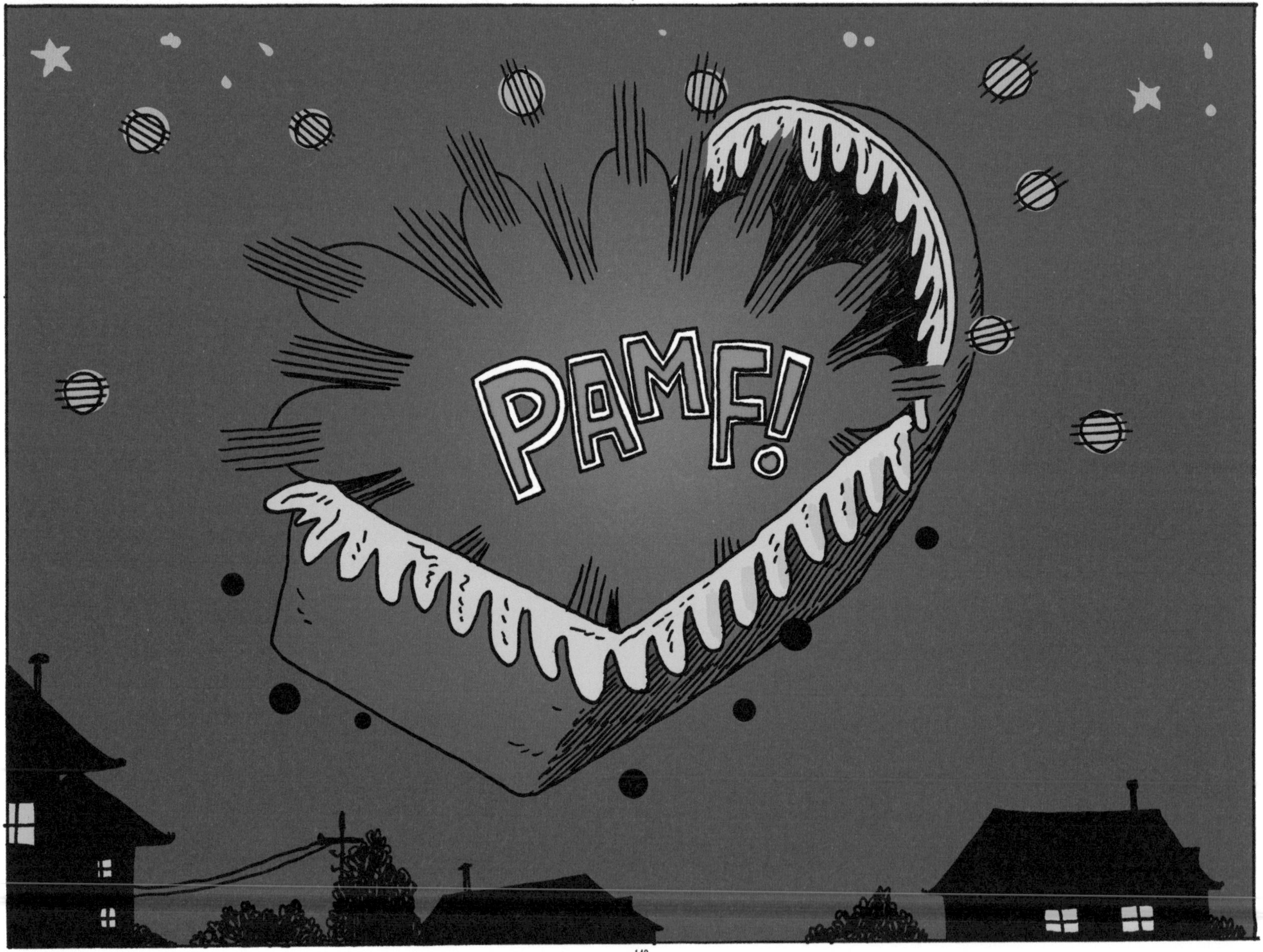
PAMF!

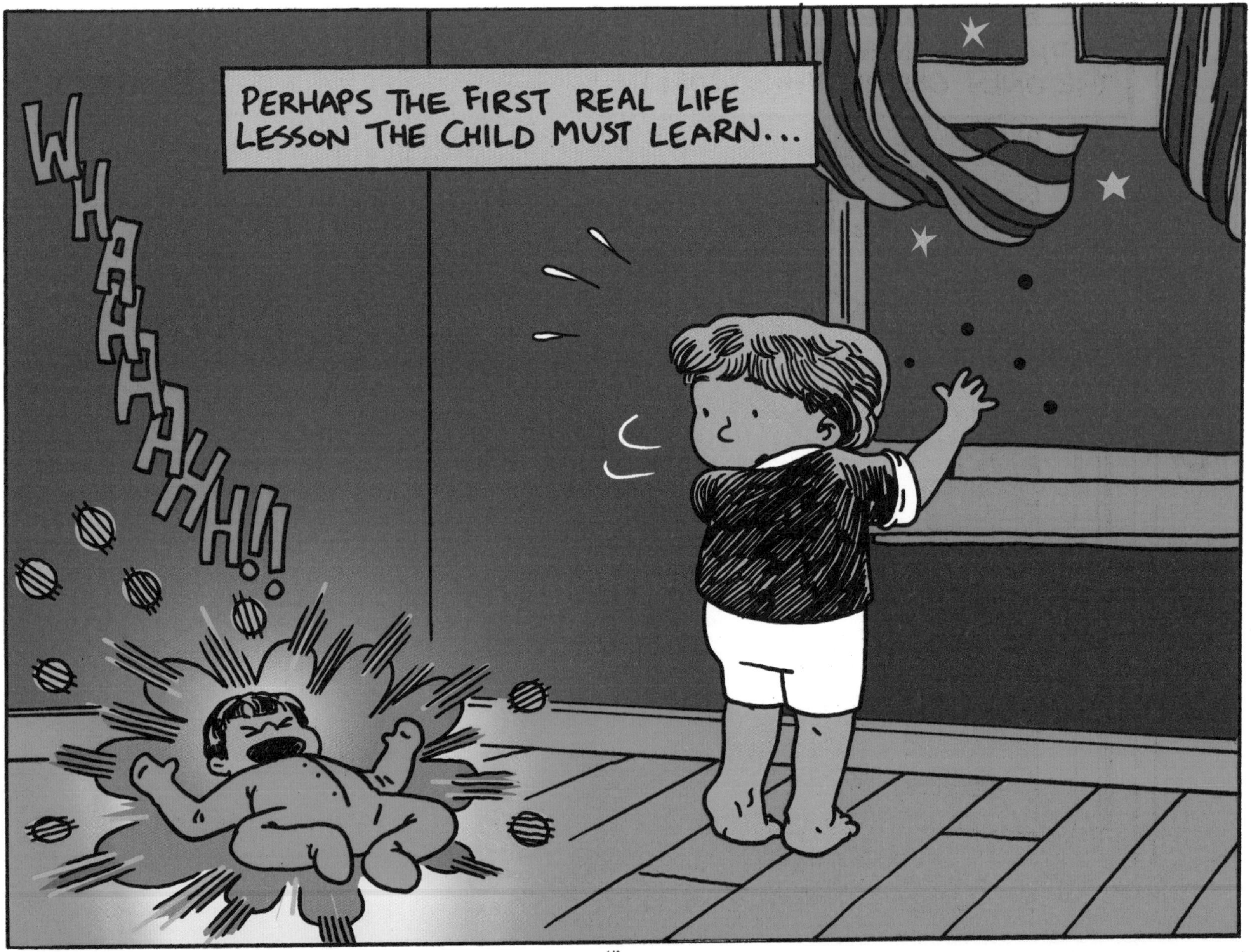
PERHAPS THE FIRST REAL LIFE LESSON THE CHILD MUST LEARN...
WHAAAAAAHH!!

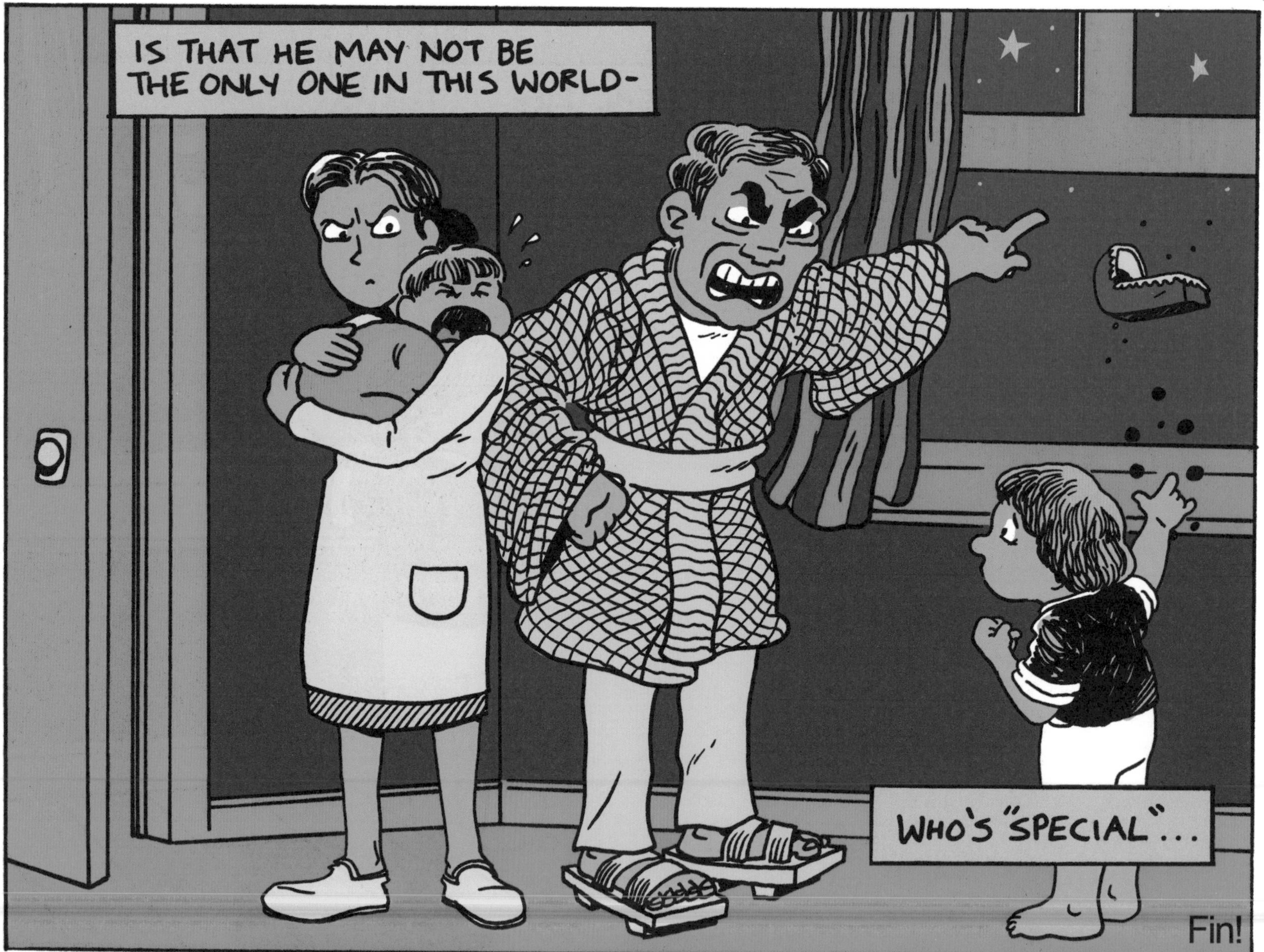
IS THAT HE MAY NOT BE THE ONLY ONE IN THIS WORLD-
WHO'S "SPECIAL"...
Fin!

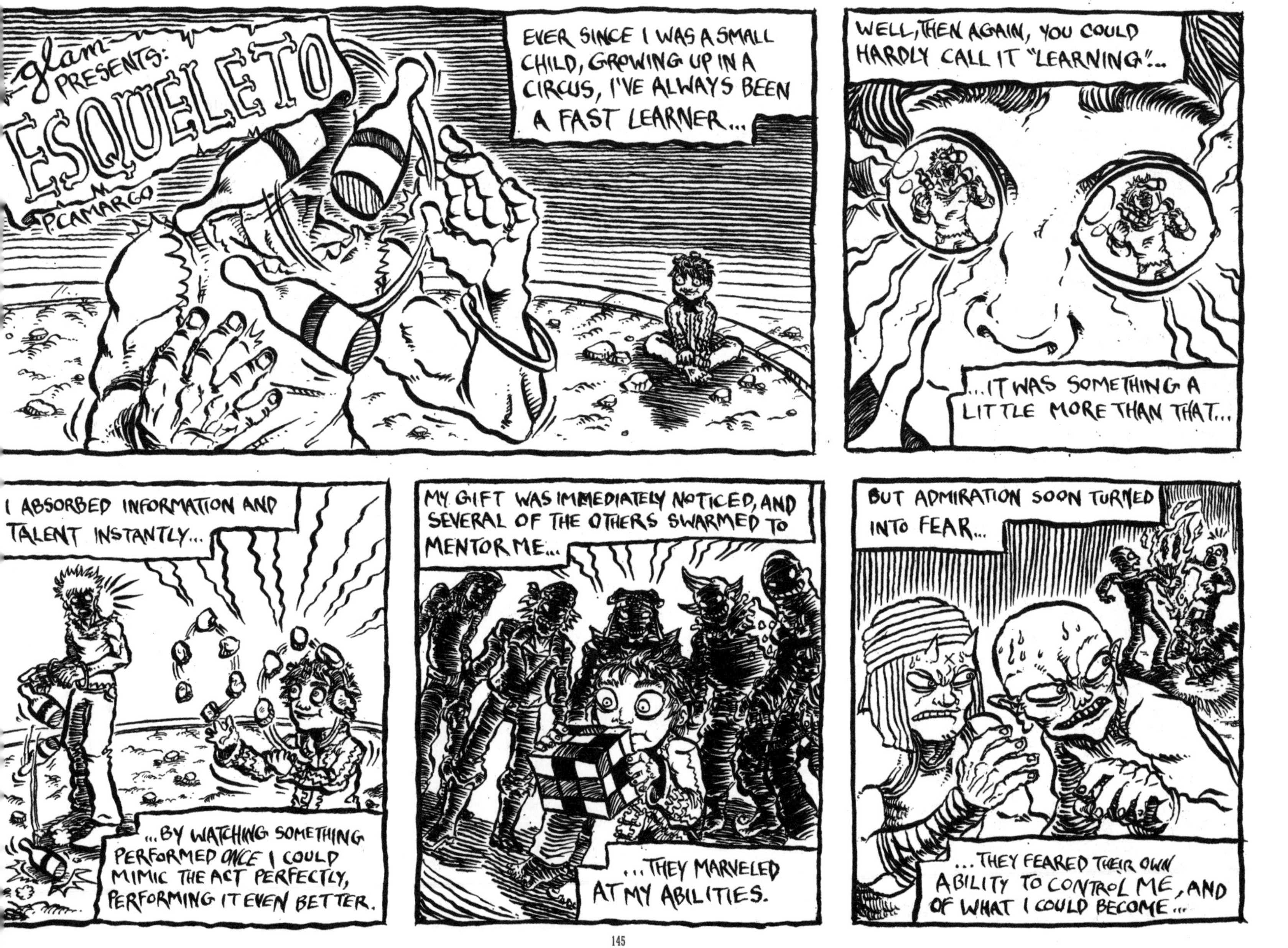
glam PRESENTS:
ESQUELETO
P. CAMARGO
EVER SINCE I WAS A SMALL CHILD, GROWING UP IN A CIRCUS, I'VE ALWAYS BEEN A FAST LEARNER...
WELL, THEN AGAIN, YOU COULD HARDLY CALL IT "LEARNING"...
...IT WAS SOMETHING A LITTLE MORE THAN THAT...
I ABSORBED INFORMATION AND TALENT INSTANTLY...
...BY WATCHING SOMETHING PERFORMED ONCE I COULD MIMIC THE ACT PERFECTLY, PERFORMING IT EVEN BETTER.
MY GIFT WAS IMMEDIATELY NOTICED, AND SEVERAL OF THE OTHERS SWARMED TO MENTOR ME...
...THEY MARVELED AT MY ABILITIES.
BUT ADMIRATION SOON TURNED INTO FEAR...
...THEY FEARED THEIR OWN ABILITY TO CONTROL ME, AND OF WHAT I COULD BECOME...

THE CIRCUS, WHILE STILL A REAL CIRCUS, WAS ALSO A FRONT FOR ANOTHER CRIME SYNDICATE... EVERY PERFORMER A TRAINED ASSASSIN...

...BUT IN A CITY LIKE THIS, YOU COULDN'T EXPECT ANY LESS.

AS FOR MYSELF, I WAS A PART OF THE TRAPEZE FAMILY... AND THERE LAY THEIR PROBLEM. IF ANY OF THE OTHERS TRIED TO DO AWAY WITH ME, THEY'D HAVE TO DEAL WITH THE ENTIRE FAMILY.

ME

AND ALSO, THEY'D NEVER DARE DO ANYTHING BEHIND THE RING LEADER'S BACK, HE WAS THE BOSS, AND HE'D NEVER AGREE TO ONE OF THEIR SCHEMES...

...SO THEY HAD TO BE CAUTIOUS...

IT WAS ONLY A MATTER OF TIME BEFORE AN "ACCIDENT" HAPPENED.

AND THE CIRCUS LOST ITS TRAPEZE ACT.

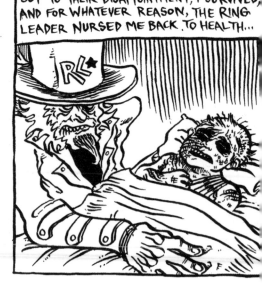

BUT TO THEIR DISAPPOINTMENT, I SURVIVED, AND FOR WHATEVER REASON, THE RING LEADER NURSED ME BACK TO HEALTH...

I SOON RECOVERED AND, THOUGH SCARRED AND ALONE, CONTINUED TO LEARN FROM MY SURROUNDINGS. INNOCENTLY BELIEVING WHAT HAD HAPPENED WAS, IN FACT, AN ACCIDENT...

AND THEY CONTINUED TO FEAR, HATE...

...AND CONSPIRE.

THIS TIME THE PLAN WAS DESIGNED BY THE ESCAPE ARTIST. HAVING ALREADY OVERCOME ALL HIS PREVIOUS DESIGNS, I WAS PRESENTED WITH HIS LATEST CHALLENGE.

YOUNG AND STUPID, I EAGERLY ACCEPTED, EXCITED TO LEARN A NEW TRICK...

TO HIS SURPRISE, I ESCAPED FROM THE SUIT WITH LITTLE DIFFICULTY...

...THE HELMET, HOWEVER, WAS NEVER DESIGNED TO BE ESCAPED FROM,

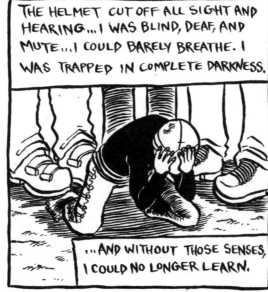

THE HELMET CUT OFF ALL SIGHT AND HEARING...I WAS BLIND, DEAF, AND MUTE...I COULD BARELY BREATHE. I WAS TRAPPED IN COMPLETE DARKNESS.

...AND WITHOUT THOSE SENSES, I COULD NO LONGER LEARN.

THEY KEPT ME HIDDEN IN THE BURNT REMAINS OF OUR CARAVAN...I WAS OUT OF SIGHT AND TOO AFRAID TO TRY AND FIND MY WAY OUT.

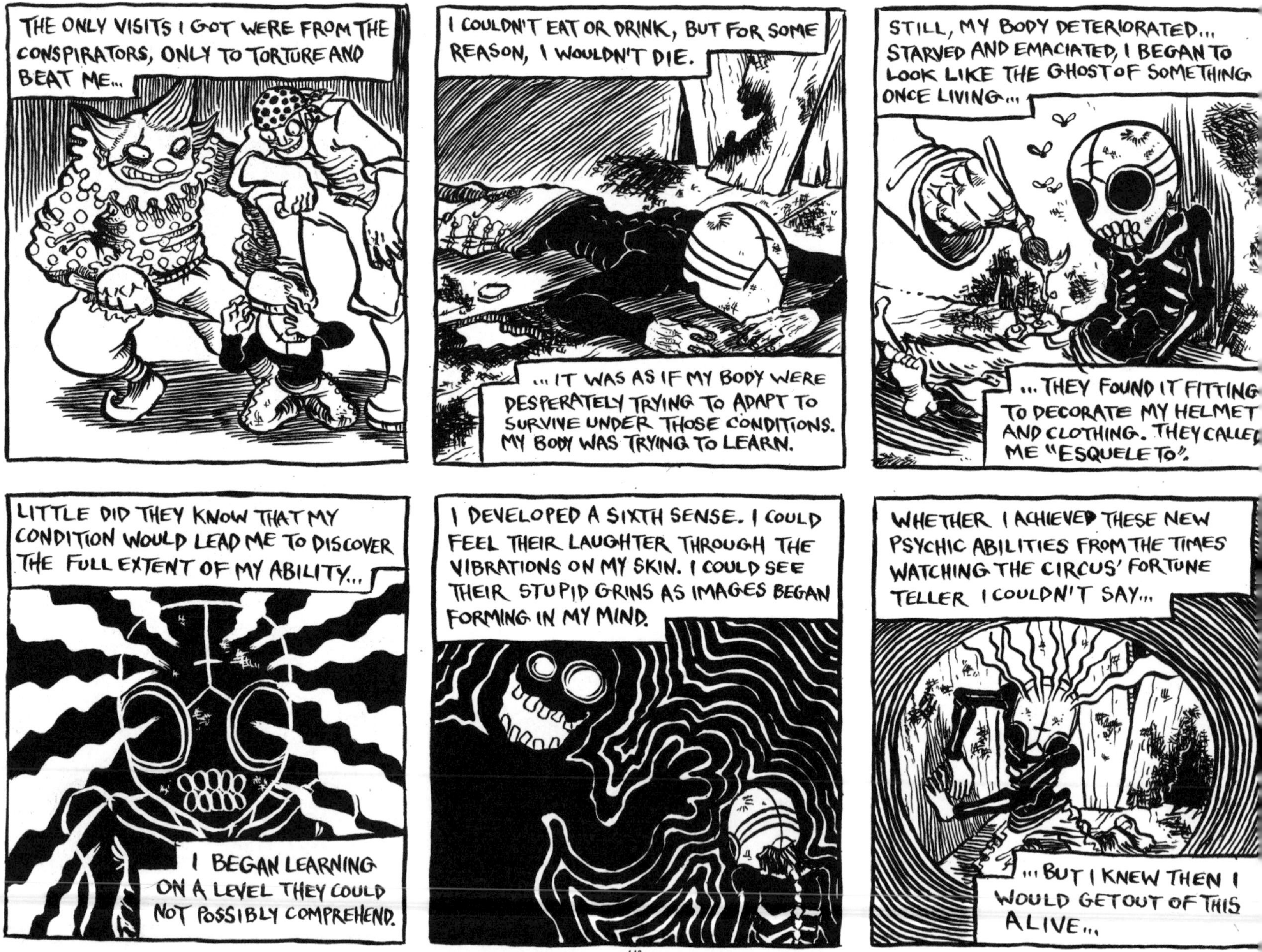
THE ONLY VISITS I GOT WERE FROM THE CONSPIRATORS, ONLY TO TORTURE AND BEAT ME...
I COULDN'T EAT OR DRINK, BUT FOR SOME REASON, I WOULDN'T DIE.
...IT WAS AS IF MY BODY WERE DESPERATELY TRYING TO ADAPT TO SURVIVE UNDER THOSE CONDITIONS. MY BODY WAS TRYING TO LEARN.
STILL, MY BODY DETERIORATED... STARVED AND EMACIATED, I BEGAN TO LOOK LIKE THE GHOST OF SOMETHING ONCE LIVING...
...THEY FOUND IT FITTING TO DECORATE MY HELMET AND CLOTHING. THEY CALLED ME "ESQUELETO".
LITTLE DID THEY KNOW THAT MY CONDITION WOULD LEAD ME TO DISCOVER THE FULL EXTENT OF MY ABILITY...
I BEGAN LEARNING ON A LEVEL THEY COULD NOT POSSIBLY COMPREHEND.
I DEVELOPED A SIXTH SENSE. I COULD FEEL THEIR LAUGHTER THROUGH THE VIBRATIONS ON MY SKIN. I COULD SEE THEIR STUPID GRINS AS IMAGES BEGAN FORMING IN MY MIND.
WHETHER I ACHIEVED THESE NEW PSYCHIC ABILITIES FROM THE TIMES WATCHING THE CIRCUS' FORTUNE TELLER I COULDN'T SAY...
...BUT I KNEW THEN I WOULD GET OUT OF THIS ALIVE...

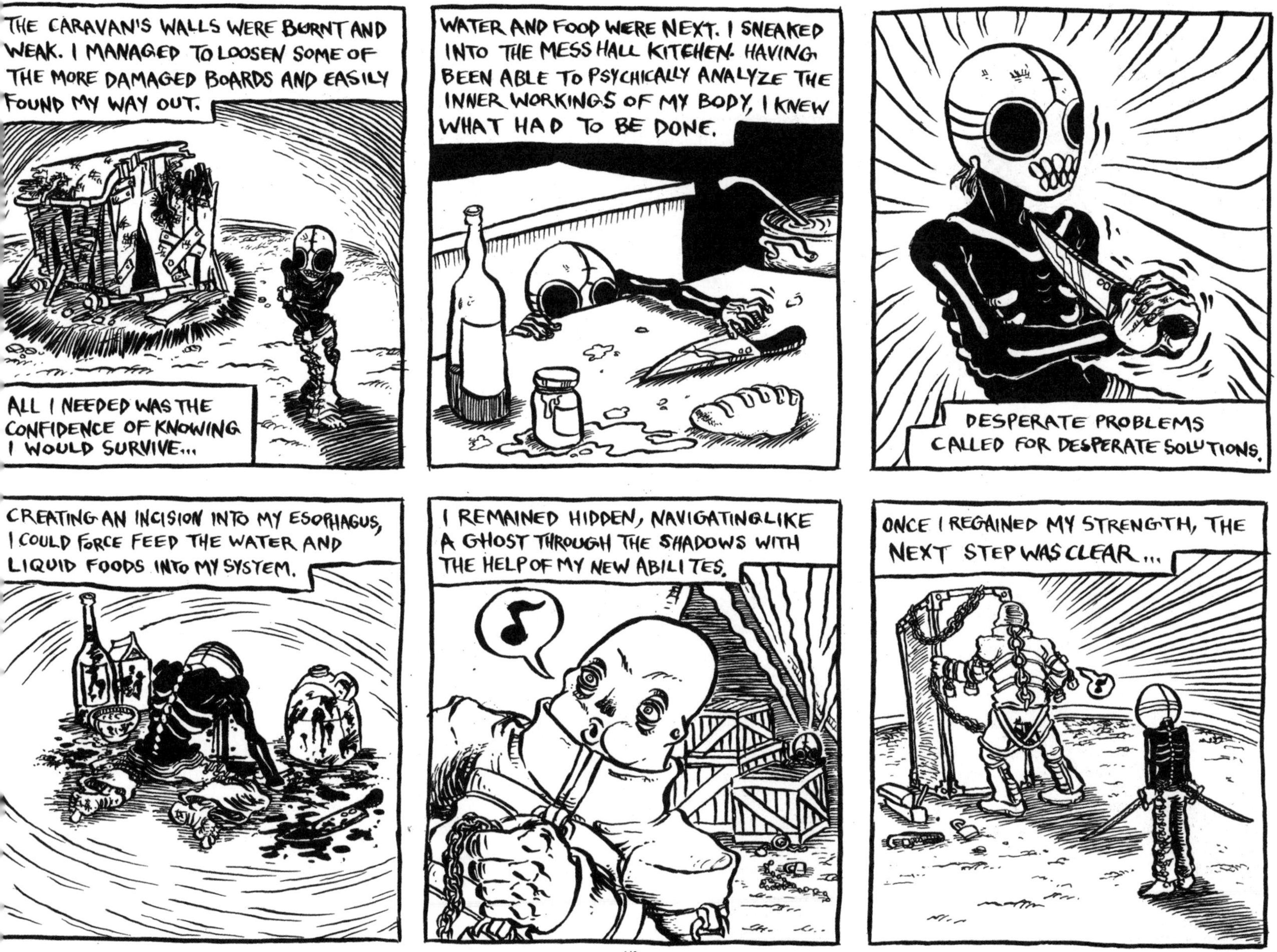
THE CARAVAN'S WALLS WERE BURNT AND WEAK. I MANAGED TO LOOSEN SOME OF THE MORE DAMAGED BOARDS AND EASILY FOUND MY WAY OUT.
ALL I NEEDED WAS THE CONFIDENCE OF KNOWING I WOULD SURVIVE...
WATER AND FOOD WERE NEXT. I SNEAKED INTO THE MESS HALL KITCHEN. HAVING BEEN ABLE TO PSYCHICALLY ANALYZE THE INNER WORKINGS OF MY BODY, I KNEW WHAT HAD TO BE DONE.
DESPERATE PROBLEMS CALLED FOR DESPERATE SOLUTIONS.
CREATING AN INCISION INTO MY ESOPHAGUS, I COULD FORCE FEED THE WATER AND LIQUID FOODS INTO MY SYSTEM.
I REMAINED HIDDEN, NAVIGATING LIKE A GHOST THROUGH THE SHADOWS WITH THE HELP OF MY NEW ABILITES.
ONCE I REGAINED MY STRENGTH, THE NEXT STEP WAS CLEAR...

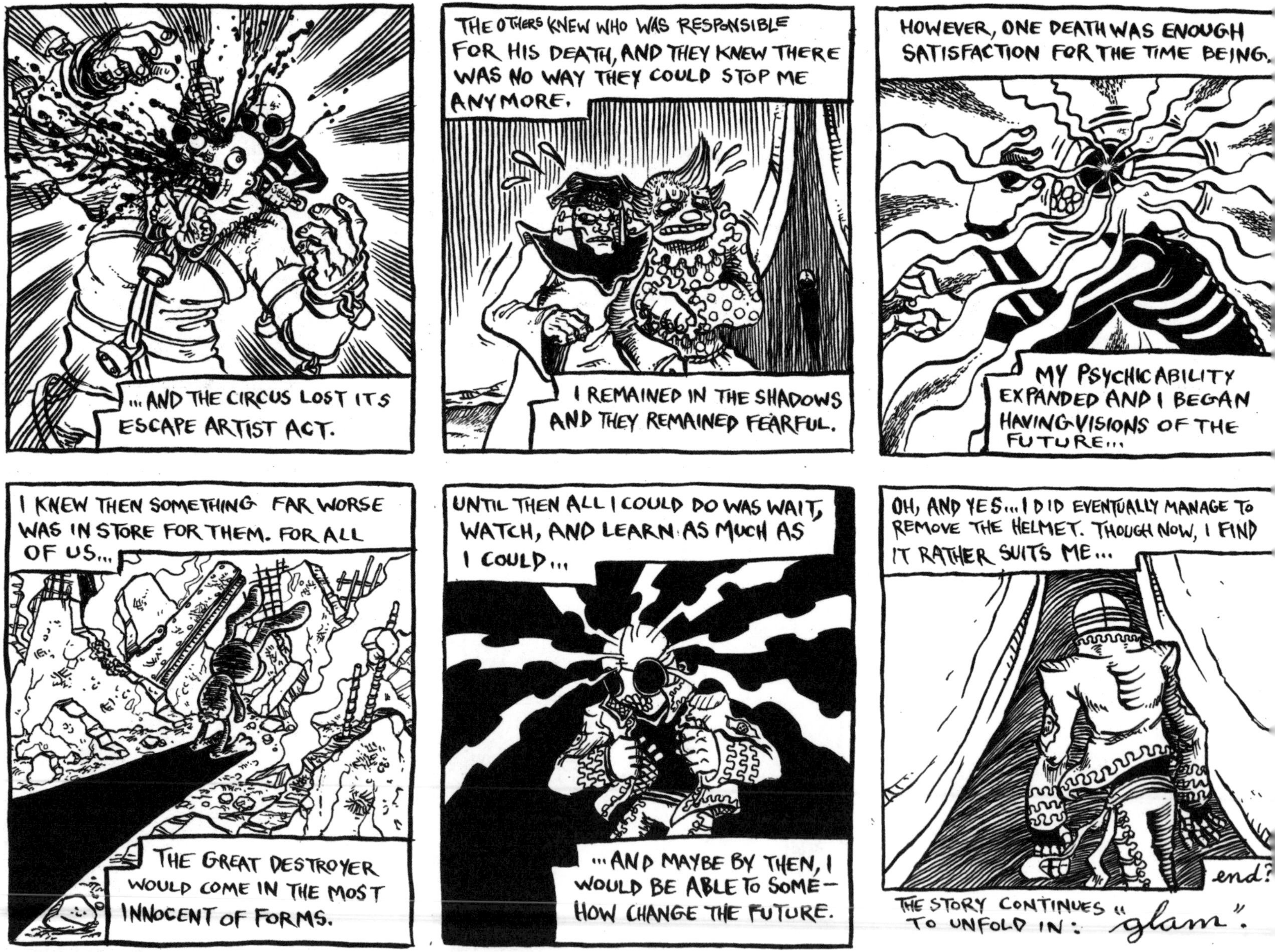
...AND THE CIRCUS LOST ITS ESCAPE ARTIST ACT.
THE OTHERS KNEW WHO WAS RESPONSIBLE FOR HIS DEATH, AND THEY KNEW THERE WAS NO WAY THEY COULD STOP ME ANYMORE.
I REMAINED IN THE SHADOWS AND THEY REMAINED FEARFUL.
HOWEVER, ONE DEATH WAS ENOUGH SATISFACTION FOR THE TIME BEING.
MY PSYCHIC ABILITY EXPANDED AND I BEGAN HAVING VISIONS OF THE FUTURE...
I KNEW THEN SOMETHING FAR WORSE WAS IN STORE FOR THEM. FOR ALL OF US...
THE GREAT DESTROYER WOULD COME IN THE MOST INNOCENT OF FORMS.
UNTIL THEN ALL I COULD DO WAS WAIT, WATCH, AND LEARN AS MUCH AS I COULD...
...AND MAYBE BY THEN, I WOULD BE ABLE TO SOME-HOW CHANGE THE FUTURE.
OH, AND YES... I DID EVENTUALLY MANAGE TO REMOVE THE HELMET. THOUGH NOW, I FIND IT RATHER SUITS ME...
end?
THE STORY CONTINUES TO UNFOLD IN: "glam".

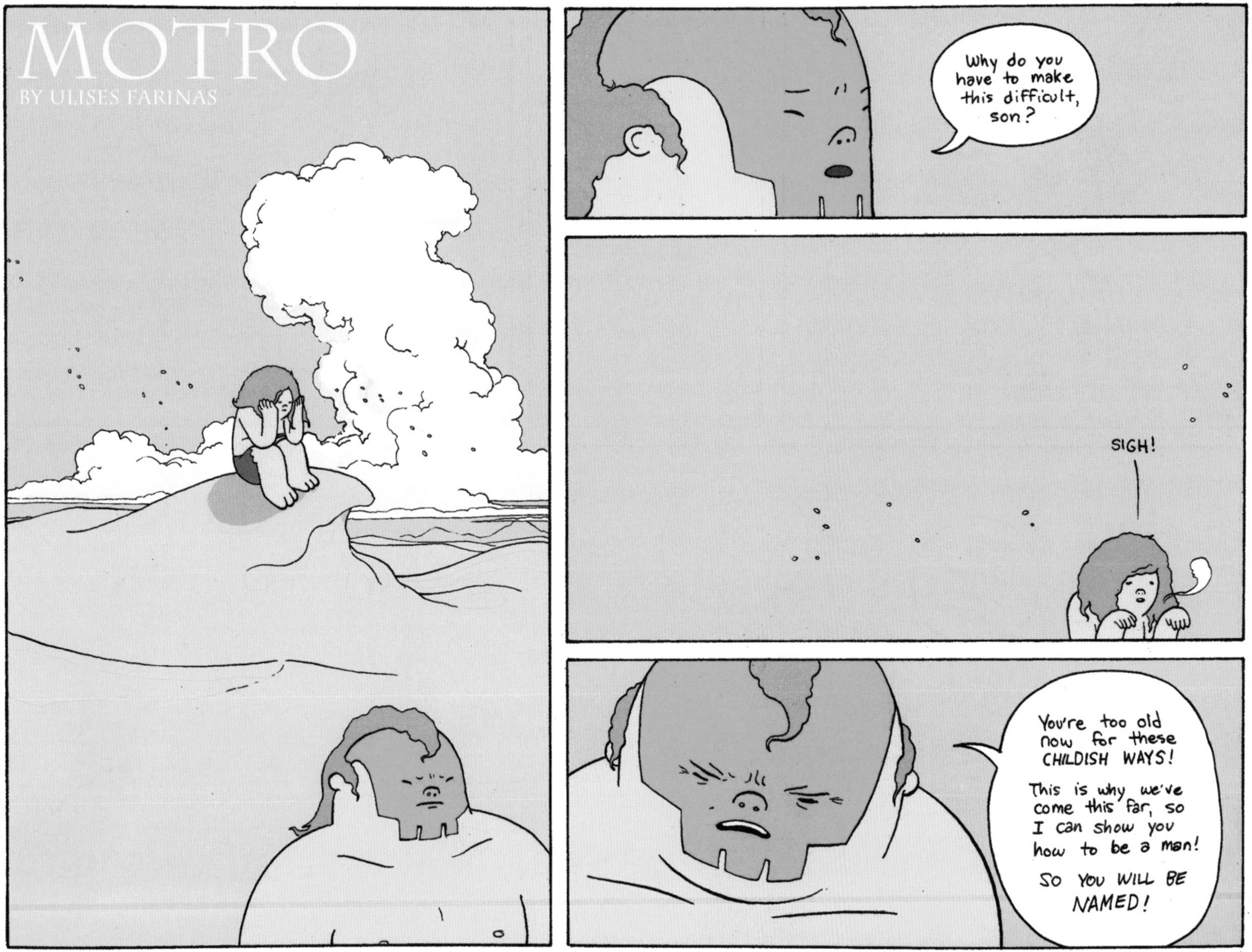
MOTRO
BY ULISES FARINAS
Why do you have to make this difficult, son?
SIGH!
You're too old now for these CHILDISH WAYS!
This is why we've come this far, so I can show you how to be a man!
SO YOU WILL BE NAMED!

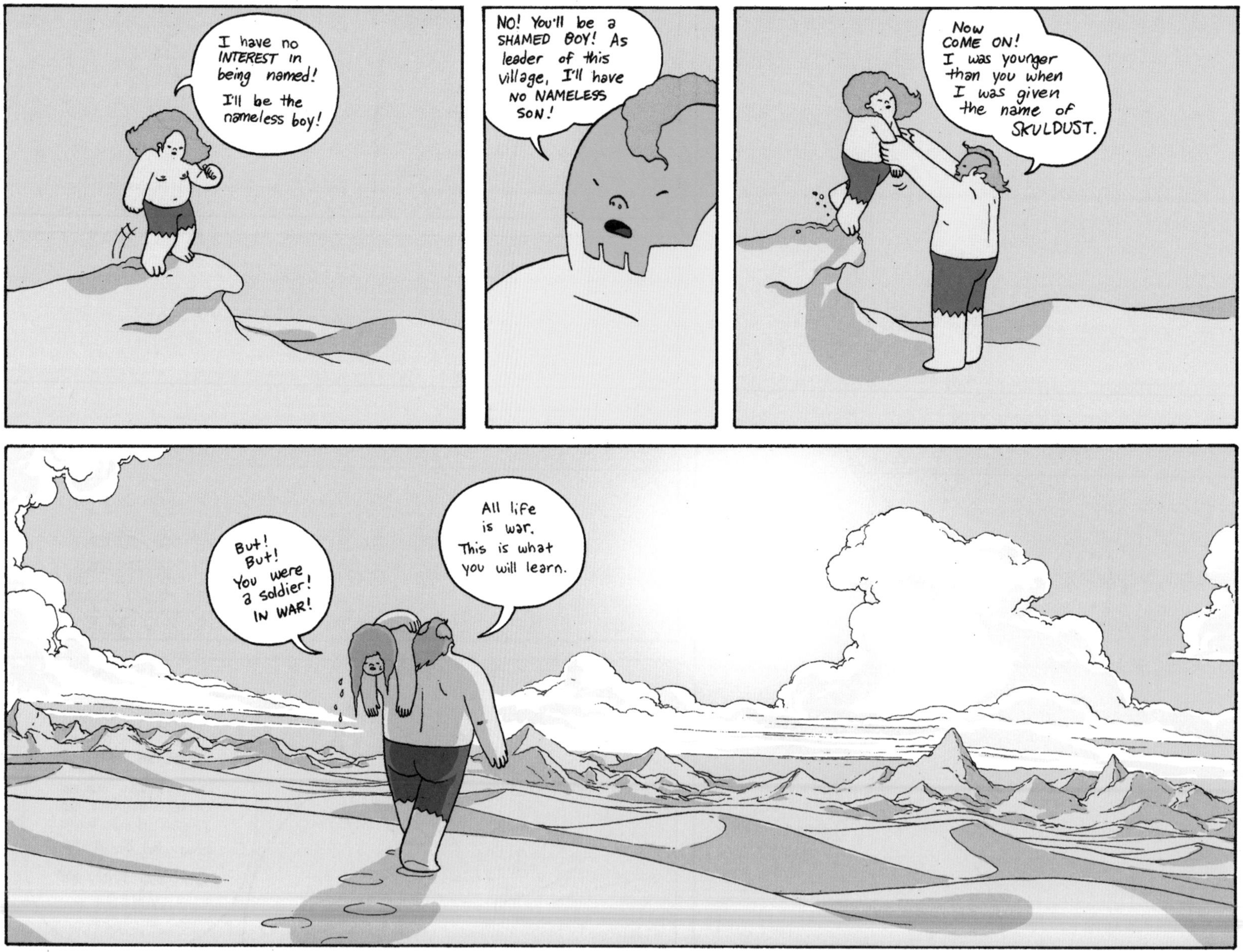
I have no INTEREST in being named! I'll be the nameless boy!
NO! You'll be a SHAMED BOY! As leader of this village, I'll have NO NAMELESS SON!
Now COME ON! I was younger than you when I was given the name of SKULDUST.
But! But! You were a soldier! IN WAR!
All life is war. This is what you will learn.

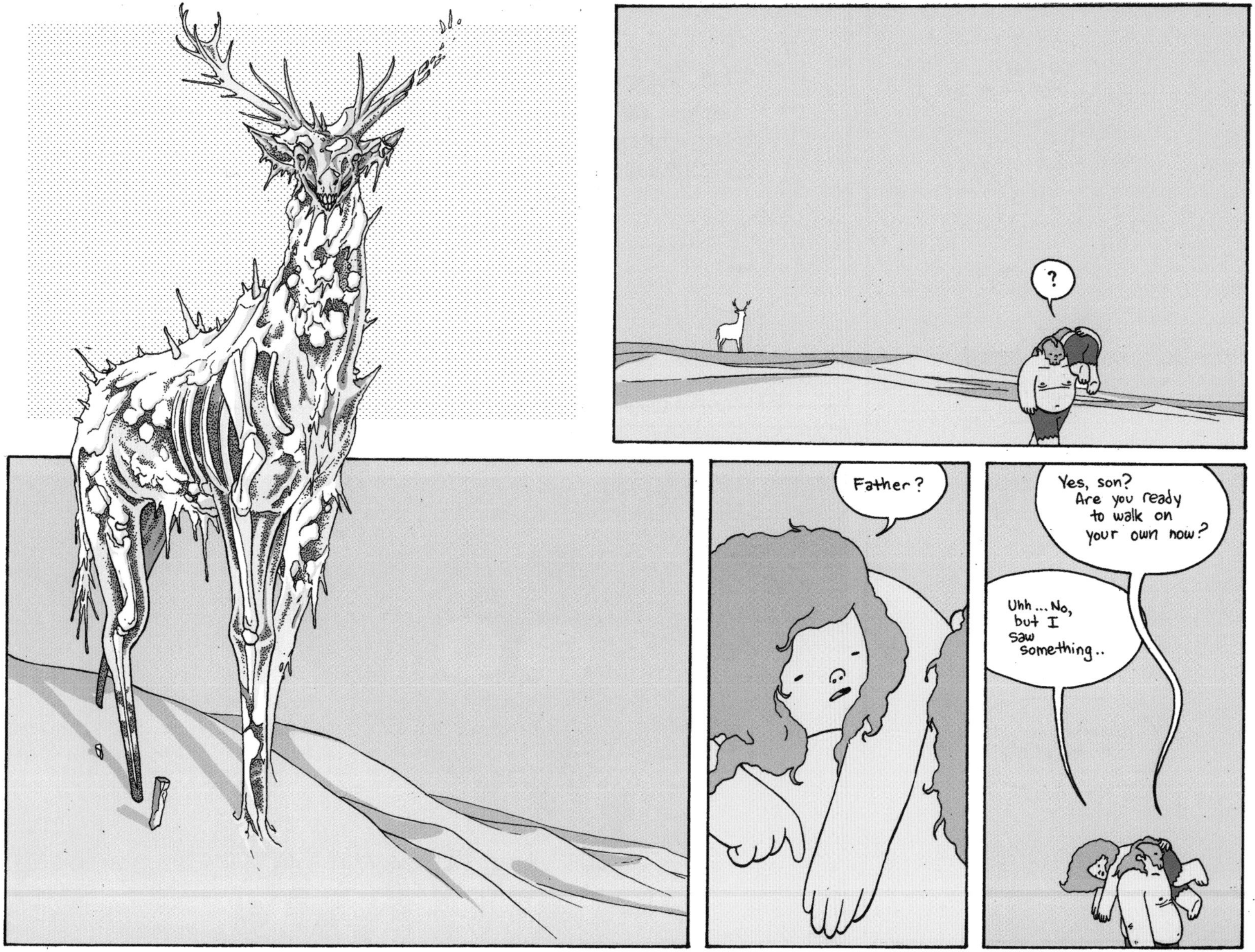
?
Father?
Yes, son? Are you ready to walk on your own now?
Uhh... No, but I saw something..

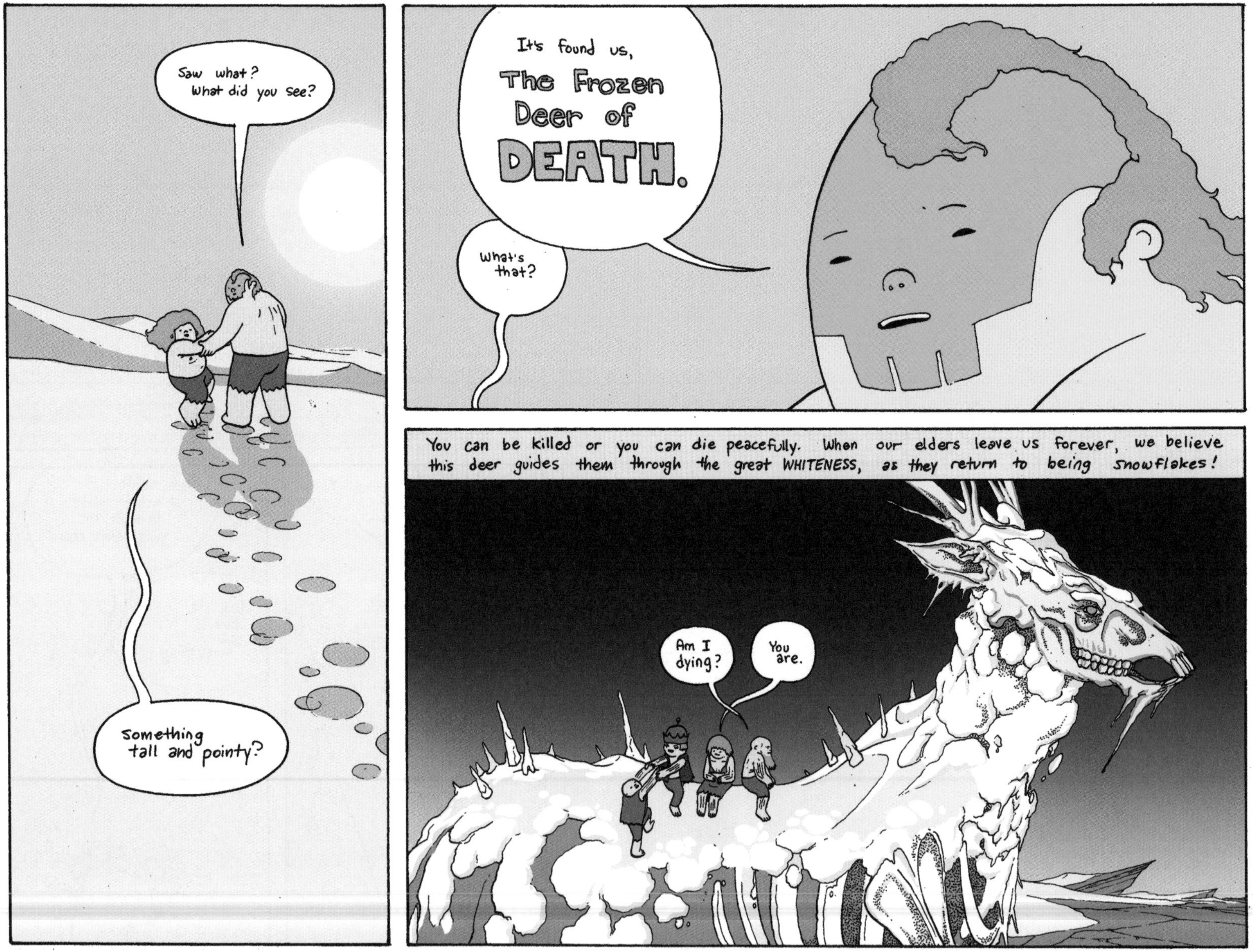
Saw what? What did you see?
Something tall and pointy?
It's found us, The Frozen Deer of DEATH.
What's that?
You can be killed or you can die peacefully. When our elders leave us forever, we believe this deer guides them through the great WHITENESS, as they return to being snowflakes!
Am I dying?
You are.

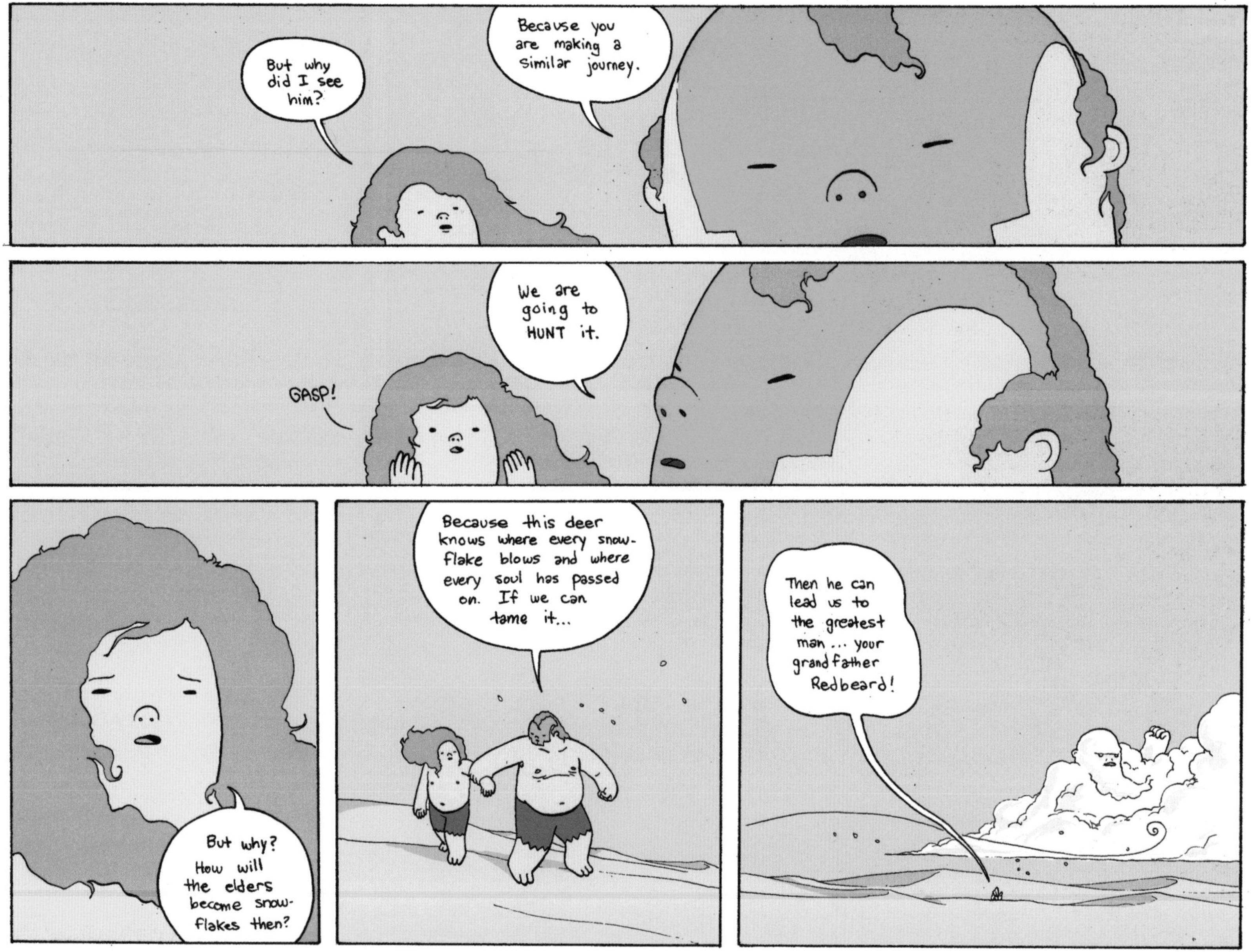
But why did I see him?
Because you are making a similar journey.
We are going to HUNT it.
GASP!
But why? How will the elders become snow-flakes then?
Because this deer knows where every snow-flake blows and where every soul has passed on. If we can tame it...
Then he can lead us to the greatest man... your grandfather Redbeard!

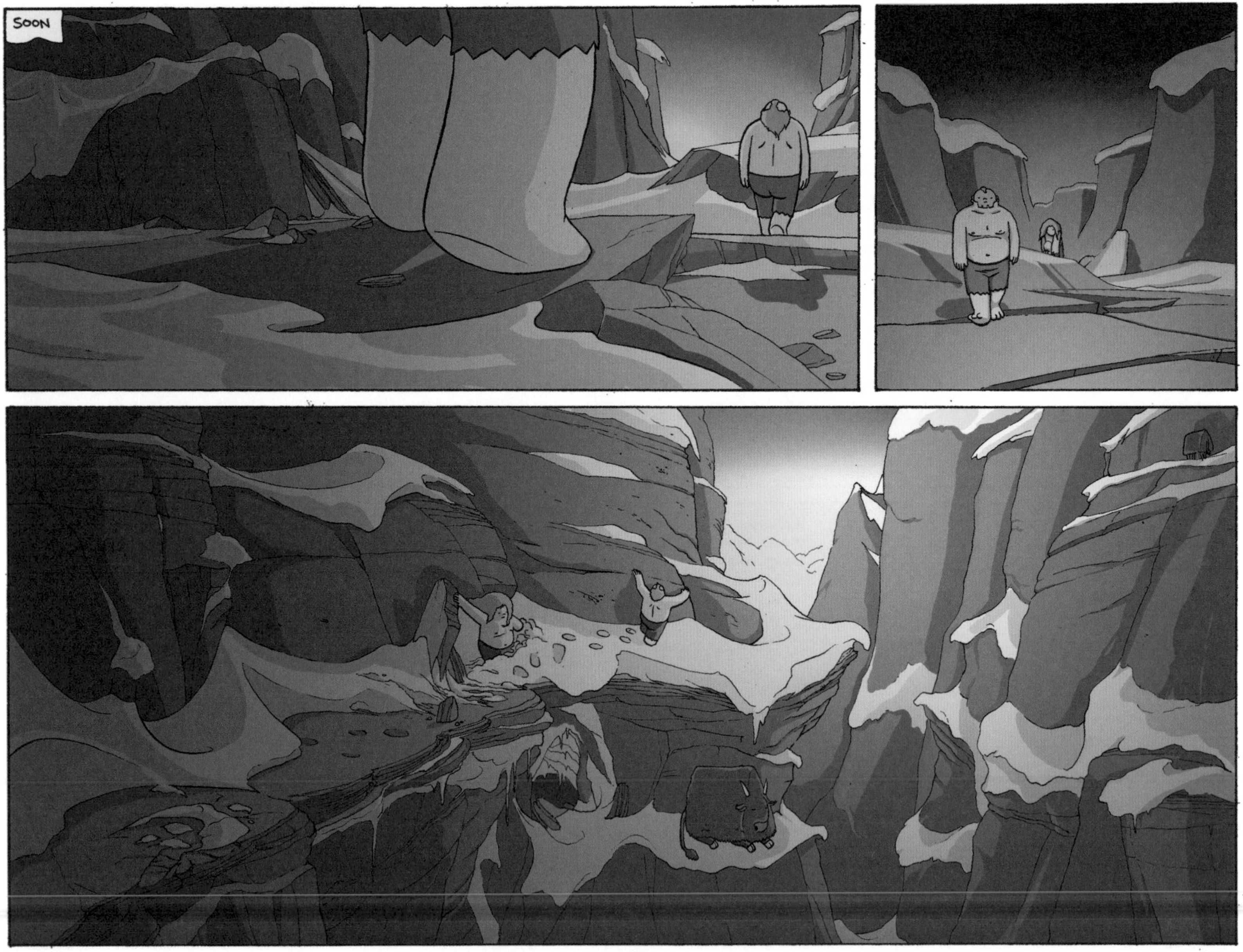
SOON

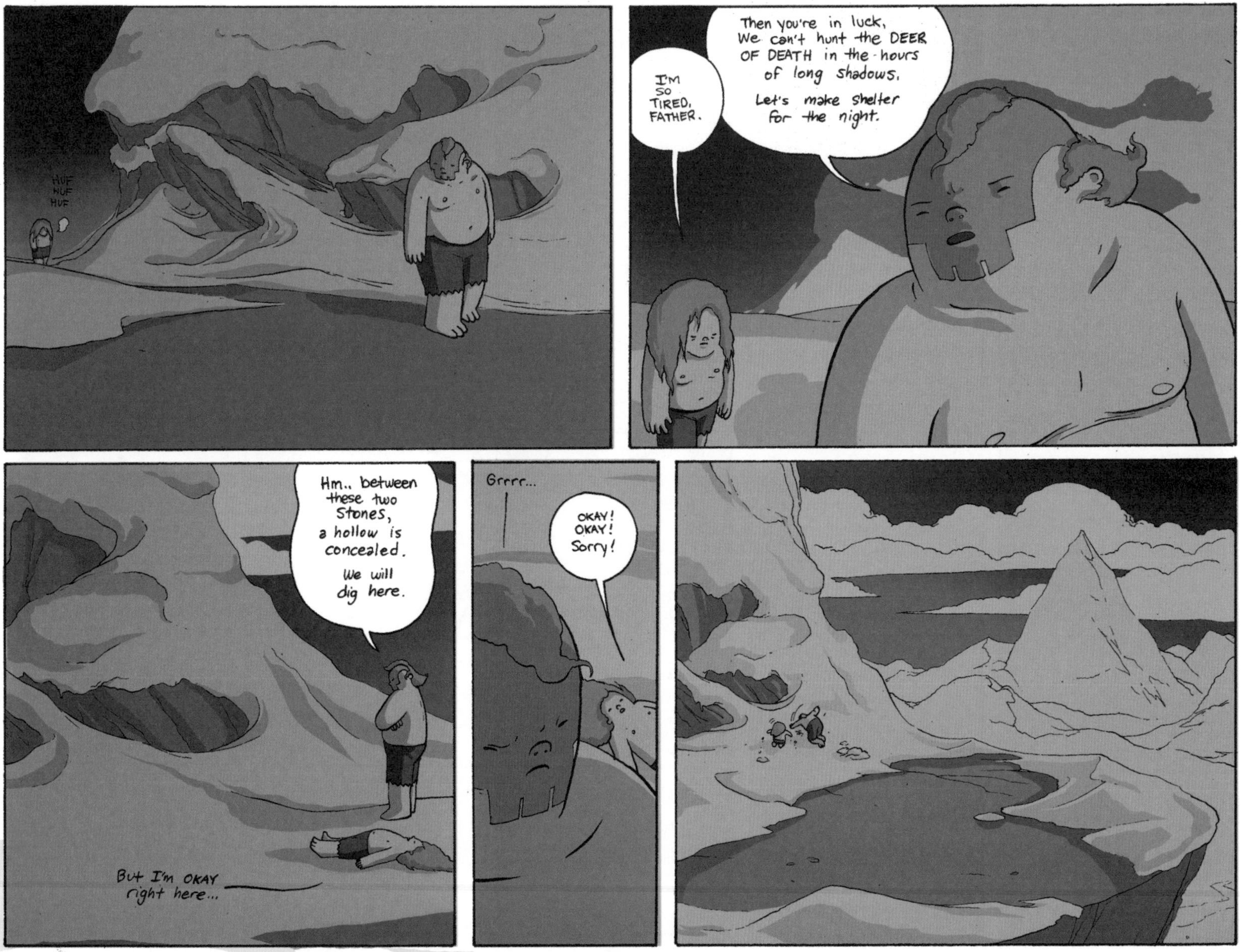
HUF
HUF
HUF
I'M SO TIRED, FATHER.
Then you're in luck, We can't hunt the DEER OF DEATH in the hours of long shadows.
Let's make shelter for the night.
Hm.. between these two Stones, a hollow is concealed.
We will dig here.
But I'm OKAY right here...
Grrrr...
OKAY! OKAY! Sorry!

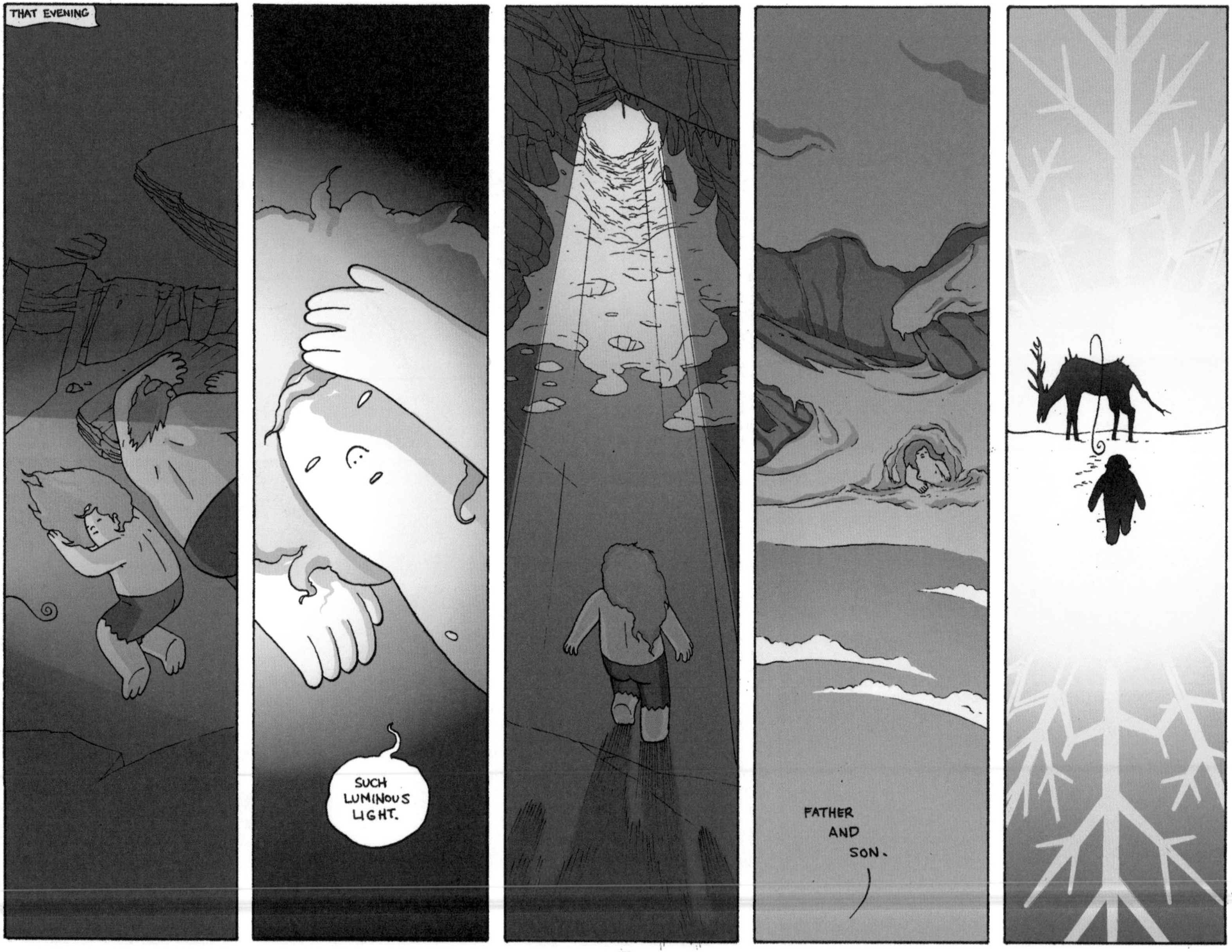
THAT EVENING
SUCH LUMINOUS LIGHT.
FATHER AND SON.

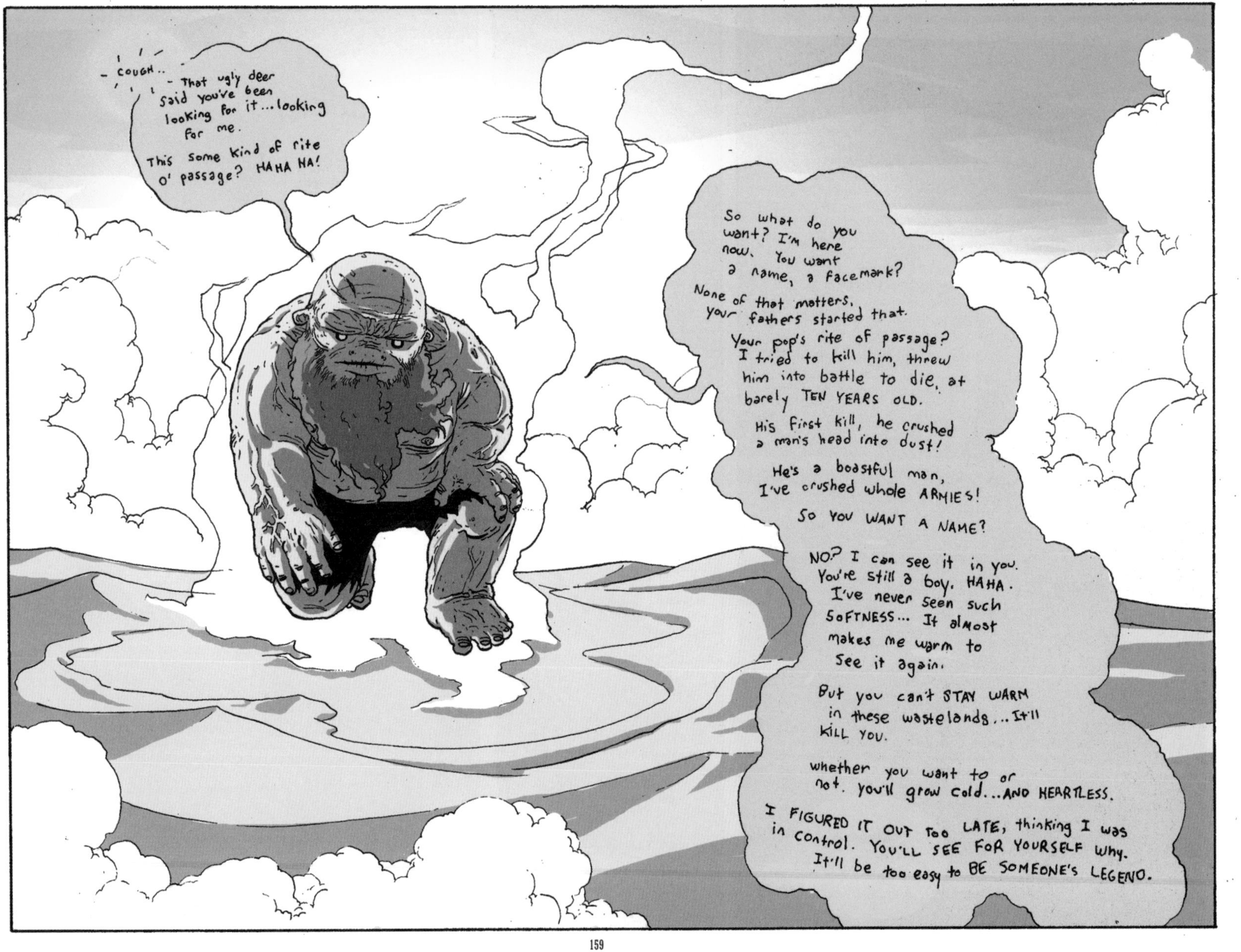
COUGH.. - That ugly deer said you've been looking for it... looking for me.
This some kind of rite o' passage? HAHA HA!
So what do you want? I'm here now. You want a name, a facemark?
None of that matters, your fathers started that.
Your pop's rite of passage? I tried to kill him, threw him into battle to die, at barely TEN YEARS OLD.
His first kill, he crushed a man's head into dust!
He's a boastful man, I've crushed whole ARMIES!
So YOU WANT A NAME?
NO? I can see it in you. You're still a boy. HAHA. I've never seen such SOFTNESS... It almost makes me warm to see it again.
But you can't STAY WARM in these wastelands... It'll KILL YOU.
whether you want to or not. you'll grow cold... AND HEARTLESS.
I FIGURED IT OUT TOO LATE, thinking I was in control. YOU'LL SEE FOR YOURSELF why. It'll be too easy to BE SOMEONE'S LEGEND.

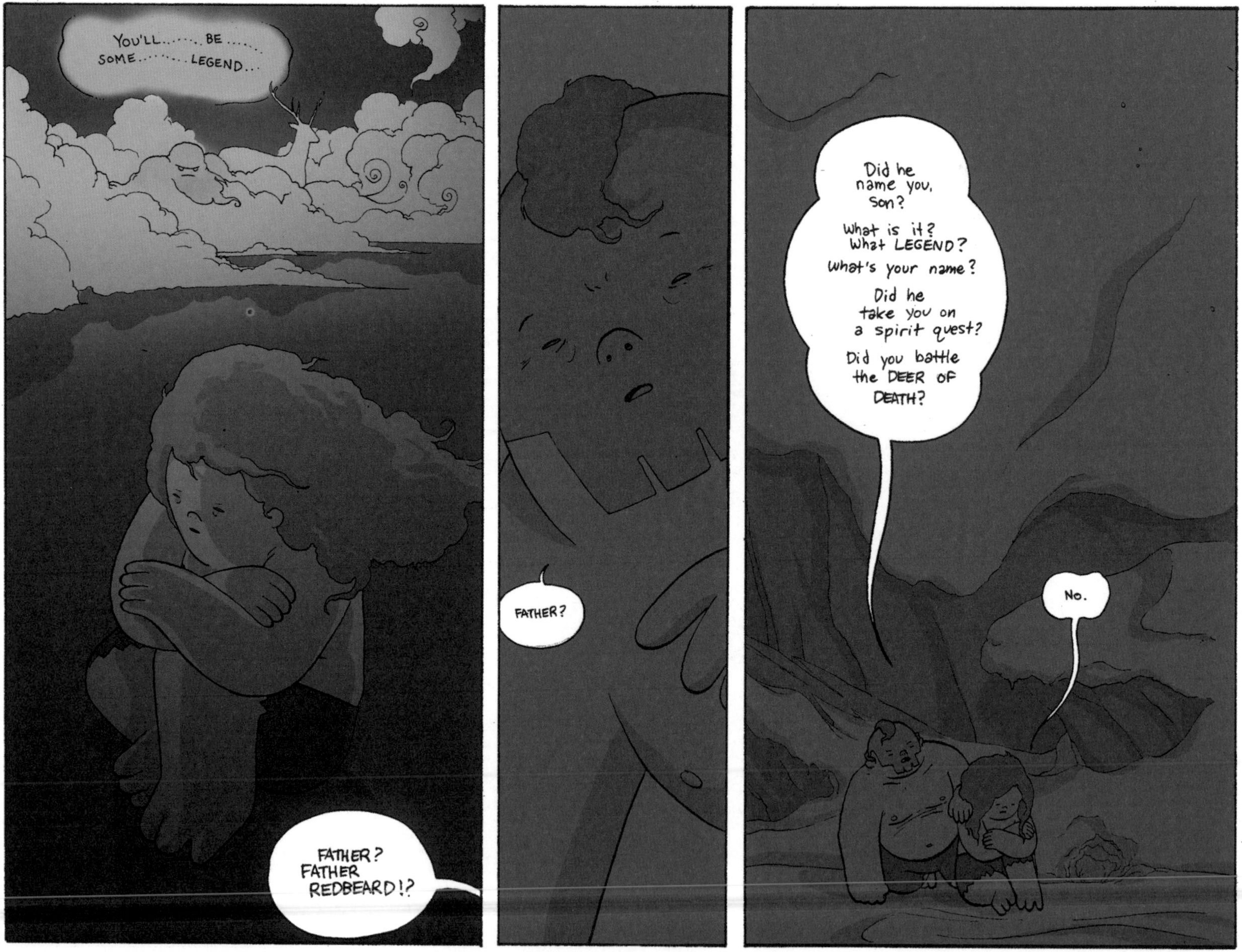
YOU'LL....... BE ....
SOME........ LEGEND...
FATHER? FATHER REDBEARD!?
FATHER?
Did he name you, son?
What is it? What LEGEND?
What's your name?
Did he take you on a spirit quest?
Did you battle the DEER OF DEATH?
No.

THE NEXT DAY

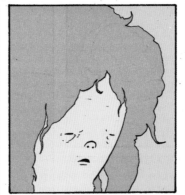

Cheer up, son. Your name must be chosen very carefully!

No. It's not that, FATHER.

..And GREAT REDBEARD himself spoke to you! I know he said you'll be the HERO of our VILLAGE!

No... but...

NEARBY

FATHER! FATHER! FATHER ZATHRU! The TRIBAL LEADER and his son have returned!

[?]

The village is coming out to greet us...

STAND AND GREET THEM WITH PRIDE.

They'll all come, expecting a name. But KNOW, you are soon to be a NEW MAN. STAND TALL AND LET THEM WONDER AND AWE!

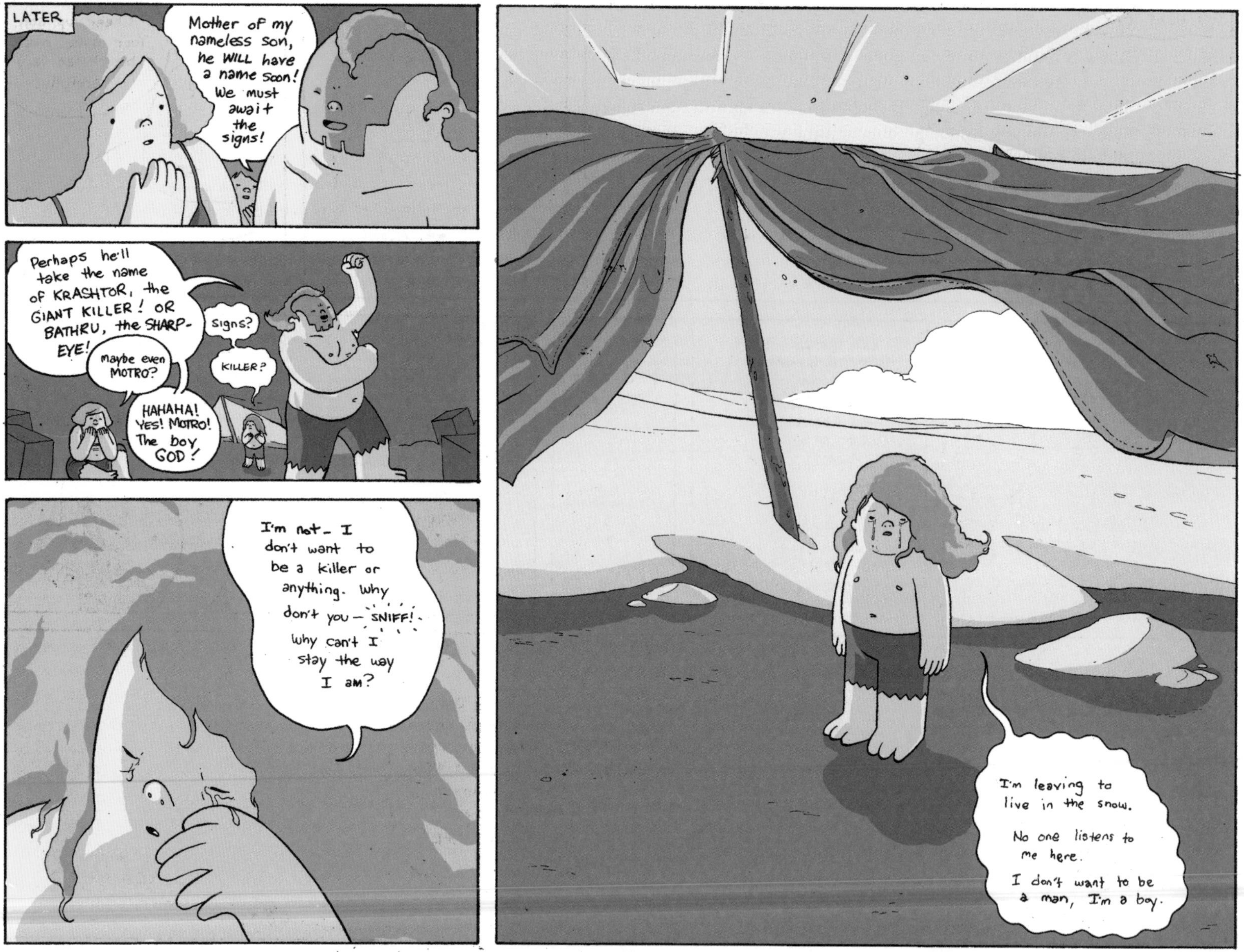
LATER
Mother of my nameless son, he WILL have a name soon! We must await the signs!
Perhaps he'll take the name of KRASHTOR, the GIANT KILLER! OR BATHRU, the SHARP-EYE!
maybe even MOTRO?
HAHAHA! YES! MOTRO! The boy GOD!
Signs?
KILLER?
I'm not - I don't want to be a killer or anything. Why don't you - SNIFF! - Why can't I stay the way I am?
I'm leaving to live in the snow.
No one listens to me here.
I don't want to be a man, I'm a boy.

CREATOR BIOS

NICK BERTOZZI

Nick Bertozzi is the author of THE SALON, a graphic novel about Picasso, the discovery of Cubism, and magical absinthe. He collaborated with Jason Lutes on the cartoon-biography HOUDINI: THE HANDCUFF KING, drew Glen (THE COLBERT REPORT) Eichler's forthcoming STUFFED! and for the past several years Nick has been teaching cartooning at NYC's School of Visual Arts.

WWW.NICKBERTOZZI.COM

PEDRO CAMARGO

Pedro Camargo hails from Brazil, but has had New York surgically implanted into his heart. Pedro first gained the attention of ACT-I-VATE with his comic SPACE SUCKS and then went on to create his second series, GLAM, both of which are still ongoing at ACT-I-VATE.

WWW.SILICONNEEDLE.LIVEJOURNAL.COM

MIKE CAVALLARO

Mike Cavallaro has been a New York-based cartoonist for almost 20 years. He's the creator of LOVIATHAN, the Eisner-Award-nominated series PARADE (WITH FIREWORKS), and the co-creator of THE LIFE AND TIMES OF SAVIOR 28. Mike has worked for Valiant Comics, DC, Marvel, Cartoon Network, MTV Animation, First Second Books, and others.

WWW.66KMPH.LIVEJOURNAL.COM

MOLLY CRABAPPLE

Molly Crabapple is an artist, author and the founder of Dr. Sketchy's Anti-Art School, a global chain of alternative drawing salons. She has been called "a downtown phenomenon" by the NEW YORK TIMES, and "THE artist of our time" by comedian Margaret Cho. Crabapple's first graphic novel, SCARLETT TAKES MANHATTAN, was published by Fugu Press in July '09.

WWW.MOLLYCRABAPPLE.COM

MIKE DAWSON

Mike Dawson is the cartoonist behind the epic graphic-memoir FREDDIE & ME: A COMING-OF-AGE (BOHEMIAN RHAPSODY), and the action-packed book of short stories ACE-FACE: THE MOD WITH THE METAL ARMS, from AdHouse Books. His newest comic, JACK & MAX ESCAPE FROM THE END OF TIME is currently being serialized at ACT-I-VATE.

WWW.MIKEDAWSONCOMICS.COM

JIM DOUGAN

Jim Dougan is the writer and co-creator of SAM & LILAH. His previous endeavors include writing CRAZY PAPERS, drawn by Danielle Corsetto, and editing NO FORMULA, an anthology of short stories from Webcomics collective The Chemistry Set. He lives in Washington, DC.

WWW.CHATTERBOX-DC.LIVEJOURNAL.COM

ULISES FARINAS

Ulises Farinas is a cartoonist living in Brooklyn, currently drawing MOTRO, an epic surrealist fantasy. He's done comics for Image comics' POPGUN Vols. 2 and 3, THE AWESOME ANTHOLOGY Vol. 2, FAESTHETIC MAGAZINE and illustrations for the NEW YORK TIMES, INC. MAGAZINE and a T-shirt for Threadless Select.

WWW.ULISESFARINAS.COM

MICHEL FIFFE

Michel Fiffe is a founding member of ACT-I-VATE, where he features ZEGAS, the surreal short stories of FUT MISO, and the erotic grotesque romance, PANORAMA. Fiffe is also working on his upcoming graphic novel, CUBA.

WWW.ZEGAS.LIVEJOURNAL.COM

MAURICE FONTENOT

Maurice Fontenot lives in Brooklyn where he writes and draws GHOST PIMP, pencils for DC Comics and creates storyboards for Disney, MTV, Cartoon Network and many others. He's a graduate of the Joe Kubert School of Cartoon Art and was a writer and editor at Valiant Comics.

WWW.GHOSTPIMP.COM

SIMON FRASER

Simon Fraser is a well-traveled Scottish comics artist and co-creator of the Eagle-Award-winning NIKOLAI DANTE character for the UK anthology comic 2000AD. He has drawn for numerous publishers on both sides of the Atlantic during his 18-year career. He likes Fish and Spaceships.

WWW.SIMONFRASER.NET

TIM HAMILTON

Tim Hamilton has produced work for The NEW YORK TIMES, CICADA MAGAZINE, King Features, DC Comics, MAD MAGAZINE, NICKELODEON MAGAZINE, Dow Jones, Lifetime, ABC Television and produced PET SITTER and THE ADVENTURES OF THE FLOATING ELEPHANT for ACT-I-VATE. Tim adapted TREASURE ISLAND into a graphic novel for Puffin Graphics, and more recently did the same with Ray Bradbury's FAHRENHEIT 451 for Hill & Wang.

WWW.HAMILTON-TIM.PAIR.COM

DEAN HASPIEL

Dean Haspiel is a native New Yorker and the creator of BILLY DOGMA, STREET CODE, and ACT-I-VATE. Dino has drawn comix for the NEW YORK TIMES and superheroes for Marvel, DC, and other publishers but is best known for his semi-autobio collaborations with Harvey Pekar on THE QUITTER and AMERICAN SPLENDOR, and with Jonathan Ames on THE ALCOHOLIC and HBO's "Bored to Death."

WWW.DEANHASPIEL.COM

JENNIFER HAYDEN

Jennifer Hayden writes and draws the Webcomic UNDERWIRE, at www.ACT-I-VATE.com. She is also working on a graphic novel called THE STORY OF MY TITS, to be published in 2011 by Top Shelf. She lives with her husband and two children in Central New Jersey.

WWW.JENNIFERHAYDEN.COM

JOE INFURNARI

Joe "the Canadian Crippler" Infurnari hails from the frozen tundras of the Great White North where he wields his Canuckle Sandwich in an unending quest for quality comics! Past glories include the Eisner-nominated Webcomics THE PROCESS and VS., as well as THE TRANSMIGRATION OF ULTRA-LAD! His handiwork can also be seen under the auspices of Oni Press, Image Comics, Marvel, ABC News, Complex Magazine, Three Rivers Press and First Second Books.

WWW.JOEINFURNARI.COM/BLOG

JOHN LEAVITT

John Leavitt is the co-author of DR. SKETCHY'S OFFICIAL RAINY DAY COLORING BOOK, SCARLETT TAKES MANHATTAN and BACKSTAGE. His cartoons have been featured in the NEW YORKER, THE MAGAZINE OF FANTASY AND SCIENCE FICTION, NARRATIVE, and THE CHRONICLE REVIEW. He lives in New York City.

WWW.JLEAVITT.NET

HYEONDO PARK

Hyeondo Park was born January 4th, 1982. He recently illustrated HUCKLEBERRY FINN MANGA EDITION for Wiley Publishing, adapted by Adam Sexton, with whom he also illustrated JULIUS CAESAR MANGA EDITION. Besides SAM & LILAH, Hyeondo also collaborated with Jim Dougan on COME THE DAWN, published in The Chemistry Set's NO FORMULA anthology.

WWW.HANARODA.NET

LELAND PURVIS

Leland Purvis started in comics as a Xeric Grant recipient for the anthology VOX. He continued with PUBO, and is the artist for the Eisner-nominated SUSPENDED IN LANGUAGE. Recent works include books in the Turning Points line for Simon & Schuster, and an upcoming graphic novel series from First Second titled RESISTANCE. Purvis is a founding member of ACT-I-VATE and DEEP6 Studios; a native of Portland, Oregon, he relocated to New York City in 2004 for Love and adventure.

WWW.LELANDPURVIS.COM

ROGER LANGRIDGE

Roger Langridge has worked for Marvel, DC, Dark Horse and various other publishers over the years, as well as on his own self-published title FRED THE CLOWN, which was nominated for several awards. He is currently writing and drawing THE MUPPET SHOW COMIC BOOK for Boom! Studios.

WWW.HOTEL-FRED.COM

TO READ THE FURTHER ADVENTURES OF THESE CHARACTERS AND MUCH MORE, FOR FREE, GO TO:

ACT·I·VATE.COM

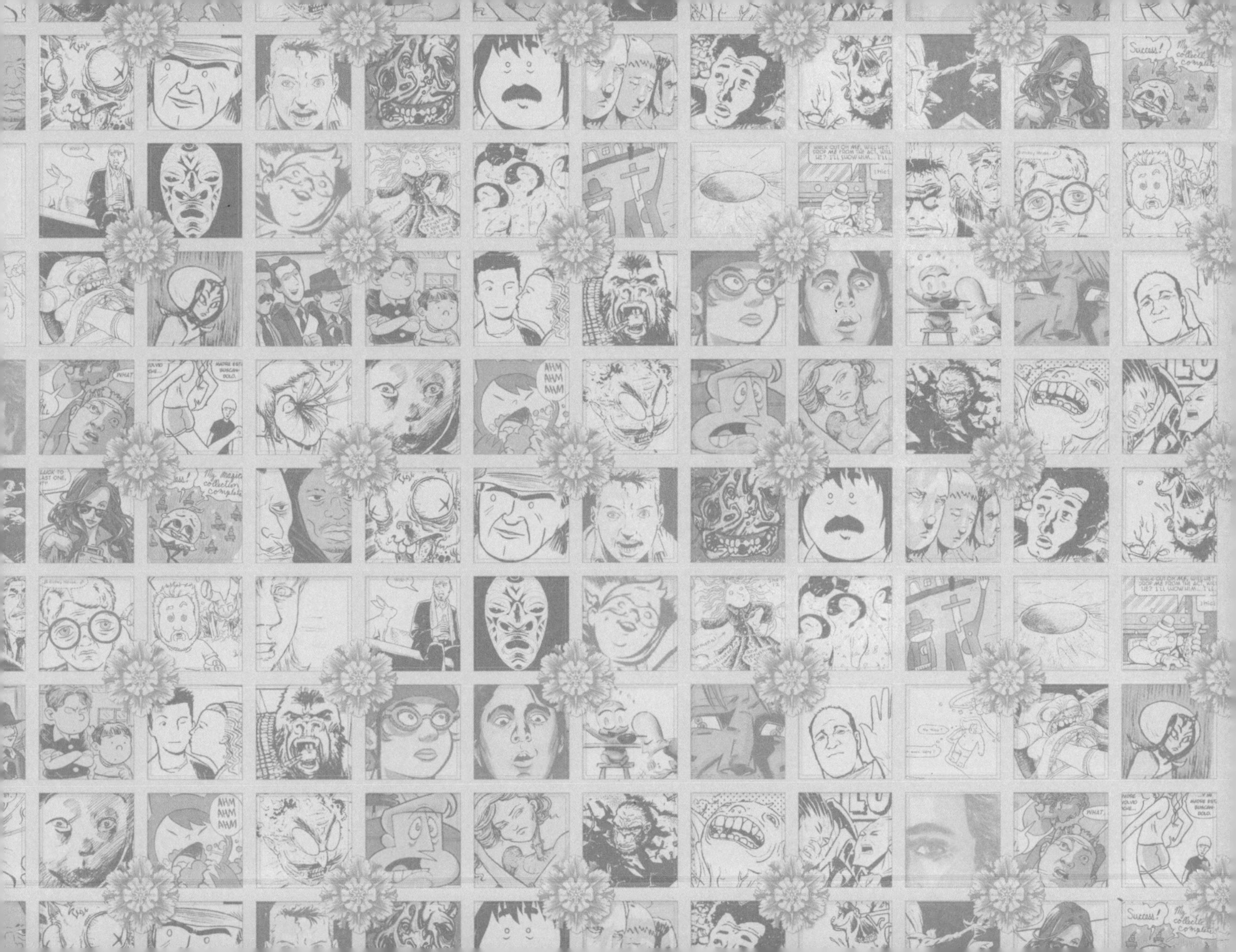
AHM AHM AHM
WHAT?

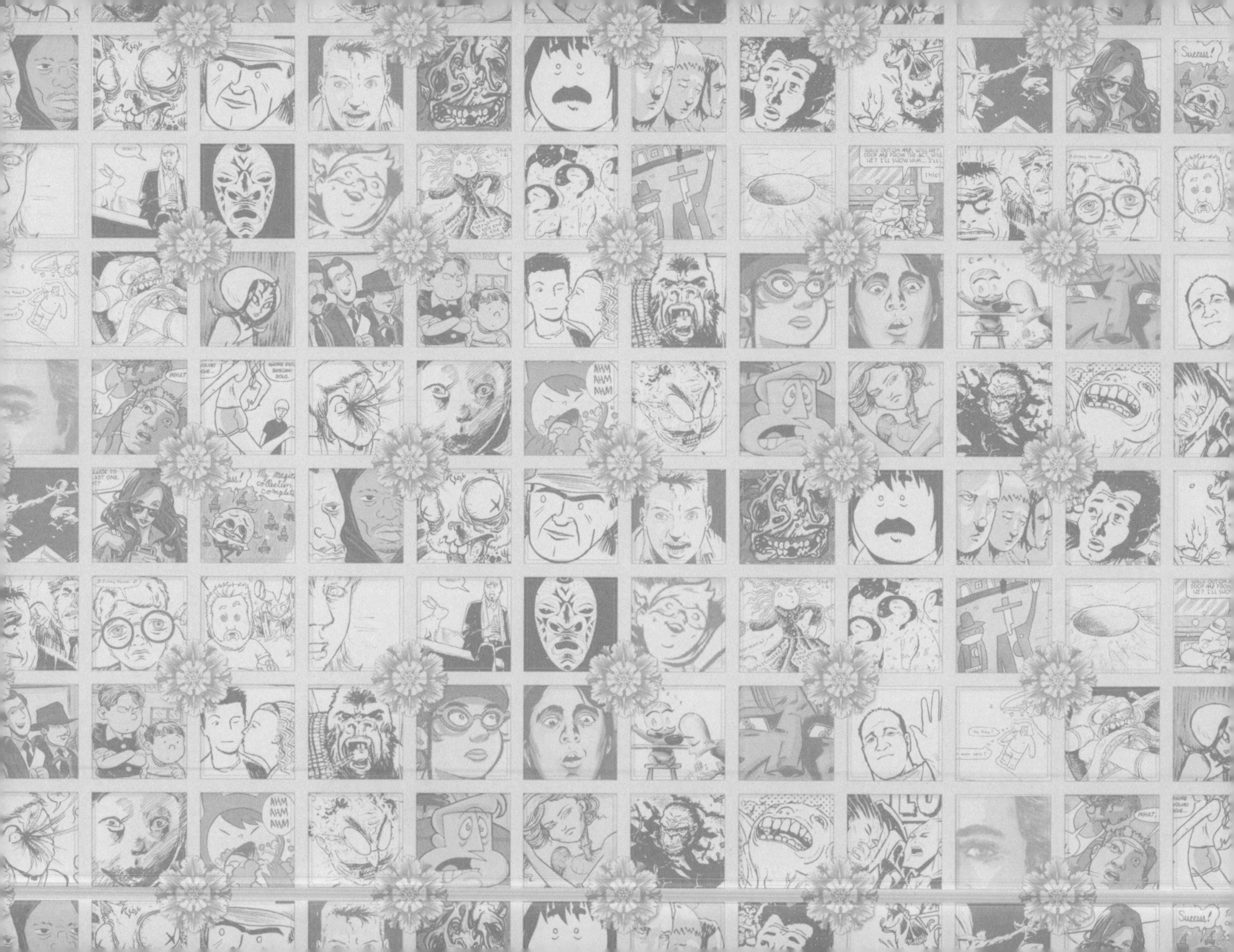
Success!
AHM
AHM
AHM